PATHWAYS TO INDEPENDENCE

PATHWAYS TO INDEPENDENCE

Reading, Writing, and Learning in Grades 3–8

Jo Worthy
Karen Broaddus
Gay Ivey

THE GUILFORD PRESS
New York   London

© 2001 The Guilford Press
A Division of Guilford Publications, Inc.
72 Spring Street, New York, NY 10012
www.guilford.com

Printed in the United States of America

This book is printed on acid-free paper.

Last digit is print number: 9 8 7 6 5 4 3 2

Library of Congress Cataloging-in-Publication Data

Worthy, Jo.
    Pathways to independence: reading, writing, and learning in grades 3–8 / Jo Worthy, Karen Broaddus, Gay Ivey.
        p. cm.
    Includes bibliographical references and index.
    ISBN 1-57230-646-7 (cloth)—ISBN 1-57230-647-5 (pbk.)
    1. Language arts (Elementary)   2. Language arts (Middle school)   I. Title: Reading, writing, and learning in grades 3–8.   II. Broaddus, Karen.   III. Ivey, Gay.   IV. Title.
LB1576 .W684 2001
372.6—dc21
                                                                              00-067681

To our Families

Don Fullerton, Jared Montague, and Jenna Fullerton

Rich, Jessica, and Eliza Broaddus

Stinson and Edith Ivey

About the Authors

Jo Worthy, PhD, is an associate professor of reading education and teacher education at the University of Texas at Austin, where she teaches graduate and undergraduate practicum courses in reading methods and reading difficulties in addition to courses on reading and language arts research. After receiving her bachelor's degree and teaching certificate in early childhood education, Dr. Worthy taught for many years in Virginia public elementary and middle schools. She continues to spend most of her time in public schools, collaborating closely with teachers, teaching her classes on an elementary school campus, and directing a literacy tutoring program. Dr. Worthy earned her doctorate in 1989 from the University of Virginia in reading education, focusing on educational research, clinical assessment, and children's literature. From 1991 to 1994, as a postdoctoral fellow at the Learning Research and Development Center with Isabel Beck and Margaret McKeown, she researched text comprehension and engagement. Her current research and teaching interests include teacher education, students' reading preferences, and reading difficulties, with a focus on grades 1 through 6.

Karen Broaddus, PhD, is an associate professor of reading education at James Madison University in Harrisonburg, Virginia. Her background experiences include teaching middle and secondary English and working as a children's librarian in school and public library settings. Dr. Broaddus received her doctorate from the University of Virginia in 1995, focusing her studies on reading, English education, and assessment. She began her college career at the University of Tulsa in Oklahoma teaching children's literature, multicultural studies in adolescent literature, language arts, and literacy assessment and intervention. In Tulsa city schools, Dr. Broaddus collaborated with preservice teachers in group research projects on children's responses to multiethnic literature and in individual case study projects of struggling readers. Since her appointment to the faculty at James Madison University in 1998, she has focused her teaching and research on reading, writing, and content area learning in the middle grades.

Gay Ivey, PhD, is an assistant professor of reading education at the University of Maryland at College Park. She began her teaching career in Albemarle County, Virginia, where she was a middle school Title I reading/language arts teacher. Dr. Ivey received her master's degree from the University of Virginia in 1990 and her doctorate from the University of Georgia in 1997. Her first university position was at the Graduate School of Education at Rutgers University before moving to the University of Maryland in 1999. She teaches courses in reading instruction and assessment, and her research interests include examining ways to make regular classroom instruction more responsive to individual development and motivation in the upper elementary and middle grades, especially for students who find reading and writing difficult.

Acknowledgments

Permission to reproduce covers and/or text excerpts from the following books has been granted by their publishers.

Cover from *Garfield Feeds the Kitty* by Jim Davis (1999). Copyright 1999 by PAWS, Inc. Reprinted by permission of Ballantine Books, a division of Random House, Inc.

Cover from *Basketball's Greatest Players* by S. A. Kramer (1997). Copyright 1997 by S. A. Kramer. Reprinted by permission of Random House Children's Books, a division of Random House, Inc.

Cover from *The Guinness Book of World Records 1999* edited by M. C. Young (1999). Copyright 1999 by Guinness Publishing, Ltd. Used by permission of Bantam Books, a division of Random House, Inc.

Cover from *Pyramid* by David Macaulay (1975). Copyright 1975 by David Macaulay. Reprinted by permission of Houghton Mifflin Company. All rights reserved.

Cover from *La Llorona/The Weeping Woman* by Joe Hayes (1987). Copyright 1987 by Joe Hayes. Reprinted with permission of Cinco Puntos Press, El Paso, TX.

Cover from *Teammates* by Peter Golenbock (1990). Illustration copyright 1990 by Paul Bacon. Reproduced by permission of Harcourt, Inc.

Cover from *The Hidden Children* by Howard Greenfeld (1993). Copyright 1993 by Howard Greenfeld. Reprinted by permission of Houghton Mifflin Company. All rights reserved.

Cover from *A Gift from Papá Diego/Un Regalo de Papá Diego* by Benjamin Alire Sáenz (1998). Copyright 1998 by Benjamin Alire Sáenz. Reprinted with permission of Cinco Puntos Press, El Paso, TX.

Cover from *The Stinky Cheese Man and Other Fairly Stupid Tales* by Jon Scieszka (1992). Copyright 1992 by Jon Scieszka. Cover illustration copyright 1992 by Lane Smith. Used by permission of Viking Penguin, a division of Penguin Putnam Inc.

Cover from *Marvin Redpost: Alone in His Teacher's House* by Louis Sachar (1994), cover illustration by Neal Hughes. Cover illustration copyright 1994 by Neal Hughes. Reprinted by permission of Random House Children's Books, a division of Random House, Inc.

Cover from *The Perilous Journey of the Donner Party* by Marian Calabro (1999). Cover illustration copyright 1999 by Leslie Evans. Reprinted by permission of Clarion Books/Houghton Mifflin Company. All rights reserved.

Cover from *Extremely Weird Primates* by S. Lovett (1996). Copyright 1996 by John Muir Publications, a division of Avalon Travel Publishing, 5855 Beaudry St., Emeryville, CA 94608. Reprinted with permission of the publisher.

Cover from *Roll of Thunder, Hear My Cry* by Mildred D. Taylor (1976). Copyright 1976 by Mildred D. Taylor. Used by permission of Dial Books for Young Readers, a division of Penguin Putnam Inc.

Cover from *Cinder-Elly* by Frances Minters (1994), illustrated by G. Brian Karas. Copyright 1994 by G. Brian Karas, illustrations. Used by permission of Viking Penguin, a division of Penguin Putnam Inc.

Cover from *Amazing Poisonous Animals* by Alexandra Parsons (1990). Copyright 1990 by Dorling Kindersley Limited. Reprinted by permission of Alfred A. Knopf Children's Books, a division of Random House, Inc.

Cover and excerpts from *The Bone Keeper* by Megan McDonald (1999), illustrated by G. Brian Karas. Copyright 1999 by Megan McDonald. Illustrations copyright 1999 by G. Brian Karas. Reprinted with permission of Dorling Kindersley Publishing, Inc.

Cover from *The Mysteries of Harris Burdick* by Chris Van Allsburg (1984). Copyright 1984 by Chris Van Allsburg. Reprinted by permission of Houghton Mifflin Company. All rights reserved.

Cover and excerpt from *The Watertower* by Gary Crew (1998), illustrated by Steven Woolman. Reprinted with permission of Crocodile Books, USA, an imprint of Interlink Publishing Group, Inc. Copyright 1998.

Cover from *Flying Solo* by Ralph Fletcher (1998). Copyright 1998 by Ralph Fletcher. Reprinted by permission of Clarion Books/Houghton Mifflin Company. All rights reserved.

Cover from *The Bone Detectives* by Donna M. Jackson (1996), illustrated by Charlie Fellenbaum. Copyright 1996 by Donna M. Jackson. Illustrations copyright 1996 by Charlie Fellenbaum. Reprinted with permission of Little, Brown and Company.

Cover from *Insectlopedia* by Douglas Florian (1998). Copyright 1998 by Douglas Florian. Reproduced by permission of Harcourt, Inc.

Excerpt from "Pleitos" in *Canto Familiar* by Gary Soto (1995). Copyright 1995 by Gary Soto. Reprinted by permission of Harcourt, Inc.

Cover from *Saving Sweetness* by Diane Stanley (1996), illustrated by G. Brian Karas. Illustrations copyright 1996 by G. Brian Karas. Used by permission of G. P. Putnam's Sons, a division of Penguin Putnam Inc.

Excerpt from *Working Cotton* by Sherley Anne Williams (1992). Text copyright 1992 by Sherley Anne Williams. Reprinted by permission of Harcourt, Inc.

Cover from *The House That Drac Built* by Judy Sierra (1995). Cover illustration copyright 1995 by Will Hillenbrand. Reproduced by permission of Harcourt, Inc.

Cover from *Search for the Shadowman* by Joan Lowery Nixon (1996). Copyright 1996 by Joan Lowery Nixon. Used by permission of Random House Children's Books, a division of Random House, Inc.

Preface

We began writing this book for ourselves. We each teach reading methods and reading practicum courses for prospective and practicing teachers of elementary and middle school literacy. In our search for books to use with our students we have found many that address a circumscribed grade range (primary, elementary, or middle) and some that focus on teaching reading in the content areas or on instructing students who find reading difficult. However, we have been unable to find a book, or even the right combination of books, that addresses all of the issues that we find important in teaching students in the upper elementary and middle school grades. Thus, we set out to write a book that provided (1) a comprehensive, in-depth treatment of research-based reading and writing instruction with attention to the unique issues of learning in the middle grades; (2) an emphasis on reading and writing as thinking in both narrative and information text; (3) a focus on building connections between instruction and students' lives, interests, strengths, needs, and diversities; (4) a balance between curriculum requirements and students' developmental levels and engagement in learning; and (5) numerous examples from classrooms and intervention programs of practical, theoretically sound, field-tested approaches using a variety of materials.

UNIQUE FEATURES OF THE BOOK

The book is grounded in the notion that the teaching and learning of all students should be tailored to suit individual needs and interests, as well as cultural, linguistic, and gender differences among students. Throughout the book, we include suggestions for using, modifying, and managing instruction for a diverse classroom of students.

Teacher and student case studies, responses, and work samples provide examples of instruction and assessments, and the voices of students and teachers are heard throughout the book. Many of the stories and all of the quotes are from teachers, parents, preservice teachers, students, and university faculty we have known through the years. Other stories and descriptions are composites of students, parents, and teachers we have known and classrooms and schools in which we have worked, observed, and conducted research.

We present a core of instructional approaches that include teacher-guided and independent reading in a wide variety of texts and writing in many formats and for varied purposes. In addition, there are chapters on components of literacy learning that are not always addressed sufficiently in instruction for older students, including teacher read-alouds, interactive reading and writing, reading fluency, language study (including spelling development and instruction), and building a classroom library collection.

We believe it is important for educators to ensure that students are exposed to a balance of high-quality, conceptually challenging literature and student-preferred materials in a range of genres, formats, and difficulty levels. Thus, throughout the book, as well as in the chapter devoted to reading materials, we address critically acclaimed literature, popular series books in fiction and nonfiction, materials that help students to develop positive views of diverse cultures and languages, and less conventional materials like magazines, joke books, and comics. Informative texts in a variety of formats are featured in every chapter. Throughout the book, we use such materials in describing instructional approaches. Further, we provide numerous lists, throughout the book and in appendices, of appropriate, engaging materials.

ABOUT THE AUTHORS

We are all former classroom teachers with professional experiences ranging from primary to high school, including work in predominantly low-income, ethnically diverse settings as well as extensive experience in clinical work with students who have persistent reading and writing challenges. Each of us continues to teach and learn from preservice teachers, inservice teachers, and students in elementary through secondary school. The book includes our insights from reading and conducting research, teaching, talking to each other and other colleagues, and discussing (sometimes heatedly) the important issues in literacy instruction.

We each bring overlapping knowledge, experiences, and passions to the teaching of literacy that aided in writing a comprehensive book for the instruction of students in grades 3 through 8. Karen, a former middle school and high school English teacher, focuses on literature and writing with adolescents. Gay's teaching and research in middle school concerns the unique individual, social, and motivational issues affecting literacy and learning in students of this age. Jo's research and teaching in primary through middle school has led to her interests in curriculum-based assessment and students' reading preferences. Each of us has a passion for supporting preservice and inservice teachers in productive field work and reflection on literacy engagement and learning, including a special focus on students who find reading and writing challenging.

The most important lesson we have learned in working with students in the upper elementary and middle school grades is that even the best instructional methods and materials will work only if students find them relevant to their lives. We recognize that no two students are alike. A student who experiences challenges in one area will shine in other areas. Likewise, students have different interests, needs, and motivations. Finding and embracing these areas in all students is essential for engaging students in learning. Thus, we have kept our main focus on students, and throughout the book you will hear the voices of real students expressing their views about literacy practices and materials.

INTENDED AUDIENCE AND USES OF THE BOOK

Writing this book was not just a matter of writing down what we knew about teaching reading and writing. We started with what we knew and learned more from each other. The process included examining our past and present lives, our research, and our teaching and learning from professors, colleagues, teachers, and students. This book is about recognizing the varied pathways to literacy taken by upper elementary and middle school students. We can make that journey engaging, welcoming, and productive for all students.

The book we began writing for ourselves became a book for prospective teachers, practicing teachers, literacy specialists, teacher educators, and others who work with literacy in the middle grades. It is appropriate as a text for undergraduate and graduate courses in reading instruction and assessment, language arts methods, content area literacy, and literacy foundations, as well as for formal professional development and teacher study groups. We hope you find it useful.

ACKNOWLEDGMENTS

We particularly wish to thank the people whose original writing and ideas are included in the book: Janet Bloodgood, Susan Buchanan, Barbara Corbin, Kim Duhamel, Marilyn Elrod, Colleen Fairbanks, Sheila Felber, Julee Hart, Jim Hoffman, Dora Jarrard, Brian Lundstrom, Brandy McCombs, Megan McDonald, Nancy Roser, John Reese, Loretta Stewart, and Michelle Williams. We also acknowledge the many unnamed teachers and students who provided inspiration for instructional vignettes.

Teachers, principals, graduate students, preservice teachers, and colleagues read and commented upon drafts of the book and gave us invaluable advice. We wish to thank the following reviewers and advisers: Janet Bloodgood, Ann Duffy, Dee Grimm, Brian Lundstrom, Marg Mast, David Schwarzer, Mallory Smith, Loretta Stewart, Susan Strecker, Greg Swimelar, and Sylvia Thompson.

The foundations of this book were developed through our work together at the University of Virginia, and we would like to thank the past and present faculty, students, and children from the McGuffey Reading Center. We also acknowledge our current colleagues at the University of Texas at Austin, James Madison University, the University of Maryland at College Park, and the children and teachers of Allison Elementary School. We are especially grateful for the inspiration provided to each of us by various members of the literacy education community: Dick Allington, Jim Baumann, Isabel Beck, Pat Crook, Edmund Henderson, Peter Johnston, Darrell Morris, and Cathy Roller.

Contents

APPENDICES

PATHWAYS TO INDEPENDENCE

INTRODUCTION

Understanding Students
in the Middle Grades (3–8)

Literacy education in grades 3–8—the "middle grades"—spans a wide range of individual and developmental needs. Some students will be just beginning to read or to write fluently, while other students will be experienced writers and strategic readers of content information. Even within a single classroom, you will find a wide range of interests and abilities. Take a look at these comments from students in grades 3–8 about reading and writing. What do their answers suggest to you about these students as learners?

Brian: "I like to read newspapers and magazines more than chapter books. . . . I like reading about research and trying to figure stuff out. . . . Lately I've been going to the sports [section in the newspaper] because of the playoffs, the Stanley Cup."

Sammy: "I like when you get to pick your own topic. Let's say there's one topic on the board, and it says you can write about a dog, but you don't want to write about a dog. You can write about a frog or something. You want to do your own thing."

Fernanda: "The books in my classroom are too hard. When I read a book in there, I can read it over and over, but I don't get it. I can't concentrate. But I like scary stories, *Bailey School Kids* [e.g., *Dracula Doesn't Rock and Roll*—Dadey & Jones, 2000], *Henry and Mudge* [e.g., *Henry and Mudge under the Yellow Moon*—Rylant, 1998], and *Fox* [e.g., *Fox at School*—Marshall, 1983]. And I like *The Stinky Cheese Man* [*The Stinky Cheese Man and Other Fairly Stupid Tales*—Scieszka, 1992] and other cool books like that. They're cool and interesting. *Those* I pay attention to."

Amy: "*American Girl* books, Samantha's adventure [*Samantha Saves the Day*—Tripp, 1988]. And sometimes I just check out baby books from here [school library] for my little cousin because sometimes I have to watch him. And I read to my niece too. They just like the pictures."

Ellie: "Before, I really didn't read that much, unless it's a really good book that you can get into really fast. If it's a book that's really boring for the first few chapters, I really don't like it. But if it jumps right into something good, then I'll read it. *Spirit Seeker* [Nixon, 1997], it's a mystery book. It's kind of a scary book. I like those kind of books—historical kind of books—*The Life and Death of Crazy Horse* [Freedman, 1996]. That was a really good one."

Tuan: "I'm good at being an author. I like writing stories on the computer and doing research. I like to write, but I don't really like to read."

Anna: "I really didn't know I liked adventure books and stuff like that, and now I love them. When I started reading *Cracker Jackson* [Byarsm 1985], which was in third grade, I was like, 'Wow, this is a good book!' "

Angelique: "Now I can read more chapter books than I used to. I used to get so bored because I couldn't read the words. And now I'm doing more chapter books, and I'm starting to understand them better."

Wesley: "I learn a lot of new words when I hear other kids say their writing out loud, and sometimes I'll go into the dictionary to find out a few words that could be in my book I'm reading."

Rocio: "I remember the book *Roll of Thunder, Hear My Cry* [Taylor, 1976]. It makes you feel like you're in the book. When these kids get hit, you can feel the pain and stuff."

Mei: "I like going to the PreK class and just reading to little kids. Sometimes my friends tease me, but I like those little kid books like *Arthur* [e.g., *Arthur's Eyes*—Brown, 1986] and *Berenstain Bears* [e.g., *The Berenstain Bears and the Truth*—Berenstain & Berenstain, 1988]."

Jamie: "Novels about the war and all that. Magazines, *PSM—PlayStation Magazine*; it's PlayStation games and all that. *A Bridge Too Far* [Ryan, 1974], World War II, a Vietnam magazine."

What is important to these students about reading and writing? How can you describe the diversity that you see in their reading? These students mention different genres (e.g. historical fiction, picture books, realistic fiction, science fiction, information books) and clearly spend time reading varied types of materials (e.g., newspapers, magazines, comic books, series books). Their reading includes a wide selection of book levels and a range of complexity (e.g., easy series books, high-interest fiction, biographies for upper middle grades, adult nonfiction). The students talk about reading for entertainment, social interaction, and personal involvement (e. g. comic books, mystery and horror stories, adventure books, easy chapter books, historical fiction, funny picture books, and even "little kid books"), and reading to learn (e.g., using the newspaper to find information about sports, looking at magazines on special topics, reading about history). When you look at these students' different purposes for reading and their varied choices of materials, it may seem overwhelming to plan for reading and writing instruction that addresses all of their individual interests in one classroom. At the same time, it is necessary to address the fact that these students have different purposes for reading and varied academic needs.

Keep this idea about individual differences in mind as you take a look at the case descriptions in Box I.1 of four students in a fifth-grade classroom. As you read, use the chart in Box I.2 to focus your thinking. Jot down some notes about each student in the following categories: (1) background and personal qualities; (2) interests and engagement in literacy; (3) strengths in reading and writing; (4) concerns about reading and writing; and (5) ideas for appropriate instruction. After reading, write down some ideas for each of the discussion questions at the bottom of the chart, and then discuss your answers with a group of your peers.

Even with this information about four students, you can see how complex a process it is to teach reading and writing to different types of students. Why is considering the personal and academic needs of individual students so important? In our own experiences of teaching and conducting research in elementary and middle school classrooms, we often find a mismatch between what individual students in grades 3–8 need from literacy instruction and the instruction they typically receive (Ivey & Broaddus, 2000). First, although students in the middle grades represent a wide range of abilities and interests, teachers rarely differentiate instruction in response to this variation (Tomlinson, Moon, & Callahan, 1998). Second, students may be unlikely to find their preferred reading materials in school (Worthy, Moorman, & Turner, 1999) since teachers may rely on a narrow range of materials for instruction, such as the required textbook and class novels, which many students may be uninterested in reading or unable to read on their own. Third, students are most motivated to read and write when they have a say in the development and direction of the curriculum (Oldfather, 1993). However, decisions about what and how students will learn are usually left to teachers and other adults. Fourth, students in the middle grades often get few real opportunities to read in school, despite the evidence for the powerful influence of time spent reading on students' reading development (Anderson, Wilson, & Fielding, 1988) and cognitive growth (Stanovich, 1986). In addition, students desire this time to read on their own for the sake of learning and pursuing personal interests (Ivey & Broaddus, in press). Recently, we have observed teachers spending much of their valuable instructional time preparing students for high-stakes tests and covering content subjects (science, social studies, math, etc.) without letting students read or write about them, and with little instruction about how to read and write effectively in the content areas.

In this book, we describe how teachers move past these dilemmas to design instruction that is responsive to individual readers and writers, and that helps all students accelerate their learning. Box I.3 summarizes these issues, the alternatives we explore in this book, and some questions to keep in mind as you are reading.

PERSONAL AND SOCIAL ISSUES THAT AFFECT EDUCATION FOR STUDENTS IN THE MIDDLE GRADES

As we have seen in the case studies, there are numerous issues to consider about individual characteristics and academic diversity for students in the middle grades. At the same time, we can also explore some of the typical concerns that students have as they make the transition between elementary school and high school. Read the book ex-

BOX I.I. Sketches of Four Students in a Fifth-Grade Classroom

Marie loves scary stories like the *Goosebumps* series, or books about girls like *The Babysitters Club* series, even though those books are difficult for her to read. Cheerful and outgoing, she has a great attitude about school, and she loves reading. She doesn't enjoy writing, however, and when she has a school assignment, she usually makes a list rather than tells a story. She is one of nine children in a Mexican American family (with siblings ranging from age 1 to age 23), and she takes a lot of responsibility for housework after school. Spanish is spoken in her home. She began school in Mexico, but she attended both third and fourth grades in the United States. She can read books with good accuracy at the second-grade level, but she reads extremely slowly, and she has problems with comprehension in third- and fourth-grade-level texts. She can also read in a third-grade Spanish text, but her speed is even slower than when she reads English, although her comprehension is very good in Spanish. She enjoyed the picture book *Chato's Kitchen* (Soto, 1995) because it includes both English and Spanish terms.

Drew is an African American student who just came to the class from a school in another state. This will be the third school he has attended this year. He is living with his grandparents, but he says he is only staying there temporarily. Drew is tall, slender, and quiet. Drew tries to avoid reading in school, but when he is required to read orally, he reads with both fluency and solid comprehension in grade-level texts. Drew's passion is art, and he often gets into trouble in class because he is drawing when he is supposed to be writing. He creates detailed drawings on scientific topics, such as showing how things work or labeling specific parts. Although he claims that he doesn't read any of the text, Drew spends a lot of time studying the photographs or illustrations in books, making his own sketches, and taking notes about the information he needs. His two favorite resources in his classroom are *The New Way Things Work* (Macaulay, 1998) and *Stephen Biesty's Incredible Cross-Sections* (Platt, 1992). His teacher brought in the book *A Street through Time* (Millard, 1998), and recently Drew has shown some interest in historical illustrations.

Ian is interested in dogs, particularly pointers. He is the only child in a European American family, and he spends most of his time at home watching television or playing computer games. Ian enjoys Western books, magazines with poems, and comic books about Batman. He writes silly poems and long stories just for fun, but these stories are usually hard to decipher because he doesn't use any punctuation. Ian is relaxed and productive at school, and he is always helpful around the classroom. He is bigger than any of the other students, but he seems comfortable with his size. Although he can read almost perfectly in third- and fourth-grade-level texts, he is unable to understand most of what he reads. However, he enjoys activities that involve words, and he can easily read a list of words at the fifth-grade level.

Jana is another student in this class. She is the only girl in an African American family; she lives with her father and two younger brothers. She reads with her 5-year-old brother every night in books he brings home from his kindergarten class and from their own collection of picture books at home. Jana's favorite author is Christopher Curtis, because he writes about real things that happened and still has funny parts in his books. She loved his book that is set during the civil rights movement, *The Watsons Go to Birmingham—1963* (Curtis, 1995), and his book about the Depression, *Bud, Not Buddy* (Curtis, 1999). This year she finished reading all of the *Harry Potter* books by J. K. Rowling, and for fun she rereads *The Friendship Ring* series by Rachel Vail and the *Anastasia* books by Lois Lowry. Jana keeps a journal at home, but she hates to write at school. In fact, she is not interested by most of the activities at school, and she generally brings a novel to read during English class.

BOX 1.2. Information Chart for Collecting Case Study Data
for Four Fifth-Grade Students

Areas of literacy	Background and personal qualities	Interests and engagement in literacy	Strengths in reading and writing	Concerns about reading and writing	Ideas for appropriate instruction
Marie					
Drew					
Ian					
Jana					
Discussion questions (write answers on back of this page)	How will you honor individual student differences in background during literacy instruction?	How can you use all of these diverse interests to engage students in reading and writing?	What will you do to be sure that each of these students uses an area of strength to develop other literacy areas?	How will you teach students of differing abilities in one classroom?	How can these instructional ideas fit together in a classroom curriculum?

BOX I.3. Aligning Reading and Writing Instruction to Meet the Needs of Diverse Middle Grades Students

Problematic instruction: Common practices in reading and writing instruction that do not take into account individual student needs	*Alternative approaches:* Recommended approaches that build a solid foundation in literacy for a wide range of students	*Questions:* Issues to consider as you are reading this book about how teachers can integrate reading and writing instruction across the curriculum
"One-size-fits-all" curriculum (whole-class teaching on required topics, lack of differentiation for individual learners in fluency and comprehension instruction)	Approach reading and writing instruction as a developmental process by reading aloud to students, developing fluency through performance, linking reading with writing, and promoting word analysis skills.	How can teachers address learning to read (developmental reading practices) and reading to learn (content area reading strategies) at the same time?
Use of a narrow range of materials for instruction (required textbooks, class novels, limited exposure to diverse genres, reading materials on grade level)	Provide access to a wide range of materials on different reading levels, including informational books, poetry, scripts, picture books, novels, newspapers, and other sources.	How can teachers encourage students to read in materials that interest them and motivate them to continue to read, yet still expose students to required curriculum in language arts and other content areas?
Lack of student ownership in the literacy curriculum	Learn about individual students as readers and writers (exploring student interests, using informal assessments, working individually with students) and provide opportunities for purposeful reading and writing.	How do teachers find out personal information about students and administer assessments when time is limited in the classroom? If students are allowed to make choices about their reading and writing, how can the teacher determine whether these choices are appropriate?
Ineffective prioritizing of instructional time (focus on high-stakes testing, content instruction without student reading or writing)	Move purposeful, individual reading and writing to the forefront of the curriculum, with teacher guidance and coaching.	How do teachers make sure that they are teaching effective literacy strategies in an environment where students are pursuing individual reading and writing projects?

cerpts in Box I.4 about students starting school across the middle grades, beginning with third graders Judy Moody and Cody Michaels, and ending with Melinda Sordino as she enters high school. What do these students have in common? How are their concerns different across age groups?

You can see from these selections that certain social and emotional issues related to school show up across grades. Just "fitting in" is a key concern for students. Although each student has unique issues, there are some general issues closely related to engagement in learning that touch most students. These include (1) the quest for independence and control; (2) diversity of background, language, culture, and individuality; (3) differences in instructional needs; (4) diversity in personal interests and preferences; (5) the need for social interaction; and (6) the need for personal connections and an accepting community. These issues are discussed in the following sections, along with suggestions for how teachers can meet students' needs while holding expectations for learning high.

BOX 1.4. Examples from Children's Literature of Middle Grades Students Beginning School

- Judy Moody in *Judy Moody*: "One of the worst things about the first day of school was that everybody came back from summer wearing new T-shirts that said DISNEY WORLD or SEA WORLD or JAMESTOWN: Home of Pocahontas. Judy searched her top drawer and her bottom drawer and even her underwear drawer. She could not find one shirt with words." (McDonald, 1999, p. 13)
- Cody Michaels in *Hey, New Kid!*: " 'This is our new student, Cody Michaels.' Cody was standing in front of his new class with his new teacher, Ms. Harvey. A classroom full of strangers looked back. His heart was beating fast—faster, he was sure, than it ever had before. He imagined again that he was a prisoner. Twenty pairs of eyes were fixed on him like the guns of a firing squad. . . . 'Tell us something about yourself, Cody,' Ms. Harvey said. 'Where are you from?' He rubbed his hands together to stop them from shaking. Topeka sounded so boring. It was time to create the new Cody. 'Alaska,' he said instead. 'We lived in an igloo.' 'My,' his teacher said." (Duffey, 1996, pp. 11–12)
- Katie Roberts in *The Private Notebook of Katie Roberts, Age 11*: "The principal sent a letter. WELCOME TO MEADOWLAWN SCHOOL. They make you take a school bus. No one will sit next to me or talk to me, which is all my mother's fault. SHE doesn't care that I am miserable in Texas. SHE doesn't care that I will never have a best friend—or any friend—for the rest of my life. All SHE cares about is her new husband PRINCE CHARMING." (Hest, 1995, p. 13)
- Joey Pigza in *Joey Pigza Swallowed the Key*: "At school they say I'm wired bad, or wired mad, or wired sad, or wired glad, depending on my mood and what teacher has ended up with me. But there is no doubt about it. I'm *wired*." (Gantos, 1998, p. 3)
- Maleeka Madison in *The Skin I'm In*: "The first time I seen her, I got a bad feeling inside. Not like I was in danger or nothing. Just like she was somebody I should stay clear of. To tell the truth, she was a freak like me. The kind of person folks can't help but tease. That's bad if you're a kid like me. It's worse for a new teacher like her." (Flake, 1998, p. 1)
- Paul Fisher in *Tangerine*: "With the schedule had come a map of the high school–middle school campus, which I appreciated, and a hand-written note to Mom from Mrs. Gates, which I did not. It said, 'Vision-impaired students should report to the office for assistance.' That made me mad. What did she plan to do? Assign me a dog and cane?" (Bloor, 1997, p. 35).
- Yolonda Mae Blue in *Yolonda's Genius*: "Back in Chicago, most of the kids in her school, in her neighborhood, were black. Everyone had learned not to name-call or bait her. Even older boys steered clear. . . . Here you had to be careful. The bus driver could turn you in for fighting. The atmosphere, with more white kids than black, was tame and murky. Yolonda studied it carefully." (Fenner, 1995, p. 13)
- Melinda Sordino in *Speak*: "It is my first morning of high school. I have seven new notebooks, a skirt I hate, and a stomachache. . . . The bus picks up students in groups of four or five. As they walk down the aisle, people who were my middle-school lab partners or gym buddies glare at me. I close my eyes. This is what I've been dreading. As we leave the last stop, I am the only person sitting alone." (Anderson, 1999, p. 3)

Issue: The Quest for Independence and Control

What Teachers Can Do: Increase Expectations and Student Responsibility for Behavior and Learning

Preadolescents and adolescents don't like to be controlled. "[T]eetering between the world of the child and the world of the young adult" (Hynd, 1997, p. 3), they are beginning to test their independence. Choice, an important factor in young children's motivation for learning (Turner, 1995), plays an even greater role as older students move toward independence in learning. Students need to have a sense of autonomy and personal control, and they need to know that their opinions are valued. There may be increased tension between what teachers assign and the reading and writing activities students choose for themselves. It is a hard balance, but students need both support and independence. They need to take part in planning their instruction, and they need to be able to make choices (Hynd, 1997). Rather than fighting over who is in charge, teachers can take advantage of the middle graders' quest by providing opportunities for these students to take responsibility for their own learning. Practices that foster self-responsibility include (1) teachers' and students' working collaboratively to set goals and plan instruction; (2) teachers' encouraging students to assess and evaluate their own learning; and (3) teachers' helping students to gain independence in learning.

Students are more likely to "buy into" academic learning when they can participate in planning their instruction, with many opportunities to choose among appropriate instructional formats and materials. In our experience, students who feel in control of their learning are more likely to push themselves to their own limits, accelerating their learning even more than a teacher might. The teacher is a coplanner or consultant—an idea that fits well with social constructivist views of learning (Vygotsky, 1978) and apprenticeship models (Rogoff, 1990). In such a model, a more experienced teacher or learner guides students with explanations, modeling, guided practice, and independent practice as they move toward self-reliance (Taylor, Harris, Pearson, & García, 1995). When focusing on fluency, for example, teachers explain to students the reasons for building fluency, demonstrate instructional approaches, and then guide students as they try each approach. Students have some choice in independent practice activities. Marla, for example, chose to focus mainly on timed repeated readings for building her rate, because she liked using the stopwatch and graphing her own rate of reading. To work on smoothness and expression, she practiced easy, fun books to read to her younger cousin. Luis found that timing his reading was very stressful, and he chose instead to focus on Readers' Theater. Both of these formerly reluctant readers increased their reading outside of school and made significant gains in achievement.

As another example, many students in upper elementary and middle school say they hate to read. From research and our experiences, we have learned that many so-called "reluctant" readers very often do like to read when they have a say in what they're reading or doing in school (Bintz, 1993; Ivey, 1999; Worthy & McKool, 1996). When they feel that they are a part of the process, students are more likely to take responsibility for their own learning. Struggling learners carry additional burdens related to previous unsuccessful learning experiences, including negative self-concept, depressed motivation, and fear of failure (Kos, 1991; McCormick, 1994). While addressing these issues, we have also found it important to impress upon students the fact that their progress in literacy is not dependent on their teachers, tutors, or parents, but on their own engagement with reading and writing. Children's literature is filled with stories about middle grades students who read and write for real purposes. Box I.5 provides examples of easy-reading books, short chapter books, and novels in which students use literacy for personal reasons. Trip logs, letters, scary stories, poetry, and a class newspaper are just a few of the activities students share in these books.

Issue: Diversity of Background, Language, Culture, and Individuality

What Teachers Can Do: Recognize, Learn about, and Affirm Individual Differences

Strickland (1994) and many others have called for alternatives to a "one-size-fits-all" curriculum that clearly does not work in today's diverse classrooms. This idea is especially crucial as students move through adolescence. Individual differences become

---

BOX I.5. Books that Provide Models of Students as Writers, Readers, and Storytellers

Adedjouma, D. (Ed.). (1996). *The palm of my heart: Poetry by African American children* (ill. G. Christie. New York: Lee & Low.

Byars, B. C. (1988). *The burning questions of Bingo Brown*. New York: Viking.

Bunting, E. (1989). *The Wednesday surprise* (ill. D. Carrick). New York: Clarion.

Cameron, A. (1998). *The secret life of Amanda K. Woods*. New York: Foster.

Cleary, B. (1983). *Dear Mr. Henshaw* (ill. P. O. Zelinsky). New York: Morrow.

Clements, A. (1999). *The Landry News*. New York: Simon & Schuster.

Creech, S. (1990). *Absolutely normal chaos*. New York: HarperCollins.

Creech, S. (2000). *The wanderer* (ill. D. Diaz). New York: HarperCollins.

Danziger, P., & Martin, A. M. (1998). *P.S. longer letter later*. New York: Scholastic.

Fine, A. (1996). *Step by wicked step*. Boston: Little, Brown.

Giff, P. R. (1991). *The war began at supper: Letters to Miss Loria* (ill. B. Lewin). New York: Bantam Doubleday.

Grimes, N. (1998). *Jazmin's notebook*. New York: Dial. (For mature readers)

Hest, A. (1998). *The great green notebook of Katie Roberts: Who just turned 12 on Monday*. Cambridge, MA: Candlewick.

Jones, R. C. (1990). *Germy blew the bugle*. New York: Arcade.

Klise, K. (1998). *Regarding the fountain: A tale, in letters, of liars and leaks*. New York: Avon.

Lowry, L. (1979). *Anastasia Krupnik*. Boston: Houghton Mifflin.

McDonald, M. (2000). *Beezy and Funnybone* (ill. N. Poydar). New York: Orchard.*

Marshall, E. (1985). *Four on the shore* (ill. J. Marshall). New York: Dial.*

Marshall, E. (1994). *Three by the sea* (ill. J. Marshall). New York: Puffin.*

Marshall, J. (1986). *Three up a tree*. New York: Dial.*

Moss, M. (1995). *Amelia's notebook*. Berkeley, CA: Tricycle.

Moss, M. (1996). *Amelia writes again*. Berkeley, CA: Tricycle.

Moss, M. (1997). *Amelia hits the road*. Berkeley, CA: Tricycle.

Moss, M. (1998). *Amelia takes command*. Berkeley, CA: Tricycle.

Myers, W. D. (2000). *Monster*. New York: HarperCollins. (For mature readers)

Snyder, Z. K. (1990). *Libby on Wednesday*. New York: Delacorte.

*Easy-reading books.

more pronounced, and personal interests take on greater importance. This book is grounded in the notion that the teaching and learning of all students should be tailored to suit individual needs and interests, as well as cultural, linguistic, gender, and economic differences among students. Nieto (2000) suggests, "Our increasingly diverse society demands that all of us, but especially those of us who interact with students every day, 'tune in' to the voices of those who are different from ourselves. . . . The need for schools to do this is particularly urgent" (p. 13).

Issues of cultural, community, gender, and linguistic diversity are addressed in this book through varied reading and writing formats and materials, through instruction that relates to students' lives, and through suggestions for connecting instruction with students' families and homes. A common project in our classroom and intervention programs, for example, is for students to write their autobiographies over the course of several weeks. The students use a variety of sources, including photos, artifacts, and interviews with family members, to research their projects.

Issue: Differences in Academic Needs

What Teachers Can Do: Diversify Instruction for Individual Learners

An example from a single classroom (Ivey, 1999) illustrates the diversity in instructional strengths and challenges among students of the same age. Allison struggled greatly with word identification and fluency, but thrived as a thinker and listener and loved to listen to and discuss books read aloud. Allison certainly needed focused intervention in her challenge areas; however, a program that focused only on her weaknesses would have been disastrous for her motivation and continued conceptual learning. Another student, Ryan, was pegged as a reluctant learner because he refused to complete his out-of-school reading assignments. Although his in-class attitude and grades did not reflect it, Ryan was actually a competent reader who needed some individual guidance in selecting materials to read on his own. Although there were several other students with obvious challenges, most of the students in the classroom were achieving at or above grade level in most subjects and did not appear to have major social or personal challenges. Yet each needed individual attention in one way or another. It was critical for their teacher to know each student as an individual so that she could address their diverse needs. In keeping with this theme, the instructional approach we describe should in no way be considered a "one-size-fits-all" program to be followed to the letter. Rather, instruction should be multifaceted to address the individual diversities, instructional needs, personal interests, and motivational issues of the still-developing learner in the middle grades.

Issue: Varied Personal Interests and Preferences

What Teachers Can Do: A Balance of Requirements and Choices

Traditional instruction tends to focus solely on curriculum requirements, with few opportunities for students to explore their interests or concerns. In our experience, students are more motivated to learn when educators listen to their interests and provide choices in instruction, while retaining a major focus on high-quality literature and accepted curricula. Many teachers try to plan units of study and research projects with the interests of students in mind. However, students' interests can be so varied that an assigned topic cannot possibly be engaging to every student in the classroom. For example, students in Sharon Washington's language arts class were nearing the end of a unit on baseball. They had spent 4 weeks doing research in the library on a basic topic of their choice, and now they were putting the finishing touches on their reports. Ms. Washington was concerned about one group of boys who had read and written almost nothing, even though a month of class sessions had been devoted to the project, and she had taken the class step by step through the research process. She had some hunches about why these students had made little progress. For one thing, all of these boys were struggling readers, and even though she and the librarian had gathered over 300 books on baseball, most of the texts were still too difficult for many students, not to mention dry and outdated. Ms. Washington also began to wonder about the topic. Even though students were encouraged to choose their own specific topic (e.g., women's leagues, the World Series), they were still bound by the general theme of baseball.

A conversation with a couple of the boys confirmed her hunches, and she learned more about her students than she expected. As the rest of the students were finishing their final drafts, Ms. Washington sat with the boys and asked them about their projects.

Ms. W: What do you think of this project?

JAKE: It's all right. I mean, I don't like to read and write

Ms. W: You don't like to read and write *anything*?

JAKE: No. I mean, I'd like, this is—we could do wrestling.

Ms. W: Do you read about wrestling?

JAKE: I don't know.

Ms. W: What do you think about that wrestler who just died during a match?

JAKE: I think it was his fault. Oh, you asked me if I read about wrestling. I do. I heard that [the wrestler] fell from this wire when he was doing a stunt. My mom told me, so I started reading all these things in the newspaper, and it said it was his fault.

At this point in the conversation, another student joined in.

STEVEN: No, it wasn't his fault! It was faulty wiring. I read it!

JAKE: That's not what it said when I read . . .

This debate continued as other students shared information they had gathered about the wrestler's death. Ms. Washington learned her assumption that baseball would be interesting for most students was wrong. Her conversation with the boys suggested that they would have been much more engaged if the topic had been one of their own choosing, and she decided to let students pick their topics for the next research unit. In addition to wrestling, students focused on current family and community issues (e.g., gangs, divorce, responsible pet ownership, drugs, gangs), careers (e.g., the armed services, screenwriting, marine biology), favorite authors and musicians, and many other topics. With the help of the librarian, students used a variety of sources, including interviews, the World Wide Web, and books. They worked individually, in pairs, or in groups, according to their interests. Considering student interests along with curriculum requirements has great potential for stemming the tide of negative attitudes that seem so common among upper elementary and middle school students (Worthy, 1998). The students' appreciation for Ms. Washington's flexibility was reflected in their improved behavior and willingness to do traditional schoolwork. We are not suggesting that students should control the curriculum, but that decisions about instruction and materials can be collaborative. When the curriculum requires that particular topics must be studied, teachers can "think outside of the box," and allow a choice of focus areas and materials.

Issue: The Need for Social Interaction

What Teachers Can Do: Provide Time and Opportunity for Productive Social Learning

There's probably nothing more important to students in the middle years than socializing. Luckily, we know that social learning approaches can be very effective for learning and motivation. Social relationships, important for learning at every age, focus heavily on peers in preadolescence and adolescence. Not every learning situation is right for social interaction; however, work with peers used judiciously and appropriately can aid in learning and motivation. Some examples are collaborative research, word study games, performance activities, book recommendations, and conversations about in-school and extracurricular reading and writing (Almasi, 1996; Manning & Manning, 1994; Raphael & McMahon, 1994). Doing important, engaging work with peers leads not only to cognitive and academic growth, but also to social and personal growth. When peers can spend time working and talking together in informal and academic situations, they have the opportunity to get to know each other, to develop friendships and a sense of community, and to feel safe and valued among their peers. Other opportunities for social interactions centered around literacy include reading to younger students.

Issue: The Need for Personal Connections and Community

What Teachers Can Do: Get to Know Students Personally; Build a Community

In a cafeteria filled with hundreds of noisy, cheerful children and adults, Darlene Grayson watches James as he eats alone. James has developed a reputation for being a difficult student. He never does assignments or homework, and he spends his class time calling out and distracting other students. His quick temper, verbal abusiveness, and angry fists frighten his classmates as well as other students in the school. Ms. Grayson has herself often been on the receiving end of James's bad moods and harsh words, and she avoids him as much as possible. She knows it would be easier to go to her room and do her paperwork and planning than to interact with James. He is not her responsibility, but it is the end of the year, and she feels guilty that she has not taken the time to know him personally and has never exchanged pleasant words with him. Sitting down next to James, Ms. Grayson asks him why he is sitting by himself. Expecting to be snubbed, she is surprised by his reply, delivered in an emotionless, matter-of-fact tone: "Everybody here hates me." His words are startling, but Ms. Grayson quickly reaches the disturbing conclusion that he is absolutely right. He has built a tough wall of anger around himself that seems impenetrable, making it easy to blame him, his parents, his poverty, the school from which he has transferred, anything to keep the responsibility from the shoulders of the school. In just 2 weeks, he will leave this school and will attend middle school in the fall. Ms. Grayson wonders: "What will happen to James in middle school? Will someone take responsibility for him? What could the school have done differently to reach James and other students like him?"

As schools get bigger and bigger, and as departmentalization moves into elementary schools, students like James become even harder to reach. Beyond the nurturing of the primary grades, schools can be hectic and lonely places. In middle schools especially, when students change classes for virtually every subject and when their classes do not eat together in the cafeteria, students have to make or find their own places to feel comfortable. This is a difficult and confusing process for many students, and it can damage students' sense of belonging and self-worth. Block scheduling and the team approach that many middle schools have adopted are steps in the right direction. However, even when a student has only three or four teachers instead of six or seven, it's still hard to establish personal connections with 60 or more students. Schools need to be places where students can make personal, human connections with adults as well as with peers. Getting to know students individually, as people as well as learners, is the focus of our first chapter.

A GUIDE TO THIS BOOK

How can a teacher provide high-quality content area instruction when students still need to learn about reading and writing? What are effective and engaging methods of instruction that reach individual students? Our inspiration to write this book grew from these types of questions from teachers and preservice teachers about how to organize instruction in upper elementary and middle school classrooms. We saw the need for a text that addressed content area literacy instruction (reading to learn) within the context of developmental reading instruction (learning to read). As you begin reading this book, we ask you to keep the following principles in mind:

- Teachers need to learn about individual students' interests and academic abilities. Early in the year, time should be spent building personal relationships in a learning environment.
- Teachers need to model fluent reading and the ways in which a strategic reader comprehends text.
- Students need time to read. The teacher acts as both coach and strategist during focused, independent reading and group fluency practice.
- Engaging instruction and reading materials should be focal points in the classroom and should vary by genre, type, level, and complexity. Instruction and materials should support the cultural, linguistic, and academic diversities of all students.

• Writing requires teacher modeling and student practice, and the writing process should be closely linked with reading. Books may provide models of forms of writing or information to use in a piece of writing.

• Language play and word analysis should be integral parts of literacy activities.

We have organized this book to demonstrate that all types of content can be taught within a developmental framework that moves from teacher demonstration to student expertise. We have also provided our readers with diverse examples from children's literature of appropriate picture books, information books, poetry, fiction, biographies, and other reading materials, and with many examples of classroom stories. Box I.6 provides an overview of each chapter with key points and unique features.

CHILDREN'S BOOK REFERENCES

Anderson, L. H. (1999). *Speak.* New York: Farrar, Straus, Giroux.

Berenstain, S., & Berenstain, J. (1988). *The Berenstain Bears and the truth.* New York: Random House.

Bloor, E. (1997). *Tangerine.* San Diego, CA: Harcourt Brace.

Brown, M. (1986). *Arthur's eyes.* Boston: Little, Brown.

Byars, B. (1985). *Cracker Jackson.* New York: Viking.

Curtis, C. P. (1995). *The Watsons go to Birmingham—1963.* New York: Delacorte.

Curtis, C. P. (1999). *Bud, not Buddy.* New York: Delacorte.

Dadey, D., & Jones, M. (2000). *Dracula doesn't rock and roll.* New York: Little Apple.

Duffey, B. (1996). *Hey, new kid!* New York: Viking.

Fenner, C. (1995). *Yolonda's genius.* New York: McElderry.

Flake, S. G. (1998). *The skin I'm in.* New York: Hyperion.

Freedman, R. (1996). *The life and death of Crazy Horse* (ill. A. Bad Heart Bull). New York: Holiday.

Gantos, J. (1998). *Joey Pigza swallowed the key.* New York: Farrar, Straus, Giroux.

Hest, A. (1995). *The private notebook of Katie Roberts, age 11* (ill. S. Lamut). Cambridge, MA: Candlewick.

McDonald, M. (1999). *Judy Moody* (ill. P. Reynolds). Cambridge, MA: Candlewick.

Macaulay, D. (1998). *The new way things work.* Boston: Houghton Mifflin.

Marshall, E. (1983). *Fox at school.* New York: Dial.

Millard, A. (1998). *A street through time* (ill. S. Noon). New York: Dorling Kindersley.

Nixon, J. L. (1997). *Spirit seeker.* New York: Laurel Leaf.

Platt, R. (1992). *Stephen Biesty's incredible cross-sections* (ill. S. Biesty). New York: Knopf.

Ryan, C. (1974). *A bridge too far.* New York: Simon & Schuster.

Rylant, C. (1998). *Henry and Mudge under the yellow moon.* New York: Simon & Schuster.

Scieszka, J. (1992). *The stinky cheese man and other fairly stupid tales* (ill. L. Smith). New York: Viking.

Soto, G. (1995). *Chato's kitchen* (ill. S. Guevera). New York: Putnam.

Taylor, M. D. (1976). *Roll of thunder, hear my cry.* New York: Dial.

Tripp, V. (1988). *Samantha saves the day: A summer story.* Madison, WI: Pleasant Company.

REFERENCES

Almasi, J. A. (1996). A new view of discussion. In L. B. Gambrell & J. Almasi (Eds.), *Lively discussions!: Fostering engaged reading* (pp. 2–24). Newark, DE: International Reading Association.

Anderson, R. C., Wilson, P. T., & Fielding, L. G. (1988). Growth in reading and how children spend their time outside school. *Reading Research Quarterly, 23*(3), 285–303.

BOX I.6. What's in This Book?

Chapters	What are the key features and practical points of this chapter?	What is unique about this chapter?
Chapter I. Assessment: Getting to Know Students as People and Learners	• Working with families • Activities for collecting information about students during the first weeks of school • Guiding students in book selections • Instructional techniques and assessments	This chapter provides the foundation for our focus on knowing individual learners. We present techniques that allow teachers to get to know students personally and academically through engaging instructional practices and individualized assessments.
Chapter 2. What Students Read and How to Get It	• Student preferences in reading • Selecting materials for a classroom collection • Finding resources	This chapter sets up an area that we emphasize throughout the book—how to motivate students as readers. Textbooks rarely mention materials except to use specific books as examples. We want the classroom library to be a central feature of our book.
Chapter 3. Reading Aloud to Students	• Teaching students about genre and informational topics • Engaging students through read alouds • Modeling fluent reading • Supporting comprehension	This chapter introduces the concept of teacher modeling. We explore read-alouds as an engaging practice that allows teachers to model the use of reading techniques that support comprehension of important content. Students will use these techniques during independent reading.
Chapter 4. Just Reading	• Organizing instruction around silent, independent reading • Balancing student choice in reading with wide reading • Ways teachers can support, teach, and assess reading comprehension, vocabulary, and word identification	This chapter is the heart of our book—how teachers can guide students to become strategic, independent readers. Our approach is unique in that we put "just reading," with focused instruction by the teacher, at the forefront of the reading curriculum.
Chapter 5. Building Reading Fluency	• Instruction that supports oral fluency development • Reading performance activities • Developing students' fluency in silent reading	Fluency is often mentioned in beginning reading, but a focus on fluent reading is an unusual feature for a middle grades text. Fluency is closely tied to comprehension and deserves careful attention in instruction. We share practical ideas for looking at meaning through rehearsed oral reading and focused silent reading.

(continued)

BOX 1.6. *(continued)*

Chapter 6. Guiding Students to Read as Writers	• Process writing: Focusing on details and thinking through writing • Using models from literature • Promoting engagement and personal writing	In this chapter, we work with a published author to examine how an actual writer collects information and uses it in different forms. We explore the process of developing fluency in writing and thinking through writing.
Chapter 7. Exploring Words	• Analyzing how language is used in poetry and prose • Creating new works from existing models of language usage • Learning about how words are spelled • Word analysis and word play that support word recognition and spelling	This chapter takes a new look at words by introducing spelling with a playful analysis of language usage. Our approach includes assessing students' development of spelling knowledge and using instructional techniques such as word analysis and word play.
Chapter 8. Guiding Students to Act as Researchers	• Conducting research, reading across sources • Using the writing process with instructional support • Integrating research into the instructional framework • Creative publishing • Evaluation of research	Our focus in this chapter is reading and writing about information. We link conducting research with the writing process and consider alternatives to lengthy projects. Research is integrated within the developmental framework that we use in this book.
Chapter 9. Tailoring Instruction for Individual Students	• Steps for modifying and individualizing classroom instruction for challenged learners • Case studies of middle grades students • Suggestions for teachers' professional growth	We complete this book with an explicit plan for meeting the needs of less skilled readers and writers. We provide our readers with the opportunity to apply their skills by considering case studies of students who are not succeeding in school.

Bintz, W. P. (1993). Resistant readers in secondary education: Some insights and implications. *Journal of Reading, 36,* 604–615.

Hynd, S. (1997). *On the brink: Negotiating literature and life with adolescents.* New York: Teachers College Press.

Ivey, G. (1999). A multicase study in the middle school: Complexities among young adolescent readers. *Reading Research Quarterly, 34,* 172–193.

Ivey, G., & Broaddus, K. (in press). "Just plain reading": A survey of what makes students want to read in middle school classrooms. *Reading Research Quarterly.*

Ivey, G., & Broaddus, K. (2000). Tailoring the fit: Reading instruction and middle school readers. *The Reading Teacher, 54,* 68–78.

Kos, R. (1991). Persistence of reading disabilities: The voices of four middle school students. *American Educational Research Journal, 28,* 875–895.

Manning, G. L., & Manning, M. (1984). What models of recreational reading make a difference? *Reading World, 23,* 375–380.

McCormick, S. (1994). A nonreader becomes a reader: A case study of literacy acquisition by a severely disabled reader. *Reading Research Quarterly, 29,* 156–177.

Nieto, S. (2000). *Affirming diversity: The sociopolitical context of multicultural education.* New York: Longman.

Oldfather, P. (1993). What students say about motivating experiences in a whole language classroom. *The Reading Teacher, 46,* 672–681.

Raphael, T. E., & McMahon, S. I. (1994). Book Club: An alternative framework for reading instruction. *The Reading Teacher, 48*(2), 102–116.

Rogoff, B. (1990). *Apprenticeship in thinking: Cognitive development in social context.* New York: Oxford University Press.

Stanovich, K. (1986). Matthew effects in reading: Some consequences of individual differences in the acquisition of literacy. *Reading Research Quarterly, 24,* 7–26.

Strickland, D. S. (1994). Educating African American learners: Finding a better way. *Language Arts, 71,* 323–336.

Taylor, B., Harris, L. A., Pearson, P. D., & GarcUa, G. (1995). *Reading difficulties: Instruction and assessment* (2nd ed.). New York: McGraw-Hill.

Tomlinson, C., Moon, T. R., & Callahan, C. (1998). How well are we addressing academic diversity in middle school? *Middle School Journal, 3,* 3–11.

Turner, J. C. (1995). The influence of classroom contexts on young children's motivation for literacy. *Reading Research Quarterly, 30,* 410–441.

Vygotsky, L. S. (1978). *Mind and society.* Cambridge, MA: Harvard University Press.

Worthy, J. (1998). "On every page someone gets killed!": Book conversations you don't hear in school. *Journal of Adolescent and Adult Literacy, 41,* 503–517.

Worthy, J., & McKool, S. S. (1996). Students who say they hate to read: The importance of opportunity, choice, and access. In D. J. Leu, C. K. Kinzer, & K. A. Hinchman (Eds.), *Literacies for the 21st century: Research and practice* (pp. 245–256). Chicago: National Reading Conference.

Worthy, J., Moorman, M., & Turner, M. (1999). What Johnny likes to read is hard to find in school. *Reading Research Quarterly, 34,* 12–27.

PART I

Getting Ready for the School Year: Assessment and Materials

Whether you are a new or an experienced teacher, you probably begin each school year with similar questions: "What will my students be like? How can I get to know my students, build a classroom community, and assess students' skills? How should I start the school year? What kinds of materials should I have in my classroom?" In this first section of the book, we address these and other issues with chapters about assessment and building a classroom book collection.

CHAPTER 1

Assessment: Getting to Know Students as People and Learners

It is language arts time on the first day of school, and Mrs. Walker has just finished going over the class rules. Now her third-grade students are sitting in their desks quietly working on "What I Did over the Summer" essays, while Mrs. Walker works through a stack of paperwork. Next, students will silently read the first story in their basal readers. Down the hall, Ms. Singh and her sixth-grade students are sitting in pairs around the room laughing, chatting, and jotting down notes as they interview each other about favorite movies and music, events of the summer, hobbies, families, and so on. They will introduce their interview partners to the class and make a "Who's Who" bulletin board with highlights from the interviews. Next, they will browse through a set of varied reading materials that Ms. Singh has displayed and will talk together about their favorite things to read. What are your thoughts about how these two teachers approach the beginning of the school year?

WHAT'S IN THIS CHAPTER?

What Is Assessment and Why Is It Important?
Getting to Know Students as People
Getting to Know Students as Learners
Issues in Choosing Appropriate Books
Analyzing Students' Reading
Continual Assessments during Classroom Instruction

WHAT IS ASSESSMENT AND WHY IS IT IMPORTANT?

In *The Literacy Dictionary* (Harris & Hodges, 1995), *assessment* is defined as "the act or process of gathering data in order to better understand the strengths and weaknesses of student learning, as by observation, testing, interviews, etc." (p. 12). Effective assessment does not stop with the gathering of information, however. Equally important are (1) carefully evaluating the data for strengths, challenges, and issues that may be impeding or contributing to students' growth; and (2) using the evaluations to plan and refine instruction that will help students progress as engaged, independent learners. Without assessment and evaluation, instruction is a hit-or-miss affair. Careful assessment and evaluation will help teachers to better individualize instruction, meet students' needs, and help students accelerate their learning.

In recent years, educators have moved away from a view of reading and writing as separate, skills-based subjects to a view that encompasses the language arts as integrated and reciprocal processes. This change in thinking has also led to changes in ideas about literacy assessment, especially in regard to who are the best judges of students' literacy and what sorts of procedures are most useful. It is only logical that the best judges of students' literacy development are classroom teachers who observe them engaged in literacy tasks day after day (Johnston, 1987), and that the best assessments are those yielding information that can be used in planning instruction (Farr, 1992).

In this book we focus on *curriculum-based assessments*, defined by Harris and Hodges (1995) as "the appraisal of student progress by using materials and procedures directly from the curriculum taught" (p. 51). For a brief discussion of *norm-referenced* and *criterion-referenced* tests, please see Box 1.1. Curriculum-based assessments are useful and practical because they are based on classroom activities and they inform instructional planning. In this chapter, we describe initial assessments that can be used to get to know students as people and as learners. Each instructional chapter in this book includes examples of assessments and guidelines for evaluating and grading students' work. Students should be involved in every aspect of assessment as they continue on the road toward independent learning. Assessments should be shared with students so that they will know what the rationale behind them is, how to use them, and how they can be used in evaluating their own learning and building strategies.

Our practical experiences, along with educational research, have convinced us that academic assessments should be combined with listening to students—gathering information about their lives, their interests, and what is important to them (Ivey, 1999; Worthy & McKool, 1996). When students know their teachers and each other as people, they can benefit from the diverse knowledge and experiences that all bring to the classroom, feel comfortable taking risks in learning, and achieve at their highest potential. Thus we use an approach to initial assessment that is geared toward knowing students *personally* as well as *academically*. In this chapter, we describe (1) activities that help teachers and students get to know each other personally and begin to build a classroom community, and (2) assessments to be conducted during the first weeks of school that will help teachers get to know students as literacy learners and provide a baseline for students' skills. More focused assessments are included in the instructional chapters. Depending on their ages and skills in reading and writing, students will need varying degrees of support to complete the activities described in this chapter. Feel free to modify them as appropriate for your students and context.

GETTING TO KNOW STUDENTS AS PEOPLE

Building a community is the first order of business for every classroom, regardless of subject or grade level. To do this, teachers and students must first learn about each other as people. Begin the assessment process at the beginning of the school year (or be-

BOX 1.1. Norm-Referenced, Criterion-Referenced, and Informal Assessments

Our book focuses mainly on *curriculum-based assessments* (see Chapter 1). However, it is important for teachers to be aware of the other kinds of assessments that are used in schools: *norm-referenced* and *criterion-referenced*.

Norm-Referenced and Criterion-Referenced Achievement Tests

Two types of assessments that are usually far removed from classroom instruction are norm-referenced and criterion-referenced. Group-administered norm-referenced tests, including the Iowa Test of Basic Skills and the Standardized Achievement Test, compare students' academic achievement with others of the same age or grade. Students' scores on these tests may be reported in terms of standard scores, percentiles, stanines, and/or grade equivalents. These terms are explained in books about tests and measurements and in the manuals for specific tests. Norm-referenced tests have a place in informing education stakeholders about the achievement of large groups of students, and in comparing groups of students. However, group-administered norm-referenced tests rarely inform classroom instruction. There are many individually administered norm-referenced tests that focus on achievement in a variety of content areas, including reading and writing; these tests afford more detailed information about a specific child's strengths and areas of challenge.

An individually administered norm-referenced test for ages 7–19 that focuses solely on reading is the Gray Oral Reading Test—3 (Wiederholdt & Bryant, 1992), which provides information about a student's oral reading accuracy, rate, and comprehension. Although such tests can be useful components of an assessment plan, the short, context-limited passages, and multiple-choice or short-answer formats do not afford useful information about students' achievement in classroom reading and writing tasks. Such tests are usually administered by reading specialists but are not particularly helpful for classroom teachers, except to provide rough estimates of reading achievement levels and areas of challenge and strength.

Criterion-referenced assessments, including most state minimum-competency tests, measure students' skills against preset criteria or standards. These tests can be useful for determining whether groups or individuals are meeting minimum basic skills in a variety of areas. However, like the information in norm-referenced tests, the information in criterion-referenced tests is rarely useful for teachers in planning instruction. Rather than measuring what is being taught in ways that reflect instructional practice, the tasks on most of these tests are quite unlike those found in most classrooms. Consequently, many teachers feel the need to spend large amounts of time outside of regular classroom instruction preparing students to do well on the tests. Test season is accompanied by anxiety among principals, teachers, and (by extension) students, as illustrated in the following comment by the mother of a fourth grader:

> "You know the tests that they have? Maya would just start crying if she knew that that was a week they were gonna have a test or a practice test. She was already dreading it. . . . It bothered us all at home. It was getting so stressful she didn't even want to come to school."

Informal Assessments

A step closer to classroom practice, and thus more useful for teachers, are informal assessments. Reading specialists and some classroom teachers have long used individually administered tests called *informal reading inventories* to assess the skills of students who struggle with reading. Although they're called "informal," and the passages are longer and often more contextualized than those on norm-referenced and criterion-referenced tests, there is actually a good deal of formality in these

(continued)

BOX 1.1. *(continued)*

tests; the directions and administration are standardized, and the tests are time-consuming to administer. Most informal reading inventories begin with graded lists of words (preprimer through junior high or high school) to assess students' automatic word identification and word analysis skills. Next students read graded passages orally or silently, followed by a retelling and/or comprehension questions. The tester calculates the rate of reading (words per minute), the number and type of reading errors (if the student is reading orally), and the number of passage units retold and/or questions answered correctly. An example of an informal reading inventory is the Qualitative Reading Inventory (Leslie & Caldwell, 1995), for reading levels from beginning to junior high. It features word lists, both narrative and information passages, retelling and comprehension questions, a prior knowledge assessment for each passage, and several different forms for repeated administrations.

A major goal of informal reading inventories is to find the levels at which students' reading is considered to be in the independent (appropriate for reading without assistance), instructional (appropriate for reading with instructional support), and frustrational ranges (too difficult for the students to read). These categories are important to understand, because students' progress in reading is dependent in part on the types of texts they read. However, even the longer passages in an informal reading inventory do not always translate well to "real books" that students are actually reading. The text of this chapter provides more information on the benefits of using curriculum-based assessments with classroom materials.

fore) by gathering personal information about students and getting to know their families. This information will help you as a teacher to gear your instruction toward what your students bring with them to school. Box 1.2 lists areas of interest, along with tools and strategies for gathering personal information about students. There are many "getting-to-know-you" activities described in this chapter; pick the ones that are most appropriate for you and your students. Before school begins, prepare an assessment folder or portfolio for every student in your classroom. The portfolio will include information from initial assessments, samples of continuous assessments, and student work from throughout the year. Gathering and evaluating this information regularly will help you to plan appropriate instruction for students and monitor their progress.

BOX 1.2. Gathering Information about Students as People

Areas	Tools and strategies
• Personal information about students and teachers	• Letters, visits, and/or phone calls to parents
• Information about families and home literacy	• Interviews and observations
• Information about personal interests	• "I wish" poems
• Important Book	• Guess my fib
	• Student–teacher dialogue journals (see chapter text for a description)

Contacting Students and Their Families

Building a classroom community can start before the first day of school, as teachers establish contact with students and their families. Along with a welcome letter to students, many teachers send a letter of introduction to parents over the summer or early in the year, requesting information about students and inviting parents to visit, volunteer, offer input, or help the class in other ways. At the least, teachers should make personal contact with parents by phone either before or during the first weeks of school. Many teachers find that home visits enhance their teaching. If you do not speak the language that is spoken in a student's home, find someone in your school or community who can accompany you on the home visit to translate and advise you about the family's culture. Home visits should be considered a time for teachers, students, and their families to get to know each other better informally and to establish home–school partnerships that will benefit all involved.

Parents can provide information about their child's interests, development, and educational history that can be useful in planning instruction. Taking the time to listen to parents' views can provide a valuable perspective that is not typically available from school records or from talking to previous teachers. For example, the quotes in Box 1.3 are excerpts from interviews with upper elementary and middle school parents about their children who have had academic difficulties in school. Their statements illustrate an intense interest in and knowledge about education that some people may assume are lacking in parents of struggling learners. How might a teacher use the information from these parents in working with the students?

Partnering with parents can make a real difference in your relationships with students as well. The week before school started, an eighth-grade language arts teacher, Carmen Barrera, found that her new class included a student, Joseph, who had a school-wide reputation as a troublemaker. Before school started, Mrs. Barrera called Joseph's parents to introduce herself and chat with them about their son. Joseph's mother mentioned that he had been in constant trouble in previous years. Both parents made it clear to Mrs. Barrera that they had high expectations for Joseph's behavior and learning, and that the teacher should call if there was ever a problem. At the first serious sign of classroom disruption, Mrs. Barrera called home and handed the phone to Joseph to explain what he had done. It only took one more phone call for Joseph to realize that his teacher was serious. Mrs. Barrera also made sure to call Joseph's parents with good news about his learning and attitudes. Several weeks later, when one of Joseph's previous teachers dropped by Mrs. Barrera's classroom, she was amazed to see Joseph working productively and wondered what had led to the drastic change. "Oh, that," replied Mrs. Barrera. "Joseph and I are best buddies now. I know his parents, and he knows that we are all serious about his learning and behavior in the classroom." Joseph's parents were grateful that the teacher had included them as partners, and that Joseph's school days were now spent learning rather than wasting time. Mrs. Barrera discovered, as do many teachers, that when first contacts are positive, parents will be more receptive to collaborating with teachers. Continue to have regular contacts throughout the year, through class newsletters, phone calls, visits, personal notes, and so forth. Making frequent "good news" calls for all of your students is an excellent investment in the classroom climate.

BOX 1.3. Excerpts from Parent Interviews

"I did a lot of reading with Marcus when he was young. The topic varied from sports to animals and scary stories. He showed a real interest in books."

"After we got Maya's last report card, I went to see the school counselor to tell her the pressure was getting to Maya. She didn't even want to come to school anymore. She would get up and tell me she was dumb. I wouldn't think it was right for her to be going through all that."

"Omar did okay in first and second, but the problem started in third grade. He was too quick to be labeled. The teacher said he was hyperactive, and she referred us to a doctor for Ritalin. At this point I never believe we should have done that. . . . The Ritalin didn't change him. In fact, he started doing worse in school. I finally said I don't want him taking that any more."

"At home, Noah loves to read to his brothers and sisters, but at school he's frustrated. He says the books are too hard. The teacher wants to test him for a learning disability."

"I buy David every book and magazine he asks for. He has a stack of *Boys' Life* and *Sports Illustrated for Kids*. But when he gets them he won't read them. He never reads them. I just don't get it."

"One time Lucia was in a class where they spoke Spanish and English, and I think that may have confused her because she didn't know Spanish. We think they put her in that class to interpret; they assumed she knew Spanish, since she was a Mexican. To this day, I think that's what caused her to fall behind."

"Matthew had some trouble getting started in reading because he was very young when he started first grade. Finally in fifth grade he got hooked on reading books and magazines about football. That's what got him started. Nowadays he reads all the time."

"Michelle has always liked books as long as I can remember. She showed an early interest in animal books. At 3 years of age, she would pick up books and even though she would only recognize one word, she would make up a story just by reading the pictures. She loves to read, and her teacher says her reading is almost on grade level. But her spelling—wow—it's awful!"

Activities for the First Weeks of School

The activities we describe in the next sections are appropriate for virtually any age and grade level in elementary and middle school. Be sure, however, to model all activities first, and to offer additional modeling, guided practice, and support for younger students and for struggling readers and writers.

Interviews and Observations

There are various ways for students and teachers to learn about each other during the first days or weeks of school. In a first-day interview, for example, all members of the class interview each other in pairs, and then partners introduce each other to the class. An example of such an interview is provided in Appendix B. For students needing literacy support, teachers may need to go through the interview step by step, reading each question aloud. It is also helpful for teachers to talk to each student individually during the first week or two of school, even if it's only for a few minutes. This can be done at lunch or recess time (if applicable) or when students are reading or writing independently. Teachers can also gain valuable information about students from observing them as they interact with other students and adults, engage in instruction and free-time activities, and participate in class.

"I Wish" Poem

We like to borrow Kenneth Koch's "wishes" poem format (Koch, 1970, pp. 64–86) as a getting-acquainted writing activity. Each student writes one sentence that adheres to the following rules: (1) It must begin with the words "I wish"; and (2) it must include three specific items, such as favorite celebrity, favorite pastime, and favorite dessert (students can help come up with ideas for the categories). After students have written their sentences, they are compiled into one long poem, which the teacher can read aloud for the group. It is fun to read the poem in its entirety, and then to read it again one line at a time with the author of each sentence identifying her- or himself. Here is an excerpt from a collaborative "I wish" poem written by Gay Ivey's sixth graders. The categories students had to include were favorite sports hero, favorite snack, and favorite book.

> I wish I could eat a Fruit Roll-Up with Michael Jordan and read *Willy the Wimp*.
> I wish I had an ice cream cone to eat while I listened to Andre Agassi read *Fantastic Mr. Fox* to me.
> I wish I could shoot baskets with Dawn Staley and then we could eat pizza and take turns reading *Where the Sidewalk Ends*.
> I wish I could play football with my brother and then we could read *Sports Illustrated* and drink Gatorade.

Important Poems

Another first-week writing activity in which students use a simple pattern to write about their interests and favorite activities is based on *The Important Book* (Brown, 1949). Each poem in the book describes an object, starting and ending with the "important thing" about the object, with supporting details between the first and last line. "The important thing about a spoon," according to the book, "is that you eat with it." Details include that it is flat and hollow and "like a little shovel." The teacher can read the book or share some "important" poems (like the one below, written by a fifth grader), help students discover the pattern, and guide them to write their own poems for a class "important" book. Again, more modeling and support will be needed for some students.

> **The Important Thing about James Evans**
> The important thing about me is that I love drawing.
> I like to make exciting stories
> And stories about people
> I'm always in a tree
> I like to pick pecans
> I think school is fun
> But the important thing about me is that I love drawing.

"Guess My Fib"

Another activity that involves students' writing is "Guess my fib." In this activity, each student writes three true statements about him- or herself and one untrue statement. The trick is to think of truths that are so unusual that class members think they couldn't be true (e.g., "I have a cat who is 20 years old"). Kim Duhamel then has her fourth-grade students sit in small clusters of four or five. Other small-group members must decide which statement is a fib. Students then regroup until everyone has heard all of the lists. Often students trick each other with interesting and unexpected information about themselves. For instance, many students in Ms. Duhamel's class were amazed to learn that the family of one of their classmates owned a hotel.

GETTING TO KNOW STUDENTS AS LEARNERS

In addition to learning about students personally, teachers need to gather information related to their literacy learning. Some areas to think about are these: What can students do? What are their areas of strength and challenge? What are their attitudes and self-concepts in regard to reading and writing? What do they like to read and write about? Box 1.4 lists areas of interest related to literacy, and tools and strategies for gathering data about students as learners. At the beginning of the year, we start with whole-class activities and observations of students as they engage in reading and writing.

For planning appropriate instructional activities and gathering appropriate materials, it is helpful for teachers to know about students' attitudes toward reading and writing, and about their preferences, habits, and experiences in both areas. Include multiple tools and strategies for assessment in all areas, such as surveys, open-ended questions, observations, interviews, and regular instructional activities. We have included the following surveys in Appendix B. Again, keep in mind that students will need varying amounts of support to complete these surveys:

- A reading attitude survey in which students respond to items about reading on a Likert scale
- A reading preference survey
- Open-ended questions about reading and writing habits

Student–Teacher Dialogue Journals

Dialogue journals are "conversations on paper," or informal letters exchanged between a student and the teacher in a journal/log. Since each student entry is based on personal interests and stories about experiences, a dialogue journal is an excellent way to learn more about individual students at the beginning of a new school year. In addition, you will collect informal assessment information on how quickly a student writes, choices about content, complexity of writing, attitudes toward writing, use of vocabulary, and mechanics (discussed more thoroughly in Chapters 6, 7, and 8). When you respond to a student, you will not be addressing grammatical errors or spelling mistakes. Since the purpose of a dialogue journal is to encourage students to write fluently about personally meaningful topics, you will be responding to the content of the writing. You

---

BOX 1.4. Gathering Information about Students as Learners

Areas	Tools and strategies
• Reading and writing attitudes and preferences	• Talking to parents • Observing and taking notes as students tour the library and choose books, and as students write • Talking to students about what they read and write • Surveying students • Reading and responding in student–teacher dialogue journals
• Reading comprehension, listening comprehension, fluency, and word identification in a variety of texts and contexts (silent reading, oral reading, teacher read-aloud), and with varying levels of teacher support • Appropriate book choices	• Listening to students read, and analyzing their word analysis and fluency • Observing students read • Listening to students as they discuss teacher read-alouds • Analyzing students' written, oral, or graphic responses • Observing and talking to students about the books they choose
• Writing content and mechanics in a variety of writing contexts and with varying levels of teacher support	• Reading and responding in student–teacher dialogue journals • Analyzing multiple writing samples, using rubrics (see Chapter 6 and Appendix B) and qualitative spelling analysis (see Chapter 7)

---

will be sharing information about yourself as a person and as a writer and reader, so your letters should contain more than responses and answers to questions posed by students. Although the initial entry with your introduction of yourself may be the same for each student, you will need to vary the dialogue journals in response to each individual student's entries. Whenever possible, try to send the journals back and forth several times a week in the beginning of the year. The frequency with which you respond to students will depend on your teaching situation. With a small self-contained classroom, you may be able to respond to all students several times per week; when you are in a departmentalized program with multiple classes, your responses will not be as frequent. Be sure, however, to respond to students at least once every 2 weeks, keeping a record of when you do. As the year progresses, students may respond to their peers' journals as well. Here are some suggestions for setting up dialogue journals:

1. Be sure to design an actual journal. Students need to know that this correspondence will be an ongoing process. Simple construction paper books with brackets work well, or print a cover with a title and graphics on the computer.

2. Type or write clearly. As you write your first entry, consider what information

you might like to know about the student. Introduce yourself, and describe those things about yourself in your entry.

3. Read your first journal entry to your students and discuss ideas for their responses. Allow 15 minutes of class time for the students to write. If there is a student who has extremely limited writing ability, you can offer to take a dictation from the student for the first response. Ask the student to reread the dictation to you after it is complete. Then ask the student to draw and label or write a caption for the drawing about the dictation.

4. Keep any questions open-ended (avoid questions that can be answered with yes–no or one-word responses). Focus on writing about a specific topic rather than creating a list of questions for the student.

5. For the first week or two of school, the major focus of dialogue journals is learning about students. As the school year progresses, dialogue journals will become tools for modeling and guiding students' writing. Be sure that you explicitly model the type of response you are expecting from students. For example, if you want a student to move beyond simple answers to a narrative format, write your response in that way. Ask questions that will help the student write about the beginning, middle, and ending of a memory about a personal experience, for example.

Read-Aloud and Response

One of the most efficient and informative whole-class or small-group assessments is a read-aloud followed by discussion and written response. By observing and listening to students as they participate in a discussion, teachers can note how the particular students conduct themselves as a group during a discussion, as well as how individual students react to both the read-aloud and the discussion. Through an open-ended written response, teachers can begin to get a feel for students' listening comprehension, writing content and form, and attitudes toward reading and writing. More in-depth assessments and instruction for each of these areas are found in later chapters.

To conduct this assessment/instructional activity, choose an interesting picture book, chapter book, newspaper or magazine article, or information book appropriate for your grade level and read it aloud to the class. After reading the book, chapter, or segment, ask students a simple open-ended question (e.g., "What do you think?") to prompt discussion. During the discussion, observe and take notes about students' participation and interaction, reactions to the read-aloud, comments, questions, and so on. After a few minutes of discussion, ask students to write whatever came to their minds as they were listening to the text, and observe them as they write. Of course, one written response does not provide enough information for you to make generalized judgments about anything, but this is a good way to achieve an initial assessment for several areas. Copy each writing sample and examine it. Box 1.5 shows a sample of general areas and questions to consider in examining students' responses.

Having introduced students to written responses to read-alouds, continue to make this a regular activity, choosing a variety of genres, topics, and response options for the read-aloud (see book lists in Chapter 3). In examining students' responses, make notes about how their writing differs in response to different kinds of books. Please note, however, that students should not be required to respond to every read-aloud. There should also be read-alouds for pure enjoyment and other purposes, as described in Chapter 3.

BOX 1.5. Examining Written Responses to a Teacher Read-Aloud

• *Listening comprehension*: Does the response indicate a general understanding of the book or chapter? Does the response make sense?

Is the response a literal retelling, or does the student make interpretations, connections to personal experiences, and connections to other books she or he has read? Does the student make predictions and evaluations?

• *Writing*: Evaluate for fluency, coherence, voice.

• *Mechanics*: Evaluate for spelling, punctuation, grammar.

• *Attitudes*: Did the student approach the task willingly or with complaints? Did he or she ask many questions or tackle the assignment independently? During the writing, did the student spend time thinking? Did she or he appear frustrated?

Interacting with Students as They Read on Their Own

To gain an early sense of students' reading preferences, attitudes, and skill, teachers should begin immediately giving students daily opportunities to choose and read books and other materials. This reading time will gradually become more focused on instruction and fluency (see Chapters 4 and 5); however, early in the year, independent reading time gives teachers an opportunity to gather initial assessment information as they listen to individual students read and talk about their books. Before the reading time, set up several tables for book browsing, with books from every topic and genre imaginable—including typical school materials (e.g., novels, information books, short stories, school magazines, series books, multicultural materials, poetry), as well as less conventional materials (newspapers, trade magazines), being sure to include topics that particularly interest students in the middle grades (horror, sports, jokes, animals, humor, etc.). See Chapter 2 for suggestions. Make sure all students have books that  are easy and interesting to read, and enough books to keep them reading for the agreed-upon time. After they have chosen, ask them to tell or write the answers to these or similar questions about each item they choose:

"Why did you choose this?"

"Have you read this or something like it before?"

"Is this easy for you to read? Something you would like me (or someone else) to help you with? Too challenging for you to read on your own? Why?"

Observing students as they choose books and recording and evaluating their answers to these questions, will help you to learn whether students already have some independence in reading and choosing appropriate books and how much support they will need to find and choose books. Getting students started in reading independently is a valuable way to begin the year. Most likely, you will find that many students need assistance in choosing appropriate books. In the next section, we discuss how to help students choose books with the right amount of support and challenge to help them grow in reading proficiency and enjoyment.

ISSUES IN CHOOSING APPROPRIATE BOOKS

Reading at the Independent Level

Successful reading experiences lead to more enjoyment of reading, and thus to more reading. All students should have access to materials they can read independently—materials that provide success and enjoyment. In reality, however, skilled readers have many opportunities to read in independent-level materials, while students who struggle with reading rarely have such opportunities. Which ones do you think will be more likely to pick up a book in their spare time? We believe that the lack of easy, interesting reading materials is the major reason for the slow progress and negative attitudes of lower-achieving readers.

What kinds of materials do you read when you are on vacation? Before going to sleep? For pure enjoyment or to learn more about a topic with which you are already very familiar? Do you read news, sports, entertainment, gardening, or other magazines? Mystery, science fiction, romance, humorous, or other novels? The newspaper? These materials are most likely on your *independent* reading level. You have no difficulty understanding what you are reading. Virtually all of the words are familiar, and you can easily figure out those that aren't. Reading in independent-level materials helps to develop fluency and motivation; when students can read almost all of the words correctly, they can concentrate on smoothness, expression, enjoyment, and understanding rather than spending their brainpower decoding words.

So why don't we just give all students plenty of materials on their independent reading levels? The problem is that finding independent-level materials that struggling readers will read is very difficult. If we only considered reading level or fit, we could probably provide plenty of materials that would be easy. However, while some students may feel relieved that they can read without struggling, others are embarrassed about reading books meant for younger students. Furthermore, the excitement of books that "fit" wears off for some students after reading many books that are not age-appropriate. Finally, to make progress, students need to stretch their reading proficiency with books that provide more challenge. Thus the concept of fit is far more complex than that of reading level.

Roller (1996) discusses ways to make "easy books acceptable." One way is to help students find real purposes for reading easy books, such as practicing to read to a younger sibling or to younger students at school. Lafayette, a seventh-grade struggling reader, would never read the repetitive pattern book *Once, a Lullaby* (Nichol, 1986) for his own pleasure. However, after practicing it several times, he was proud to be able to read it fluently to his second-grade reading buddy, who eventually convinced him to "sing" the book with her. Teachers can also make students comfortable with reading easy books by introducing and reading aloud simple texts and recommending them as possible reading choices for *all* students in the class. It is easy for teachers to be enthusiastic about many of these books, since they appeal to readers of all ages and skill levels. For instance, we love *Squids Will Be Squids* (Scieszka, 1998) and *Earl's Too Cool for Me* (Komaiko, 1990). It is also important to talk honestly with students about the importance of reading independent-level books; for some students, this is enough to make them persist until they can read more age-appropriate materials.

Ways to make "difficult books accessible" are allowing students to explore difficult books independently and with other students, reading out loud to students, taped reading, partner reading, and rereading. Roller (1996) also recommends starting with easy books and gradually moving to more difficult books on the same topic. For example, a student who wants to read about a current sports star might start with an easy-reading biography. Next, having been exposed to the basic information and vocabulary, he can move to gradually more difficult books. In any case, teachers should give extra attention to students who have reading challenges, making sure that they are finding plenty of books that they can read independently. All students need to feel the experience of being "lost in a book" (Nell, 1988).

Reading at the Instructional Level

What kinds of texts are a little more difficult for you? Are you a member of a book club in which you read and discuss books that are more challenging than your usual vacation books? Do you read professional journals such as *The Reading Teacher* or the *Journal of Adolescent and Adult Literacy* (published by the International Reading Association), *Language Arts* or *English Journal* (published by the National Council of Teachers of English), and *The Horn Book Magazine*? Books and articles that your professor assigns for class reading (if you are a student) or other professional texts that you read to learn new approaches to teaching, including this book, would probably be on your instructional level. Instructional-level materials provide opportunities to learn new information, to experience new forms of language and vocabulary, and (for developing readers) to learn and practice reading strategies with support. Supports for adults may include your own prior knowledge and experience with the text topic, other materials about the same topic, and/or support from colleagues or an instructor. Mature readers can sometimes learn on their own from instructional-level materials, because they have the reading skills and maturity to persist even when tasks are difficult. Young students who are developing in reading, and more advanced students who are learning new content material, will probably need support to benefit from text at the instructional level. If students are interested in what they're reading and if the challenges aren't too great, instructional-level books can be very motivating; we all like to learn new information and test our limits when we know help is available.

Reading on the Frustration Level

Independent-level materials help students to develop fluency and confidence; instructional-level materials help students to learn new ideas and strategies. Frustrational level materials give students exactly what the term implies—frustration. Frustrational-level texts may be too difficult in terms of new concepts and vocabulary, unfamiliar text type or language structure, and/or word identification demands. If you've ever tried to read a research article on an unfamiliar subject (neuroanatomy? physics? philosophy?), you can identify with students reading on the frustrational level. Reading on the frustrational level is one of the most, well, frustrating experiences that a student can have, and many students have these experiences every day. In Box 1.6, a preservice teacher (who is now teaching in a Texas public school) reflects upon his experience with a fourth-grade student as she read a frustrational level text. Ebony was a skilled, motivated reader, but in those few moments of reading, she experienced what it is like to struggle with reading.

Clearly, the text was not appropriate for Ebony to read on her own, even with support. This was probably her first experience with a text this difficult, since she was one of the best readers in her class. Imagine how repeated experiences with frustrational-level texts would affect Ebony's motivation for learning. Now consider the reality that for students who struggle with reading, the majority of their reading experiences are exactly like Ebony's, if not worse (Allington, 1983). Furthermore, grade-level textbooks are on the frustrational level of many students, yet some teachers persist in requiring

---

BOX 1.6. A Skilled Reader Experiences Text at Her Frustrational Level (by John Reese)

Yesterday I had a most insightful experience. Ebony and I were doing a supported reading activity [the student reads with teacher assistance]. As Ebony is an excellent reader and can pretty much handle any of the books in the reading club library, I decided to try a more challenging text than we usually read: Martin Luther King Jr.'s "I Have a Dream" speech (*I Have a Dream*; King, 1997). If you haven't read it lately, read it; it's very uplifting. Anyway, recall that it is a speech and uses "speech language." It paints a striking verbal picture for a listener or reader, due to the elaborate use of the English language. Anyway, after I introduced the text and made some links to Ebony's existing knowledge of MLK, we began to read (me a page, her a page). Even before she finished her first page, she was "lost." I got to see firsthand how a text that is too difficult can snuff out the desire to read (now I know why it's called the FRUSTRATIONAL level). Whereas we usually talk, make predictions, try to get meaning from context or pictures (it's a picture book, by the way), or make real-life connections to what we are reading as we read, we were unable to do this because she had NO comprehension of the "meaning" of the speech as it is written. She lost her enthusiasm (she usually loves to tell you about links she makes to what she reads); she began to mumble at unfamiliar words instead of decoding them; she began to only sound out the first part of an unfamiliar word (e.g., "mmmmm" for *manacles*), then immediately turn and look at me and wait.

Her attention continually waned. Her expression changed to sullen (I'm not exaggerating! Ebony is normally the least sullen child who ever lived) as she continually stumbled in almost every sentence. We stumbled through a few more pages; then I stopped her and told her this was a mistake on my part, that I chose a book way too hard for her. I reminded her that she was an excellent reader, etc., etc. Anyway, I got to see firsthand how readers become demotivated (very quickly) by text that is not on their level and how, if it is too hard, not even supported reading can help them make their own connections in regard to comprehension because all you're doing is decoding words and that's no fun. Just ask Ebony. When it was over, she said to me, "I have no idea what I just read. It was too hard." Yes, Ebony, it was, and thank you, dear heart, for teaching me a valuable lesson.

students to read them. This is all the more reason to become familiar with and provide a wide range of materials, and to remember that a textbook is just a resource.

Although we do not want students to read materials that cause frustration, students can often comprehend books read aloud that are too difficult for them to read. Thus it is essential for them to have access to texts that may be at their frustrational *reading* level (but still interesting to them and conceptually appropriate) through teacher read-alouds (see Chapter 3) and taped books (see Chapter 5).

Readability Formulas and "Leveled" Book Lists

Look on the back of many novels and other books for young readers, and you will see a level stated in years and months (e.g., 2.4 equals the fourth month of second grade). It is tempting to believe that these levels are precise. However, while they can often provide a ballpark estimate of a book's difficulty, it is important to know that these levels are based on readability formulas (e.g., Fry, 1987), which measure text difficulty only through sentence and word length. Books with long sentences and big words are rated as more difficult, regardless of the difficulty of the vocabulary and concepts.

Lists of "leveled books" (Pinnell & Fountas, 1999), which include a wide variety of books categorized for difficulty, are currently all the rage. These lists are based on the notion that students should read books at an appropriate level of difficulty—which, as we have discussed earlier, is a great idea. The leveling in some of these programs goes beyond readability formulas to include such features as match of illustrations and text for emerging and beginning readers, language (e.g., use of patterns, sophistication, dialect), size of print, number of words per page, vocabulary, and sophistication of concepts (Peterson, 1991; Rhodes, 1981). It is important for teachers to understand how these factors relate to text difficulty, so they can help their students select books rather than simply relying on published lists. Sheila Felber, an elementary language arts specialist in California, has explained how teachers in her school worked in a team to develop their understanding of text difficulty: "By first dividing your books into obvious piles from easiest to most challenging and then subdividing and then subdividing again, you learn an insider's view of how to level books. We found it very effective."

However, preleveling books is necessarily limited to text features. The appropriateness of a text for a particular student also depends on the *reader* (familiarity and experience with the topic and type of text, prior vocabulary and conceptual knowledge, interest) and on the *context* in which the reading occurs (see Box 1.7 for more complete information). Leveled book lists can certainly be useful tools in directing students to books that may be within their reading comfort range. However, we and other teachers have found repeatedly that a student assessed as reading on a particular level may find that some of the books in that level are appropriate while others are not. Similarly, the same book may pose completely different challenges for two students who supposedly read "on the same level." With a heavy focus on level, students' interests and prior knowledge may be neglected in considering appropriate books. Furthermore, using only leveled books does not give students an active role in assessing the "fit" of a book, leading many students to become dependent on the levels or the teacher's help in choosing books. When one teacher began to hear her students make comments like "You can't read that book; it's not on your level," and "There's no more books on my level, so I don't have anything to read," she decided that it was time to back off from

---

**BOX 1.7. Factors That Influence Ease of Reading or Readability,
from a Student's Point of View**

Reader Factors

1. Interest/familiarity/prior knowledge
    - Have I seen this text or a similar text before?
    - Do I know something about this subject?
    - Is this about something interesting to me?

2. Vocabulary knowledge
    - Are the words in my speaking vocabulary?
    - If the word is not in my speaking vocabulary, does it refer to a familiar concept? (An example is the word *furious* which may be an unfamiliar word for a familiar concept.)

Text Factors

1. Structure and language of text
    - How many words and lines are there per page?
    - How closely do the pictures match the print (for early readers)?
    - Is the text a narrative (story) or information?
    - Are the sentences phrased the way I would normally say them?

2. Decodability/predictability
    - Is the text written in rhyme, or is there a pattern (e.g., a repeated phrase) that I can easily remember?
    - Are there many words in my reading vocabulary (e.g., "sight" or "anchor" words, or words that I have studied)?
    - Do unfamiliar words contain patterns that help me to decode them?

Context Factors

1. Independence versus assistance
    - Am I reading by myself?
    - Am I reading with a teacher's help?

2. Purpose of reading
    - Am I reading for fun?
    - Am I reading to study?

---

her dependence on leveled texts. She explained to her students that levels were only one way of choosing books, and she showed them strategies that they could use themselves.

Students who are dependent on teachers and levels to choose their books may be less likely to become independent readers. When students learn to choose their own books and can read independently, teachers have more freedom to focus on individual book conferences and assessment (see Chapter 4). In the next section, we discuss a strategy for student book choice.

A Strategy for Students to Use in Choosing Books

Rather than using specific levels, we prefer thinking of books in terms of a range of difficulty. Especially for students beyond the earliest stages of reading, it is important to choose books within a range rather than on one level. It is most essential that students develop their own book-choosing skills. The system we use with students is simple yet effective. With modeling and guided practice, even young students can learn the system easily and can learn why a particular book is appropriate, rather than depending on rules, formulas, the teacher, or a leveling system. Olhausen and Jepsen (1992) developed the "Goldilocks" system to help students learn to choose their own books based on comprehension, fluency, and word recognition. In the Goldilocks system, students rate books as "too easy" (independent level, in Betts's [1946] terms), "just right" (instructional level), and "too hard" (frustrational level). We have slightly modified the Goldilocks scheme by changing the labels, and adding the dimensions of interest and instructional or social context (see Box 1.8). Feel free to reword the descriptions for your students if needed. *Easy* books (independent level) are easy to understand and read, appropriate for reading independently for enjoyment, fluency practice, or sharing with a friend or younger child. *Instructional* books are those that students will need some assistance to read and understand; these books are appropriate for a Readers' Workshop or book club format if the teacher is available for support. *Challenge* books (frustrational

---

BOX 1.8. A Strategy for Students to Use in Choosing Books

Easy books (books I can handle by myself):

I have read the book several times before or I have read books like it.
I understand what the book is about.
I understand almost all of the words and I can figure out the hard words
I can read smoothly and with expression.
I would be feel comfortable reading this book out loud to someone.
I am interested in reading this book.

Instructional (books I can handle with some help):

The book or type of book is new or pretty new to me.
I understand most of the book.
There are a few words on each page that I'm not sure of, but not too many.
I can read parts of the book smoothly, and I only have a few trouble spots.
Someone can help me if I have challenges.
I am interested in reading this book with some help.

Challenge (books that are too difficult to read on my own):

I am confused about what is happening in the book.
There are many words I don't know.
My reading is choppy and slow.
I get easily frustrated while reading.
I would like to save this book for later or have someone read it to me.

---

level) are those that are too difficult for independent or even assisted reading. These books challenge children's conceptual understandings and may be ideal for teacher read-aloud and discussion. Challenge books should be available for student browsing, for teacher read-alouds, and for possible eventual reading by students after they develop the necessary skill.

In teaching any strategy, students need explanation, modeling, guided practice, and independent practice. On the first day of school, begin by explaining and modeling for students what books in the three categories are like for you, showing them examples. Read excerpts from the books aloud, and think aloud as you share with students the various issues and challenges in reading the three types of books. Make a poster or chart explaining the different types of books and the criteria used to select them, and give students personal copies of the categories and descriptions. Engage students in a whole-class discussion of books that fall into each category for themselves, followed by guided practice in choosing books in each category. Ask students to choose materials that they would like to read by themselves or check out to read at home (easy), materials that they would like to read in school (instructional), and materials that they would like the teacher to read aloud (challenge).

Skill in choosing the right books does not happen overnight. It is a gradual process. Some students, especially younger students and those who have had challenges with reading, will need many experiences with a variety of genres and levels of books before they will be able to choose appropriate books consistently (Fielding & Roller, 1992). Keep the criteria poster in the room for the entire year, and refer students to it as needed. Review the strategy periodically as you introduce and recommend new books. When you have conferences with students (Chapter 4), ask them to tell you which category the book is in (often, there's an overlap). In our experiences, students quickly learn how to judge a book's appropriateness, and can then choose books that will help them develop fluency and make accelerated progress. In the next section, we discuss how you can use independent reading time to assess students' reading both informally, through observation, and more systematically, through reading analysis.

ANALYZING STUDENTS' READING

A Broad Initial Examination of Students' Reading

Many teachers begin reading assessments with an oral reading analysis, running record, or informal reading inventory. It is important to use these tools to examine students' reading proficiency in depth, and we discuss them later in the chapter. However, we like to start out the year with a broader examination of students' reading—one that focuses not just on reading proficiency, but also on engagement, interests, and attitudes. While students are engaged in their independent reading, go around to individuals and ask them to tell you about their books (focus on "real reader" questions like "What's your book about?" and "How do you like it so far?"). Ask each student to read aloud a favorite segment of the book while you take notes.

Your notes can take a variety of forms, from anecdotal notes and charts to rubrics or checklists that you construct or borrow from other professionals. A common way of taking anecdotal notes is to use self-stick, plain mailing labels (we use the 2 × 3-inch size). Place a sheet of labels on a clipboard and walk around the room to talk with students. Each time you talk with a student, write the student's name, the date, and your notes on a label or labels. You will probably be able to talk with only four or five students per class period. During your next break or at the end of the day, affix the labels to a sheet of paper in the student's assessment folder. Students in our teacher education classes start taking anecdotal notes from the first day they begin observing and assisting in classrooms. Box 1.9 shows an example of a preservice teacher's anecdotal notes during one semester when she was observing in a third-grade classroom twice per week. She also explains how her notes evolved from very general to more focused, and how she learned about both students and literacy from the experience. As a classroom teacher, you will take notes more frequently, at least once every 2 weeks for each student. Begin this process with students about whom you have immediate concerns—for example, those who have difficulty choosing appropriate books and/or those who appear to struggle with reading or reading attitudes.

An alternative way to record your observations about students is to construct a chart, like the one in Box 1.10. The chart is divided into comments about engagement and comments about reading. Within these two categories, you can include attention to specific aspects of reading and engagement, including books students read, how quickly they read, whether they finish their books, body language, level of engagement, fluency (pausing, phrasing, expression, and speed of reading), comprehension, word identification, and any other aspect you notice. As with anecdotal notes, most teachers find it easier to focus on four or five students per day, so that the initial observations for all students can be completed within about 2 weeks. A chart such as this is particularly helpful during the beginning of the year, when students are learning to choose appropriate books.

Oral Reading Analysis: A Closer Examination of Students' Reading Proficiency

After one or two informal observations, you will begin to note where students' challenges and strengths lie in reading and will have a good idea about where to begin instruction. Next, you will want to begin analyzing students' reading more systematically, to gather more information about their specific challenges in word analysis and comprehension (in Chapter 4, we add more information about assessment). This information will help you fine-tune your instruction to accelerate students' progress. The form of reading analysis that we use evolved from informal reading inventories (Betts, 1946), running records (Clay, 1993), and miscue analysis (Goodman, 1969). See Boxes 1.11 and 1.12 for explanations.

Oral Reading Analysis Strategies for Older Students

Through our many years of analyzing reading in classroom and clinical settings, we have found running records very helpful for use with early readers. However, when students begin to develop some reading speed, we find it difficult to keep up with their reading in a running record format, making checkmarks for every word read correctly in addition to recording every error or deviation from print. Instead, we recommend

BOX 1.9. Anecdotal Notes and Comments (by Michelle Williams)

1-24-00

- a icy, plays drums on desk, fiddles, raises hand occasionally.
- Incredible reader · 5th or 6th grade level quiet but eager to share
- So Smart!

2-10

Reading: Andy's Wild Animal Adventure won for most reading points in all of second grade. Also won honor roll, attendance + PIP. He is labeled GT.

3-6

- new haircut!
- very cooperative · negotiates roles
- leaves at 12:45 w/ mrs. L (with _____) to do math enrichment

3/27

- didn't want to read aloud to me but did talk about his book, The Junkyard Dog. Said it was boring at first, but now it was more exciting. Pointed out the word "hell" + said there were other bad words too! preferred to read silently.

4-10

- My Teacher Fried My Brains
- really into book - reading every spare minute - even waiting for the bus outside - read to me today - Yeah!!
- * needs more info on radio waves, smells, molecules traveling through space · radios, t.v.
- Awsome reader · very fluent, great compct made predictions · not as many personal connectns
- we could work on making those personal connections more → extend his thinking

Michelle's Comments about Using Anecdotal Notes

When I first began keeping the notebook, it was hard to know exactly what to write. I found myself writing general descriptions of the children (which translates into how I perceived their personalities to be). I wrote things about how sweet, quiet, or active they were. I also wrote about their mood and their attendance. I found it difficult to write something about everyone. For some I would think, "They just don't *do* anything . . . what am I supposed to write?" As the semester continued, I began spending more one-on-one conversation time with the five on my list for the day. I circulated more and got to know those "quiet" children who somehow blend into the room. This led to the first major change in my notes. I began writing about their interests, their families, and anything else personal about them. This was so much more meaningful stuff I could look back on and reference. Not only was I getting to know them as individuals, I was learning about ways I could

(continued)

connect to them and connect them to learning. Learning about David's crowded house, Laura's car accident, and Ana's first language helped me see a more complete little person—not just a student I want to take out a pencil for a spelling test. I could connect behaviors with experiences they were having outside of school. With these personal entries, I also began to write everything I heard from other teachers (home situations, special needs, learning difficulties).

The next evolution for my notes came when I began reading with my five students each day. The anecdotal notes provided such a great way to record my thoughts on their reading: techniques they were using, their comprehension, their fluency. I could actually use this info! I could track progress and know what strategies the student could use in a minilesson. I also could make notes to myself about additional resources I could provide (e.g., "needs more info on radio waves"). I realized this could be expanded to all other subjects as well.

Keeping the anecdotal notes was a major learning process for me. When I look back at them, I can see the transition from general judgments to tangible and meaningful information. They were also a monitor for my interactions with each student (am I reaching everyone enough?) I know I will continue to utilize anecdotal notes as a way of ongoing assessment, to track patterns, record personal information, and to connect to my students. It seems to me that using the notes doesn't take up much time, but it does makes a huge difference in connecting to and reaching every individual in the classroom. It's a great tool!

BOX 1.10. Sample Chart for Recording Reading Observations

Name of student:	Sandra	Language arts teacher:	Salvatore

Date	Book	Engagement	Reading proficiency
8/25	Sideways Stories from Wayside School (Sachar)	Seems bored. Looks around the room. Says the book is "okay." She chose it because she had heard it was funny. Log entries are short and fuzzy.	Her oral reading is choppy. Misses lots of words. Doesn't understand the premise of the book. I need to help her find another book. She's been wasting time! Arggh!
8/27	Amber Brown Is Not a Crayon (Danziger)	She chose the Amber Brown series.* I've noticed her laughing about it. She asked me if she could take it home and finish it.	This book is perfect for Sandra! Her reading is smooth and expressive and she has no trouble understanding, as shown by her reading log (great predictions) and our book conferences.
9/2	Amber Brown Goes Fourth (Danziger)	She's been taking Amber books home. This is her third one and she's almost finished. Says she wants to start reading Judy Blume books next (e.g. Freckle Juice)	Her confidence has really picked up. She called me over so she could read me her favorite part.

Other comments: * I noticed that some students were reading books that were too hard, so I introduced several fun series books and read parts of them out loud. I took several books around with me during free-reading time. Several students, including Sandra, chose one of the books.

BOX 1.11. Informal Reading Inventories

The *informal reading inventory* is an individualized reading assessment instrument that was originally designed to be administered by a reading specialist or diagnostician. Students read words from graded lists. Students then read orally and answered questions about a series of passages, while the administrator marked their errors (or "deviations from print") on the text. Students continued to read passages, both silently and orally, in order to determine reading achievement level and appropriate placement in a graded basal reading series. Betts (1946) recommended that reading level should be a range from *independent* (able to read without assistance), to *instructional* (appropriate for reading with support from a teacher), to *frustrational* (too difficult for the student to read). The levels were determined by the percentage of words read correctly and the percentage of comprehension questions answered correctly. In their book entitled *Reading Diagnosis for Teachers*, Barr, Blachowicz, and Sadow (1995) offer criteria, based on Betts's recommendations, for independent, instructional, and frustrational reading levels (shown below). Some educators recommend more lenient criteria for early readers (Clay, 1993). It is important to realize that these levels are not precise, because word recognition and comprehension do not always match, and students' reading skill may vary in different texts.

The *word recognition score* refers to the percentage of words read correctly (divide the words read correctly by the total number of words in the passage):

    Independent: 98–100
    Instructional: 95–97
    Borderline: 90–94
    Frustrational: Below 90

The *comprehension score* is the percentage of questions answered correctly (divide the number of questions answered correctly by the total number of questions):

    Independent: 90–100
    Instructional: 75–89
    Frustrational: Below 75

---

two modified strategies for students who are past the primary grades. In the first, described in the next section, teachers take notes about students' reading and mark errors on a copy of the text the student is reading. This is a particularly helpful strategy to use

at the beginning of the year, when you want to assess all of your students' reading in grade level texts. In the second strategy, which can be used at any time with any text, teachers use a blank sheet of paper, similar to a running record, but record only errors (not words read correctly).

BOX 1.12. Miscue Analysis and Running Records

Prior to the research of Goodman (1969) on *miscue analysis*, deviations from print in oral reading were simply counted as errors. Miscue research pointed out that there is a qualitative difference among reading errors, and that errors (or *miscues*) provide a window into students' attempts to make meaning of the text. For example, if a student reads "dad" for *father*, it is likely that she or he is attending to the meaning of the text. Reading "house" for *horse*, on the other hand, signals an interruption in meaning, even though the words are visually similar. Instead of simply counting reading errors, then, it is important to record errors exactly as read by the student, by writing them phonetically. After the reading, miscues are analyzed as *semantic* (meaning), *syntactic* (word order or grammatical rules), and *graphophonic* (the relationships between the look and sound of a word). Miscue analysis, now a common practice, provides information about students' reading strategies and comprehension *during* reading, and helps teachers to plan appropriate instruction. Most current commercially published informal reading inventories encourage teachers to analyze students' miscues rather than simply counting their errors.

The *running record* (Clay, 1993) has made it easier for teachers to assess students' reading on the spot, without advance planning and preparation, using only paper and pencil and the book the student is currently reading. Instead of recording students' reading directly on a copy of the text, a blank sheet of lined paper can be used. Each line on the paper corresponds to a line of text. Words read correctly are recorded as a check; deviations from print are marked with a code developed by Clay. Miscues, analyzed after the reading, help teachers to decide what kinds of instruction the student needs.

Analyzing Reading When You Have a Copy of the Text

We recommend that this strategy be used for all students at the beginning of the school year and later as teachers see fit. Learning to use the strategy takes time and practice, just as any form of reading analysis does. Instructors using this book may be able to provide practice in class, but this is not always possible, so we will go through the procedure step by step. You will need a tape recorder and tapes, as well as books for students to read (explained below). It is important for you to know that there are many different ways to mark errors, and there is no *right* way. If you are a preservice teacher, or graduate student your instructor may ask you to use his or her method; if you have already learned a different method, your instructor or supervisor may allow you to use it. The most important thing is that you use a consistent method that works for you. The method that we use is shown in Box 1.13. Notice that some errors are scored and others are marked but not scored (e.g., repetitions, self-corrections, pauses, and omission of punctuation).

1. Study and practice the error-marking method you will use.
2. Select a passage from a short novel or series book appropriate for your grade level. Although some students may have difficulty, it will be easier to use the same text for every student as you are learning the strategy, and it is important to see how students read and comprehend text that is on their approximate grade level. The passage should be 100–200 words long, depending on the age and approximate reading level of your students, and should contain enough story elements (setting, characters, plot) for

BOX 1.13. Marking System for Oral Reading Errors

The following errors are scored when calculating the percentage of words read correctly:	
Omission of a word: Circle the omitted word in the text.	She was (almost) ready to go to the dance.
Insertion of a word: Draw a caret (^) and write the word where it was inserted.	She was almost ready to go ^out to the dance.
Teacher help: If the teacher supplies the word or gives help, write "Ⓣ" above the word. Note: Wait 4–5 seconds before supplying the word.	Ⓣ She was almost ready to go to the dance.
Substitution of an incorrect word: Write the substitution phonetically above the word. If the student spontaneously corrects the substitution, do not score it as an error (see below).	raydy reedy She was almost ready to go to the dance.

The following errors are marked in the text, but are not scored:	
Correction of a substitution or omission: Write "Ⓒ" next to or above the substitution.	Ⓒ really She was almost ready to go to the dance.
Repetition: Draw a squiggly line underneath the repeated word(s).	She was almost ready to go to the dance.
(*Optional*: Mark pauses with a slash for each second of hesitation. Circle omitted punctuation.)	She was/almost ready/to go to the dance.

a retelling and prediction. The beginning of a book works best. Count the number of words in the passage and write it on the text. Make copies of the text for each student. You will use the copies to record errors while students read from the actual text. For our demonstration passage, we chose several paragraphs from the beginning of *The Kid Who Ran for President* (Gutman, 1996).

3. Call each student to a quiet corner of the room, ask her or him to read the title of the book and make a prediction ("What do you think this book will be about?"), and to read the passage into the tape recorder. Students should read from the actual book while you follow along in the copied text. After the reading, assess comprehension by asking the student to discuss what he or she read and to predict what might happen next. If the student's understanding of the passage is not clear, ask her or him to retell the passage, offering prompts if needed. Ask the student to define one or two vocabulary words. Listen to the tape afterward and try out the error-marking system. If you are inexperienced, you will need to listen to the tape several times to catch all of the errors. Also make notes about how easily and confidently the student reads the passage, including phrasing, pauses, expression, and speed of reading.

4. The left column of Box 1.14 shows the passage with deviations from print

marked according to the transcript. The right column of Box 1.14 shows how the same reading was marked on blank lined paper (we explain this method later in the chapter). The middle column shows which errors were scored in calculating percentage of words read correctly.

5. Calculate the percentage of words read correctly. Below, we calculate this information for the student's reading marked in Box 1.14.

BOX 1.14. Marking Oral Reading Errors

Marking errors on a copy of the text	Scored	Marking errors on lined paper
brainy It was right after /election day, 1999. Lane Brainard	✓	⊤ brainy/Brainard
basement and I were down in his basement shooting /pool when we	✓	basment/basement
present first came up with the /idea of a kid running for President.		© present/President
television The TV was on. A bunch of boring grown-ups in	✓	television/TV
at suits and ties were sitting around a table. I wasn't	✓	at/around
jabbing paying much attention, but they were jabbering	✓	jabbing/jabbering
democrat something about what the /Democratic Party and the	✓	democrat/Democratic
Republican Party are going to have to do if they want to/		
win the election next year in 2000.		
©*ordinary* Ordinarily, I would grab the /remote control and		© ordinary/ordinarily
water switch to something more interesting (to me the /Weather	✓	water/weather
©*is* *be* Channel would have been more interesting). But Lane's	✓	© is/would be/have been
©*genie* sort of a /weird /genius who wants to know everything		© genie/genius
about everything. His /favorite show is *Meet the Press!*)		
because Besides, it was *his* house.	✓	because/besides
Number of words = 135 Scorable errors (see Box 1.8) = 9 (*Brainard, basement, TV, around, jabbering, Democratic, water, have been, besides*) Percentage of words read correctly = 93.3 (93%)		Teacher's notes: • Phrasing ok but many pauses • Somewhat tentative in his reading, but not really frustrated • Very little expression • Fairly slow

Number of words in passage = 135
Number of scorable errors = 9
Number of words read correctly (total words minus scorable errors) = 135 – 9 = 126
Percentage of words read correctly (number of words read correctly divided by total number of words = 126/135 = 93.3% (round down to 93%). This is a borderline-level score for word identification (see Box 1.11).

6. Analyze comprehension and word-reading errors. Determine the "fit" of the passage (see next sections).

7. When you can mark errors quickly and accurately, the next step is to try the strategy "live," using the tape recording as a backup as long as you need to.

Analyzing Comprehension. Listen to what the student says about the passage (including discussion, predictions, retelling, and/or answers to questions), and decide whether his or her comprehension is very good (independent), adequate (instructional), or inadequate (frustrational). Here is a conversation between the teacher and the student whose reading is marked in Box 1.14. How would you evaluate the student's comprehension?

TEACHER: What did you think about that?

STUDENT: Well, it was about these two guys who were watching TV, a show about the president—I mean about the election.

TEACHER: And?

STUDENT: Well, this one guy was real smart and he liked watching stuff about the election and stuff, and the other guy thought it was boring.

TEACHER: What do you think will happen next?

STUDENT: I think one of them is going to run for president.

TEACHER: Do you see the word jabbering? What does that mean in the story?

STUDENT: Talking.

TEACHER: Do you think you'd like to read this?

STUDENT: Yeah, I guess so.

TEACHER: Do you think it would be easy for you to read by yourself, or do you think you'd want some help reading it?

STUDENT: I'd probably need a little help. I didn't get all of it.

The student's initial response included the two characters and an accurate description of them, although the teacher had to probe for details. He omitted some details, including where the boys were and that they were playing pool, but these details are not central to the gist of the passage. The student's prediction was plausible and showed that he understood the major point of the segment, although this prediction would be fairly easy to make, given the title of the book. His definition of the word *jabbering* was technically accurate but surface-level. The student's familiarity with the concepts in the book was a little shaky. For a very good retelling, we might have expected the student to discuss or retell without prompting, to talk about the two political parties and candidates (especially if this was during an election year), and possibly to comment about a kid running for president. However, we would consider the student's comprehension adequate. We agree with the student's assessment that he would need some support with the book. It might be helpful to have an oral discussion of the political parties and candidates for office, either with the entire class or in a book conference.

Analyzing Oral Reading Errors. When analyzing the errors that students make during reading, the goal is to figure out their strategies for identifying words and for making sense of the text (see Box 1.15). A first pass at analyzing oral reading for all students is to look at whether or not each oral reading error preserves the meaning of the text. In general, a few non-meaning-changing errors, such as those the student in this passage made, will not cause major problems. However, many such errors may signal word analysis challenges that can become much larger problems in more complex text with new information and vocabulary. Next, analyze the student's decoding strategies for each word (even those for which the meaning is not changed) to see whether patterns exist. Also consider aspects of fluency such as pauses, phrasing, and expression. All of the information collected will help determine the "fit" of the passage for the student.

BOX 1.15. Analyzing Miscues

Answer these questions about the errors.

1. *Does the error change the meaning of the passage?* In this example *Brainy/Brainard, television/ TV, at/around,* and *have been/be* did not change the meaning, and several words were self-corrected. Self-corrections are non-meaning-changing errors and are not usually considered serious if not frequent. Teachers may choose to analyze them to affirm patterns.
   Jabbing/jabbering, democrat/democratic, water/weather, and because/besides *do* change the meaning.
2. *Is the word unfamiliar (i.e., unknown vocabulary)?* In this case, *jabbering* was probably an unfamiliar word, and *Democratic* might have been an unfamiliar form of *democrat.* The other words were most likely familiar, although the student might not have been familiar with *The Weather Channel.*
3. *Does the student correctly decode the beginning of the word? The middle? The end?* In most cases, this student correctly decoded the beginning sound. In several words, the middle (*weather, around, jabbering,* and *besides*) and ending sounds (*around, besides, Brainard*) were not correctly decoded.
4. *Can you identify patterns in how students attempt unfamiliar words?* This student had some difficulty with the middles and endings of words.
5. *Are there many pauses while the student attempts to decode words? Does the student attend to punctuation?* This student made several pauses, and skipped over one period. According to the teacher's notes in the right column of Box 1.14, he read with mostly appropriate phrases but with little expression.

Deciding on the "Fit" of the Passage. Based on the information you have gathered, decide whether the passage is on the student's independent, instructional, or frustrational level. In the example above, we consider this passage on the low end of the student's instructional reading level; his word recognition score was in the borderline instructional range, but his fluency was shaky and he had difficulty decoding the middles and endings of unfamiliar words. His comprehension was skimpy but adequate after prompting. After more reading and conferences with the teacher, it's likely that this text would become easier for the student. For a more complete picture of his reading skills, the teacher would also want to hear the student read in different types of texts and perhaps more in this particular text. Keep all assessment information in a portfolio, which you can evaluate frequently for patterns of strengths and challenges that will help in planning and modifying instruction.

Analyzing Students' Reading When You Do Not Have a Copy of the Text

After you are comfortable with the strategy described above, you may go a step further and begin recording miscues on a blank sheet of lined paper (see right column of Box 1.14). This system is different from Clay's running records because only errors are recorded; checks are not used to record words read correctly. As shown, each line on your sheet of paper corresponds to a line in the text. This procedure is especially helpful when you are analyzing students' reading "on the spot" as they are reading independently in books of their choosing. This is very valuable for classroom teachers, since most students will be reading different texts during this time. You may choose to go back to the text and count the number of words if you want to calculate a word recognition score. However, after you have listened to many students read, you will begin to have a good idea about the "fit" of the text. Furthermore, with practice in choosing and reading books independently, most students will be able to tell you how comfortable they are with the texts they are reading. Analyzing students' oral reading is not an easy procedure to learn, and it takes much practice. Don't give up on this valuable assessment tool!

When to Do Oral Reading Analysis

The concept of text level (independent, instructional, and frustrational) is essential for teachers to understand, and teachers must know how to listen analytically to students as they read and determine the appropriateness of books. However, it is impossible for classroom teachers to count words and figure out percentages of words read correctly for all of their students in everything they read. Nor is it preferable. The purpose of reading instruction is for students to become independent readers. If they rely on their teachers to choose or approve books of the appropriate level, it will only take longer for them to gain independence. Furthermore, although teachers must learn to judge students' accuracy and fluency, the number of words read correctly or incorrectly is only one dimension of a text's appropriateness.

At the beginning of the year, you will want to analyze every student's reading using the system described earlier, starting with those who seem to have challenges. After that, the frequency of oral reading analysis will depend on your schedule and your stu-

dents. A third- or fourth-grade teacher with many challenged readers will need to analyze students' oral reading more often than a middle school teacher whose students are
advanced, independent readers. Use your judgment and be careful not to overdo it. If
students are reading in books that fit, in terms of both interest and difficulty level, they
will benefit most from independent reading with regular teacher conferences, and you
will be primarily monitoring their silent reading comprehension (see Chapter 4). During that time, you will occasionally ask them to read favorite or important portions
aloud as a check on fluency and ease of reading. After you have had much practice in
marking and analyzing miscues, you will begin to think about the components of oral
reading analysis every time you confer with students, and systematic oral reading analysis will become less necessary.

Reading Analysis with Context Textbooks

Ask a teacher of almost any grade level what causes her or his students the most difficulty in reading, and many will say, "Information texts." Many of the books that students have been exposed to in the primary grades are narrative stories, most of which
have a predictable story structure (setting, characters, plot, resolution). In contrast, information books come in a variety of text structures and formats, which are often unfamiliar to students. Teachers don't use nonfiction as much as fiction texts, so students
don't have adequate experience with them (Olson & Gee, 1991). Content textbooks often pose additional problems, in that they (1) assume that students have background
knowledge and experiences that many don't have; (2) often lack coherence; and (3) are
often boring (Beck, McKeown, & Gromoll, 1989). Ask students what their least favorite
subject is, and many will say that it is science or social studies—not because of the subject matter, but because teachers of these subjects often depend heavily on textbooks.
Poorly written, dull textbooks and a strong dislike for a subject often result in students'
having difficulty in content subjects even if they read on grade level.

It is important to assess how students approach content textbooks and how well
they read, understand, and can use the information in them. Assessment shows the
specific challenges that individual students have with textbooks and helps teachers
plan instruction that will support them. The initial assessment described here follows a
procedure similar to the oral reading analysis described earlier. Begin this assessment
by previewing a textbook chapter from a science or social studies textbook, deciding
how you will introduce the information to students. Plan to read and discuss a portion
from the beginning of the chapter with students, selecting a succeeding 100- to 200-
word segment of text that each student will read individually. Make a copy of this text
for every student. As in the previously described oral reading assessment, you will
mark each student's oral reading errors on the copy while the student reads from the
actual book. Follow this procedure:

1. Read aloud and discuss the first part of the section with students, stopping just
before the segment you have chosen for students to read.
2. While the class is doing independent work, call each student individually to a
quiet place in the room. Help the student review the first segment and ask him or her to
predict what the next segment will be about.

3. Then ask the student to read aloud the first half of the copied segment of text (the student reads from the book). As the student is reading, listen and take notes on your copy, focusing on vocabulary, knowledge of the topic, and understanding of the text. Although you do not need to do a full oral reading analysis, note the words that the student misreads or does not know, along with the quantity of errors, the smoothness and comfort level of the student's reading, and the student's understanding of what is read.

4. If the student's understanding of the oral reading is adequate, check silent reading comprehension by having the student finish reading the text silently and then discussing it with her or him. Alternatively, have the student finish reading the text out loud, and check for comprehension.

5. Evaluate these assessments for individual students and for the whole class. How easy is this book for most students to read? What specific kinds of challenges do individual students have with the text (e.g., vocabulary, word recognition, ability to synthesize information, knowledge about the topic)? What kinds of support will students need to read and learn from this textbook? Your answers to these and other similar questions will help determine how you use the textbook and how you supplement it with other materials and other instructional activities.

Chances are good that many of your students will have difficulty with content textbooks. It is important for all teachers to be aware of the challenges inherent in content textbooks and to support students in reading them. Even if the book is easy for the majority of students, we recommend using the content textbook as a reference rather than as the core of reading for content areas. Every classroom should have a wide variety of high-quality information books on a range of difficulty levels. Fortunately, there has been a virtual explosion in recent years in the varieties and quality of information trade books appropriate for students in the middle grades (see Chapters 2, 3, 4, 5, and 8, and Appendix C).

CONTINUAL ASSESSMENTS DURING CLASSROOM INSTRUCTION

Assessments gathered from the first several weeks of school will guide you in formulating general instructional plans for reading, writing, fluency, and word study. In addition, rather than taking time away from instruction, the kinds of assessments described in this chapter set the stage for a classroom filled with reading and writing. Teachers need to assess and evaluate students' skills and knowledge continually, in order to provide students with the most appropriate instruction, independent work, and materials and to make necessary modifications in these. As you become more familiar with various instructional approaches like those described in the following chapters, you will see that they afford many opportunities for assessment of students. Each instructional chapter includes suggestions for continual, curriculum-based assessments. The assessments suggested in this book are not intended to be fully comprehensive. You will want to include additional assessments in your program, based on your students' needs and your own preferences. Think about and experiment with the examples of assessments in this chapter and the other chapters; consider your instructional goals for your class and for each student; read professional materials; and talk to other educators as you build your assessment plan.

CHILDREN'S BOOK REFERENCES

Blume, J. (1971). *Freckle juice*. New York: Four Winds Press.

Brown, M. W. (1949). *The important book*. New York: Harper.

Danziger, P. (1994). *Amber Brown is not a crayon*. New York: Putnam.

Danziger, P. (1995). *Amber Brown goes fourth*. New York: Putnam.

Gutman, D. (1996). *The kid who ran for president*. New York: Scholastic.

King, M. L., Jr. (1997). *I have a dream*. New York: Scholastic.

Komaiko, L. (1988). *Earl's too cool for me*. New York: HarperCollins.

Nichol, B. P. (1986). *Once, a lullaby*. New York: Greenwillow.

Sachar, L. (1993). *Sideways stories from Wayside School*. New York: Avon.

Scieszka, J. (1998). *Squids will be squids: Fresh morals for beastly fables*. New York: Viking.

REFERENCES

Allington, R. L. (1983). The reading instruction provided readers of differing reading ability. *Elementary School Journal, 83,* 543–559.

Barr, R., Blachowicz, C. L. Z., & Sadow, M. W. (1995). *Reading diagnosis for teachers: An instructional approach* (3rd ed.). White Plains, NY: Longman.

Beck, I., McKeown, M., & Gromoll, E. (1989). Learning from social studies texts. *Cognition and Instruction, 6,* 99–158.

Betts, E. A. (1946). *Foundations of reading instruction*. New York: American Books.

Clay, M. (1993). *Reading Recovery: A guidebook for teachers in training*. Portsmouth, NH: Heinemann.

Farr, R. (1992). Putting it all together: Solving the reading assessment puzzle. *The Reading Teacher, 46,* 26-37.

Fielding, L., & Roller, C. (1992). Making difficult books accessible and easy books acceptable. *The Reading Teacher, 46,* 673-685.

Fry, E. (1987). A readability formula that saves time. *Journal of Reading, 11,* 587.

Goodman, K. S. (1969). Analysis of reading miscues: Applied psycholinguistics. *Reading Research Quarterly, 5,* 9–13.

Harris, T. L., & Hodges, R. E. (1995). *The literacy dictionary: The vocabulary of reading and writing*. Newark, DE: International Reading Association.

Ivey, G. (1999). A multicase study in the middle school: Complexities among young adolescent readers. *Reading Research Quarterly, 34,* 172–193.

Johnston, P. (1987). Teachers as evaluation experts. *The Reading Teacher, 40,* 744–748.

Koch, K. (1970). *Wishes, lies, and dreams: Teaching children to write poetry*. New York: Chelsea House.

Leslie, L., & Caldwell, J. (1995). *Qualitative Reading Inventory—II (QRI-II)*. New York: HarperCollins.

Nell, V. (1988). *Lost in a book: The psychology of reading for pleasure*. New Haven, CT: Yale University Press.

Olhausen, M., & Jepsen, M. (1992). Lessons from Goldilocks: Somebody's been choosing my books, but I can make my own choices now! *The New Advocate, 5,* 36.

Olson, M. W., & Gee, T. C. (1991). Content reading instruction in the primary grades: Perceptions and strategies. *The Reading Teacher, 45,* 293–307.

Peterson, B. (1991). Selecting books for beginning readers. In D. DeFord, C. Lyons, & G. S. Pinnell

(Eds.), *Bridges to literacy: Learning from Reading Recovery* (pp. 119–147). Portsmouth, NH: Heine-mann.

Pinnell, G. S., & Fountas, I. C. (1999). *Matching books to readers: Using leveled books in guided reading K–3*. Portsmouth, NH: Heinemann.

Rhodes, L. K. (1981). I can read!: Predictable books as resources for reading and writing instruction. *The Reading Teacher, 34,* 511–518.

Roller, C. (1996). *Variability, not disability: Struggling readers in a workshop classroom.* Newark, DE: International Reading Association.

Wiederholdt, J., & Bryant, B. (1992). *Gray Oral Reading Test—3 (GORT-3).* Austin, TX: Pro-Ed.

Worthy, J., & McKool, S. (1996). Students who say they hate to read: The importance of opportunity, choice, and access. In D. J. Leu, C. K., Kinzer, & K. A. Hinchman (Eds.), *Literacies for the 21st century: Research and practice* (pp. 245–256). Chicago: National Reading Conference.

CHAPTER 2

What Students Read and How to Get It

In our research with students in grades 3–8, we have found that even students who say they hate to read in school would be willing to read if they had access to materials of interest to them (Ivey & Broaddus, in press; Worthy, Patterson, Salas, Turner, & Prater, 1997). What we find in schools, however, is that there is often a glaring mismatch between what students like to read and what schools provide, which is especially marked for reluctant readers (Baines, 1994; Worthy, Moorman, & Turner, 1999). From his interviews with resistant readers, Blintz (1993) concluded that a major reason for resistance to school reading is that students "are forced to read materials that they have no voice in selecting" (p. 612). The following comments from a sixth grader illustrate that even highly motivated, skilled readers are often dissatisfied with books provided at school:

> "I used to love to read. But this year it's not as enjoyable. I don't know why, but I plainly don't like it any more. I guess it is because I have better things to do. Another reason may be that I can't find a book in the library that interests me. I mean, the school library would be the only place I could get books right now. I have already read my books at home."

Research about the importance of interest in learning tells us that providing students with access to books that appeal to them is a crucial aspect of reading instruction (Fractor, Woodruff, Martinez, & Teale, 1993; Tunnell & Jacobs, 1989). People who have ready access to books and magazines are more likely to read than those who don't (Greaney & Hegarty, 1987; Neuman, 1986). Students read more when there are more books in the classroom, when the books are physically accessible, and when they can take books home (Morrow & Weinstein, 1982). Access to books, then, is a prerequisite to reading. Although providing access to a wide range of books does not guarantee students will read, having the right books helps.

It is essential for educators to ensure that students have access to a balance of both high-quality, conceptually challenging literature and student-preferred materials to enhance development of reading, writing, content knowledge, thinking, and positive attitudes toward reading and learning. The purpose of this chapter is to offer guidelines for building a classroom book collection that matches the instructional needs, interests, and reading skills of students, as well as the curriculum of language arts and other content areas. You may wonder why we are focusing on classroom collections instead of school libraries. The number of school librarians, or media specialists, is steadily shrinking. With demands for technology expertise for school librarians increasing rapidly, more graduates in library science are opting for more lucrative jobs in private companies rather than taking demanding, lower-paying jobs in education. As school librarians retire, there is often no one to take their place. If the current situation continues, "By 2005, researchers project a need for nearly 25,000 media specialists" (Lord, 2000, p. 53). Thus, in future years, the responsibility for being sure that students have access to books will rest even more on the shoulders of classroom teachers. Although we believe that it is the responsibility of schools to provide reading materials for students, we know that this does not always happen. Teachers need to be armed with research about what materials to provide and about the importance of access.

What kinds of materials do you think students like to read? What kinds of materials do you think teachers want students to read? Before you read further, make a list. As you read the chapter, compare your ideas with ours.

WHAT'S IN THIS CHAPTER?

Building a Classroom Collection to Support Learning and Engagement
Other Important Features of a Well-Balanced Classroom Collection
Books That "Fit": Guiding Students in Choosing Appropriate Books
The Hardest Part: Acquiring Materials for Classroom Collections

BUILDING A CLASSROOM COLLECTION
TO SUPPORT LEARNING AND ENGAGEMENT

What Do Students Like to Read?

Students in grades 3–8 like to read what their peers are reading, especially books and magazines that focus on popular culture (and don't forget song lyrics!). The popularity of such materials is widespread (Kulleseid, 1994–1995; McKenna, Kear, & Ellsworth, 1991). The most popular materi-

als among more than 600 elementary through middle school students surveyed (Worthy et al., 1997, 1999) were books and stories with a scary or horror theme (e.g., the *Goosebumps* series by R. L. Stine); cartoon collections (e.g., *Garfield Feeds the Kitty*—Davis, 1999); comics (e.g., *X-Men, Superman, Archie*); popular magazines (e.g., entertainment, teen issues, sports, video games, cars and trucks); and sports biographies (e.g., *Basketball's Greatest Players*—Kramer, 1997). Joke and riddle books were favorites of almost all the students we surveyed. Others that topped the lists were information books about animals, drawing books, materials about cars and trucks, current series books, *The Guinness Book of World Records* (Young, 1999) and other almanacs, and funny picture books (e.g., Scieszka's [1989] *The True Story of the Three Little Pigs*) and novels (e.g., Rockwell's [1953] *How to Eat Fried Worms*, Clement's [1996] *Frindle*). Some of the favorite authors mentioned were Roald Dahl, Beverly Cleary, Judy Blume, Shel Silverstein, Marc Brown, Jon Scieszka, R. L. Stine, Stephen King, and Louis Sachar. Keep in mind that these were the *most* popular materials among the students surveyed. It's important to survey your own students, using

closed-ended and open-ended surveys (see forms in Appendix B), and to remember that not all students like what the majority prefers. As Howes (1963) cautioned, "Each child is himself no matter what the generalization about the reading patterns and interests for his age may be" (p. 492).

What Do Educators Want Students to Read?

Although many teachers and librarians are aware of students' preferences and do their best to provide materials that students want to read, many stakeholders in education insist on the importance of *high-quality literature*. What *is* high-quality literature? In our interviews with teachers and librarians, we have heard it defined as "something from the library," "something with educational content," "an award-winning book," "classic literature," "something wholesome," "something appropriate," or at least "not something frivolous" (Worthy et al., 1999). Favorites with teachers were *Bridge to Terabithia* (Paterson, 1977), *Hatchet* (Paulsen, 1987), *Island of the Blue Dolphins* (O'Dell, 1960), and *Tuck Everlasting* (Babbitt, 1975). Teachers spoke of pressure to "make the most of class time," and thus many insisted that students read "honest-to-goodness books." Although many teachers were open to students' reading series books and scary books during self-selected reading time, many felt real or perceived pressure to rely on critically acclaimed materials (such as Newbery and Caldecott

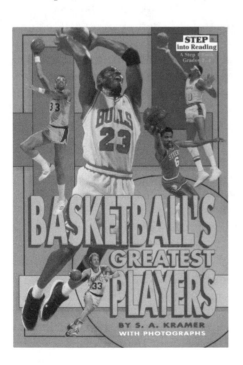

Award winners) and to prepare students for standardized tests. In many of the classrooms, then, time for reading student-selected materials was not a priority (Worthy,
Turner, & Moorman, 1998). Certainly there are some reading materials, even "higher-
quality" materials, that are inappropriate for students at certain ages. Teachers, families, administrators, and librarians should research and discuss issues related to appropriateness of all materials, keep an open mind while carefully examining materials that
may be considered offensive, and determine what is best for all involved in the specific
situation. It is also important for teachers to be familiar with the books in their classroom collections. Consult a book on children's or young adults' literature (e.g., Nilsen
& Donelson, 2001) or the National Council of Teachers of English Web site (http://
www.ncte.org) for guidelines if you are concerned about the appropriateness of a particular book.

Surprisingly, librarians were less insistent on so-called "high-quality" than teachers, as one librarian remarked: "I'm not so concerned with *what* they're reading. I'm just
thrilled that they're reading." However, most drew the line at comics, cartoons, and
popular magazines (e.g., anything other than school-related magazines); these were
seen by many teachers and librarians as "fine for reading at home" but inappropriate
for school.

Striking a Balance

Should educators attempt to arrest what some see as a "decline in literary standards"
by providing only "high-quality" literature in school? Should the academic curriculum
be set aside in favor of providing students with materials related to their current individual interests? We say no to both questions, and suggest a more moderate approach
that we feel all educational stakeholders should accept.

Student choice and control in reading materials and instruction play important
roles in involvement with and enjoyment of reading and in fostering voluntary reading
(Bintz, 1993). Therefore, in addition to providing critically acclaimed materials, it is crucial that students' preferences be addressed in order to capture their attention and engagement, and thus to foster learning. Fortunately, there are both academic and affec-
tive benefits to using materials that students prefer. Many times students' chosen
materials are more complex than teacher-assigned materials (Southgate, Arnold, &
Johnson, 1981). Even light materials promote fluent reading and vocabulary development, and help to develop the linguistic competence, confidence, and motivation necessary for reading more sophisticated materials (Carlsen & Sherrill, 1988; Dorrell &
Carroll, 1981; Parrish & Atwood, 1985). For example, while many people think of comic
books as "junk" and would prefer to ignore their vast popularity, comics have many re-
deeming qualities that support students' literacy development as well as motivation
(see Box 2.1). In studying reading habits in middle school, Ujiie and Krashen (1996)
found that seventh-grade boys who were avid comic book readers were "more likely to
enjoy reading in general, read more, and read more books than boys who read fewer
comic books or none at all" (Krashen & McQuillan, 1996, p. 14).

Comics and cartoons are popular genres among all ages. Well over half of the elementary students surveyed by McKenna et al. (1991) reported reading comic books and
newspaper comics. Many of the avid adult readers interviewed by Carlsen and Sherrill
(1988) reported being hooked on comics (e.g., superheroes, *Archie*, classic comics) at one

BOX 2.1. The Scoop on Comics

At the mere mention of comic books, many parents and educators turn up their noses in indignation: "Let kids read junk like that in school? I think not!"

Why do so many people object to students reading comics in school and even at home? Why do comics have such a bad rap? A look at the history of comic books tells us why (Brocka, 1979). When the first comics were published in the 1940s, the only standard of quality and censorship was that "anything goes." Many comics truly were junk, filled with violence and racial slurs. In the 1950s, during a heyday of censorship, comic book publishers realized it was time to "clean up their acts," and they established a set of guidelines for comic book publishing. The first comics based on these guidelines played it a little too safe; they were yawners about ghosts and animals that no one bought. The future of comics looked dim.

Fortunately, in 1961 Stan Lee, then the publisher of Marvel Comics, came to the rescue! Lee began writing realistic action stories about superheroes (Spiderman, The Incredible Hulk, Captain America, etc.), leading to an explosion in comic book popularity. As Brocka (1979) has explained, "The basic ingredients were still there: heroes, villains, action, fantastic plots, astounding inventions and gizmos. But the new ingredient was realism. This combination of ingredients made comics the equal of other creative media" (p. 31). Following Lee's lead, there are now five major U.S. publishers of comics that are appropriate for use in schools. All adhere to strict standards, outlined by the Comics Code Authority (Wright, 1979).

Other points in favor of using comics as reading materials in schools are as follows:

- Comics contain sophisticated language, vocabulary, plots, and character development.
- Comics are written in a wide range of readability levels, from 1.4 to 8.3 (see Wright, 1979). Archie and Casper, the Friendly Ghost are among the easiest; X-Man is among the most difficult.
- Comics are motivational for readers of all skill levels.
- Many avid readers grew up on comics (Carlsen & Sherrill, 1988).
- According to one of the most influential educators of the 20th century, comics are excellent for exposing students to new vocabulary: " . . . research on reading and comic books found that a student reading one comic book a month for a nine-month school year would be exposed to as many new words as reading the standard fourth or fifth grade reader" (Thorndike, 1941, cited in Dorrell & Southall, 1982, p. 398).

time. The presence of illustrations and the less dense text make comics nonthreatening for struggling readers. The plots, vocabulary, and characterization can be quite complex. In fact, there are highly sophisticated comic books, or graphic novels, that address historical and political issues. In *Maus: A Survivor's Tale* (1986), winner (together with its 1991 sequel) of a special 1992 Pulitzer Prize, Art Spiegelman tells the fascinating but harrowing story of his father, a Jewish survivor of the Holocaust (this book is not appropriate for elementary children). Comic-style books for children have been written by acclaimed children's author/illustrators such as Maurice Sendak (*We Are All in the Dumps with Jack and Guy*, 1993), Brian Pinkney (*The Adventures of Sparrowboy*, 1997), Joanna Cole (*The Magic School Bus inside the Earth*, 1987), James Stevenson (*That Terrible Halloween Night*, 1980; *Don't Make Me Laugh*, 1999), and Jules Feiffer (*Meanwhile . . .* , 1999). These kinds of materials also provide inspiration for students' writing.

Teachers have a responsibility to expose students to a wide range of exemplary fiction and information books. When students are not permitted to exercise choice, however, they may avoid teacher-selected books as a matter of principle. Thus, when students say they don't like to read, part of this opinion may be due to their perceived lack of voice in the school curriculum. Especially in upper elementary and middle school, then, teachers should negotiate the curriculum with students. Fortunately, elementary and middle school students value their teachers' recommendations and help in choosing books if the teacher shows genuine interest in the materials (Csikszentmihalyi & McCormack, 1986; Ivey & Broaddus, 2000; Roettger, 1980). Furthermore, students' personal interests do not need to be static; teachers can stretch students' topic interests through instructional approaches and materials that are motivating (Schiefele, 1991). The transition from light materials to more complex texts can be hastened by providing student-preferred materials for free-choice reading, using more sophisticated works on similar topics for read-alouds, and encouraging students to adopt a critical stance when they read.

Educators should be aware that parents, administrators, and community members may not immediately approve of popular materials. Ignoring such materials, however, may lead to declines in reading attitudes, in voluntary reading, and ultimately in achievement. Providing all concerned parties with explanations proactively, backed by research findings that support the use of student-preferred materials, may head off the complaints that could accompany such a move. With the balance between curriculum and students' interests in mind, we have constructed a list of materials that should be available for students to read in school and to check out for home reading (see Box 2.2).

BOX 2.2. Reading Materials In a Balanced Classroom Collection

- Easy-reading books
- Series books
- Transitional chapter books
- Current popular magazines with appropriate language and topics (e.g., *Sports Illustrated*, *Sports Illustrated for Kids*, *Nickelodeon*, entertainment magazines)
- Simple and more sophisticated picture books
- Song lyrics
- Short story collections
- Age-appropriate fiction and award-winning books
- Reference books (e.g., thesaurus, dictionary, encyclopedia)
- High-quality information books and magazines (e.g., *Discovery*, *Cobblestones*) on a variety of interesting topics
- A variety of current news and information sources (e.g., record books, almanacs, newspapers, news magazines, Internet)
- Materials that encourage language play (jokes, riddles, puns, palindromes, word games, "madlibs")
- Poetry
- Student-authored works
- School publications
- Cartoons and comics with appropriate language and concepts
- Readers' Theater scripts (see Chapter 5)
- Books arranged in text sets by author, genre, or topic

OTHER IMPORTANT FEATURES OF A WELL-BALANCED CLASSROOM COLLECTION

In addition to student and teacher preference, there are many other considerations in building a good classroom library collection, as we discuss in this and later sections. A crucial consideration, which we discuss later in the chapter, is that students must have access to books that "fit"—books that they can read and that are appropriate for a variety of reading situations. Another important issue in upper elementary and middle school is the use of picture books. Often seen as inappropriate for older students, picture books are great sources for independent reading, vocabulary development, introducing new concepts and topical studies, teacher read-alouds, and research (Miller, 1998). In each chapter of this book, we provide lists of engaging, high-quality picture books and discuss a variety of ways to incorporate such books throughout the literacy curriculum.

Books That Present Positive Cultural and World Views

Students should have opportunities to read materials about a wide range of cultures, communities, and people. These materials should present strong, accurate, nonstereotypical portraits that help children to develop a positive world view (Bishop, 1992; Day, 1994). A selection of authors who write about diverse cultures and communities are provided in Box 2.3. Such books should be naturally infused throughout the curriculum rather than showcased as multicultural selections.

BOX 2.3. Authors Who Present Strong Portraits of Diverse Cultures

Hispanic and Hispanic American: Alma Flor Ada, Gary Soto, Arthur Dorros, Sandra Cisneros (mature), Judith Ortiz Cofer (mature), Carmen Lomas Garza, David Diaz

African and African American: Beverly Naidoo, Mildred D. Taylor, John Steptoe, Langston Hughes, Eloise Greenfield, Jacqueline Woodson (mature), Lucille Clifton, Virginia Hamilton, Faith Ringgold (author/illustrator), Jerry Pinkney (illustrator), Brian Pinkney (illustrator), Tom Feelings (author/illustrator), Walter Dean Myers, Patricia McKissack, Frederick McKissack, Verna Aardema

Native American: Joseph Bruchac, Michael Dorris, Byrd Baylor, Virginia Driving Hawk Sneve, John Bierhorst, Shonto Begay, Paul Goble, Russell Freedman, Michael Caduto

Asian and Asian American: Toshi Maruki (mature), Allan Say, Huynh Quang Nhuong, Sook Myul Choi, Ed Young, Laurence Yep, Bette Bao Lord (mature), Yoshiko Uchida, Sherry Garland, Mintong Ho

Jewish and Jewish American: Barbara Cohen, Johanna Hurwitz, Carol Matus, Isaac Bashevis Singer (mature)

Multiple cultures: Arnold Adoff, Juanita Havill, Patricia Polacco, Ina Freedman, Jama Kim Rattigan, Vera B. Williams, Milton Meltzer, Roger Lipsyte (mature), Francis Temple, Diane Hoyt-Goldsmith, Jane Yolen

---

Information Books

Students love to read about a variety of "real things," including entertainment, animals, the Civil War, football, basketball, wrestling, cars, cooking, low-rider cars, horses, and the armed forces, to name only a few. However, current information books and materials are often not available in classroom collections. Many teachers rely on novels and fiction picture books for classroom instruction, read-alouds, and free reading, to the exclusion of information texts. As a result, students often have limited experience with books that present content information, which leads to difficulty with content textbooks in later years. On the other hand, giving students access to a wide variety of visually engaging, current information texts supports the content curriculum. Students of all ages should have frequent opportunities to examine and read information materials, and teachers should introduce and provide information on the topics when students' prior knowledge is low or incomplete. Whereas high-quality information books used to be rare, currently there are many thousands of fine books available for young readers. See Box 2.4 for a list of authors, categorized by subject area, who specialize in writing information books. Examples are Patricia McKissack and Fred McKissack's (1992) *Sojourner Truth: Ain't I a Woman?*; Joanna Coles's *The Magic School Bus* science series; David Schwartz's (1989) *If You Made a Million*; and David Macaulay's technology-focused books, such as *The New Way Things Work* (1998) and *Pyramid* (1975).

It is also important to include in the collection other information sources, such as newspapers, computer software, almanacs, reference books, and materials covering topics that are personally interesting to students. Magazines are another valuable information source. With the wide variety of specialized magazines available, all students should be able to find something of interest. Publications that are particularly popular are magazines about sports (e.g., *Sports Illustrated for Kids* and *Sports Illustrated*), video games, music and entertainment, cars, and humor. Students' tastes and magazine top-

---

BOX 2.4. Authors Who Write Information Books

Science, mathematics, and technology: Patricia Lauber, David Schwartz, Joanna Cole, Kathryn Lasky, Seymour Simon, Laurence Pringle, S. Lovett, David Macaulay, Jim Arnosky, Gail Gibbons, Caroline Arnold, Jim Brandenburg, Aliki

Social studies: Jean Fritz, Russell Freedman, Diane Stanley, Milton Meltzer, James Giblin, Jerry Stanley, Patricia McKissack and Frederick McKissack, Walter Dean Myers, Aliki, Jim Murphy, Peter Sis, James Haskins, Rhoda Blumberg

ics change like the wind, so keep up. The Internet is a constantly evolving source for a vast range of current information.

Transitional Chapter Books and Series Books

A fortunate few students seem to make the transition from beginning reading to full-length novels almost overnight. Most of us, however, learned to read gradually over several years before finally acquiring the skills to read honest-to-goodness sophisticated novels and information books. Those years were probably filled with easy picture books that provided strong support through pictures and context, followed by easy reading books (e.g., *I Can Read, I Can Read It All by Myself*, and *Step into Reading* books). For many students, series books and short, transitional chapter books provide a gradual introduction to sustained silent reading and a bridge between easy-reading books and novels. Such books are especially important for struggling readers, who may never have read an entire book from start to finish and may be intimidated by the length of novels.

The series book has been a solid reading staple for both adults and children for many years. Mackey (1990) believes that the popularity of series books may be due partly to the fact that they provide readers with a sense of mastery over the conventions of reading. With characters, language, and content that grow more familiar with every book read, "even a reader inexperienced in an absolute sense has the opportunity to behave like an experienced reader in this one regard at least" (p. 484). Series books, which are especially beneficial for students with limited reading practice, come in a variety of levels that are appropriate for students in grades 3–8, from easy-reading chapter series (e.g., Marshall's *Fox* series) to more difficult series books (e.g., Applegate's *Animorphs*). Series from long ago, such as *The Hardy Boys* (Dixon), *Nancy Drew* (Keene), and *The Boxcar Children* (Warner), are still around in original and updated forms, and more recent series are always among the bestsellers in children's bookstores. In the past, series focused almost exclusively on fiction mystery, adventure, or drama. Fortunately for today's young readers, there are dozens of new series on a variety of additional subjects including humorous fiction, sports, science fiction, adventure, animals, scary stories, and many others. It is important to note that many critically acclaimed books and children's classics are part of a series, including Taylor's (1976) *Roll of Thunder, Hear My Cry* and Voigt's (1981) *Homecoming*.

Marilyn Elrod, a literacy specialist in Texas who works with students and teachers in grades 3–6, highly recommends series books. Through more than 35 years of teaching, Mrs. Elrod has seen many struggling and reluctant readers become hooked on reading and make accelerated progress through reading in series. Mrs. Elrod reads the books herself and then enthusiastically introduces each series. She helps students find a series that's right in terms of difficulty level and interests, and monitors students' fluency and comprehension progress as they are reading the books. Mrs. Elrod gives students regular opportunities to discuss their books and read their favorite parts out loud, which gives students practice in fluency as well as in picking out important events and characters. The characters in the books become frequent topics of conversation. Mrs. Elrod has explained, "I get as excited as they do when a new book in one of our favorite series like *Marvin Redpost* [Sachar] or *Captain Underpants* [Pilkey] comes out, because I enjoy them myself, and I know the kids can't wait to get their hands on them."

A cousin to the series book is the transitional chapter book. Students who are intimidated by longer books are often willing to read a book with fewer pages (from under 50 to just over 100). Like series books, transitional chapter books come in a wide variety of topics and difficulty levels, including Moore's (1998) *Koi's Python* and Manes's (1982) *Be a Perfect Person in Just Three Days*. See Box 2.5 for a list of selected book series and transitional chapter books, ranging from easier to more difficult. Some series and transitional books contain multiple short stories about the same character (e.g., Sobol's *Encyclopedia Brown* series) or topic (e.g., Schwartz's [1981] *Scary Stories to Tell in the Dark*). More transitional books, short novels, and story collections are listed in Appendix C.

Text Sets

The features of series books and transitional chapter books that make them easier to read can also be found when students read a variety of texts on the same topic. Classroom collections should include text sets, books, and other materials grouped by author, genre, topic, theme, and/or format (e.g., poetry, jokes). Materials within the sets should span a wide range of difficulty level and should include materials other than books. Students should become familiar not only with a variety of genres, but also with the range of reading and writing formats and strategies (discussed in later chapters) that mature readers use for enjoyment, gain information, and effectively do their jobs. A teacher, for example, may read the newspaper (news articles, horoscopes, comics, editorials, statistics, graphs, charts, etc.), magazines, professional articles, novels, and books for students. The teacher will probably also read and write lesson plans and procedures, as well as student information presented in different formats (e.g., anecdotal notes, cumulative folders, notes from parents). Moreover, she or he may check and send professional or personal e-mail and look up information on the Web for a variety of reasons.

To help students gain practice in using different kinds of print sources, as well as to improve fluency, we recommend combining student-preferred materials, nontraditional text sources, and more sophisticated or conventionally accepted texts within a topical study. See Box 2.6 for some examples of text sets on two popular topics. Model and encourage students to adopt a critical stance as they read and write about the texts.

A Unit on Shakespeare

The use of sets that include nonprint and nonconventional texts along with conventional texts can turn a teacher-selected book or course of study into an exciting literature unit. For example, a study of Shakespeare, whose works are often introduced in late elementary to middle school, can be enhanced by using varied resources to support students' comprehension. Text sets that relate to students' lives help student to learn about the literature in more depth and build the background knowledge to read and appreciate Shakespeare's plays. For example, a middle school text set on *Romeo and Juliet* might include analysis and comparison of one or more of the early film versions and the more recent and very different 1990s version with Claire Danes and Leonardo DiCaprio, as well as other movies with similar themes (e.g., *West Side Story*). Printed text can include, in addition to the play, books about Shakespeare's life and times (e.g., Aliki, 1999), movie scripts, movie reviews, books with similar themes and plots, and song lyrics.

BOX 2.5. Book Series and Transitional Chapter Book in Approximate Order of Difficulty

Book series

Henry and Mudge by C. Rylant. New York: Simon & Schuster (and other publishers).
Fox by E. Marshall. New York: Dial and Puffin.
Mr. Putter and Tabby by C. Rylant. San Diego, CA: Harcourt Brace.
Eek! Stories to Make You Shriek by various authors. New York: Grosset & Dunlap.
Horrible Harry by S. Kline. New York: Puffin.
Junie B. Jones by B. Park. New York: Random House.
Arthur by Marc Brown. New York: Scholastic. (Picture books, easy-reading books, and easy chapter books.)
Eyewitness Readers by various authors. New York: Dorling Kindersley. (Levels 3 and 4 are for students reading at the second- to fourth-grade level.)
Nate the Great by M. W. Sharmat. New York: Puffin.
Eyewitness Juniors ("Amazing Animals" series) by various authors. New York: Knopf.
Kids of the Polk Street School by P. R. Giff. New York: Yearling.
Marvin Redpost by L. Sachar. New York: Random House.
Cam Jansen by D. Adler. New York: Viking.
Magic Tree House by M. Osborne. New York: Random House.
The Magic School Bus by Joanna Cole. New York: Scholastic. (Picture books and chapter books.)
World of Adventure by Gary Paulsen. Various publishers.
Clue Jr. by P. Hinter. New York: Scholastic.
Choose Your Own Adventure by various authors. New York: Skylark. (These come in two difficulty levels.)
Amelia by M. Moss. Berkeley, CA: Tricycle.
Amber Brown by P. Danziger. New York: Putnam and Scholastic.
The Adventures of Captain Underpants by Dav Pilkey. New York: Blue Sky Press.
The Time Warp Trio by J. Scieszka. New York: Putnam and Scholastic.

Transitional chapter books

Schwartz, A. (1999). *How to catch an elephant.* New York: Dorling Kindersley.
Byars, B. (1996). *Tornado.* New York: HarperCollins.
Blume, J. (1969). *The one in the middle is the green kangaroo.* Chicago: Reilly & Lee.
Moore, M. (1998). *Koi's python.* New York: Hyperion.
Howe, J. (1990). *Hot fudge.* New York: Avon.
Duffey, B. (1996). *Hey, new kid.* New York: Viking.
Auch, M. J. (1999). *I was a third grade science project.* New York: Bantam.
Coville, B. (1992). *Space brat.* New York: Minstrel.
Hesse, K. (1998). *Just juice.* New York: Scholastic.
Blume, J. (1971). *Freckle juice.* New York: Four Winds Press.
George, J. C. (1999). *Incredible animal adventures.* New York: HarperTrophy.
Byars, B. (1990). *Beans on the roof.* New York: Yearling.
Bruchac, J. (1997). *Eagle song.* New York: Dial.
Bulla, C. R. (1975). *Shoeshine girl.* New York: Crowell.
Cleary, B. (1990). *Muggie Maggie.* New York: Morrow.
Estes, E. (1944). *The hundred dresses.* New York: Harcourt Brace.
Bledsoe, L. J. (1995). *The big bike race.* New York: Avon.
Cuyler, M. (1991). *Weird wolf.* New York: Holt.
Reinhard, J. (1998). *Discovering the Inca ice maiden: My adventures on ampato.* Washington, DC: National Geographic Society.
Taylor, M. D. (1987). *The gold Cadillac.* New York: Puffin.
MacLachlan, P. (1991). *Journey.* New York: Dell.
Rockwell, T. (1953). *How to eat fried worms.* New York: Yearling.
Paulsen, G. (1989). *The winter room.* New York: Yearling.
Smith, R. K. (1972). *Chocolate fever.* New York: Coward, McCann & Geoghegan.

(continued)

BOX 2.5. *(continued)*

Book series

Bullseye Step into Classics, and *Bullseye Chillers* by various authors. New York: Random House.

Judy Moody by M. McDonald. Cambridge, MA: Candlewick Press.

Extremely Weird Animals by S. Lovett. Santa Fe, NM: John Muir.

Friendship Ring by R. Vail. New York: Scholastic.

On the Court With ... by M. Christopher. Boston: Little, Brown. (Christopher writes information and narrative sports series on many levels.)

Goosebumps by R. L. Stine. New York: Scholastic. (These come in two levels.)

Animorphs by K. A. Applegate. New York: Apple.

Harry Potter by J. K. Rowling. New York: Scholastic.

California Diaries by A. M. Martin. New York: Scholastic. (Middle school.)

Series Based on Films and TV:

Easier series include *Rugrats, Doug, Full House, Scooby-Doo.*

Slightly more difficult series include *Star Wars, X-Files,* and *Wishbone.*

Transitional chapter books

Levy, E. (1983). *Dracula is a pain in the neck.* New York: Harper & Row.

Schwartz, A. (1981). *Scary stories to tell in the dark.* New York: Lippincott.

Gardiner, J. R. (1980). *Stone Fox.* New York: HarperTrophy.

Anaya, R. A. (1999). *My land sings: Stories from the Rio Grande.* New York: Morrow.

Dahl, R. (1978). *The enormous crocodile.* New York: Knopf.

Dahl, R. (1966). *Fantastic Mr. Fox.* New York: Knopf.

Pinkwater, D. (1977). *The Hoboken chicken emergency.* Englewood Cliffs, NJ: Prentice-Hall.

Kline, S. (1997). *Marvin and the mean words.* New York: Putnam.

Lowry, L. (1979). *Anastasia Krupnik.* Boston: Houghton Mifflin.

Bauer, M. D. (1986). *On my honor.* New York: Clarion.

Manes, S. (1982). *Be a perfect person in just three days.* New York: Clarion.

Walter, V. (1998). *Making up megaboy.* New York: Dorling Kindersley. (Mature middle school readers only.)

Other recommended books for a Shakespeare unit include Coville's (1996) retelling of *A Midsummer Night's Dream* and Krull's (1994) *Lives of the Writers: Comedies, Tragedies (and What the Neighbors Thought).* In Cooper's (1999) fantasy novel, a boy in a theater company travels back in time to 1599 and trades places with a young Shakespearean actor. Such a study could culminate in a trip to see a local performance of a play, along with a student-directed performance. A good read-aloud book to introduce Shakespeare is Blackwood's (1998) suspenseful *The Shakespeare Stealer,* in which a young orphan boy is ordered by his master to steal the script of *Hamlet.* Sources for teachers (Christenbury, 1996; Daniel, 1995) are included in the References list for this chapter.

A Unit on Legends and Tales

Every culture and country has a variety of legends and tales, available in picture books like the Mexican legend *La Llorona/The Weeping Woman* (Hayes, 1987) and story collections like *The Brocaded Slipper and Other Vietnamese Tales* (Vuong, 1992). Worthy and Bloodgood (1992–1993) describe a litera-ture unit on variants of the Cinderella story, used with students in classrooms and in a uni-versity reading center. The unit includes sto-ries from many different cultures—for exam-ple, *Mufaro's Beautiful Daughters* (Steptoe, 1987) from Africa, and *Yeh-Shen* (Louie, 1982) from China. Humorous transformations include *Ugh* (Yorinks, 1990), the story of a cave boy Cinderella figure and *Cinder-Elly* (Minters, 1994), a humorous modern version written in verse, which is perfect for Readers' Theater. Students of all ages enjoy comparing familiar stories with transformations or variants. Sipe (1993) describes a literature unit appropriate for upper elementary and middle school stu-dents. The students who worked with Sipes compared traditional versions of a fairy tale with books in which elements of the stories, including language, theme, plot, characters and/or setting, had been transformed. Exam-

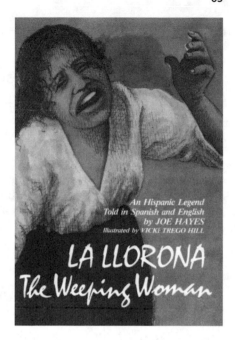

An Hispanic Legend
Told in Spanish and English
by JOE HAYES
Illustrated by VICKI TREGO HILL

LA LLORONA
The Weeping Woman

BOX 2.6. Constructing Text Sets for Two Topics Popular with Students

Sports

- Materials about wide range of both men's and women's sports; focus on sports that are in the news and/or that your students participate in
- Biographies and current information about past and current sports figures (e.g., Pelé, Jackie Joyner-Kersee, Roberto Clemente, Mia Hamm, Shaquille O'Neal, Bruce Lee, Lance Armstrong, Venus and Serena Williams)
- Sports magazines
- How-to-play books
- Novels, short stories, poetry, picture books, historical fiction
- Sports page and Internet (check daily; use Internet to find out how to write to current sports figures)
- Bulletin board with articles, current sports events (including students' game schedules)
- Student-written stories, articles, poetry, and jokes about sports

Scary/mystery:

- Scary story collections by noted authors' such as Alvin Schwartz, ranging from very easy to more sophisticated
- Books of scary riddles, jokes, and poetry
- Novels by acclaimed children's and young adult authors such as James Howe, Mary Downing Hahn, and Lois Duncan
- Popular series books
- Picture books
- "Classic" horror stories and books by authors such as Edgar Allan Poe, Mary Shelley, and Bram Stoker
- True crime books or magazines
- Ghost stories and legends from a variety of cultures

ples of the fairy tale transformations read by these students were *The Frog Prince Continued* (Scieszka, 1991), *The Principal's New Clothes* (Calmenson, 1989), *The Chocolate Touch* (Catling, 1981), *Sleeping Ugly* (Yolen, 1981), and *The Three Pigs/Los Tres Cerdos: Nacho, Tito, and Miguel* (Salinas, 1998). Students compared the books and wrote transformations of their own.

Author and Illustrator Studies

There are hundreds of authors who write for students in the middle grades. Author studies can focus on language, theme, style, or influences. Students can also analyze illustrators' styles and influences. Publishers' Web sites often include information about authors and illustrators and links to their personal Web sites. Box 2.3 lists authors who write about different cultures; Box 2.4 lists authors of information books. In Box 2.7, we list some of our other favorite authors by genre, along with some illustrators.

BOOKS THAT "FIT": GUIDING STUDENTS IN CHOOSING APPROPRIATE BOOKS

The Concept of "Fit"

There is wide agreement among reading educators that students will make the most progress when the books they read "fit" their skill level, providing just the right amount of challenge and success (McGill-Franzen, 1993; Roller, 1996). When students read text that "fits," their error rate is low, making it easier to focus on comprehension and fluency (Gambrell, Wilson, & Gantt, 1981; McCormick, 1994). Students who experience success in an endeavor feel more competent and are more likely to engage in more reading, to expend more effort, to persist in the face of challenges, and to achieve at higher levels (Bandura, 1981). Factors that influence ease of reading include language patterns and structure, conceptual demands of the text, and familiarity of the text to the reader (Peterson, 1991; Rhodes, 1981). In order to practice learned reading skills and to continue making progress in reading achievement and enjoyment, *all* students need access to books that are easy to read, books that provide a moderate degree of challenge, and books that are demanding (presented through teacher read-alouds and on tape, for example). In Chapter 1, we have discussed strategies for helping students choose books that fit (easy, instructional, and challenge books), as well as teacher strategies for assessment.

Providing Materials of Varied Difficulty

Every student in every classroom needs to read in easy books and in texts that are appropriate for instruction. Students also need exposure to books that stretch their knowledge and thinking through teacher read-alouds. Balancing text demands with students' interests is tough with students in upper elementary and middle school. Although even first graders have a range of reading skill, it is generally true that the higher the grade in school, the wider the range in readers. A fifth-grade student whose instructional reading level is fourth grade, for example, will need books for independent reading

---

BOX 2.7. More Authors to Study (See Also Boxes 1.2 and 1.3)

Historical fiction: Karen Cushman, James and Christopher Collier, Michael Dorris, Kathryn Lasky, Scott O'Dell, Katherine Paterson, Mildred D. Taylor

Illustrators (AI = author/illustrators): Chris Van Allsburg (AI), Anthony Browne (AI), Leo Dillon, Diane Dillon, David Diaz (AI), Richard Egielski, Kevin Henkes (AI), Ruth Heller (AI), Thomas Locker (AI), Tomie de Paola (AI), Brian Pinkney, Jerry Pinkney (AI), Allan Say (AI), Lane Smith, William Steig (AI), Ed Young (AI)

Fantasy: Natalie Babbitt, Lloyd Alexander, Roald Dahl, Susan Cooper, Arthur Yorinks, J. K. Rowling, Philip Pallmar

Poetry: Alma Flor Ada, Joanna Cole, Eloise Greenfield, Lee Bennett Hopkins, Paul Janeczko, Gordon Korman, Naomi Shihab Nye, Jeffrey Moss, Jack Prelutsky, Shel Silverstein, Gary Soto

Folk and fairy tales: Paul Goble, William Hooks, James Marshall, Rafe Martin, Rosemary Minard (mature), Robert D. San Souci, Diane Wolkstein

Realistic fiction: Eve Bunting, Betsy Byars, Jean Craighead George, Paula Fox, E. L. Konigsburg, Phyllis Reynolds Naylor, Gary Paulsen, Louis Sachar, Jerry Spinelli

Across genres: Joanna Cole, Pam Conrad, Virginia Hamilton, Karen Hesse, Lois Lowry, Patricia McKissack, Walter Dean Myers, Cynthia Rylant, Louis Sachar, Gary Soto, John Steptoe, Judith Viorst, Jane Yolen

Humor: Roald Dahl, Stephen Manes, Dav Pilkey, Daniel Pinkwater, Louis Sachar, Jon Scieszka, Mike Thaler, Arthur Yorinks

Sophisticated picture books: Anthony Browne, Eve Bunting, William Steig, Chris Van Allsburg, Jane Yolen, Arthur Yorinks

Scary/horror: Alvin Schwartz, James Howe, Lois Duncan (mature)

(perhaps ranging from second- to third-grade level), books to read with teacher support (perhaps ranging from third- to fifth-grade level), and conceptually challenging books to "grow into" or for teacher read-alouds (ranging from perhaps fifth- to seventh-grade level). Consider that every class has students reading on a range of levels; figure in students' diverse interests; and you begin to understand the need for a varied classroom collection. If only grade-level texts are included in the classroom library, students will get the message that it is only acceptable to read such books. Students who do not read on grade level will then be embarrassed to check out easier books from the library. Under these circumstances, most of these students will not read at all or will attempt to read frustrational-level texts. The teacher who includes a wide range of texts in his or her classroom and enthusiastically introduces books of all difficulty levels will set the tone for acceptance of all readers. Box 2.8 shows just a sample of the range of books found in a sixth-grade classroom with a good collection. Notice that there are information and fiction easy picture books, easy-reading books, series books, sophisticated picture books, poetry, transitional chapter books, and a variety of more sophisticated books. A third-grade classroom would include more easy books and beginning readers, and an eighth-grade classroom would include more sophisticated books, but *all* classrooms need a wide variety of print sources on many topics covering many difficulty levels.

BOX 2.8. The Range of Reading Materials in a Sixth Grade Classroom

Easy-to-Read Picture Books

Branley, F. M. (1988). *Tornado alert.* New York: Harper & Row.
Brown, M. (1999). *Arthur's teacher trouble.* Boston: Little, Brown.
Rylant, C. (1997). *Henry and Mudge in the family trees.* New York: Simon & Schuster.
Sandin, J. (1989). *The long way westward.* New York: HarperCollins.
Smith, L. (1993). *The happy Hocky family.* New York: Puffin.
Thaler, M. (1999). *The gym teacher from the black lagoon.* New York: Scholastic.

Sophisticated Picture Books

Aliki. (1979). *Mummies made in Egypt.* New York: Harper & Row.
Garza, C. L. (1996). *In my family/en mi familia.* San Francisco: Children's Book Press.
Mahy, M. (1989). *The great white man-eating shark.* New York: Dial.
Mochizuki, K. (1993). *Baseball saved us* (ill. D. Lee). New York: Scholastic.
Mora, P. (1997). *Tomás and the library lady.* New York: Knopf.
Seuss, Dr., & Prelutsky, J. (1998). *Hooray for diffendoofer day.* New York: Knopf.
Simon, S. (1992). *Snakes.* New York: HarperCollins.
Soto, G. (1995). *Chato's kitchen* (ill. S. Guevara). New York: Putnam.

Transitional Chapter Books

Ackerman, K. (1994). *The night crossing.* New York: Scholastic.
Christopher, M. (1997). *Stranger in right field.* Boston: Little, Brown.
Scieszka, J. (1995). *2095.* New York: Scholastic.
White, E. B. (1952). *Charlotte's web.* New York: Harper & Row.

More Sophisticated Fiction and Nonfiction

Baker, J. (1995). *The story of Rosy Dock.* New York: Random House.
Clements, A. (1996). *Frindle.* New York: Simon & Schuster.
Conly, J. L. (1993). *Crazy lady.* New York: HarperCollins.
Filipovic, Z. (1994). *Zlata's diary: A child's life in Sarajevo.* New York: Viking.
Giff, P. R. (1997). *Lily's crossing.* New York: Delacorte Press.
Krull, K. (1998). *Lives of the presidents: Fame, shame (and what the neighbors thought).* San Diego, CA: Harcourt Brace.
Park, B. (1995). *Mick Harte was here.* New York: Scholastic.
Rubin, S. G. (1998). *Toilets, toasters, and telephones: The how and why of everyday objects.* San Diego, CA: Harcourt Brace.
Stanley, D. (1998). *Joan of Arc.* New York: Morrow.

Poetry

Alarcón, F. X. (1997). *Laughing tomatoes and other spring poems/Jitomates risueños y otros poemas de primavera.* San Francisco: Children's Book Press.
Greenfield, E. (1978). *Honey, I love.* New York: Crowell.
Merriam, E. (1969). *The inner city Mother Goose.* New York: Simon & Schuster.

(continued)

Myers, W. D. (1993). *Brown angels: An album of pictures and verse.* New York: HarperCollins.

Prelutsky, J. (1989). *Poems by A. Nonny Mouse.* New York: Random House.

Rosenberg, L. (Ed.). (1998). *Earth-shattering poems.* New York: Holt.

Silverstein, S. (1996). *Falling up.* New York: HarperCollins.

Turner, A. (1993). *Grass songs: Poems of women's journey west.* San Diego, CA: Harcourt Brace.

Volavkova, H. (Ed.). (1993). *I never saw another butterfly: Children's drawings and poems from Terezin concentration camp.* New York: Schocken.

Note. Adapted from Ivey, G., & Broaddus, K. (2000). Tailoring the fit: Reading instruction and middle school readers. *The Reading Teacher, 54* 68–78. Copyright by the International Reading Association. Adapted with permission.

THE HARDEST PART: ACQUIRING MATERIALS FOR CLASSROOM COLLECTIONS

The Need to Allot Instructional Money for Reading Materials

Although most schools have plenty of materials that adults want students to read, the availability of student-preferred materials lags far behind (Worthy et al., 1999). In interviews with teachers and librarians, we have found that the most difficult part of providing students with reading choices is obtaining reading materials. Many of the librarians and teachers we interviewed wanted to provide materials that appealed to students; however, they found it very expensive to keep up with popular, current materials. Series and scary books were in all of the libraries and in a few classrooms, but were so popular that they were always checked out. Comics and cartoon collections (e.g., *Garfield* books) and popular magazines were expensive, had limited durability, and were easily lost. Sports books were widely available in libraries but less so in classrooms. According to one librarian, many sports heroes are "here today, gone tomorrow," making many such books obsolete in a short time. Each year librarians were required to spend more of their budgets on technology, in addition to keeping reference materials up to date (Miller & Shontz, 1995). Most schools spend a great deal of instructional money on textbooks, basals, and class novel sets, but they spend very little on building classroom libraries. Many schools now also invest a great deal of money in computer-based reading incentive programs (e.g., Accelerated Reader), which include mainly fiction books, leaving very little money to buy student-preferred materials and current information books like those described in this chapter.

There are many areas in which money that could be spent on reading materials is used on other things. We recently visited a school in an upper-middle-class suburb. We saw state-of-the art facilities and equipment, including a newly remodeled classroom wing and refurbished sports fields. Each classroom and the library had an abundance of the latest computer hardware and software available. Yet students had to participate in a lottery to check out popular and award-winning *paperback* novels from the library, and were unable to take home the books they were reading for language arts because there were not enough books in the classroom libraries. Although we do not discount the importance of facilities and technology, books should be a priority in schools. Fortunately, most of the students in this school are able to obtain books outside of school. Their parents are able to provide them with money to buy books and/or with transportation to visit public libraries. Most students have shelves of reading materials at home, including the latest series books, magazines, and comics. Our concern is for students who may not have discretionary money, and thus are more dependent on school sources for reading materials (Worthy et al., 1999). For students in poor communities, access to books at school is even more limited (Constantino, 1995).

In interviews with teachers who work in low-income communities, we have found that many spend their own time and money acquiring materials for their classroom libraries because they know it is necessary, and there is often limited money in school budgets to do so. As one teacher said, "If you have to do it, you have to do it. It's no big deal, because if you're a teacher, I think you want to provide things that the kids can't wait to get to." Students in the classrooms of teachers such as this one are the fortunate few. However, we worry about students who do not have books of their own *and* whose teachers either do not have the resources to buy books or object to spending their own money for materials that schools should provide. Whatever the reasons, the bottom line is that some students have more access to books than others. Limited availability of preferred materials in school leaves students with three choices: reading something outside of their interests, obtaining their preferred materials outside of school, or not reading. Students who cannot afford to obtain their preferred materials have fewer choices, and thus are less likely to read and less likely to do well in school.

Ways of Acquiring Reading Materials

Teachers should not be required to spend their own money for reading materials that are necessary for their students. This is the responsibility of schools. School personnel can work together to see that available resources are spent wisely. For example, since many language arts teachers do not use basals and textbooks or use them only occasionally (Worthy et al., 1998) one or two sets can be shared among a grade level or kept in the library. Software and reference books can also be shared, rotated, or bought only as needed. Your school should be able to find other ways to cut back on instructional materials budgets. Another suggestion is to solicit donations of books for your school from the parents of your students or from the community. Many families have books in their homes that their children have outgrown. The National Junior Honor Society at a middle school in Texas organized a book drive for area elementary schools. The yield was an astounding 6, 000 books, most in good to excellent shape, in a wide variety of genres. Box 2.9 lists these and other suggestions for acquiring reading materials.

Making Access to Reading Materials Your Top Priority

Time spent reading is crucial for reading and writing development as well as for learning in general. We recommend that teachers, principals, parents, and librarians meet to plan ways that will work for their own situations to ensure that every classroom has an excellent, inviting collection of materials, and that *all* students in the school have abundant access to books they can and want to read.

BOX 2.9. Suggestions for Acquiring Reading Materials (Cheap or Free)

- Set up book swaps for students to exchange books, magazines, and comics among themselves.
- Visit thrift stores and discount book stores frequently.
- Ask publishers, bookstores, and comic book stores for discards.
- Attend garage sales, publishers' warehouse sales, and library book sales.
- Request school copies of the local newspaper.
- Send a wish list of books to parents and/or suggest that parents donate books to the classroom for their children's birthdays or for holidays.
- Copy song lyrics from the Web and/or from CD jackets.
- Use book clubs (e.g., Scholastic, Trumpet). The books are cheap and popular with students, and teachers can earn bonus points to buy books.
- Use the school and public libraries to keep your classroom collection evolving; check out many different kinds of books for browsing. (Keep these books separate from your own collection.)
- Take your class to visit the public library and get library cards.
- Use money that's now used to buy whole-class sets for a variety of paperbacks.
- Rotate classroom collections with other teachers.
- Organize a book drive, start a school bookstore.
- Ask school sponsors to contribute to a book fund; use the money to build classroom collections.
- If your school gives students rewards for reading, make the rewards books rather than items unrelated to reading.

CHILDREN'S BOOK REFERENCES

Aliki. (1999). *William Shakespeare and the Globe*. New York: HarperCollins.
Babbitt, N. (1975). *Tuck everlasting*. New York: Farrar, Straus, Giroux.
Blackwood, B. L. (1998). *The Shakespeare stealer*. New York: Dutton.
Calmenson, S. (1989). *The principal's new clothes*. New York: Scholastic.
Catling, P. (1981). *The chocolate touch*. New York: Bantam.
Clement, A. (1996). *Frindle*. New York: Simon & Schuster.
Cole, J. (1987). *The magic school bus inside the earth*. New York: Scholastic.
Coville, B. (1996). *William Shakespeare's A midsummer night's dream, retold by Bruce Coville*. New York: Dial.
Cooper, S. (1999). *King of shadows*. New York: Simon & Schuster.
Davis, J. (1999). *Garfield feeds the kitty*. New York: Ballantine.
Feiffer, J. (1999). *Meanwhile. . .* New York: HarperCollins.
Hayes, J. (1987). *La llorona/The weeping woman*. El Paso, TX: Cinco Puntos Press.
Kramer, S. A. (1997). *Basketball's greatest players*. New York: Random House.
Krull. K. (1994). *Lives of the writers: Comedies, tragedies (and what the neighbors thought)*. San Diego, CA: Harcourt Brace.
Louie, A. (1982). *Yeh-Shen: A Cinderella story from China*. New York: Philomel.
Macaulay, D. (1975). *Pyramid*. Boston: Houghton Mifflin.
Macaulay, D. (1998). *The new way things work*. Boston: Houghton Mifflin.
Manes, S. (1982). *Be a perfect person in just three days*. New York: Clarion.

McKissack, P. C., & McKissack, F. (1992). *Sojourner Truth: Ain't I a woman?* New York: Scholastic.

Minters, F. (1994). *Cinder-Elly.* New York: Viking.

Moore, M. (1998). *Koi's python.* New York: Hyperion.

O'Dell, S. (1960). *Island of the blue dolphins.* Boston: Houghton Mifflin.

Paterson, K. (1977). *Bridge to Terabithia.* New York: Crowell.

Paulsen, G. (1987). *Hatchet.* New York: Bradbury Press.

Pinkney, B. (1997). *The adventures of Sparrowboy.* New York: Simon & Schuster.

Rockwell, T. (1953). *How to eat fried worms.* New York: Yearling.

Salinas, B. (1998). *The three pigs/Los tres cerdos: Nacho, Tito, and Miguel.* Alameda, CA: Piñata.

Schwartz, A. (1981). *Scary stories to tell in the dark.* New York: Lippincott.

Schwartz, D. (1989). *If you made a million.* New York: Lothrop, Lee & Shepard.

Scieszka, J. (1989). *The true story of the three little pigs.* New York: Viking.

Scieszka, J. (1991). *The frog prince continued.* New York: Viking.

Sendak, M. (1993). *We are all in the dumps with Jack and Guy: Two nursery rhymes.* New York: HarperCollins.

Steptoe, J. (1987). *Mufaro's beautiful daughters: An African tale.* New York: Lothrop, Lee & Shepard.

Stevenson, J. (1980). *That terrible Halloween night.* New York: Greenwillow.

Stevenson, J. (1999). *Don't make me laugh.* New York: Farrar, Straus, Giroux.

Taylor, M. D. (1976). *Roll of thunder, hear my cry.* New York: Dial.

Voigt, C. (1981). *Homecoming.* New York: Simon & Schuster.

Vuong, L. D. (1992). *The brocaded slipper and other Vietnamese tales.* Reading, MA: Addison-Wesley.

Yolen, J. (1981). *Sleeping ugly.* New York: Coward, McCann & Geoghegan.

Yorinks, A. (1990). *Ugh.* New York: Farrar, Straus, Giroux.

Young, M. (Ed.). (1999). *The Guinness book of world records 1999.* New York: Bantam.

REFERENCES

Baines, L. (1994). Cool books for tough guys: 50 books out of the mainstream of adolescent literature that will appeal to males who do not enjoy reading. *The ALAN Review, 22*, 43–46.

Bandura, A. (1981). Self-efficacy: Toward a unifying theory of behavioral change. *Psychological Review, 84*, 191–215.

Bintz, W. P. (1993). Resistant readers in secondary education: Some insights and implications. *Journal of Reading, 36*, 604–615.

Bishop, R. S. (1992). Multicultural literature for children: Making informed choices. In V. J. Harris (Ed.), *Teaching multicultural literature in grades K–8* (pp. 37–54). Norwood, MA: Christopher-Gordon.

Brocka, B. (1979). Comic books: In case you haven't noticed, they've changed. *Media and Methods, 15*, 30–33.

Carlsen, R., & Sherrill, A. (1988). *Voices of readers: How we come to love books.* Urbana, IL: National Council of Teachers of English.

Christenbury, L. (1996). Race, racism, and racial harmony: Using classic and young adult literature to teach *Othello, the Moor of Venice.* In J. F. Kaywell (Ed.), *Adolescent literature as a complement to the classics* (Vol. 3, pp. 93–103). Norwood, MA: Christopher-Gordon.

Constantino, R. (1995). Two small girls: One large disparity. *The Reading Teacher, 48*, 504.

Csikszentmihalyi, M., & McCormack, J. (1986). The influence of teachers. *Phi Delta Kappan*, 415–419.

Daniel, P. L. (1995). Relationships and identity: Young adult literature and the tragedy of *Julius Caesar.* In J. F. Kaywell (Ed.), *Adolescent literature as a complement to the classics* (Vol. 2, pp. 145–161). Norwood, MA: Christopher-Gordon.

Day, F. A. (1994). *Multicultural voices in contemporary literature.* Portsmouth, NH: Heinemann.

Dorrell, L. D., & Carroll, E. (1981). Spider-Man at the library. *School Library Journal, 27*, 17–19.

Dorrell, L. D., & Southall, C. T. (1982). Captain America: A hero for education! *Clearinghouse, 55*, 397–399.

Fractor, J. S., Woodruff, M. C., Martinez, M. G., & Teale, W. H. (1993). Let's not miss opportunities to promote voluntary reading: Classroom libraries in the elementary school. *The Reading Teacher, 46,* 476–484.

Gambrell, L. B., Wilson, R. M., & Gantt, W. N. (1981). Classroom observations of task-attending behaviors of good and poor readers. *Journal of Educational Research, 24,* 400–404.

Greaney, V., & Hegarty, M. (1987). Correlates of leisure-time reading. *Journal of Research in Reading, 10,* 3–20.

Howes, V. (1963). Children's interests—a key note for teaching reading. *Education, 8,* 491–496.

Ivey, G., & Broaddus, K. (2000). Tailoring the fit: Reading instruction and middle school readers. *The Reading Teacher, 54,* 68–78.

Krashen, S., & McQuillan, J. (1996). *The case for late intervention: Once a good reader, always a good reader.* Culver City, CA: Language Education Associates.

Kulleseid, E. R. (1994–1995). EL K–12 bestsellers. *Emergency Librarian,* January/February, 1994 through May/June, 1995.

Lord, M. (2000, June 12). Where have all the librarians gone? They've gone to dotcoms, one by one. *U.S. News and World Report,* p. 53.

Mackey, M. (1990). Filling the gaps: The Babysitters Club, the series book, and the learning reader. *Language Arts, 67,* 484–489.

McCormick, S. (1994). A nonreader becomes a reader: A case study of literacy acquisition by a severely disabled reader. *Reading Research Quarterly, 29*(2), 156–177.

McGill-Franzen, A. (1993). "I could read the words!": Selecting good books for inexperienced readers, *The Reading Teacher, 46,* 424–426.

McKenna, M., Kear, D., & Ellsworth, R. (1991). Developmental trends in children's use of print media: A national study. In J. Zutell & S. McCormick (Eds.), *Learner factors/teacher factors: Issues in literacy research and instruction* (pp. 319–324). Chicago: National Reading Conference.

Miller, M., & Shontz, M. (1995). The race for the school library dollar. *School Library Journal, 41,* 22–33.

Miller, T. (1998). The place of picture books in middle-level classrooms. *Journal of Adolescent and Adult Literacy, 41,* 376–381.

Morrow, L. M., & Weinstein, C. (1982). Increasing children's use of literature program and physical design changes. *Elementary School Journal, 83,* 131–137.

Neuman, S. (1986). The home environment and fifth-grade students' leisure reading. *Elementary School Reading, 86,* 335–343.

Nilsen, A. P., & Donelson, K. L. (2001). *Literature for today's young adults* (6th ed.). New York: Longman

Parrish, B., & Atwood, K. (1985). Enticing readers: The teen romance craze. *California Reader, 18,* 22–27.

Peterson, B. (1991). Selecting books for beginning readers. In D. DeFord, C. Lyons, & G. S. Pinnell (Eds.), *Bridges to literacy: Learning from Reading Recovery* (pp. 119–147). Portsmouth, NH: Heinemann.

Rhodes, L. K. (1981). I can read!: Predictable books as resources for reading and writing instruction. *The Reading Teacher, 34,* 511–518.

Roettger, D. (1980). Elementary students' attitudes toward reading. *The Reading Teacher, 33,* 451–453.

Roller, C. M. (1996). *Variability, not disability: Struggling readers in a workshop classroom.* Newark, DE: International Reading Association.

Schiefele, U. (1991). Interest, learning, and motivation. *Educational Psychologist, 26,* 299–323.

Sipe, L. R. (1993). Using transformations of traditional stories: Making the reading–writing connection. *The Reading Teacher, 47,* 13–26.

Spiegelman, A. (1986). *Maus: A survivor's tale.* New York: Pantheon.

Southgate, V., Arnold, H., & Johnston, S. (1981). *Extending beginning reading.* London: Heinemann.

Tunnell, M., & Jacobs, J. S. (1989). Using "real" books: Research findings on literature based reading instruction. *The Reading Teacher, 42,* 470–477.

Ujiie, J., & Krashen, S. (1996). Is comic book reading harmful?: Comic book reading, school achievement, and pleasure reading among seventh graders. *California School Library Association Journal,* *19,* 27–28.

Worthy, J., & Bloodgood, J. (1992–1993). Enhancing reading instruction through Cinderella tales. *The Reading Teacher, 46,* 290–301.

Worthy, J., Moorman, M., & Turner, M. (1999). What Johnny likes to read is hard to find in schools. *Reading Research Quarterly, 34,* 12–27.

Worthy, J., Patterson, E., Salas, R., Turner, M., & Prater, S. (1997, December). *Reading preferences of elementary students in a school-based tutoring program.* Paper presented at the National Reading Conference, Scottsdale, AZ.

Worthy, J., Turner, M., & Moorman, M. (1998). The precarious place of self-selected reading. *Language Arts, 76,* 296–305.

Wright, G. (1979). The comic book: A forgotten medium in the classroom. *The Reading Teacher, 33,* 153–161.

RESOURCES FOR SELECTING BOOKS

Ammon, B., & Sherman, G. (1996). *Worth a thousand words: An annotated guide to picture books for older readers.* Littleton, CO: Libraries Unlimited.

Barrera, R. B., Thompson, V. D., & Dressman, M. (1997). *Kaleidoscope: A multicultural booklist for grades K–8.* Urbana, IL: National Council of Teachers of English.

Day, F. A. (1994). *Multicultural voices in contemporary literature.* Portsmouth, NH: Heinemann.

Donelson, K. L., & Nilsen, A. P. (1996). *Literature for today's young adult.* New York: HarperCollins.

Sutton, W. K. (Ed.). (1997). *Adventuring with books: A booklist for pre-K through grade 6.* Urbana, IL: National Council of Teachers of English.

RESOURCES THROUGH THE WORLD WIDE WEB

• The Miss Rumphius Award (link from www.reading.org), sponsored by the International Reading Association (Newark, DE), honors "educators who develop and share exceptional Internet resources for literacy and learning. It honors teachers who make our world a more beautiful place, like the title character in the book *Miss Rumphius* by Barbara Cooney" (New York: Viking Penguin, 1982).

• Outstanding Science Trade Books (link from www.nsta.org), sponsored by the National Science Teachers Association (Arlington, VA) in conjunction with the Children's Book Council, features an annotated book list (published yearly) of excellent science books for prekindergarten through eighth grade, arranged by topic.

• Spaghetti Book Club (www.Spaghettibookclub.org), sponsored by Happy Medium Publications of New York City, features "book reviews by kids for kids" in kindergarten through sixth grade.

• The International Reading Association's online journal, *Reading Online,* links to Web sites featuring book review columns, professional books, author Web sites, and reviews of individual books (www.readingonline.org/reviews/literature/). There are also reviews of software by education faculty at Georgia State University (www.readingonline.org/electronic/McKenna).

• Publishers' sites usually have information about authors, as well as book reviews from a variety of sources.

PART II

Reading and Writing Instruction

Now that we have discussed how to begin the school year by assessing students and building a classroom book collection, it is time to address instruction in reading, writing, and word analysis. One issue to consider in all areas of instruction is how to organize students for learning. How often and under what circumstances should whole-class instruction take place? Small-group? Paired? Individual? These are difficult questions with complex answers that are dependent on your students, your purpose, your materials, and the context of instruction. Teachers must be aware that grouping students by so-called ability or achievement for a large portion of the school day can be very damaging, especially for students in the "low groups" (Allington & Walmsley, 1995; Berghoff & Egawa, 1991; Oakes, 1986). Instruction for remedial or low-achieving students is typically of lower quality and delivered at a slower pace, further increasing achievement gaps. Although you may occasionally bring groups of students together to work on a skill, be careful not to overdo this practice. As you read and think about appropriate instruction for your students, consider the suggestions for organizational formats in the box below.

REFERENCES

Allington, R. L., & Walmsley, S. A. (Eds.)(1995). *No quick fix: Rethinking literacy programs in America's elementary schools*. New, DE: International Reading Association and Teachers College Press.

Bergoff, B., & Egawa, K. (1991). No more "rocks." Grouping to give students control of their learning. *The Reading Teacher, 44*, 536–541.

Oakes, J. (1986). Keeping track: Part I. The policy and practice of curriculum inequality. *Phi Delta Kappan, 68*, 12–17.

Organizing for Instruction: Literacy Practices in Different Settings

Instructional focus/grouping	Reading fluency	Reading comprehension	Word knowledge	Writing
Whole class	Teacher modeling of fluent reading	Teacher read-aloud with think-aloud, directed listening–thinking activity (DL-TA), or book discussion; model graphic analysis of text structure	Word wall; modeling of word sorts and other word analysis activities; content vocabulary study	Brainstorming; modeled writing; supported writing; editing demonstration; Author's Chair
Mixed ability groups	Readers' Theater and poetry performance	Readers' Theater and poetry performance; graphic analysis of text structure	Poetry performance; word play and writing (riddles, rhymes, games)	Brainstorming; interactive writing; recording information for writing on a graphic organizer; peer editing groups
Groups set up by skills or interests	Thematic reading on topics of study	Book discussion groups; research study groups setting up a data chart	Teacher-directed minilessons and word analysis sorts; word hunts; word study games about specific features	Teacher-directed minilessons on writing techniques; content editing groups
Student pairs	Partner reading in independent to instructional text; reading dialogue or interviews for performance	Think-aloud; recording research data on chart; graphic analysis of text structure	Practicing word analysis sorts for automaticity; word hunts; word study games about specific features	Interactive writing of dialogue or letters; interviews; editing checklists
Individual students	Independent reading in easy, high-interest materials; listening to taped recordings while following in the text	Directed reading–thinking activity (DR-TA) with written predictions; graphic analysis of text structure	Word study notebook collection of word sorts, word hunts, and word play games	Individual writing (all stages of the writing process)

CHAPTER 3

Reading Aloud to Students

Missy is a student in Ms. Lewis's fourth-grade inclusion classroom. She began the year reading on approximately a first-grade level. Although Ms. Lewis knew that Missy needed to read books on her instructional level to become a more fluent and confident reader, she also sympathized with Missy's desire to experience the higher-interest materials enjoyed by her peers. Free-reading times were especially difficult for Missy, and during the first several weeks of school, Ms. Lewis watched as Missy struggled through every other word in books like *It Takes Two* (Krulik, 1995), a book based on a popular movie, and something many of the girls in her class were reading. Through a process that took several weeks, she worked with Missy during free-reading times to help her choose books she could read more comfortably. In the end, Missy found herself enjoying *Harry and the Terrible Whatzit* (Gackenbach, 1979) and other easy picture books she could manage with ease. But Ms. Lewis could not shake the image of Missy trying hopelessly to read what she really wanted to read, especially since Missy could understand the content of the book, and limited decoding skill was the only barrier to her comprehension. Missy has every right to know and discuss age-appropriate books that are of high interest, but the bottom line is that she cannot read them, even with strong support from her teacher.

How do you think Ms. Lewis might respond to Missy's dilemma?

WHAT'S IN THIS CHAPTER?

Why Read Aloud in the Middle Grades?
Exposing Students to a Variety of Topics and Genres by Reading Aloud
Promoting Engagement in Reading through Reading Aloud
Giving Students Access to Materials They Cannot Yet Read on Their Own
Creating a Context for Sharing Expertise about Reading and Writing
Providing Opportunities for Personal Response, Discussion, and Inquiry
Making Time for Reading Aloud

WHY READ ALOUD IN THE MIDDLE GRADES?

Few would argue about the benefits of teachers reading aloud to young children: learning about concepts of print, developing a sense of story, building language and vocabulary, and cultivating a curiosity about books. In fact, reading aloud to children may be the single most important way for them to acquire fundamental knowledge about reading (Anderson, Hiebert, Scott, & Wilkinson, 1985). It is no surprise that read-alouds, even several times during the day, are common in preschool and the early grades.

What about the middle grades? Although the amount of time teachers spend reading to their students is uncertain, there are clear advantages, which are hinted at by these sixth-grade students who talked about why they appreciate read-alouds:

"I want to read in this class when the teacher reads a little part of the book. If it is interesting, I want to find out about the rest of the book."

"What makes me want to read is when there is an author or book that the teacher starts to read in class, and when they read it they make their voice sound exciting."

"When the teacher reads, it sounds more explainable."

"Sometimes my teacher reads from big books with small writing and makes it interesting. She makes us want to read it."

In our survey of over 1,700 sixth-grade students (Ivey & Broaddus, in press), the teacher read-aloud was cited as one of the most preferred reading activities in school. In the remainder of this chapter, we discuss some reasons for this popularity and some ways for teachers to make the most of reading aloud to their students.

EXPOSING STUDENTS TO A VARIETY OF TOPICS AND GENRES BY READING ALOUD

Cunningham and Allington (1999) suggest that teachers should read four types of material to children every day: information books, grade-level favorites, poetry, and easy books. Middle grades teachers should also read aloud additional materials students need and prefer, including picture books, newspapers, and magazines.

Information Books

In the middle grades, it is more important to share nonfiction materials than at any other time. Not only are students faced with expository text most of the school day in their content area subjects, but they are also looking for information about personal interests in their pleasure reading. Nonfiction read-alouds can be connected to a topic of study undertaken by the class. For instance, *Hiroshima No Pika* (Maruki, 1980) documents the bombing of Hiroshima through the experiences of a Japanese girl and her family. But teachers can also include read-alouds of texts to tap students' interest in reading about new topics, or just to expose them to unfamiliar forms of writing. Rubin's (1998) *Toilets, Toasters, and Telephones: The How and Why of Everyday Objects* provides a sampling of information about a variety of topics.

Teachers need not read aloud all information texts in their entirety. In our own real reading, we would seldom read an entire encyclopedia, almanac, or book of sports statistics, or even a newspaper from cover to cover. Teachers might want to show students how to use the index or table of contents to find the information they want to read to them from a particular text. Reading just an excerpt from a nonfiction text might also give students an incentive to read that text on their own. The Internet can provide current information on topics of interest to read aloud to students.

Grade-Level Favorites

If you have spent any time in middle grades reading or language arts classrooms, chances are you have heard some of these titles: *Maniac Magee* (Spinelli, 1990), *Hatchet* (Paulsen, 1987), *There's a Boy in the Girls' Bathroom* (Sachar, 1987), *Bridge to Terabithia* (Paterson, 1977), and *Dear Mr. Henshaw* (Cleary, 1983). These are books usually earmarked for whole-class studies through either independent silent reading or round-robin oral reading, but we suggest that they are perfect for reading aloud (and, of course, students may choose these books for independent reading). Although we encourage teachers to expose students to the old favorites, we strongly recommend that teachers keep students abreast of new titles that are destined to become classics. For instance, as Kim Duhamel, a fourth-grade teacher from New Jersey, was finishing a read-aloud of *Harry Potter and the Sorcerer's Stone* (Rowling, 1998) to her class near the end of the school year, the second book in the series, *Harry Potter and the Chamber of Secrets* (Rowling, 1999), had just hit bookstore shelves and was already listed on *The New York Times* bestseller list. They started the new book but did not finish it before the last day of school. Nevertheless, a number of students asked their parents for their own copies to finish over the summer, and Ms. Duhamel advised parents to take her place in reading aloud to their children. Read-alouds of novels and grade-level favorites provide the perfect opportunity for introducing a particular author or series and for promoting further reading.

Poetry

Perhaps no genre begs to be read aloud more than poetry. Furthermore, short readings can be very effective even though they take up very little class time. We recommend poetry read-alouds spread throughout the day and across the curriculum. No doubt teachers will want to include humorous old favorites by Shel Silverstein (*A Light in the Attic*, 1981; *Where the Sidewalk Ends*, 1974; *Falling Up*, 1996) and Jack Prelutsky (*The New Kid on the Block*, 1984; *Something Big Has Been Here*, 1990). In fact, many students will already know these collections when they enter middle grades classrooms. Although hearing familiar selections will engage students in their listening, teachers will also want to introduce students to many different kinds of verse, including multicultural collections like *Brown Angels: An Album of Pictures and Verse* (Myers, 1993) and *Neighborhood Odes* (Soto, 1992), and poems about personal experiences, such as *Waiting to Waltz: A Childhood* (Rylant, 1984). Other collections can be easily connected to science topics (*I Am Phoenix: Poems for Two Voices*—Fleischman, 1985; *Bone Poems*—Moss, 1997) and social studies topics (*Grass Songs: Poems of Women's Journey West*—Turner, 1993; *I Never Saw Another Butterfly: Children's Drawings and Poems from Terezin Concentration Camp*—Volavkova, 1993).

Easy Books

Read-alouds of easy books serve a number of purposes. First, it is a way for teachers to make "easy books acceptable" (Fielding & Roller, 1992) not only for students who struggle with reading difficult texts, but also for students who need to read easy books to build their fluency, as well as for good readers who enjoy easy books. Second, the reading of easy books is an ideal way to model fluent reading, which we discuss later in this chapter. Third, the fact that a book is easy does not mean that it is not an interesting or engaging book. Some of our favorite books are very simply written. We like to use easy picture books such as *The Stupids Die* (Allard, 1981), *Miss Nelson Is Missing* (Allard, 1977), and *Henry and Mudge under the Yellow Moon* (Rylant, 1998), and especially books with a predictable or repetitive pattern, such as *Bringing the Rain to Kapiti Plain* (Aardema, 1981) and *Guess What*? (Fox, 1990). It is equally important to read aloud easy or transitional chapter books, such as *Happily Ever After* (Quindlen, 1997) and *The Magic Finger* (Dahl, 1966). For older students, read-alouds can be used to introduce high-interest, short chapter books such as *Making Up Megaboy* (Walter, 1998).

Picture Books

The value of reading aloud picture books in the middle grades seems infinite. Besides the fact that they are short and can be completed within a single class period, they provide a myriad of uses for instruction. Content-related picture books can be used to introduce a unit of study. For instance, *Counting on Frank* (Clement, 1991) offers a colorful and

engaging glimpse into measurement, volume, and capacity, and *Teammates* (Golenbock, 1990) raises issues about civil rights through the story of Jackie Robinson's debut in major league baseball. Other selections can be used to introduce concepts about text structure, theme, and other literary elements. For example, a series of read-alouds of alternative versions of Cinderella, such as *Ugh* (Yorinks, 1990), *Mufaro's Beautiful Daughters* (Steptoe, 1987), and *Prince Cinders* (Cole, 1987), can lead to a study of familiar plot structures and common themes. In addition, picture books are good models for students' writing, as we discuss in detail in Chapter 6.

Popular Newspapers and Magazines

Recent surveys (Ivey & Broaddus, in press; Worthy, Moorman, & Turner, 1999) indicate that magazines are among middle school students' most preferred reading materials. Students' interests span a wide range, depending on their hobbies and interests, but many of them enjoy magazines about automobiles, video games, music, television and movie stars, and sports. This is no surprise, since adult readers also read a variety of magazines for entertainment and information. Read-alouds of newspaper and magazine articles not only give teachers a chance to pique students' interest in reading on their own, but also provide opportunities for studying what it takes to write these kinds of materials, but in engaging ways. For instance, one fourth-grade teacher read aloud a newspaper article in which the author critiqued a popular musical group's performance at a recent concert—a topic that grabbed the interest of the students—and then had students focus on the kinds of descriptive words the author used and how those word choices contributed to an overall positive review.

PROMOTING ENGAGEMENT IN READING
THROUGH READING ALOUD

Read-alouds inspire middle grades students to read on their own. Even when they are surrounded by a rich and varied classroom library with colorful covers and interesting titles displayed, students do not always seek out new materials. On the other hand, when a teacher practices what Linda Gambrell calls "blessing a book"—enthusiastically introducing a new book to the class—the book suddenly appeals to students. This is particularly true when the teacher has built a reputation for knowing the good books.

Sometimes when teachers read just a portion of a book, students are inspired to read the rest of the book. For instance, many students need only to hear the unusual and quirky opening of *The Twits* (Dahl, 1980) to become hooked into reading it on their own:

> What a lot of hairy-faced men there are around nowadays.
> When a man grows hair all over his face it is impossible to tell what he really looks like. Perhaps that's why he does it. He'd rather you didn't know.
> Then there's the problem of washing.
> When the very hairy ones wash their faces, it must be as big a job as when you and I wash the hair on our heads.
> So what I want to know is this. How often do all these hairy-faced men wash their faces? Is

it only once a week, like us, on Sunday nights? And do they shampoo it? Do they use a hairdryer? Do they rub hair tonic in to stop their faces from going bald? Do they go to a barber to have their hairy faces cut and trimmed or do they do it themselves in front of the bathroom mirror with nail scissors?

I don't know. But next time you see a man with a hairy face (which will probably be as soon as you step out onto the street) maybe you will look at him more closely and start wondering about some of these things. (p. 3)

Middle grades students are also inspired to revisit books that have been read by teachers in their entirety. For instance, after listening to his sixth-grade teacher read *Officer Buckle and Gloria* (Rathmann, 1995), Zachary borrowed another copy from the school library for his own pleasure reading. Similarly, students learn about authors they like, as in Ms. Duhamel's fourth-grade class, where hearing *My Teacher Is an Alien* (Coville, 1990) led many students to find other books by Bruce Coville and even to write their own sequels to his series.

The allure of the read-aloud is created by not only the distinctive and engaging voice of the text, but also the expressive voice of the reader, which is difficult for many students to find on their own. On the other hand, unenthusiastic read-alouds can have the opposite effect, discouraging students from reading. Katie, a sixth grader, explained how she knew when a teacher was not interested in a particular book: "You could tell it in her voice. It was like, 'Uhhhh. I don't like this.' And it was like, 'Why do you make us read it if you don't like it?' "

But teachers are not the only readers in the class who can inspire interest in books. Students also relish the opportunity to read aloud to their classmates. Struggling readers, in particular, enjoy reading aloud books they have practiced on their own (Ivey, 1999b). In fact, in some middle school classes, student read-alouds are so popular that teachers have to create schedules so that everyone will get a chance to read. One of our preservice teachers came up with the idea of "open-microphone" sessions (borrowed from the format used in stand-up comedy clubs), so that students, one after another, may stand up and read their current favorite things.

GIVING STUDENTS ACCESS TO TEXTS THEY CANNOT YET READ ON THEIR OWN

Remember Missy from the beginning of the chapter? In early December of the school year, Gay Ivey visited Missy's classroom to read aloud Anthony Browne's (1998) *Voices in the Park*, a picture book that had been just recently published. Gay assumed that this book, which tells of a park visit from the points of view of four different characters, might be challenging for fourth graders because of the shifts in perspective and the sophisticated and complex illustrations, both of which are integral to understanding the story. Both Gay and Missy's teacher, Ms. Lewis (who sat behind the students as they listened), noted the whole class's interest in the book, which was apparent in their questions, comments, and undivided attention to the reading. But it was Missy who led the class in building an understanding of the book. She was the first student in the group to realize that the book was written from four different perspectives, and she was also able to elaborate on the story by drawing important inferences from the illustrations, even making some connections that neither Gay nor Ms. Lewis had noticed. For instance, Missy pointed out to the class that contrasting illustrations on two separate pages represented the changes that occurred in two characters after a brief visit to the park: In the first illustration, Smudge and her father, who is unemployed and frustrated, walk to the park on a littered street, past wilting trees, tall, dark buildings, a homeless man dressed in a Santa Claus suit with a sign asking for money, and a portrait of a crying Mona Lisa, all under a gloomy gray sky. The second illustration shows Smudge and her father walking back through this area after an uplifting trip to the park. This time, however, the streets are spotless, and the trees are adorned with glistening white lights. The buildings are lit up with colorful heart- and star-shaped windows, and the homeless man and Mona Lisa are dancing happily on the sidewalk.

As the school year progressed, Ms. Lewis paid special attention to Missy's participation and thinking during read-alouds, and what she observed was similar to what she and Gay had observed during the reading of *Voices in the Park*. Although Missy was just beginning to develop as a reader, she was already a deep thinker and a skilled listener. When she was freed from the burden of having to decode difficult words, there seemed to be no limit to what she could understand. Ms. Lewis was working diligently with Missy to build her word identification skills and fluency, and Missy still had much to learn. But it was equally important for her to focus on what Missy *could* do. Reading aloud was clearly an ideal way for Missy to experience the texts she could understand and relate to, but that she could not yet read on her own. Although Ms. Lewis read aloud frequently and understood the benefits for all of her students, she was certain that it was a critical component of literacy development for students like Missy.

Missy's experiences confirm some previous research on struggling readers and listening comprehension. Gay's multicase study of sixth-grade students (Ivey, 1999a) included one student, Allison, who was frustrated with oral reading, but demonstrated high-level comprehension behaviors when she listened to the teacher reading aloud: predicting, monitoring her comprehension by asking the teacher to reread a section, asking critical questions, and relating the text to other texts and to her personal experiences. In another study (Horowitz & Samuels, 1985), both the reading comprehension and listening comprehension of students who were proficient at decoding words were compared with those of students who had decoding problems. Although the good decoders had better reading comprehension, there were no differences between the two groups on listening comprehension.

Teachers would be selling their students short if they assumed that those who struggle with decoding cannot understand complex concepts and vocabulary, or if they set boundaries on the kinds of materials that can be used with these students for instruction. Remember that reading is not just a matter of figuring out words. Students bring a broad repertoire of knowledge to any texts, including not only their own experiences and what they know about the world, but also understandings about the complexity of texts, including plot twists, reading between the lines, shifting perspectives, and foreshadowing. The key is to know which texts students can read on their own and which texts should be read aloud.

One text often erroneously designated for independent reading is the class novel, particularly when there is a range of reading abilities in the class. Teachers give various reasons for assigning class novels. For instance, they may have a state-, district-, or school-mandated list of books to be covered at each grade level, or they want students to have a common reading experience for the purpose of discussion or writing. While we do not believe that there is a canon of the *right* books to be read at any particular grade level, or that reading choices should be made without input from students and teachers, we do agree that students can benefit from common reading experiences. However, matching students with texts that are both interesting and on appropriate levels of difficulty is of primary importance when it comes to reading fluency and engagement. Thus it is doubtful that any single text would be appropriate fare for the independent reading of all or even most of the students in a class. For this reason, teachers ought to consider reading aloud any texts that are critical in terms of content, yet too difficult for some students to read on their own.

The read-aloud is especially critical for students who are learning English as a second language. These students not only must carry the burden of deciphering the code and trying to make sense of what they read, but they are also dealing with new vocabulary and sometimes new cultural concepts all at once. We have heard many teachers say that limited background knowledge and vocabulary are the biggest barriers to reading progress for second-language learners. If this is the case, then why not plan some experiences with text that focus just on building this kind of knowledge? Imagine how much these students could learn from being exposed to a variety of topics through frequent teacher read-alouds, during which all they are asked to do is think about the content.

CREATING A CONTEXT FOR SHARING EXPERTISE ABOUT READING AND WRITING

Reading is a complex process, during which the reader applies many different kinds of knowledge and various strategies all at the same time. In fact, Pearson, Roehler, Dole, and Duffy (1992) have suggested seven characteristics of expert readers:

- They make connections between what they already know and what they read.
- They monitor their comprehension as they read.
- They take steps to repair their comprehension when it breaks down.
- They distinguish between important information and less important information in texts.
- They synthesize information as they read.
- They draw inferences as they read.
- They ask questions as they read.

We also know that good readers recognize words automatically (Adams, 1990), and as we discuss in depth in Chapter 5, good readers read smoothly, accurately, and with appropriate expression. In fact, expert readers expend very little energy on figuring out words, and they focus most of their attention on building meaning.

However, these characteristics do not equate to skills that students learn one at a time. Rather, it is important to understand that expertise in reading is a developmental process, and that becoming an independent reader is a gradual process that begins even before formal schooling begins. We believe that students develop these characteristics over time primarily by having lots of opportunities to engage in reading interesting materials. However, there are many ways teachers can guide students toward expertise along the way. Here we discuss how reading aloud provides the perfect context for doing so. As you read these next few pages, also take a look at Box 3.1, which provides some ways to assess students' reading development as you read aloud and discuss books and other materials.

Providing a Model of Fluent Reading

If students never hear fluent, expressive reading, they have no way of knowing how it sounds, and they have nothing to strive for in their own reading. Often students only get to hear the reading of other students who are also still developing as readers. The best model for fluent reading in the class is the teacher. Thuong, a preservice teacher, wrote about how quickly students became attuned to and mimicked the way she read:

> "I read *The Judge* by Harve Zemach [1969] to a small group of students in my practicum. By the third prisoner, one of them asked me if he could read the next one, so I said, 'Sure!' I read the short part and then he read the repetitive part. After he finished, the others wanted to read it too! The students were trying to read it the way I had read it. I was their model."

Fluent reading by the teacher gives students a good sense of how they can sound when they read books that are of an appropriate level of difficulty. Kaitlin, another preservice teacher, realized the importance of modeling when she read to fourth grader Samuel a portion of *The Book That Jack Wrote* (Scieszka, 1994), and then had him echo her reading:

> "This was an amazing experience for both of us. . . . The last time he read it (I faded into the background about halfway through), he actually sounded like a fluent reader. He got a big smile on his face and said, 'That was good reading!' He told me that this was the coolest book and he wanted to do it again."

BOX 3.1. What You Can Learn about Students' Reading as You Read Aloud

1. Are students engaged in listening as you read? Are there certain kinds of texts or topics that interest particular students?
2. Do students ask questions as you read? Do these questions reflect an understanding of the text? Do these questions reflect strategic listening (e.g., clarification, anticipation)?
3. Do students make spontaneous comments as you read? Do these comments reflect an understanding of the text? Do these comments reflect strategic listening (e.g., predictions, connections with other texts or experiences)?
4. Do any students differ in their comprehension or engagement when listening to texts read aloud versus their comprehension or engagement when reading on their own? If so, how so?

Although speed and accuracy are important features for teachers to model in their reading, it is also important to stress the role of expression and intonation when reading aloud. Students need to be reminded that the purpose of reading is to create meaning, not just to pronounce words quickly and correctly. When students focus on word identification only, they miss not only the point of the passage, but also the subtleties of texts that make them come alive. One of our favorite picture books for middle grades students is *Louis the Fish* (Yorinks, 1980), but many students would miss its dry, low-key humor if they read it on their own. Take, for instance, the following excerpt describing Louis's discontented life as a third-generation butcher:

> . . . Louis was not a happy man. He hated meat. From the time he was a little boy he was always surrounded by meat. Whenever he would visit his grandfather on Sundays it was always, "Louis, my favorite grandson. What a good boy. Here's a hotdog." On his birthdays his beaming parents would hand him a gift-wrapped salami. When he was thirteen they gave him a turkey. (p. 6)

Think about how you might read this passage in a way that captures the voice intended by the author. Box 3.2 lists other books with strong voices that are ideal for reading aloud.

Providing a Format for Instruction about Reading

Imagine two different instructional scenarios. In the first setting, Mr. Bruno is reading *Welcome to Dead House* (Stine, 1997) to one student, Jason, and after each chapter he asks

---

BOX 3.2. Books with Strong, Distinctive Voices for Reading Aloud

Picture Books

Ringgold, F. (1991). *Tar Beach*. New York: Crown.
Scieszka, J. (1989). *The true story of the three little pigs*. New York: Viking.
Smith, L. (1993). *The happy Hocky family*. New York: Puffin.
Yorinks, A. (1983). *It happened in Pinsk*. New York: Farrar, Straus, Giroux.

Chapter Books

Myers, W. D. (1975). *Fast Sam, Cool Clyde, and stuff*. New York: Puffin.
Park, B. (1995). *Mick Harte was here*. New York: Scholastic.
Sachar, L. (1998). *Holes*. New York: Farrar, Straus, Giroux.
Spinelli, J. (1997). *Wringer*. New York: HarperCollins.

Poetry

Carson, J. (1989). *Stories I ain't told nobody yet*. New York: Orchard Books.
Dahl, R. (1983). *Roald Dahl's revolting rhymes*. New York: Knopf.
Graves, D. (1996). *Baseball, snakes, and summer squash: Poems about growing up*. Honesdale, PA: Boyds Mills Press.
Viorst, J. (1981). *If I were in charge of the world and other worries*. New York: Atheneum.

Jason to retell what he has just read. When Jason cannot generate a coherent retelling, Mr. Bruno asks specific comprehension questions (e.g., "What did they hear in the house?", "And then what happened?"). This task is laborious and frustrating for both teacher and student as they trudge through each detail of the chapter. In the second setting, Ms. Kim and another student, Rosa, are reading the very same book. After a couple of paragraphs, the teacher stops reading and says, "I wonder what those noises are in the house. Let's look back at the title. It's called *Welcome to Dead House*." She continues with "So the voices must be . . . " but before she can finish her sentence, Rosa chimes in with "The voices are from dead people." Ms. Kim adds, "I think they're from people who lived in the house a long time ago. I've read books and seen movies like that." Then Rosa says, "It's like *Casper*."

What are the differences between these two scenarios? In the first instance, Mr. Bruno is testing Jason's comprehension without really providing any instruction. Jason may pick up a few points he missed during the reading, and although the teacher may help him get the gist of this particular book, it is doubtful that this activity will help him comprehend the next book he reads. In the second example, Ms. Kim is actually providing a model of strategic reading and inviting Rosa to participate, all within a naturally occurring conversation about the book. For instance, Ms. Kim asks herself a question ("I wonder what those noises are in the house"), and she uses the text and her own background knowledge to make predictions and inferences about the story ("Let's look back at the title. It's called *Welcome to Dead House*. So the voices must be . . . I've read books and seen movies like that"). Unlike in the first example, here the teacher actually provides some instruction during the reading. She not only models good reading processes, but she also shares and participates in the construction of meaning with her student. Furthermore, there is no need to check this student's comprehension, since discussions like these reveal whether or not there is understanding.

As the second example demonstrates, teaching comprehension strategies is most effective during the actual reading of a text, since that is mainly when students build their understandings. That is not to say, of course, that students cannot enrich their understandings of a text through postreading discussions, as we discuss later in this chapter. However, most of what proficient readers read, they read alone, and they need strategies and habits that enable them to make sense of things while they read.

When teachers and students discuss what they are reading in certain ways, such as when they talk about a confusing portion of text or when they make predictions about what is going to happen, they need to be at the same point in the text. There are only two reading activities that create this situation: teacher read-alouds and round-robin reading. In Chapter 5, we discuss some reasons why we do not recommend round-robin reading. On the other hand, read-alouds provide the perfect opportunity for engaging students in instruction on comprehension processes. Here we describe two instructional activities that combine reading aloud and learning to comprehend: *think-alouds* and the directed listening–thinking activity (DL-TA).

Think-Alouds

Some aspects of reading are readily observable and therefore easy to model—for instance, the act of reading for pleasure or reading aloud with fluency and expression. On the other hand, other dimensions of a person's reading process cannot be seen or heard.

When you read silently, you ask yourself questions, hypothesize and predict, make connections to other texts you have read or heard, relate the text to personal experiences, and keep a check on what you do and do not understand. These are all behaviors that contribute to comprehension. However, an outside observer is not privy to these thought processes.

One way for teachers to make students aware of how they build meaning is to think aloud about what they are reading as they read aloud to the class. The general idea is that the teacher reads a portion of text and then pauses to describe his or her thinking before continuing the next portion of text. Box 3.3 gives an example of how one teacher explains some of her reasoning when reading the first chapter of a book. Notice how the teacher talks specifically about this particular book, as opposed to giving general guidelines or steps about how to comprehend.

Duffy, Roehler, and Herrmann (1988) have made a clear distinction between modeling mental processes of reading and modeling procedures for reading. They emphasize that each reading experience is different, and that each individual processes information in different ways. Consequently, the mental processes of reading or the use of strategies cannot be summed up in a set of steps presented on a skills worksheet or drilled by the teacher. Thinking aloud about a variety of real texts demonstrates that the reader must be flexible and adaptable in employing good strategies. Box 3.4 includes a list of additional readings on thinking aloud.

Directed Listening–Thinking Activity

An effective way for students both to interact with each other and the teacher, and to practice using good reading strategies, is the DL-TA (Stauffer, 1976). The DL-TA teaches students to use what they already know to help understand the new information they encounter in text. Students learn to set purposes for reading by predicting what the text will be about, and then listening to confirm or revise their predictions. Having the teacher read the text frees the students from the burden of figuring out difficult words,

---

**BOX 3.3. A Teacher Shares Her Own Reading Processes
through Thinking Aloud about The Music of Dolphins (Hesse, 1996)
as She Reads to the Class**

1. *Making predictions or formulating hypotheses.* "From the title and cover, I think this book might be about a girl who has an unusual connection with dolphins."

2. *Using imagery to make sense of the text.* "I am picturing a lean, healthy girl with long wet hair who is swimming among the dolphins. She is very fit because she swims all day and she has been raised amidst nature. Her hair is long because she probably has never cut it."

3. *Connecting the text to what you already know.* "This makes me think of Tarzan because he was raised in the jungle by apes instead of by humans."

4. *Monitoring your comprehension.* "The girl said that her dolphin mother doesn't eat much because of her. I don't understand what she means."

5. *Fixing your comprehension.* "I need to reread that section to see if there are any clues about why the girl would keep the dolphin mother from eating enough."

BOX 3.4. Sources for Reading More about Think-Alouds and Modeling Strategic Reading

Baumann, J. F., Jones, L. A., & Seifert-Kessell, N. (1993). Using think alouds to enhance children's comprehension monitoring abilities. *The Reading Teacher, 47*, 184–193.

Davey, B. (1983). Think-aloud: Modeling the cognitive processes of reading comprehension. *Journal of Reading, 27*, 44–47.

Duffy, G. G., Roehler, L. R., & Herrmann, B. A. (1988). Modeling mental processes helps poor readers become strategic readers. *The Reading Teacher, 41*, 762–767 .

Jimenez, R. T., & Gamez, A. (1996). Literature-based cognitive strategy instruction for middle school Latina/o students. *Journal of Adolescent and Adult Literacy, 40*, 84–91.

Keene, E. O., & Zimmerman, S. (1997). *Mosaic of thought: Teaching comprehension in a reader's workshop.* Portsmouth, NH: Heinemann.

---

and they can concentrate on building meaning-based strategies they can apply in their own independent reading.

Before reading aloud any text for a DL-TA, you should read the text on your own. Mark points in the text that would serve as good stopping points for discussion—for example, a place where you would naturally make a prediction in your own mind. When you are familiar with the text, follow these steps with students.

1. Show students the cover and title of the selection. Ask, "What do you think this might be about?" Accept all responses as possibilities, but have students provide rationales for their predictions.

2. Prompt students to listen as you read the first portion of the text to see if their predictions were correct. At a predetermined stopping point, ask, "Were you correct?" or "What do you think now?" Give students an opportunity to revise their predictions if necessary. Encourage students to cite proof from the text to support their new or revised predictions.

3. Read the next section of the text to the next logical stopping point. Again, ask students to evaluate their last predictions. Continue this cycle of reading and predicting to the end of the text. The reading may culminate with an extended discussion of the text, guided by students' own questions.

Materials that work well for DL-TAs are those that build suspense and curiosity in the listener. Short stories and picture books with foreshadowing or plot twists are especially effective, as are familiar stories with a new twist, such as contemporary versions of fairy tales. See Box 3.5 for a list of books that meet these criteria.

DL-TAs also work well with nonfiction texts. In fact, knowing that students are more likely to have difficulty with expository text than with narrative text is all the more reason to use nonfiction for instruction. The DL-TA process will differ slightly with nonfiction texts. For instance, instead of asking students to predict the outcome of a text, have them focus first on what they know about the particular topic and then listen to compare that prior knowledge to what they learned from the text.

BOX 3.5. Books to Use for Directed Listening–Thinking Activities (DL-TAs)

Picture Books with Plot Twists

Mahy, M. (1989). *The great white man-eating shark*. New York: Dial.
Van Allsburg, C. (1981). *Jumanji*. New York: Scholastic.
Van Allsburg, C. (1983). *The wreck of the Zephyr*. Boston: Houghton Mifflin.
Van Allsburg, C. (1992). *The widow's broom*. Boston: Houghton Mifflin.
Wood, A. (1987). *Heckedy Peg*. New York: Harcourt Brace Jovanovich.
Yorinks, A. (1986). *Hey, Al*. New York: Farrar, Straus, Giroux.

New Versions of Familiar Tales

Calmenson, S. (1989). *The principal's new clothes*. New York: Scholastic.
Gwynne, F. (1990). *Pondlarker*. New York: Simon & Schuster.
Hooks, W. H. (1987). *Moss gown*. New York: Clarion.
Lowell, S. (1992). *The three little javelinas*. New York: Scholastic.
San Souci, R. D. (1989). *The talking eggs*. New York: Scholastic.
Young, E. (1989). *Lon Po Po: A Red-Riding Hood story from China*. New York: Philomel.

Here we draw an example from a read-aloud of *The Hidden Children* (Greenfeld, 1993), a book describing the experiences of Jewish children who went into hiding during the Holocaust to avoid being sent to concentration camps. After having students examine the title and cover of the book, and after reading the first several pages, the teacher asked students what they were curious about learning from this book. As mentioned previously, it is important to model for students during read-alouds that not all information books must be read from start to finish, particularly if the reader is seeking specific information. In this particular incident, students wanted to know what the children ate while they were in hiding. Logical questions to ask at this point were "What do you think they ate?" and "Why do you think so?" Students were encouraged to base their hypotheses both on what they already knew (including what they had read, seen, or heard previously) and on any clues provided thus far in the text (including the title and cover).

Next, the teacher modeled how to look in the index under "food" to find places in the text where that topic is mentioned. In this particular book, there is an index entry called "Food eaten in hiding (p. 116)," and 11 different pages or sections are listed. The teacher then explained how she would start with references to longer sections of text (as opposed to a single page), since that is where the topic is most likely to be covered in detail (e.g., a reference to pages 40–41 or pages 74–75, rather than a reference to page 20 or page 39).

Next, the teacher turned to page 40 of *The Hidden Children* and found that the text on this page is printed in italics, even though most of the book is printed in a more standard roman font. She explained to students that sometimes text is written in italics to convey a different perspective. In this particular book, italics are used when the text is being narrated from the perspective of one of the children who was forced into hiding. On this page there is a photograph of a group of children next to the italicized section with a caption reading "Gisele (first row, second from the left), in Sugny," which the teacher showed to the class.

Next the teacher read the first couple of sentences of the section that tells Gisele's story:

> Our group arrived at a girls' boarding school called L'Institut de la Reine Elizabeth. The school had been closed several years before, at the beginning of the war. The main house was occupied by a group of nuns—several had taught at the Institut—whose services were no longer used. (p. 40)

The teacher then stopped and asked, "Do you have a hunch yet about what these girls ate while they were in hiding?" Several students responded that maybe they ate good food, since the nuns were there to cook for them. Others suggested that nuns might serve boring food.

The teacher continued to read until she reached the section about what the children ate: vegetables, meat, and other rich foods. This information surprised most students, since they had predicted that food was scarce for children in hiding, and that what was available was probably bland and unappetizing. As the teacher checked other sections referenced in the index so that students could test their revised predictions, they actually found that the students' original hypotheses were true in some cases, especially for children hiding in different kinds of places such as orphanages and in the woods. This realization that children hid in a variety of places—not just in hidden compartments in houses—evoked a stronger curiosity about the topic in general for many students, with one student even asking to read the book on her own.

PROVIDING OPPORTUNITIES FOR PERSONAL RESPONSE, DISCUSSION, AND INQUIRY

During engaging read-alouds, teachers rarely get through the entire text without students stopping to ask questions or share their thoughts, and typically these comments stem from personal experiences. When students listen instead of reading, they can completely concentrate on meaning, and usually this leads them to make connections to what they know. This is particularly true when teachers read books that evoke strong images or memories of family. In *A gift from Papá Diego/Un regalo de Papá Diego* (Sáenz, 1998), a young boy longs to see his grandfather, who lives across the border in Mexico—an experience that is common for students whose families have immigrated to other countries.

When Gay Ivey's sixth-grade students in rural Virginia heard Cynthia Rylant's *Appalachia* (1991) and *When I Was Young in the Mountains* (1982), they talked and wrote about the homes of their grandparents and great-grandparents. Jill, a preservice teacher, reported similar experiences when she read another book to her sixth-grade class:

> "I began to read [a book about a pet that died] out loud to the class. I was sure to show them all the pictures and read with excitement. Every eye around the room was glued to the book. Every student seemed interested and curious about the book. After I finished reading the book, hands went up immediately. The students wanted to look at the book and read it themselves. Some wanted to take it home to read to their sisters and brothers. . . . After I began passing the book around, hands started going up again. Students were sharing stories of their own pets that have died, along with their neighbors' dogs and cats that died. The book is about losing a pet and how it happens and you have to move on. The students loved it, and the teacher was amazed at their interest."

Although students will spontaneously respond to read-alouds, teachers can also use these opportunities to ask critical, thoughtful questions for discussion or for writing. However, these questions should extend students' thinking, rather than require students to give a summary of what they heard or recall insignificant details from the text. Closed-ended questions such as "What was this story about?" and "How old was Nellie's sister?" serve only to end a discussion, since the point of these questions is to get a correct answer. In fact, these kinds of questions actually test a student's comprehension on a superficial level, rather than enrich a student's understanding.

Open-ended questions, on the other hand, encourage students to talk to each other and to consider multiple possibilities. By the time children reach the middle grades, they are able to think about texts in more analytical ways than when they were in the early grades. As Huck and her colleagues have suggested, older children "begin to test fiction against real life and understand it better through the comparison" (Huck, 1997, p. 63). The questions teachers ask should reflect this cognitive maturity. Here are some questions that may help ignite a productive discussion or a rich written response:

- What message was the author trying to send in this story?
- What did you think was the most important line in the story? Why?
- What confused you in this story?
- Do you think there is more to tell at the end of the story? What?
- Would you change the ending of this story in any way? How?
- What was interesting about the way the author wrote this story?
- What sort of person do you think the author is?
- Does anyone in this story remind you of someone you know? Tell us about it.
- Are you like anyone in this book? Explain.
- Does this story remind you of something else you have heard or read? Tell us about it.

The questions above should be part of a larger repertoire of general, open-ended questions. However, teachers might also want to create open-ended discussion starters or writing prompts that pertain to a specific book or story. In Box 3.6, we include some questions teachers might ask after reading *Hey, Al* (Yorinks, 1986). Note that the first

BOX 3.6. Questions for Discussing *Hey, Al* (Yorinks, 1986)

- Soon after Al and Eddie settled into their new lives on the island in the sky, the author wrote, "But ripe fruit soon spoils." What did Arthur Yorinks mean?
- Will Al and Eddie be content with their lives back on the West Side at the end of the story? Why or why not?
- Do Al and Eddie remind you of anyone you know? Tell us about that.
- What is your idea of paradise? Would it be everything you imagine? Why or why not?

two questions to start the discussion keep students focused on the book, while the last two questions encourage students to consider their own experiences.

Teachers also need ways to help students think about the nonfiction texts that are read aloud. Freeman and Person (1998) suggest that open-ended questions following a nonfiction read-aloud can be used to initiate an inquiry-based study of a particular topic. For example, they suggest that you might ask the following questions after reading *Immigrant Kids* (Freedman, 1980):

- How are these children coping with learning a new language, new customs, new holidays?
- What should schools, communities, social agencies, do to help these children and their families adjust to life in a new society?
- Should new immigrants surrender their old ways, learn to speak English only?
- Should the United States continue to broaden its immigration policies and admit people of diverse colors and races who are different from the original European colonists? (p. 64)

The goal of any questioning, of course, is to encourage students to ask these questions on their own, during both class discussions of read-alouds and their own independent reading and writing. When crafting questions to ask before, during, and after read-alouds, teachers should keep in mind that whatever they ask is a model for how students begin to think about what they read. Box 3.7 includes a list of additional readings on response and discussion.

MAKING TIME FOR READING ALOUD

When we talk about reading aloud in the middle grades, the response we often get from teachers is that they do not feel they have time for it, particularly with the demand to cover content requirements and to teach relevant skills. As you have probably figured out from reading this chapter, reading aloud is actually a way to accomplish those things, while at the same time to promote enthusiasm for reading. Teachers who read aloud regularly will tell you that this time is an instructional priority. Take a look at Barbara Corbin's experiences with reading aloud in Box 3.8.

As you consider your reading and writing instruction, you should think about reading aloud not as a luxury, a class reward, or a way to pass a few extra minutes, but instead as an integral part of your teaching. We imagine that you will read aloud not just once a day, as many teachers do after lunch or recess, but across the school day, in all of your subject areas, and for a variety of purposes.

BOX 3.7. Sources for Reading More about Response and Discussion

- Cianciolo, P. J. (1995). Teaching and learning critical aesthetic responses to literature. In M. Sorenson & B. Lehman (Eds.), *Teaching with children's books: Paths to literature-based instruction* (pp. 144–158). Urbana, IL: National Council of Teachers of English.
- Gambrell, L. B., & Almasi, J. F. (Eds.). (1996). *Lively discussions!: Fostering engaged reading.* Newark, DE: International Reading Association.
- Leonard, R. (1995). Guiding children's critical aesthetic responses to literature in a fifth-grade classroom. In M. Sorenson & B. Lehman (Eds.), *Teaching with children's books: Paths to literature-based instruction* (pp. 160–168). Urbana, IL: National Council of Teachers of English.
- Moss, B., Leone, S., & Dipillo, M. L. (1997). Exploring the literature of fact: Linking reading and writing through information trade books. *Language Arts, 74,* 418–429.
- Probst, R. (1998). Reader-response theory in the middle school. In K. Beers & B. G. Samuels (Eds.), *Into focus: Understanding and creating middle school readers* (pp. 125–138). Norwood, MA: Christopher-Gordon.
- Roser, N. L., & Martinez, M. G. (Eds.). (1995). *Book talk and beyond: Children and teachers respond to literature.* Newark, DE: International Reading Association.

CHILDREN'S BOOK REFERENCES

Aardema, V. (1981). *Bringing the rain to Kapiti plain.* New York: Dial.
Allard, H. (1977). *Miss Nelson is missing.* Boston: Houghton Mifflin.
Allard, H. (1981). *The Stupids die.* Boston: Houghton Mifflin.
Browne, A. (1998). *Voices in the park.* New York: Dorling Kindersley.
Cleary, B. (1983). *Dear Mr. Henshaw.* New York: Morrow.
Clement, R. (1991). *Counting on Frank.* Milwaukee, WI: Gareth Stevens.
Cole, B. (1987). *Prince Cinders.* New York: Putnam.
Coville, B. (1990). *My teacher is an alien.* Seattle, WA: Minstrel Books.
Dahl, R. (1966). *The magic finger.* New York: Harper & Row.
Dahl, R. (1980). *The twits.* New York: Knopf.
Fleischman, P. (1985). *I am phoenix: Poems for two voices.* New York: Harper & Row.
Fox, M. (1990). *Guess what?* San Diego, CA: Harcourt Brace.
Freedman, R. (1980). *Immigrant kids.* New York: Dutton.
Gackenbach, D. (1979). *Harry and the terrible whatzit.* New York: Clarion.
Golenbock, P. (1990). *Teammates.* San Diego, CA: Harcourt Brace Jovanovich.
Greenfeld, H. (1993). *The hidden children.* New York: Ticknor & Fields.
Hesse, K. (1996). *The music of dolphins.* New York: Scholastic.
Krulik, N. (1995). *It takes two.* New York: Scholastic.
Maruki, R. (1980). *Hiroshima no pika.* New York: Lothrop, Lee & Shepard.
Moss, J. (1997). *Bone poems.* New York: Workman.
Myers, W. D. (1993). *Brown angels: An album of pictures and verse.* New York: HarperCollins.
Paterson, K. (1977). *Bridge to Terabithia.* New York: Crowell.
Paulsen, G. (1987). *Hatchet.* New York: Bradbury Press.
Prelutsky, J. (1984). *The new kid on the block.* New York: Greenwillow.
Prelutsky, J. (1990). *Something big has been here.* New York: Greenwillow.
Quindlen, A. (1997). *Happily ever after.* New York: Puffin.
Rathmann, P. (1995). *Officer Buckle and Gloria.* New York: Putnam.
Rowling, J. K. (1998). *Harry Potter and the sorcerer's stone.* New York: Scholastic.

BOX 3.8. A Story about the Importance of Reading Nonfiction Aloud (by Barbara Corbin)

When I taught second grade, I had a self-contained class. I used to integrate reading into all the content areas. I would bring my crate to the library and rob them blind. Everyday I had at least 20 minutes to read to my class, and I would often introduce books then. During language arts, I would frequently read a book to them, and we would do a response activity of some kind. We performed Readers' Theater, wrote class poems, drew and labeled pictures of the rainforest, etc. . . . I know I've moaned about this many times, but I feel incredibly crunched for time at my school now. So, what tends to go are the projects that take a lot of time. Also, I don't teach my class social studies, but rather teach all of the science for the third grade. I must admit, during the first 2 years here, I was moving away from using literature in the content areas. I always had books related to the topics we were studying on the shelves and in special crates, but the students weren't drawn to them. I wondered why the third-grade students weren't interested in these books, as my second graders had been.

After taking an elementary literature class this summer, I began to see how removing the literature from my instruction took away such an important, dynamic element from my teaching. Now I incorporate the literature regularly into my science lessons. Also, I keep a stack of great picture books on my bookcase, ready to be pulled out and read whenever we have a few extra moments. In the beginning of the year, I consciously planned time for reading aloud, but I am finding that now it is a part of the class. The kids ask me to read all the time. Of course, if I read a book, they all clamor to get their hands on it, so I now have a "new-release" basket that is constantly being replenished. That way the kids don't have to sort through the hundreds of books on the shelves to find the book I read to them yesterday.

By reading picture books in the content areas, the kids are able to grasp more of the concepts. They can reread if there's something they missed. Sometimes they just want to look through the pictures because they couldn't see them very well when I was reading the book aloud. Students who are drawn to the "new-release" basket in search of a title I have read often come away with a different book on the same topic. They enjoy reading the related book and sharing new information with the class.

I really feel much better about the literacy environment in the classroom this year compared to the 2 previous years. The kids are excited, and I'm more excited. Incorporating literature into the content areas and reading aloud are the catalysts for the energy I feel in my classroom this year.

Rowling, J. K. (1999). *Harry Potter and the chamber of secrets.* New York: Scholastic.

Rubin, S. G. (1998). *Toilets, toasters, and telephones: The how and why of everyday objects.* San Diego, CA: Harcourt Brace.

Rylant, C. (1982). *When I was young in the mountains.* New York: E. P. Dutton.

Rylant, C. (1984). *Waiting to waltz: A childhood.* Scarsdale, NY: Bradbury Press.

Rylant, C. (1991). *Appalachia.* San Diego, CA: Harcourt Brace Jovanovich.

Rylant, C. (1998). *Henry and Mudge under the yellow moon.* New York: Simon & Schuster.

Sachar, L. (1987). *There's a boy in the girls' bathroom.* New York: Knopf.

Sáenz, B. A. (1998). *A gift from Papá Diego/Un regalo de Papá Diego.* El Paso, TX: Cinco Puntos Press.

Scieszka, J. (1994). *The book that Jack wrote.* New York: Viking.

Silverstein, S. (1974). *Where the sidewalk ends.* New York: HarperCollins.

Silverstein, S. (1981). *A light in the attic.* New York: HarperCollins.

Silverstein, S. (1996). *Falling up.* New York: HarperCollins.

Soto, G. (1992). *Neighborhood odes.* San Diego, CA: Harcourt Brace.

Spinelli, J. (1990). *Maniac Magee.* New York: Scholastic.

Steptoe, J. (1987). *Mufaro's beautiful daughters: An African tale*. New York: Lothrop, Lee & Shepard.

Stine, R. L. (1997). *Welcome to dead house* (*Goosebumps*, No. 1). Milwauke, WI: Gareth Stevens.

Turner, A. (1993). *Grass songs: Poems of women's journey west*. San Diego, CA: Harcourt Brace.

Volavkova, H. (Ed.). (1993). *I never saw another butterfly: Children's drawings and poems from Terezin concentration camp*. New York: Schocken.

Walter, V. (1998). *Making up megaboy*. New York: Dorling Kindersley.

Yorinks, A. (1980). *Louis the fish*. New York: Farrar, Straus, Giroux.

Yorinks, A. (1986). *Hey, Al*. New York: Farrar, Straus, Giroux.

Yorinks, A. (1990). *Ugh*. New York: Farrar, Straus, Giroux.

Zemach, H. (1969). *The judge*. New York: Farrar, Straus, Giroux.

REFERENCES

Adams, M. J. (1990). *Beginning to read: Thinking and learning about print*. Cambridge, MA: MIT Press.

Anderson, R. C., Hiebert, E., Scott, J. A., & Wilkinson, I. A. G. (1985). *Becoming a nation of readers*. Washington, DC: National Institute of Education.

Cunningham, P. M., & Allington, R. L. (1999). *Classrooms that work: They can all read and write*. New York: Longman.

Duffy, G., Roehler, L., & Herrmann, B. A. (1988). Modeling mental processes helps poor readers become strategic readers. *The Reading Teacher, 41*, 762–767.

Fielding, L., & Roller, C. (1992). Making difficult books accessible and easy books acceptable. *The Reading Teacher, 46*, 678–685.

Freeman, E. B., & Person, D. G. (1998). *Connecting informational children's books with content area learning*. Boston: Allyn & Bacon.

Horowitz, R., & Samuels, S. J. (1985). Reading and listening to expository text. *Journal of Reading Behavior, 17*, 185–198.

Huck, C. S. (1997). *Children's literature in the elementary school* (6th ed.). Madison, WI: Brown & Benchmark.

Ivey, G. (1999a). A multicase study in the middle school: Complexities among young adolescent readers. *Reading Research Quarterly, 34*, 172-192.

Ivey, G. (1999b). Reflections on teaching struggling middle school readers. *Journal of Adolescent and Adult Literacy, 42*, 372–381.

Ivey, G., & Broaddus, K. (in press). "Just plain reading": A survey of what makes students want to read in middle school classrooms. *Reading Research Quarterly*.

Pearson, P. D., Roehler, L. R., Dole, J. A., & Duffy, G. G. (1992). Developing expertise in reading comprehension. In S. J. Samuels & A. E. Farstrup (Eds.), *What research has to say about reading instruction* (pp. 145–199). Newark, DE: International Reading Association.

Stauffer, R. (1976). *Teaching reading as a thinking process*. New York: Harper & Row.

Worthy, J., Moorman, M., & Turner, M. (1999). What Johnny likes to read is hard to find in school. *Reading Research Quarterly, 34*, 12–27.

CHAPTER 4

Just Reading

Ms. Williams observed three different students in her fifth-grade language arts class on a typical day. Their assignment was to read a story from the literature anthology and then answer the questions at the end of the story. Ethan sat with the book open, but he was not reading. He looked at the first page for a while, but Ms. Williams could tell from the frustrated look on his face and from his restlessness that he was not getting anywhere with it. He was obviously frustrated. His frustrated expression turned into an absent-minded stare, and eventually he picked up a pencil and began to doodle in the margin of his book. Shannon immediately got out a blank sheet of paper. She numbered it 1–10, and flipped back to the end-of-story questions before reading. She skimmed to find the answer to each question without reading the story in its entirety. Will read the story quickly, wrote answers to the questions just as hurriedly and without looking back at the story, stuffed his paper in his notebook, and then pulled out his copy of *2095*—a book from Jon Scieszka's (1995) *The Time Warp Trio* series. For most of the period, he read his own book.

Ms. Williams began to wonder, "What are my students getting out of this assignment?" She made the assignment because she wanted all of her students to read. She wanted them to like the story and to understand it; most of all, she hoped that having them read this story and others like it would help them become more proficient and more motivated to read. But obviously, as Ms. Williams knew, this assignment did not have the effects she intended. The story was too difficult for Ethan to read. Shannon's purpose was just to get the answers to the questions. Will was more interested in his own book.

If you were Ms. Williams, what would you do differently to make sure all of the students in your class get opportunities to read? What would you do to make reading time count for all students?

In this chapter, we describe the benefits and nature of *just reading* in the reading/language arts classroom. We suggest that self-selected, independent reading—as opposed to a set of novels, a literature anthology, or a set of skills—should be the core of the reading curriculum. Consequently, during most of the time in a period or class designated as reading, students should be *just reading*. That is not to say that there is no instruction or that there is never a time for whole-class or small-group activities. These are discussed primarily in other chapters of the book. The main purpose of this chapter, and one of the main foci of this book, is to describe the benefits of independent reading and ways to bring it to the center of the reading program.

WHAT'S IN THIS CHAPTER?

Why Prioritize Independent, Self-Selected Reading?
The Importance of Self-Selection: What Students Read on Their Own
Independent Reading in the Content Areas
What Teachers Do during Reading Time: Supporting, Teaching, and Assessing

WHY PRIORITIZE INDEPENDENT, SELF-SELECTED READING?

We all know students who would do almost anything before picking up a book to read on their own. As students move beyond the primary grades, more and more develop resistance and negative attitudes toward academic and recreational reading (McKenna, Kear, & Ellsworth, 1995). This is illustrated in the following statement by Marta, a fourth grader:

> "When I was a little girl, I loved to read. I mean, I was so smart. I was excellent. I was reading the newspaper when I was 8. When I was a little girl, I would just read and read every night. I would read a whole book every night. I'd read one page and Mom would read one page. Every night. But then when I got older, I got interested in a lot of other things and I just put that aside, and I started forgetting how to read. . . . When I got older, I just hated to read."

Middle school students in particular are notorious for having negative attitudes toward reading and for limited voluntary reading (Anderson, Tollefson, & Gilbert, 1985; Cline & Kretke, 1980). Because time spent reading is tied to reading and writing competence, many students who do not read in their free time often eventually lose academic ground even if they are not initially remedial readers (Anderson, Wilson, & Fielding, 1988; Mullis, Campbell, & Farstrup, 1993). On the other hand, when students, even struggling readers, spend time reading voluntarily, they can become very accomplished readers. Rosalie Fink interviewed successful adults who had been labeled "dyslexic" in school and found that all had reached the highest level of reading competence through voluntary reading in areas of personal interest (Fink, 1995–1996). Fink's research is good news for teachers and students. It seems like such a simple solution to "just encourage students to read."

Recognizing the benefits of time spent reading, and realizing that students may not have the opportunity, motivation, or materials necessary to read voluntarily in their free time at home, schools nationwide have endorsed free-choice reading times scheduled into the school day to increase the likelihood that students will have ample time to practice their reading. In the two most popular programs, Drop-Everything-And-Read (DEAR) and Sustained Silent Reading (SSR), students are to put aside whatever they are doing for roughly 20 minutes and read on their own in materials they select. In some cases, DEAR or SSR is scheduled at a specific time for the entire school, and the whole school population—including students, teachers, administrators, staff, and custodians—must read. In other cases, free-reading times are designated by individual teachers. In general, school-wide independent reading programs supplement rather than replace the reading/language arts program.

While programs such as DEAR and SSR are both worthwhile and commendable, they are often insufficient in terms of ensuring that students get ample opportunities to read. Although teachers recognize the value of such programs, many find it difficult to implement them on a regular basis. Sixth-grade teachers in one study (Worthy, Turner, & Moorman, 1998) reported four general barriers to free-choice reading. First, they felt pressured to cover mandated curricula and to focus on improving test scores, and they feared that outsiders to the classroom would view just reading as an enrichment activity rather than instruction. Second, teachers had a hard time responding to students' reading interests, because they felt they needed to restrict students' book choices to those that were related either to the curriculum or to standardized tests. Also, teachers were cautious about letting students read popular novels in place of the "high-quality," award-winning books that are more likely to be sanctioned by schools. Third, teachers were concerned about meeting the wide range of instructional needs in their classrooms, especially those of struggling readers and second-language learners. Teaching the "basics" in order to prepare these students for tests often took precedence over free-reading time. Fourth, teachers reported that many students did not have their own reading materials to bring from home, and that although their schools purchased sets of textbooks and class novels, there were few funds for purchasing enough interesting and varied materials for classrooms and even for school libraries.

So, despite efforts to promote independent reading, it is likely to fall by the wayside. Instead of reading, students in many middle grades classrooms are more likely to experience instruction that, although reflecting teachers' good intentions, may do little to promote proficiency and interest in reading. Even in classrooms where worksheets and drills are nonexistent, students tire of instructional activities such as answering questions about books, listening to their classmates read out loud, doing book reports, and writing responses to every book they read. As one teacher shared,

> "I've had [students] ask me before, 'Can't we just read today, just to read?' And I say, 'Yeah, we can.' A lot of times they get into their books a lot more when they don't have a lot of work over it. They really enjoy the book a lot more. So a lot of times I let them read, just to read for enjoyment."

The situation is even worse for students who find reading difficult. The major focus of remedial reading instruction in many schools is on decontextualized basic skills, literal recall, skills worksheets, and error-free oral reading, to the neglect of strategic silent reading in connected text (Johnston & Allington, 1991). Such instruction, rather than helping students to improve their reading as intended, has been tied to slower progress (Johnston & Allington, 1991). Thus struggling readers, who need to make *accelerated* progress, fall farther and farther behind. Students who struggle with reading are often caught in a cycle of recurring failure that leads to decreasing motivation and self-confidence, and to feelings of helplessness in regard to learning (Johnston &

Winograd, 1985). Is it any surprise that such students have little desire to engage in the activity that has caused them such pain?

On the other hand, having time just to read books they can manage with ease and that they enjoy causes students to want to read even more. Although free-choice reading is not always a top priority for teachers, it is a top priority with students. In our survey of over 1,700 sixth graders (Ivey & Broaddus, in press), independent reading was named as a favorite activity in reading/language arts class more times than any other activity. These written comments from some of the students highlight their enthusiasm for time to read:

> "I like reading books by myself because I can enjoy it better by being quiet and being used to the way I read."

> "I like reading by myself that way I get done with my book and I find out what happens."

> "I like reading quietly to ourselves our own book that we get from the library or from home, but I *want* more *time* in this class to read."

Most importantly, students said they liked time to read on their own because it gave them a chance to think and learn.

Students who participate in free-reading programs in schools are more likely to read outside of school (Greaney & Clarke, 1973; Pilgreen & Krashen, 1993). Take, for instance, Gloria, who participated in a university-based reading intervention during the summer between her sixth- and seventh-grade school years. Her tutor found through informal assessments that Gloria did not have any apparent skill-related problems with reading. She could read most words, and her comprehension of most passages was acceptable. However, her sixth-grade teacher reported that she was having problems reading school assignments. What the tutor discovered was that Gloria only read when it was required. She had never read any book voluntarily. Given her inexperience with reading, it is no surprise that she would have difficulty reading and staying focused on the kinds of materials middle school students are expected to read in school.

During the 1-hour tutoring sessions, instruction was focused mainly on getting Gloria engaged in reading, and approximately 40 minutes of each session was spent on just reading books of Gloria's choice. Within 1 week, Gloria was reading voluntarily outside of the reading program. Teachers reported seeing her reading each morning before the tutoring session on the front steps of the school. Within a month, Gloria had read five chapter books, including *There's a Boy in the Girls' Bathroom* (Sachar, 1987). The keys to this success story were letting Gloria find materials she enjoyed and providing time for her to read them.

Schools can no longer pigeonhole free reading as homework or as an add-on activity to be included only when other school business, such as teaching specific skills, covering curricula, or preparing for high-stakes tests, has been addressed. Although all of those things are important and need to be addressed in the classroom, the only way for students to become good readers is to let them read (Allington, 1977). If helping every student become a good reader is the ultimate goal of the reading program, then time to read needs to be the central focus of the curriculum and the instruction.

THE IMPORTANCE OF SELF-SELECTION: WHAT STUDENTS READ ON THEIR OWN

Providing time for students to read is effective only when students actually read, as opposed to passing the time daydreaming, skimming, distracting other students, or doing other schoolwork. For years educators have tried every trick imaginable to entice students to read—from contests and rewards for students who read the most, to the threat of pop quizzes and bad grades for students who choose not to read. However, external incentives rarely work, especially for the students who are most reluctant to read.

Getting students to read may be simpler than you think. In fact, you may have trouble getting your students to stop reading when it is time to do other things. The key is to get students *engaged* in what they are reading. Think about a time when you started reading a good novel and could not put it down, or a time when you got hooked on a good magazine article. That was *engagement* in reading. No one had to promise you something in return for reading or threaten you with punishment to get you to read. Now think back to when you were in school. How often did you have this kind of positive, self-motivated reading experience? Probably seldom, if ever.

Making the Case for Student Choice

Personal involvement in a text, whether to enjoy the aesthetic experience or to gather information, is a critical component of avid reading (Csikszentmihalyi, 1990; Nell, 1988). However, personal involvement is unlikely in typical school reading contexts, where teachers tell students what, why, and when to read. Students are more likely to make a personal investment in their reading when they have some choice about what to read and when they have their own purposes for reading.

In many cases, teachers cover "independent reading" by using class novels. In other words, every student in the class is assigned to read the same book, such as *Maniac Magee* (Spinelli, 1990), but they are given time in class to read silently (usually a predetermined number of chapters or pages per day). Although in essence students are reading independently, this activity does not have the same motivating effects as self-selected, self-paced reading. Ultimately, it does not serve the same purpose. First and foremost, it is unlikely that one book will match the reading levels and personal interests of every student in the class, or even the majority of students. Second, class novels are teacher-governed, with teachers deciding what, how much, and when students will read, and even providing questions for students to answer during and after the reading. Self-selected reading puts students in the driver's seat—allowing students to pose their own critical questions as they read, to direct their own thinking about the text, and to move at their own pace.

Third, when students choose for themselves and direct their own reading, they are more likely to read a wider breadth of materials and to get through more materials. In our survey of sixth-grade classes (Ivey & Broaddus, in press), students reported reading only a narrow range of materials in school, most of which were award-winning novels of a similar genre. Also, in classrooms where the curriculum centers around class novels, students may not get to read more than a few books each year, especially when so much time is devoted to each novel. Even when students become engaged in class novels, they are sometimes told not to "read ahead," so that everyone in class will be on the same page. We have seen classrooms in which students spend up to 4 or 5 weeks, or even longer, on the same book. We know of one fifth-grade class that studied *Shiloh* (Naylor, 1991) from December until March of the school year! Very little time is spent actually reading, however, since students are inundated with projects associated with the book—such as comprehension questions, art projects, and dramatic productions—to the point of overkill. See Box 4.1 for additional instructional issues related to reading-related projects and activities.

A fourth problem with building instruction around a class novel is that it perpetuates the "rich get richer and poor get poorer" syndrome among students. On the one hand, skilled readers who have access to books outside of school are likely to read a wealth of additional materials on their own, which is how they got to be proficient in

BOX 4.1. Reading-Related Projects and Follow-Up Activities: What Really Counts?

Extension activities following class novels and independent reading are a mainstay of elementary and middle grades reading and language arts classes. Unfortunately, many projects are assigned with little or no thought given to their instructional value. Not all follow-up activities are created equal. Nancy Roser and James Hoffman, at the University of Texas at Austin, encourage their preservice teachers to consider the following questions when planning a reading-related project:

Does It Count?

- Does it relate to the essence and/or important themes of the text?
- Is it built upon language in all of its forms—reading, writing, speaking, enacting, representing?
- Does it promote learning or responding in a way appropriate to the text and its purpose?
- Does it grow naturally out of the literature?
- Does it promote enjoyment of and engagement with the literature?
- Does it promote critical thinking?
- Does it seem reasonable in its demands on teachers' and students' time?
- Have you discussed the purpose with students, and do they see it as meaningful?
- Is it the same old thing?
- Do students have some choice and control?
- Does it allow opportunities for meaningful social interaction connected with the book?

The bottom line when considering the value of follow-up activities is that you are taking away from students' time just to read and write. Be sure to evaluate whether or not that tradeoff is worthwhile.

the first place. In fact, many have already read the books the teacher assigns. Students who frequent bookstores can get new books when they are hot off the press, whereas schools are not likely to obtain these same books until a couple of years down the road.

On the other hand, students who are not as proficient, who are resistant readers, and/or who cannot afford to buy their own materials are limited to what schools offer them. If the class novel is the focus of the reading program, then that book may be the only one they read. Certainly one book per grading period or even less, in some cases, does not provide these students with enough reading experience ever to become more proficient and motivated.

Fifth, when students choose their own books, they can share ideas for reading with their classmates. Instead of knowing just one book, students can become familiar with scores of different texts. Think about how much more students could read if they were selecting their own materials and moving at their own pace.

Before moving on to the next section of this chapter, we would like to stress that although we highlight the benefits and nature of independent reading, we also want to make it clear that reading is far from being a solitary experience. Whereas independent, self-selected reading gives students a chance to read materials they can handle comfortably on their own and that they want to read, they also learn much from participating in reading activities with others. Students need to share and discuss common texts with each other. As we have mentioned in Chapter 3, teacher read-alouds provide excellent contexts for small-group and whole-class discussion because students are freed from the burden of actually reading the words, and because readers of various ability levels can all have access to the same text. Book discussion groups, in which small groups of students read and discuss the same text, are also a good way to realize the potential of the social nature of literacy learning. See Box 4.2 for some excellent resources on small-group reading and discussion.

BOX 4.2. Sources for Learning about Small-Group Reading and Discussion

Alvermann, D. E. (1991). The discussion web: A graphic aid for learning across the curriculum. *The Reading Teacher, 45*, 92–99.

Alvermann, D. E., Young, J. P., Green C., & Wisenbaker, J. M. (1999). Adolescents' perceptions and negotiations of literacy practices in after-school Read and Talk Clubs. *American Educational Research Journal, 36*, 221–224.

Daniels, H. (1994). *Literature circles: Voice and choice in the student-centered classroom.* Portland, ME: Stenhouse.

Lehman, B. A., & Scharer, P. L. (1996). Reading alone, talking together: The role of discussion in developing literary awareness. *The Reading Teacher, 50*, 26–35.

Noll, E. (1994). Social issues and literature circles with adolescents. *Journal of Reading, 38*, 88–93.

Peterson, R., & Eeds, M. (1990). *Grand conversations: Literature groups in action.* New York: Scholastic.

Raphael, T., & McMahon, S. (1994). Book Club: An alternative framework for reading instruction. *The Reading Teacher, 48*, 102–116.

Balancing Materials Selection: Honoring Student Choices and Encouraging Wide Reading

So what are students inclined to read on their own? Students may choose a wide range of materials to read on their own: humorous picture books (e.g., *The Dumb Bunnies*—Denim, 1994; *The Stinky Cheese Man and Other Fairly Stupid Tales*—Scieszka, 1992); easy chapter books (e.g., *The Magic Finger*—Dahl, 1966; *Marvin Redpost: Alone in His Teacher's House*—Sachar, 1994); popular adult fiction (e.g., Stephen King novels); and nonfiction texts in content areas such as history (e.g., *Lives of the Presidents: Fame, Shame (and What the Neighbors Thought)*—Krull, 1998; *The Perilous Journey of the Donner Party*—Calabro, 1999) or science (e.g., the *Eyewitness Juniors* series; *Extremely Weird Primates*—Lovett, 1996). Again, keep in mind that preferred materials are often very specific and unique to the individual. For instance, one of Gay Ivey's former eighth-grade students was interested in aviation, and he enjoyed nonfiction books like Freedman's (1990) *The Wright Brothers: How They Invented the Airplane.* It is also important for teachers to recognize students' desire to read materials other than books, such as newspapers, magazines, and comic books, especially

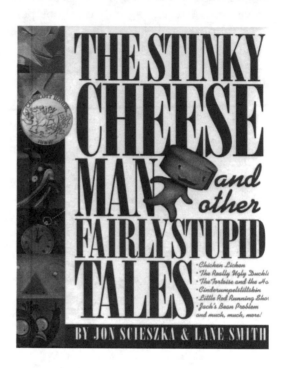

since these kinds of materials are often part of adults' preferred reading. Readers of all ages and ability levels are most likely to engage in reading when they have interesting materials that they want to read and that they can easily manage on their own. Although some students may need guidance in selecting materials, the ultimate choice should be theirs.

While we stress the importance of honoring students' personal interests, we also recognize the need for students to become experienced at reading a range of texts. Although assigning a variety of texts that represent many different kinds of writing and that cover an array of topics may seem like a viable solution, you would still encounter the problem of not having students become personally involved in the reading, and thus not engaged. Furthermore, students may not have the background knowledge necessary to read some texts on their own, particularly certain information texts. One way to expose students to new genres and

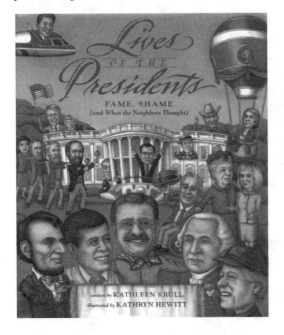

by Marian Calabro

important topics is through reading aloud to them, which we have discussed in depth in Chapter 3. Listening to the teacher read frees students from the burden of figuring out words, so they can focus on the meaning, content, and style of the text. They may then find that independent reading time is a good opportunity to reread things the teacher has read aloud, to finish reading a text the teacher has started as a read-aloud, to read another book by the author of a text that has been read aloud, or to read something from the same genre or topic. Some students may choose to read materials related to a subject they are studying in one of their content area subjects, such as science or social studies.

One way to ensure a wider range of reading experiences is to emphasize to students the importance of reading broadly, and then have them demonstrate through records of their reading that they have experimented with a variety of texts. It might be tempting to force students to read a certain number of books that fit particular categories (e.g., science fiction, poetry, fantasy), but such a requirement is likely to result in resistance or apathy, because it places too many constraints on student choice. Alternatively, we recommend that students be held accountable for reading from four broad categories: (1) "preferred fiction," (2) "fiction that expands my horizons," (3) "preferred nonfiction," and (4) "nonfiction that expands my horizons." We expect that most of students' reading will fall

into the two "preferred" categories, but that they should also be able to document trying new things. Often students' preferred materials are just as complex as or even more complex than teacher-selected materials, especially if students have been given many choices (Carlsen & Sherrill, 1988; Mackey, 1990).

See Box 4.3 for a sample reading list kept by one fifth-grade student. His preferred reading included fictional sports stories and current information about sports found in magazines and newspapers. However, he branched out from his preferred reading by trying *Everglades* (George, 1995), which is a nonfiction picture book with an environmental theme, and *Wish Giver: Three Tales of Covern Tree* (Brittain, 1983), which is a fantasy novel. Also note the volume of reading he accomplished during a period of a little over a week.

INDEPENDENT READING
IN THE CONTENT AREAS

Although we focus mainly on independent reading in reading/language arts in this chapter, we also strongly recommend time to read independently in the other academic subjects. Independent reading in the content areas has specific benefits, in addition to increasing the total amount of time students spend reading during the school day. For instance, think back to your own experiences in school. How often were you given time to explore books and other materials related to topics in science, math, or social studies? Probably seldom, other than times when you were assigned to read something

BOX 4.3. Sample Reading Log for Clay, a Fifth-Grade Student

Date completed	Preferred fiction	Fiction that expands my horizons	Preferred nonfiction	Nonfiction that expands my horizons
September 10	*Stranger in Right Field* (by Matt Christopher, 1997)		Article about baseball player, Greg Maddux, on the Internet	
September 12	*The Spy on Third Base* (by Matt Christopher, 1988)		Summaries of yesterday's National League games in *The Atlanta Journal-Constitution* sports section	
September 13			*Teammates* (by Golenbock, 1990)	*Everglades* (by Jean Craighead George, 1995)
September 18		*Wish Giver* (by Brittain, 1983) (fantasy)		

from a textbook. What if, instead, students were provided an abundance of diverse materials on a particular topic, and they were given time to explore that topic through self-selected reading without necessarily being obligated to complete any follow-up questions or assignments?

Take a look at the small sample of materials on endangered ecosystems in Box 4.4, which is part of a much larger selection of materials available on this topic. Giving students a chance to choose from these and other books on this topic would not only help them develop interest in the subject, but would also help to build the knowledge that would help them read and learn even more information about it. Furthermore, students could identify aspects of the topic that interest them through wide reading, and could then pursue additional reading, research, and writing, but with a specific focus.

Independent, self-selected reading in the content areas also gives students a chance to become familiar with and to experiment with different formats and genres used to report information about different topics, which can be used later as models in their own research and writing (see Chapter 8). To become proficient at learning from text and to make the most of the information available in text, students need lots of time to read in content area classes.

WHAT TEACHERS DO DURING READING TIME: SUPPORTING, TEACHING, AND ASSESSING

Although we acknowledge the importance of teachers serving as role models by reading on their own during independent reading times and sharing their own personal reading interests, they can and should use this time judiciously by attending to and getting to know individual students as readers. This is a good time for teachers to share expertise about reading and writing. It is also a good time to conduct informal assessments (e.g., listening to students as they read, engaging students in discussions of what they are reading) that help them focus on what students *can* do as readers rather than

BOX 4.4. Sample of Books on Endangered Ecosystems for Self-Selected, Independent Reading

Baker, J. (1995). *The story of Rosy Dock.* New York: Greenwillow.

Cherry, L. (1992). *River ran wild: An environmental history.* San Diego, CA: Harcourt Brace.

Cherry, L. (1997). *Flute journey: The life of a wood thrush.* New York: Gulliver.

Cone, M. (1992). *Come back, salmon: How a group of dedicated kids adopted Pigeon Creek and brought it back to life.* San Francisco: Sierra Club Books.

George, J. C. (1992). *The missing gator of Gumbo Limbo: An ecological mystery.* New York: HarperTrophy.

George, J. C. (1995). *Everglades.* New York: HarperCollins.

Gibbons, G. (1994). *Nature's green umbrella: Tropical rain forests.* New York: Mulberry.

Jeffers, S. (1991). *Brother Eagle, Sister Sky.* New York: Dial.

Reece, J. (1995). *Lester and Clyde running scared.* New York: Scholastic.

Wright-Frierson, V. (1999). *A North American rain forest scrapbook.* New York: Walker.

on what they cannot do, and that help them get a sense of individual students' progress over time.

Supporting Independent Reading

When you initiate independent reading in your classroom, it may be the case that some students acclimate immediately to this time, quickly finding interesting materials and rarely "coming up for air" until reading time is over, perhaps even groaning when told to put away their books. It is likely, however, that you will have a number of students who will take longer to grow accustomed to and feel comfortable with spending their time just reading, for a number of possible reasons. Students who are not experienced at reading on their own may need guidance in finding engaging materials and maintaining interest in a book for sustained periods of time. You will also run across some students, even in grades 3–8, who cannot yet read anything on their own. With the right kind of support, even these students can take full advantage of independent reading time. Box 4.5 provides an overview of what teachers can do to help struggling readers—and perhaps all readers at one time or another—get started and take control of their own reading during times set aside to just read.

Supporting Reluctant and Unpracticed Readers

It would be a mistake to assume that a student who has never read on his or her own by choice will suddenly pick up a book and start reading for any length of time. Good habits develop over time, and they grow out of having consistent positive experiences. One way to support students who have never experienced engagement in reading is to

---

BOX 4.5. What Teachers Can Do to Help Struggling Readers Get Started and Take Control of Their Own Reading during Independent Reading Times

Help students find materials they can read and want to read:	Get students started in the texts they select:	Teach students how to overcome reading dilemmas as they read on their own:
• Have individual conversations about personal interests. • Help students identify materials that are "just right" for them to read (texts they can read with near-perfect accuracy and with fairly familiar concepts and vocabulary; see Chapter 1).	• Start by reading the first few pages aloud to the student. • Start with partner reading (teacher and student reading alternate pages). • Try echo and choral reading. • Hang around with the student until he or she is "hooked" on the text.	• Teach students strategies for figuring out word pronunciations and meanings as problems come up in the reading. • Model strategies for comprehension (through thinking aloud and making the process explicit to the student; see Chapter 3).

---

help them find materials that are both interesting and manageable. By the time students reach the middle grades, they are expected to read rather sophisticated chapter books—indeed a tall order for a student who has never read anything from cover to cover. Rather than expecting students to make the long jump from reading nothing, or even from reading just picture books, to reading full-length novels, teachers can help students make small, progressive steps.

For instance, Shawn, an inexperienced seventh-grade reader, felt comfortable at first reading short, easy picture books such as those in Marshall's *Fox* series (e.g., *Fox on Wheels*—Marshall, 1983). After a few weeks of free-reading periods, he tried some transitional chapter books, like *Dracula* (adapted by Spinner, 1982) from Random House's *Bullseye Chiller* series. Before long he was ready to tackle lengthier novels such as *The Mouse Rap* (Myers, 1990). Other high-interest materials with alternative formats, such as *The Bone Detectives: How Forensic Anthropologists Solve Crimes and Uncover Mysteries of the Dead* (Jackson, 1996), allow older, unpracticed readers to read short sections of text at a time. The teacher might also sit with an unpracticed reader as she or he begins a book, taking turns with the reading until the student is hooked. These kinds of one-to-one interactions are critical to promote engagement.

Supporting Students Who Cannot Read on Their Own

If you teach in the middle grades, chances are that you will run across a student who, for whatever reason, is still at the emergent phase of learning to read. Independent reading time is not lost on these students if teachers know what kinds of support to offer them. *Echo reading* and *choral reading* are two ways of guiding the most struggling readers toward independent reading. In echo reading, the teacher reads a short section of text at a time; then the student reads what the teacher just read; and they continue in this manner until the end of the text. When the student seems comfortable with echo reading of a particular text, the teacher and student can then move to choral reading—that is, reading the same text in unison. Predictable pattern books (e.g., *Hattie and the Fox*—Fox, 1986; *It Looked like Spilt Milk*—Shaw, 1947) and short poems are very appropriate for echo and choral reading, but you can also use short nonfiction passages related to students' interests, comic strips, or even joke books. The outcomes of echo and choral reading are that eventually students not only gain confidence and a greater sight word vocabulary, but they also collect a range of materials they *can* read independently because of practice and the teacher's support. Keep in mind that building a collection of readable materials will take some time, but the results are invaluable.

Consider the case of Miguel, a fifth-grade Spanish-speaking student who was learning English as a second language. Due to both language barriers and inexperience with print in general, Miguel could not manage any text well on his own. His teacher tried echo and choral reading techniques with him during independent reading times, and before too long, Miguel had a stack of 20 books he could read without any help. Since this was Miguel's first success with reading, he was anxious to demonstrate his growing ability. Each Friday during sharing time, Miguel read aloud to the class a new pattern book that he had practiced with his teacher. One of his favorites was *More Spaghetti, I Say* (Gelman, 1987).

You might wonder whether students like Miguel are embarrassed to read easy books in front of their peers. On the contrary, Miguel was proud of his accomplishment.

It helped that Miguel's teacher conveyed to her class a theme of "making difficult books accessible and easy books acceptable" (Fielding & Roller, 1992). Miguel's teacher made difficult books accessible to him by providing support until he could read them on his own. She made easy books acceptable by introducing the books he read to the entire class as options for reading. See Box 4.6 for a list of other ways Fielding and Roller (1992) suggest that teachers can help students more comfortable with their book choices.

Independent Reading as Instructional Time

Traditionally, teachers teach to the whole class. For most people, the concept of teaching probably conjures up an image of a teacher standing at the front of the room while students sit silently listening to what the teacher has to say to the entire group. On the surface, whole-class instruction seems both efficient and equitable. The teacher can maintain control of the class, while at the same time making sure that all students get the same information. Unfortunately, whole-class instruction in reading is not very effective. As discussed earlier in this chapter, in order to motivate students to read, teachers need to relinquish some control and allow students to have a say in what, why, and how they choose to read. Furthermore, not all students benefit from the same instruction at the same time.

This is not to say that reading teachers should never conduct whole-class activities. Throughout the remainder of this book, we discuss some important skills and strategies (e.g., comprehension, fluency, spelling, and decoding) that can be addressed in a variety of groupings. However, teachers can accomplish some of their most fine-tuned and intensive instruction with individual students. Students will benefit most from lessons given just when they need them and in the context of their reading. In this section,

---

BOX 4.6. Bringing Struggling Readers Together with Books for Independent Reading

Ways to make difficult books accessible

- Allow independent reading time.
- Read to students.
- Encourage partner reading.
- Encourage rereading.
- Precede difficult books with easier books on the same topic.

Ways to make easy books acceptable

- Model use and enjoyment of easy books.
- Broaden purposes for easy reading (e.g., practice for reading to a younger student).
- Challenge preconceptions about easy books through whole-class discussions about specific books.
- Broaden the concept of acceptable reading to include genres such as poems, songs, raps, cheers, and students' own writing.
- Make simple nonfiction books available.

Note. Borrowed from Fielding, L., & Roller, C. (1992). Making difficult books accessible and easy books acceptable. *The Reading Teacher, 45*, 673–685. Copyright 1992 by the International Reading Association. Adapted by permission.

---

we detail the different kinds of instruction teachers can provide on a one-on-one basis. Also, if the teacher notices that one or more students are having a particular kind of difficulty, he or she can plan a small-group follow-up lesson during independent reading time.

Teaching Relevant Skills and Strategies

Most students undoubtedly need instruction in the essential skills and knowledge necessary to read and write. Unfortunately, skill work sometimes takes precedence over time spent reading and writing, and this should not be the case. The teaching of skills and strategies ought to *support* independent reading, not replace it. Teachers need not feel guilty or remiss about choosing to prioritize time to read, particularly if they use extended reading times to zone in on instruction for individual students. Consider, for instance, how Gay Ivey ("GI" in the dialogue below) took advantage of the opportunity to provide an on-the-spot lesson to Casey, a sixth-grade student. Casey had just gotten stuck on the word *subtle* as she read *Fifth Grade: Here Comes Trouble* (McKenna, 1991):

GI: Do you have any idea what that means? Can you figure it out?

CASEY: Is it a special word?

GI: Go back to where it's first mentioned. This is kind of an interesting way to figure out words. How do you usually figure out words you don't know? (*Casey gives no response.*) Do you skip it and go on?

CASEY: I guess.

GI: Let's see if we can figure this out. [The book] says, "Don't flop it down in the center like you're trying to show it off. Be subtle. Always be subtle."

CASEY: Be, like, just plain?

GI: Keep going.

CASEY: Don't try to—don't make it look like you're trying to show off.

GI: See if that makes sense when you use the word again.

CASEY: "Nothing about Carol was subtle." Nothing about her was plain.

GI: Yeah. That's a good way to figure out words.

CASEY: That's cool.

Although Casey did not yet have a solid understanding of *subtle*, she was beginning to grasp the concept. She would come across that word in a variety of contexts in her future reading, and eventually she would be able to narrow down its meaning. Although Gay could have presented an entire lesson on figuring out word meanings from context, this lesson was most timely and beneficial for Casey at the moment she actually needed it.

One concern of many preservice teachers in our courses is knowing when and how to intervene when students are having some difficulty reading fluently. As we discuss in Chapter 2, if a student is stumbling over every few words, then you should help the student choose another book. But if a student is reading something she or he is generally comfortable with, but still runs across difficult words, there are things you can do, as Darrell Morris (1999) suggests, to "keep the ball rolling" (p. 121). See Box 4.7 for tips on monitoring and responding to oral reading.

When you feel it is necessary to intervene in a child's oral reading, it is important to remember two additional guidelines. First, do not interrupt a student's reading in the middle of the sentence. Wait and see whether the student detects his or her own mistake and self-corrects. If this does not happen, wait until the student gets to an appropriate stopping point (such as the end of the sentence or the end of a section) before you intervene. Second, if a student makes an error that changes the meaning of a passage and you must interrupt, be sure to ask questions that will foster good reading behaviors. For instance, instead of saying, "No, that was wrong," ask, "Did that make sense to you?", since this is the kind of question you will want students to ask themselves as they read independently and you are not there.

As you move around the room during reading time, you may encounter students who need other kinds of help at the moment, such as strategies for decoding difficult words and strategies for building comprehension. For ongoing assessment of individual progress, it is a good idea to keep anecdotal records of what you discuss with students, as we have discussed in Chapter 1.

Modeling Relevant Strategies and Sharing Expertise

Likewise, one-on-one times are ideal for *modeling* reading strategies and for sharing knowledge about the reading process. One preconceived notion held by some inexperienced teachers is that students must answer questions about their reading, rather than

---

BOX 4.7. Tips on Monitoring and Responding to Oral Reading

1. *Keep the ball rolling.*
    - The teacher can read alternate pages of the book, modeling the pronunciation of new vocabulary, correct phrasing, and intonation.
    - The teacher can provide difficult words (words that are far beyond a child's decoding abilities) when the child gets stuck.

2. *The beginning reader must make sense as he [or] she reads.*
    - When a child's reading does not make sense, the teacher has some options:
    - Ask the child to read the sentence again.
    - Provide support by pointing out a letter–sound cue (e.g., a beginning consonant)
    - Reread the text up to a point, then ask the child to finish reading the sentence.

3. *The readers shall read, for the most part, the words on the page.*
    - If a child makes only a few errors and still maintains the meaning of the passage, the teacher might not want to disrupt the flow of the reading.
    - If a child makes a significant number of errors, even if he or she maintains the meaning of the passage, the teacher should have the student focus on accuracy by rereading.

Note. Adapted from Morris (1999). Copyright 1999 by The Guilford Press. Reprinted with permission.

participate with the teacher in interesting and worthwhile discussions. However, having a student answer comprehension questions that require the student to give one correct answer or to guess the answer in the teacher's head is probably fruitless in terms of improving that student's ability to read and understand. Although there may be times to *check* students' comprehension, teachers need to be sure that they *teach* students about the comprehension process. Consider this exchange between seventh grader Lola and her teacher, Beth. Lola was reading to Beth a chapter of *Scorpions* (Myers, 1988), and she came across the part where Jamal, the main character, is chastised by his principal for being late for school. Jamal is upset and unresponsive to the principal, so the principal scolds him again, "At least try to talk as if you're civilized" (pp. 16–17).

BETH: Stop there for a minute. I'm thinking Jamal is going to eventually do something drastic. Here's why I think that. People around him are constantly putting him down. A person can only take just so much, right? In my experience, lots of people who commit crimes or just make bad decisions do it because they feel bad about themselves. I'm thinking about a movie I saw where a little boy who is beaten by his father grows up to be a murderer. I don't think Jamal will do anything like that, but I think the author is setting the stage for Jamal to begin feeling desperate. His family is struggling, other boys are picking on him at school, and even adults, like the shopkeeper who said negative things about his mom, are making him feel powerless. What do you think?

LOLA: Yeah, there was this TV show that I saw that people were making fun of this kid because he was, you know, like kind of fat, so he got back at them. I think Jamal will do something. And then there's that friend—his brother's friend who just got out of jail. And he's back there, and he's messing around Jamal, and he might get him to do something bad, too.

On the surface, it may seem that Beth was giving the story away, because in the end Jamal does get himself into a precarious situation. However, Lola already had an idea about what is going to happen to Jamal. Beth's purpose was to draw Lola's attention to what *she* used to make sense of her reading: connecting to personal experiences, connecting to other texts, and examining tools the author uses to construct the storyline. Beth was primarily concerned about Lola's learning to apply good strategies to everything she read, rather than with her comprehension of this one book per se. So, when Beth sat with Lola during reading times, she focused more on the *process* of her reading than on whether or not Lola had become an expert on the content of any particular book. Also, in this particular situation, the teaching occurred in the context of a *real* conversation about a book.

One question you might have at this point is this: "If all of my students are reading different things, do I have to be familiar with all of the books, too?" To limit students' options to only those books a teacher has read from cover to cover would defeat the purpose of wide student choice. However, it is important for teachers to be at least familiar with what all students are reading—not only to judge the appropriateness of materials brought in from outside of school, but also to have meaningful discussions and instructional experiences with those materials. If you are working with a student during independent reading time, and you have not read the text the student is currently reading, a good way to start the discussion is to ask, "Catch me up on this book," "What led you to this book?", or any other real question you might have about something you have not read. Keep in mind that these are not the kinds of questions you would need to ask about a book you have read. In that case, a more logical starting point would be "Tell me where you are in this book," or "What do you think so far?" In either of these scenarios, you would then be able to join the student in the reading of the text.

Independent Reading as an Assessment Opportunity

Consider two assessment scenarios. In the first, the teacher gives everyone in the class the same 10 comprehension questions about the story they just read. After students finish the test, they turn in their papers, and the teacher checks to see how many correct answers they got. One student, named Jimmy, only gave correct answers to 5 of the questions. In the second scenario, the teacher sits with Jimmy, who reads aloud to her and talks about his book. Immediately afterward, the teacher writes some notes on what she observed. She writes that Jimmy made a lot of mistakes as he read aloud from *Bunnicula* (Howe & Howe, 1980), and that he did not try to correct his mistakes even when his errors made the sentence nonsensical. She also notes that when she tried to engage him in a conversation about the book, he did not seem to know what it was about. Further probing revealed that he did not have strong feelings about the book, but selected it because he did not know what he wanted to read.

Although the first assessment scenario has made it fairly clear that Jimmy did not get much out of his reading, it has not provided the teacher with any specific reasons for his lack of comprehension. In fact, it does not necessarily reveal a comprehension deficit at all. His failure to answer the comprehension questions correctly could be due to other factors, such as lack of interest in the material or poorly worded and confusing questions. It is also possible that Jimmy's limited background knowledge on the subject of the story made it difficult for him to make any sense of it. Since the only evidence his teacher has is a list of answers, she may never know the real problem. Where does that leave her in deciding what to do next with Jimmy?

Now think about what the teacher has learned in the second scenario. Jimmy was making word-level errors in his reading—the first clue that the book he selected might be too difficult. Coupled with that was the fact that he was not attending to meaning in the book, as evidenced by his failure to self-correct when he made errors that changed the meaning of the passage. Also, Jimmy had no interest in the book he was reading, which might even explain why he did not pay attention to what he was reading. So this scenario has enabled the teacher to make a number of solid hypotheses about why this reading experience was unsuccessful for Jimmy. She decides to focus first on helping Jimmy find a different book that he *can* read with ease and that he *wants* to read. She figures she can reserve judgment on his comprehension abilities until he finds something more engaging to read. She will revisit Jimmy on many occasions during independent reading times, each time evaluating his reading, monitoring his progress, and adjusting her instructional plans for him.

In Chapter 1, we have discussed how teachers should get to know students as readers and writers during the first few weeks of school. The assessment process should be ongoing, and the majority of assessments should be one-on-one experiences with students in the context of real reading and writing experiences. Independent reading times provide the perfect setting.

A Conceptual Framework for Assessing Students' Reading

Assessment involves not only gathering information, but also evaluating information to ascertain students' areas of strength and of need, as well as using the information to plan and refine instruction. Teachers should have these goals in mind as they observe and work with students individually during independent reading time.

When you assess, it is also important to remember that the reading experience is multidimensional, with a number of processes operating simultaneously and interactively. Rarely is a bad reading experience due solely to a student's inability to comprehend, for example. It is more likely that a number of factors interact to prevent students from reading effectively. For instance, think back to the case of Jimmy, mentioned earlier. His failure to comprehend was due to a combination of factors, including the level of difficulty of the text and Jimmy's general uninterest in the book. We discuss some tools and scales for measuring specific aspects of reading and writing (e.g., spelling, fluency) elsewhere in this book, but here we explore assessment from a more holistic perspective.

One way of organizing your assessment of individual students is the System for Teaching and Assessing Interactively and Reflectively (STAIR), a process described by Afflerbach (1993a) and specifically designed to use with students as they are engaged in real reading activities. The concept behind STAIR is a cycle of observations and reflections on individual students. For the initial observation, record the student's reading behaviors during a particular activity, and formulate a hypothesis about why the student did or did not have a successful experience with reading. Then decide what to do for that student, based on your theory.

Look at Box 4.8 for one teacher's notes on Melissa, a fifth-grade student who did not appear to be engaged in reading her book, *Ella Enchanted* (Levine, 1997). This

---

BOX 4.8. Format for Initial STAIR Hypothesis, and an Example

Student name: Melissa Date: 9/15

Hypothesis #1:

Melissa is not engaged in her reading during independent reading time.

Sources of information supporting hypothesis:

Observation of Melissa sitting with Ella Enchanted (Levine, 1997) open in front of her. She doesn't look at the page, but instead looks around the room and twirls her hair with her finger.

Instruction to address hypothesis:

Talk to Melissa about why she chose Ella Enchanted. Have her read one page aloud and talk about what is happening in the book so far to see if this book is something she really wants to read and whether or not she can read it with ease. My hunch is that it is too hard. If the book is the problem, I will help Melissa find a better fit. I think she might feel more comfortable right now with a shorter, easier book. Will gather a stack of options.

Note. The format is from Afflerbach, P. (1993). STAIR: A system for recording and using what we observe and know about our students. *The Reading Teacher, 47,* 260–263.

teacher hypothesized that Melissa's lack of enthusiasm was due to the fact that she was trying to read a book that was too difficult. She listened to Melissa read one page of her book, and sure enough, she got stuck on at least one word in almost every sentence. When she asked Melissa why she chose this book, Melissa said she liked books with girls as characters. The teacher then showed Melissa a number of easier books with young female characters, including *Muggie Maggie* (Cleary, 1990), *Amber Brown Is Not a Crayon* (Danziger, 1994), and *Shoeshine Girl* (Bulla, 1975), which was the book Melissa decided to try.

The assessment process does not end there. On subsequent days, you should continue to observe to either confirm or change your hypotheses. Look at Box 4.9 to see what Melissa's teacher observed a couple of days after the first observation. Melissa was hooked on *Shoeshine Girl*, so it appeared that the intervention was successful. Of course, you will want to watch your students throughout the entire school year and in a variety of reading contexts, and to gather even more information by engaging them in real conversations about their books.

Afflerbach (1993a) cautions that using STAIR all of the time with all of your students is impossible. More importantly, you should begin to internalize this process so that you are constantly monitoring your students' reading and linking assessment with instruction. Remember that when you evaluate students, you must also evaluate the instruction you are providing them. When a student is not having success with reading, it is up to both the student and the teacher to find texts and tasks that are more appropriate and effective. The instructional decisions you make in response to assessment can make a huge difference.

BOX 4.9. Format for Subsequent STAIR Hypotheses, and an Example

Student name: Melissa   **Date:** 9/17

Context: Independent reading time

Text: Shoeshine Girl (Bulla, 1975)

Task: Silent reading

Hypothesis: _____ Refined   X   Upheld _____ Abandoned

Sources of information:

Melissa read for at least 20 minutes without becoming distracted. She said she liked the book and asked if she could take it home to read. She said it was easy.

Instruction to address hypothesis:

Continue to introduce easy, transitional chapter books to Melissa and to the whole class as options for free reading. Keep talking to Melissa about what interests her and about the books she's reading. Also listen to Melissa read occasionally, in order to monitor her book selection.

Note. The format is from Afflerbach, P. (1993). STAIR: A system for recording and using what we observe and know about our students. *The Reading Teacher, 47,* 260–263. Copyright 1993 by the International Reading Association. Reprinted with permission.

Keeping Track of Students' Growth in Reading

Although it is important to monitor students' development and interactions with print on a day-to-day basis, it is just as important to maintain a sense of each student's overall progress. This is critical not only for instructional reasons, but also for communicating progress and areas of need to students, parents, and other teachers who hold interests in your students' reading.

For a reading curriculum in which independent reading is the central focus, however, a traditional evaluation system, such as a grade on a report card, will not work. Afflerbach (1993b) cautions that the typical report card is "something inherited from a previous generation, only partly compatible with the current reading curriculum and used without critical examination" (p. 465). We urge teachers to think of new ways to describe the range of students' reading development, based on two fundamental questions:

1. What are the primary goals for students' reading?
2. How are students developing toward these goals?

To address the first question, we see four broad goals:

- Students should increase their volume of reading.
- Students should increase their breadth of reading.
- Students should be reading fluently.
- Students should be engaged and strategic in their reading.

Note how these goals reflect the "big picture" of reading, as opposed to the miniscule skills (e.g., using context clues, drawing inferences) associated with the larger reading process. Also, these goals represent the guiding principles for reading instruction, particularly instruction that is grounded in independent reading.

To answer the second question—"How are students developing toward these goals?"—we advise teachers to rely on their impressions of students and interactions with students during independent reading times, as well as artifacts of students' experiences with reading. Anecdotal notes recorded during free-reading observations, checklists, rubrics, and student surveys (as we have discussed in Chapter 1) provide valuable evidence of student growth, as do students' reading logs and students' writing. We imagine that the most meaningful communication with students, parents, and teachers will be developed in collaboration with students, and most likely in a narrative form rather than a letter grade or checklist.

See Box 4.10 for an example of one third-grade student's progress report for independent reading. Notice the overall positive tone of the letter and the straightforward, meaningful kinds of information the teacher includes. It focuses on what this student *can* do rather than on what she cannot do. This report reflects Tara's reading development as a collaborative effort that includes Tara, the teacher, and Tara's parents. Also, notice that in Tara's report, the teacher points out not only the progress Tara has made, but also the kinds of instruction and materials that have been effective. In our experience, parents often need some guidance in helping their children find appropriate reading materials for pleasure reading at home. This kind of information is critical to parents, as well as to other teachers who may work with Tara, because it makes them evaluate some of the methods or materials they may have tried and found to be ineffective.

In some cases, teachers may not find it feasible to write such a lengthy report for each student (especially some middle grades teachers with as many as 100 students each day). An alternative is to have students write a portion or all of the letter or report after meeting individually with the teacher to discuss progress and plans. This will make the evaluation experience even more meaningful for students, and it will help them become more mindful of their development and more focused in their efforts during independent reading time.

BOX 4.10. A Narrative Report of a Third-Grade Student's Progress in Reading

Dear Mr. And Mrs. Smith:

I am writing to tell you about Tara's progress in reading during the first 6 weeks of school. Tara and I have talked about how she has improved and what she needs to focus on during the coming weeks.

Tara has come a long way in being able to read for sustained periods of time. At the beginning of the school year, she was unsure of how to choose books she was comfortable reading, so consequently it was difficult for her to become engaged in reading during independent reading time. She was selecting books that are too difficult right now, such as the short chapter book *Pinky and Rex and the New Neighbors* (Howe, 1997). Because many of the words were hard for Tara to read, she quickly became frustrated and resorted to just looking at the pictures, and eventually she would lose interest in the book. Together, we found some books Tara could read fluently and that she enjoyed. Most of these were books that have a repetitive pattern, which is just the kind of support Tara needs to have successful and productive experiences with reading—and, most importantly, to keep her reading. Some of her favorites are *Eek! There's a Mouse in the House* (Yee, 1992) and *Hattie and the Fox* (Fox, 1986). Tara finds it helpful if I read new books to her at least once before she tries them on her own.

Tara also enjoys when I read aloud to the class. It is during these times that Tara gets to hear some books and stories she cannot yet read on her own, such as *Is This a House for a Hermit Crab?* (McDonald, 1990), which is a very interesting picture book that contains some good information about the ocean and sea life, and *Chocolate Fever* (Smith, 1972), which is a chapter book. At first Tara was reluctant to join in discussions during read-aloud times, but that is starting to change. Recently she has been volunteering predictions about what might happen in the story, and sometimes she asks questions about parts of the story that confused her. I am happy that Tara has begun to speak up, because this helps me know that Tara is developing good strategies for understanding as she listens or reads.

What Tara and I need to work on now is finding some different kinds of books for her to read, especially some nonfiction or information books. I know that Tara is interested in the weather, so I will be on the lookout for books on the weather, especially those that are similar in format to the repetitive pattern books she can read so fluently. If you go to the library or bookstore with Tara, you might want to keep your eyes open for these things, too. Tara will be a big help to you in finding books she can read comfortably. If you find interesting books that are too hard for Tara right now, you might want to read them to her.

Sincerely,

Ms. Jones

CHILDREN'S BOOK REFERENCES

Brittain, B. (1983). *Wish giver: Three tales of Covern Tree*. New York: HarperCollins.
Bulla, C. R. (1975). *Shoeshine girl*. New York: Crowell.
Calabro, M. (1999). *The perilous journey of the Donner party*. New York: Clarion.
Christopher, M. (1988). *The spy on third base*. Boston: Little, Brown.
Christopher, M. (1997). *Stranger in right field*. Boston: Little, Brown.
Cleary, B. (1990). *Muggie Maggie*. New York: Morrow.
Dahl, R. (1966). *The magic finger*. New York: Scholastic.
Danziger, P. (1994). *Amber Brown is not a crayon*. New York: Putnam.
Denim, S. (1994). *The dumb bunnies*. New York: Scholastic.
Fox, M. (1986). *Hattie and the fox*. New York: Bradbury Press.
Freedman, R. (1990). *The Wright brothers: How they invented the airplane*. New York: Holiday.
Gelman, R. (1987). *More spaghetti, I say*. New York: Scholastic.
George, J. C. (1995). *Everglades*. New York: HarperCollins.
Golenbock, P. (1990). *Teammates*. San Diego, CA: Harcourt Brace Jovanovich.
Howe, D., & Howe, J. (1979). *Bunnicula*. New York: Atheneum.
Howe, J. (1997). *Pinky and Rex and the new neighbors*. New York: Atheneum.
Jackson, D. M. (1996). *The bone detectives: How forensic anthropologists solve crimes and uncover mysteries of the dead*. Boston: Little, Brown.
Krull, K. (1998). *Lives of the presidents: Fame, shame (and what the neighbors thought)*. San Diego, CA: Harcourt Brace.
Levine, G. C. (1997). *Ella enchanted*. New York: HarperCollins.
Lovett, S. (1996). *Extremely weird primates*. Santa Fe, NM: John Muir.
Marshall, E. (1983). *Fox on wheels*. New York: Dial.
McDonald, M. (1990). *Is this a house for a hermit crab?* New York: Orchard Books.
McKenna, C. O. (1991). *Fifth grade: Here comes trouble*. New York: Scholastic.
Myers, W. D. (1988). *Scorpions*. New York: HarperCollins.
Myers, W. D. (1990). *The mouse rap*. New York: HarperCollins.
Naylor, P. R. (1991). *Shiloh*. New York: Atheneum.
Sachar, L. (1987). *There's a boy in the girls' bathroom*. New York: Knopf.
Sachar, L. (1994). *Marvin Redpost: Alone in his teacher's house*. New York: Random House.
Scieszka, J. (1992). *The stinky cheese man and other fairly stupid tales*. New York: Viking.
Scieszka, J. (1995). *2095*. New York: Scholastic.
Shaw, C. G. (1947). *It looked like spilt milk*. New York: Harper.
Smith, R. K. (1972). *Chocolate fever*. New York: Coward, McCann & Geoghegan.
Spinelli, J. (1990). *Maniac Magee*. New York: Scholastic.
Spinner, S. (1982). *Dracula (Bullseye Chillers, No. 1)*. New York: Random House.
Yee, W. H. (1992). *Eek! There's a mouse in the house*. Boston: Houghton Mifflin.

REFERENCES

Afflerbach, P. (1993a). STAIR: A system for recording and using what we observe and know about our students. *The Reading Teacher, 47*, 260–263.
Afflerbach, P. (1993b). Report cards and reading. *The Reading Teacher, 46*, 453–465.
Allington, R. L. (1977). If they don't read much, how they ever gonna get good? *Journal of Reading, 21*, 57–61.
Anderson, M. A., Tollefson, N. A., & Gilbert, E. C. (1985). Giftedness and reading: A cross-sectional view of differences in reading attitudes and behaviors. *Gifted Child Quarterly, 29*, 186–189.

Anderson, R. C., Wilson, P. T., & Fielding, L. G. (1988). Growth in reading and how children spend their time outside school. *Reading Research Quarterly, 23*(3), 285–303.

Carlsen, R., & Sherrill, A. (1988). *Voices of readers: How we come to love books.* Urbana, IL: National Council of Teachers of English.

Cline, R. K. L., & Kretke, G. L. (1980). An evaluation of long-term SSR in the junior high school. *Journal of Reading, 23,* 502–506.

Csikszentmihalyi, M. (1990). Literacy and intrinsic motivation. *Daedalus, 119,* 115–140.

Fielding, L., & Roller, C. (1992). Making difficult books accessible and easy books acceptable. *The Reading Teacher, 45,* 673–685.

Fink, R. (1995–1996). Successful dyslexics: A constructivist study of passionate interest reading. *Journal of Adolescent and Adult Literacy, 39,* 263–280.

Greaney, V., & Clarke, M. (1973). A longitudinal study of the effects of two reading methods on leisure-time reading. In D. Moyle (Ed.), *Reading: What of the future?* (pp. 107–114). London: United Kingdom Reading Association.

Ivey, G., & Broaddus, K. (in press). "Just plain reading": A survey of what makes students want to read in Middle School classrooms. *Reading Research Quarterly.*

Johnston, P., & Allington, R. L. (1991). Remediation. In R. Barr, M. L. Kamil, P. Mosenthal, & P. D. Pearson (Eds.), *Handbook of reading research* (Vol. 2, pp. 984–1012). New York: Longman.

Johnston, P. N., & Winograd, P. H. (1985). Passive failure in reading. *Journal of Reading Behavior, 17,* 279–301.

Mackey, M. (1990). Filling the gaps: The Babysitters Club, the series book, and the learning reader. *Language Arts, 67,* 484–489.

McKenna, M. C., Kear, D. J., & Ellsworth, R. A. (1995). Children's attitudes toward reading: A national survey. *Reading Research Quarterly, 30*(4), 934–955.

Morris, D. (1999). *The Howard Street tutoring manual: Teaching at-risk readers in the primary grades.* New York: Guilford Press.

Mullis, I., Campbell, J., & Farstrup, A. (1993). *NAEP 1992: Reading report card for the nation and the states.* Williams, DC: U.S. Department of Education.

Nell, V. (1988). *Lost in a book: The psychology of reading for pleasure.* New Haven, CT: Yale University Press.

Pilgreen, J., & Krashen, S. (1993). Sustained silent reading with English as a second language high school students: Impact on reading comprehension, reading frequency, and reading enjoyment. *School Library Media Quarterly, 22,* 21–23.

Worthy, J., Turner, M., & Moorman, M. (1998). The precarious place of self-selected reading. *Language Arts, 75,* 296–304.

CHAPTER 5

Building Reading Fluency

John Mendoza, a fourth grader, attends a small elementary school in a mostly Mexican American community in a large urban school district. He can understand fourth-grade textbooks and grade level novels like *Tales of a Fourth Grade Nothing* (Blume, 1972), and can identify the majority of common grade-level words like *excellent* and *amazing*. Given enough time, he can use phonics and spelling patterns to decode multisyllable words like *circulation* and *manufacture*. A recent informal reading inventory, given at his teacher's request, showed that John was able to decode and comprehend a fourth-grade-level reading passage. However, this information may have been somewhat misleading. In reading the passage, John's rate was extremely slow; his reading was labored and choppy; he repeated many words and phrases; and he read with little expression and energy.

Although he is able to get through fourth-grade materials, John is not a *fluent* reader. While John has always been a hard-working student, doing well in school through the primary grades, his work is beginning to suffer the effects of his limited fluency. John's teacher says that he is often one of the last students to finish reading, and sometimes his follow-up assignments indicate a fuzzy understanding of what he's read. He made A's and B's in reading through the third grade, but this grading period he is barely able to maintain a C. He used to pick up a sports book or car magazine to read during free time, but now he has begun to avoid reading. According to his mother, John spends so much time on his homework that he hardly has time to do anything else. He rarely reads at home outside of homework. His limited fluency is beginning to interfere with his self-confidence and attitudes toward reading.

It seems likely that without intervention, John's reading difficulties will increase through the middle and high school years as the volume and demands of text continue to grow. Ironically, the most important activity in improving fluency—just reading—is becoming lower and lower on John's list of priorities. If you were John's teacher, what kinds of instructional activities would you use to help John improve his fluency and regain his enjoyment of reading?

WHAT'S IN THIS CHAPTER?

WHAT IS FLUENCY AND WHY IS IT IMPORTANT?

We all know fluent reading when we hear it, but what exactly is fluency? *Fluency* is integrally related to comprehension and is a critical component of successful reading, but even reading researchers don't agree on a single definition. In fact, fluency is not a simple concept (Rasinski, 1986). Like music, it consists not only of *rate*, *accuracy*, and *automaticity*, but also of *phrasing* and *expression*. Fluency gives language its musical quality, its rhythm and flow. Fluent oral readers make reading sound effortless; their smoothness and expression help their listeners to comprehend and become engaged. Although the term *fluency* usually refers to oral reading, a fluent reader can read silently and independently, with virtually no comprehension glitches.

Accurate word identification is an obvious structural foundation of fluent reading. Just as musicians learn common chords and melodic sequences, young readers must have a core vocabulary of common, high-frequency words, along with graphophonic skills and context strategies for identifying and understanding the meaning of new words. Meaningful reading and writing experiences that provide practice in appropriate texts help the reader to achieve automatic word identification or *automaticity*, just as practicing scales and musical pieces helps the musician to develop expertise. As the reader begins to group words together meaningfully, there is a gradual transition from "word-by-word" reading to *phrasal* reading, which more closely resembles oral language (Bear, 1991; Clay & Imlach, 1971). As automaticity develops, the reader is able to focus attention primarily on meaning rather than on features of print (Adams, 1990; Samuels, 1994; Chall, 1979; Ehri & Wilce, 1983; Stanovich, 1980), and the stage is set for *rapid reading*—a key component of fluent reading. However, just as it is possible to play a musical piece with technical accuracy but limited feeling and flow, it is possible to read with accuracy, speed, and appropriate phrasing but without fluency and understanding (Aaron, 1989; Worthy & Invernizzi, 1996). In order to put the final touches on fluent reading, a reader must comprehend and interpret text. This includes reading with appropriate timing, expressiveness, stress, and intonation (Dowhower, 1991; Strecker, Roser, & Martinez, 1999).

ELEMENTARY AND MIDDLE SCHOOL CLASSROOMS
THAT FOSTER READING FLUENCY

Fluency begins to develop with home literacy experiences and continues throughout the school years and even into adulthood (Pikulski, 1991). A classroom that fosters fluent reading development is full of interesting, well-written materials on every topic imaginable. Reading is available in a variety of formats, and materials include a wide range of difficulty levels. Instruction and texts are purposeful and interesting; the atmosphere is positive and engaging; and there are many opportunities to read and explore books individually and with peers. Teachers read aloud with expression, introduce students to interesting materials, share their enthusiasm for reading, and provide abundant successful experiences. An observer in such a classroom would know immediately that reading is a valued activity, and would see students involved and excited about learning.

WHY SOME STUDENTS DON'T DEVELOP ADEQUATE FLUENCY

Students who have limited early literacy experiences, who have difficulty learning to read, and/or who do not engage in voluntary reading may have problems developing fluency. After the primary grades, students are expected to read independently. As the amount of reading expands and the difficulty of the reading material increases, dysfluent readers have a hard time keeping up with schoolwork and often find themselves in increasing academic difficulty even if they have previously done well in school. Students with inadequate fluency are also likely to avoid reading because of fear of failure and negative attitudes. Students who don't read don't "get good" at reading (Allington, 1977; Anderson, Wilson, & Fielding, 1988); students who aren't good at reading don't read; and so it goes. Students who avoid reading have less exposure to the ideas and vocabulary in books and may be in danger of losing intellectual as well as academic ground (Stanovich, 1986). Thus, for these students, attention to fluency is critical. Instruction focusing on fluency, however, is found in few intervention programs and rarely in classroom reading programs (Hoffman, 1987; National Reading Panel, 2000; Zutell & Rasinski, 1991). Even when classroom contexts and experiences are rich, many students will need instruction and experiences that specifically target the development of fluency. Since fluency is dependent upon the meaningful interpretation of text, all students, including skilled readers, will benefit from instruction targeted toward fluency.

TRADITIONAL FLUENCY INSTRUCTION

The most common types of fluency instruction target rate and accuracy. While research studies have documented the effectiveness of addressing these components (National Reading Panel, 2000), there is danger that these narrow foci may give students the impression that reading is about "saying all the words right" and reading quickly. Students need to understand that the goal of all reading is constructing meaning. Unfortunately, much of the remedial instruction provided to struggling readers focuses on specific skills and other nonacademic activities, rather than on reading for meaning (Johnston & Allington, 1991).

Unrehearsed Oral Reading

One of the most common reading practices in language arts and content area classes is *unrehearsed oral reading* (sometimes called *round-robin reading* or "popcorn" reading), in which students read, usually unrehearsed, an excerpt from a text, while the rest of the class (theoretically) listens and follows along (see Box 5.1).

Round-robin reading focuses almost entirely upon accurate reading, rather than on constructing meaning. Reading text excerpts out loud is not a purposeful activity because it is not something "real readers" do, unless they are performing or sharing their favorite part of a story. In our opinion, round-robin reading does not benefit students. In fact, it is potentially damaging in many ways (Allington, 1983; Hoffman & Isaacs, 1991). Skilled readers are often bored by the slow pace and can sense the frustration of their classmates. Ryan, a seventh grader, explains that it takes the "slow people forever to get it done," so he volunteers to read and "get it done with." Mara, a fifth grader, says, "I get sick of listening, so I just read ahead. I'd rather just read it myself." For challenged readers, being forced to read aloud in class from frustrational-level material can be devastating. In the literacy autobiographies of preservice teachers, we have seen the enduring, damaging effects of practices such as round robin reading. Charles's memory (described in Box 5.2) makes a poignant statement and a convincing case for the abandonment of this outdated practice.

Just Say No: Alternatives to Round-Robin Reading

There are many superior alternatives to round-robin reading and other forms of unrehearsed oral reading. The best alternative depends upon the intended purpose of the reading activity. Very candid teachers tells us that one purpose of round-robin reading is "crowd control"—keeping students quiet, manageable, and (by appearances) involved. More academic reasons include assessing students' reading, ensuring that all students have access to the ideas in the text before discussing it, and practicing oral reading. Many teachers use round-robin reading when they work with small groups of students in a guided reading format. Although teachers who use round-robin reading have good intentions, we find that such reading is rarely effective for any of these purposes. When we observe the practice in classrooms (see Box 5.1), a close look shows that the teacher's control is tenuous and that it is often necessary to exhort students to follow along and pay attention. Students who are not actively reading are rarely listening or following in the text. Instead, they are practicing

---

BOX 5.1. What Really Happens during Round-Robin Reading?

You've just walked into a fifth-grade classroom. The students are sitting at their desks, each holding a copy of E. L. Konigsburg's Newbery Award-Winning novel, *The View from Saturday* (1996). Jessie is reading out loud from the book in a halting, nervous voice. She briefly hesitates on the word *superintendent*, and before she has time to open her mouth again, Mario supplies the word. "Let her try it," says the teacher, as Jessie shoots Mario an angry look. Jake's and Lupe's eyes are heavy with sleep, and Ally is hunched over her desk with her jacket covering her head and face; none of the three have their books open. "Follow along," says the teacher. Lakeisha is called on to read next, but she does not know where to begin because she has been reading ahead in the book. "Listen and pay attention," the teacher scolds. This scene continues for 20 minutes.

**BOX 5.2. A Future Teacher's Painful Memory of Round-Robin Reading
(by Charles)**

Most of my early reading experiences were very bad. Because I was a bad reader, I didn't like to read in front of anyone, because I was embarrassed. But my elementary teacher insisted that everyone read three sentences in front of the class. Whenever it was my turn to read, I would get cold sweats. I was so frustrated because I could only figure out maybe three words out of a sentence. So when I would try to read to the class, *everyone* would laugh at me. I would always try to sound words out, waiting for the teacher to go ahead and tell me the word. That experience alone inflicted deep scars on me. Still to this day (even though I am a pretty good reader now), I get nervous when I have to read out loud. But I am happy to say that I have learned from my experiences that I will never put a student through what I went through.

---

the paragraph that they will be reading, reading ahead in the text, correcting the reader's mistakes, or staring into space. We rarely see teachers take notes about children's reading or use the information to modify instruction. Furthermore, because of the range of reading levels within every classroom, some students are reading material that is above their instructional level. Frustrational-level reading does not improve oral reading fluency and can lead to negative feelings about reading (Hoffman & Isaacs, 1991; Zutell & Rasinski, 1991). Even when students are reading in instructional-level guided reading groups, only one student is reading while the others are not. This wastes valuable instruction time. There are many more effective and engaging means, described in this chapter and in this book as a whole, to accomplish any purpose a teacher might have for unrehearsed oral reading (see Box 5.3). If fluency is your goal, this chapter is devoted to practices that help students to improve their oral and silent reading fluency.

PURPOSEFUL INSTRUCTION
THAT TARGETS FLUENCY DEVELOPMENT

All forms of fluency instruction need to focus on comprehension. For students who struggle with reading, having authentic purposes is also crucial. It is important for instructional activities to have a clear purpose, and for the purpose to match the students' needs and interests. The forms of fluency instruction we describe here are as follows:

- Focused instruction in the components of fluency
- Modeled reading (choral and echo, books on tape)
- Repeated reading
- Reading performance (e.g., Readers' Theater)
- Reading to younger children or peers
- Reading series books and thematically related texts
- Making the transition to independent reading through sustained reading in manageable texts

BOX 5.3. Alternatives to Round-Robin Reading

If your purpose is . . .	Suggested instructional approaches
• Assessing oral reading	• Observe and listen to students reading individually in manageable texts; use oral reading analysis (see Chapters 1 and 4).
• Managing student behavior	• Present purposeful, engaging instruction and use interesting, engaging materials (see Chapters 2–9).
• Providing access to grade-level ideas and concepts for struggling readers	• Read challenging material aloud to students, providing a good model of expressive reading, as well as access to text (see Chapter 3). Make available books on tape or through paired reading; use materials of varying levels of difficulty for content areas (see Chapters 1, 2, and 4, and this chapter).
• Guiding students in reading instructional-level texts	• Have students read the text silently. Students can share a favorite (rehearsed) passage with the group and/or with the teacher (see Chapter 4 and this chapter).
• Helping students to build oral reading fluency	• Use Readers' Theater, modeling, explicit instruction, and other instructional activities described in this chapter.

Focused Instruction in Components of Fluency

Awareness of one's thought processes is called *metacognition*. Expert readers naturally monitor their understanding as they read, and use strategies such as rereading, predicting, summarizing, visualizing, and connecting to previous knowledge. When comprehension breaks down, expert readers are aware of their difficulty, and they take steps to solve the problem. Metacognitive strategy instruction in reading is designed to heighten students' awareness of reading processes, to teach and guide practice in strategies, and to help students become independent in monitoring their understanding. Readers become more effective in deciding what strategies to use, as well as when, where, and how to apply them. Explicit or focused strategy instruction has become a basic part of instruction in both word identification and comprehension (see Chapters 3, 4, and 7). However, metacognitive instruction is not a common practice when it comes to fluency (Strecker et al., 1999). Although the metacognitive aspects of fluency instruction should be part of instruction at any level, it seems particularly important for readers beyond the beginning stages to understand the purposes of fluency instruction. Students need to recognize that they are partners in the learning process, and that the teacher is available as a coach or consultant rather than as the director or sole bearer of information. Students who feel in control of their own learning and who know why fluency is important are more likely to engage in the sorts of repeated practice that lead to improved fluency, and eventually to learn how to adapt their reading to different situations and texts.

A minilesson format is helpful for teaching different aspects of fluency, but it is important that students understand the big picture before focusing on a specific compo-

nent. A minilesson on reading with expression—
using the book *Miss Nelson Is Missing* (Allard,
1977), for example—might begin with a read-
aloud, with the teacher demonstrating fluent
reading to students. This book is about Miss Nelson, a lovely, sweet teacher who plays a trick on
her unruly students by becoming every student's
nightmare teacher, Miss Viola Swamp. It is perfect for demonstrating how to read dialogue with
appropriate voice and expression based on character interpretation. The process begins with
modeling and discussion, with the teacher asking
students to listen carefully to her reading of the
voices of Miss Nelson (soft and syrupy sweet)
and Viola Swamp (loud and gravelly), and then
talking about how and why she read the voices
differently. The next step is guided practice, in
which students practice reading the parts them-

selves and the teacher provides feedback (e.g., "Miss Swamp, can you sound even
meaner?"). Finally, for independent practice, students may practice individually or in
groups reading other dialogue from *Miss Nelson* or other books with lively characters
and dialogue (e.g., Thaler's [1989] *The Teacher from the Black Lagoon*, Lester's [1988] *Tacky
the Penguin*). Other minilessons might focus on reading dialect, using, for example, *Roll
of Thunder, Hear My Cry* (Taylor, 1976). While learning and practicing other components
of fluency, students can continue to refine previously taught aspects. Explicit instruction in the components of fluency should be combined with opportunities to practice
oral reading fluency using manageable texts.

Modeled Reading

In *modeled reading*, students listen to an expert read, usually following the print, and either repeat the text (*echo reading*) or read along with the expert reader (*choral reading*).
Benefits of modeled reading include gains in rate, accuracy, phrasing, segmentation,
and expression (Chomsky, 1978; Dowhower, 1987; Schreiber, 1987). Modeled reading
also supports students in reading and engaging with texts that they may not be able to
handle independently, and thus enhances comprehension development. Holdaway's
(1979) shared reading approach is an example of modeled reading that is used widely
in primary grades. Shared reading is excellent for beginning readers, but it is not typically used beyond the primary grades, as most students will be moving toward independent reading. Even if they still have limited skill, some older students may be impa-
tient with the approach. However, even in upper elementary and middle school, shared
reading can be used for the purpose of helping students learn how to "season" their
oral reading with expression and to change voices for different characters.

Poetry is a natural means of building fluency because it is designed to be read
aloud, and because poets play with elements of oral language, including rhyme,
rhythm, and stress. In her sixth-, seventh-, and eighth-grade Title I reading classes, Gay
Ivey introduced a "poem of the week" each Monday, which she copied onto chart pa-

per and hung on the wall. Each class period started off with a choral reading of the poem. Students liked rereading fun poems such as Silverstein's "They Put a Brassiere on the Camel" (in *A Light in the Attic*, 1981) and "Sarah Cynthia Sylvia Stout Would Not Take the Garbage Out" (in *Where the Sidewalk Ends*, 1974). By the end of the week, the students sounded like experts, and many were able to recite the poems by heart. See Box 5.4 for a sample of poetry collections, including humorous poetry and poetry from a variety of cultures.

Books on tape also provide models of fluent reading for students. Using books on tape allows students access to a wide range of texts for independent listening and practice. Taped books "encourage less able readers to use the meaning of the language to help them decode, increase fluency and comprehend," and give second-language learners "an opportunity to hear the rhythm of the language" (Barr & Johnson, 1991, p. 403). It is important, however, that students understand their task and learn the procedures well enough to do them independently, and that teachers have a system for monitoring comprehension and progress. When they have learned the procedures, students can listen to tapes during free-reading time, during center or seatwork time, or at

---

BOX 5.4. Poetry for Modeled Reading and Performance

For All Ages

Adoff, A. (1995). *Street music: City poems*. New York: HarperCollins.

Bruchac, J., & London, J. (1992). *Thirteen moons on Turtle's back: A Native American year of moons*. New York: Philomel.

Cole, J., & Calmenson, S. (Eds.). (1990). *Miss Mary Mack and other children's street rhymes*. New York: Beech Tree.

Greenfield, E. (1991). *Night on Neighborhood Street*. New York: Dial.

Hopkins, L. B. (Ed.). (1987). *More surprises*. New York: Harper & Row.

Kuskin, K. (1992). *Soap soup and other verses*. New York: HarperCollins.

Nye, N. S. (1992). *This same sky: A collection of poems from around the world*. New York: Four Winds Press.

Prelutsky, J. (1984). *The new kid on the block*. New York: Greenwillow.

Schwartz, A. (1989). *I saw you in the bathtub*. New York: Harper & Row.

Rylant, C. (1984). *Waiting to waltz: A childhood*. Scarsdale, NY: Bradbury Press.

Silverstein, S. (1981). *A light in the attic*. New York: Harper & Row.

Soto, G. (1992). *Neighborhood odes*. San Diego, CA: Harcourt Brace.

Viorst, J. (1981). *If I were in charge of the world and other worries*. New York: Atheneum.

Vozar, D. (1993). *Yo, hungry wolf!: A nursery rap*. New York: Doubleday.

Worth, V. (1994). *All the small poems and fourteen more*. New York: Farrar, Straus, Giroux.

For Fifth Grade and Above

Carlson, L. M. (Ed.). (1994). *Cool salsa: Bilingual poems on growing up Latino in the United States*. New York: Holt.

Dahl, R. (1983). *Roald Dahl's revolting rhymes*. New York: Knopf.

Hughes, L. (1994). *The dream keeper and other poems*. New York: Knopf.

home, and practice rereading the text silently. Our adaptation of Barr and Johnson's suggested approach, based on Chomsky's (1978) method of repeated reading, is shown in Box 5.5. Taped reading is a great "combination approach" for focusing simultaneously on fluency and independent silent reading.

Repeated Reading

Perhaps the most common form of fluency instruction is repeated reading. Very young children love to share the same stories repeatedly, and early readers refine their skill by practicing the same text again and again. Repeated reading capitalizes on these natural tendencies and builds familiarity and "ownership" of stories. Other benefits of repeated reading include improved word recognition, comprehension, phrasing, and transfer of fluency improvement to new material (Carver & Hoffman, 1981; National Reading Panel, 2000).

There are several formats for repeated reading. Most involve text that is easy to understand and provides an appropriate balance of success and challenge in word recognition. The teacher reads the text aloud, discusses it with students, and provides support until students can read it independently. Next, students reread the text until they reach an appropriate level of accuracy and speed. Remember that many older students are not eager to reread the same texts without a specific purpose. Some teachers let students use a stopwatch, time their own reading, and graph their gradual increases in rate, and this is more motivating for some. However, using a stopwatch can also be stressful, and the novelty often wears out. Box 5.6 presents a formula for calculating rate, along with guidelines for oral reading rates. Be aware that reading rates will be different in various kinds of texts and reading contexts (see Chapter 1 and Box 1.7 for more information).

How different is your own reading rate for pleasure reading and for obtaining information from text? Select excerpts of about 500 words from a novel you would read

---

BOX 5.5. Modeled Reading with Taped Texts

1. Choose books that students will enjoy, written at the instructional level or slightly above.

2. Read the book at a steady but not too rapid pace, with directions to turn pages accompanied by page numbers. Commercial tapes can be used if they match the printed text (i.e., do not use abridged versions) and if they are not read too quickly.

3. Explain to students that the purpose of this activity is to increase their reading fluency and to assist them in reading more difficult books. Explain and model the procedures, and monitor students until they have learned them.

4. Explain to students that they should first listen to an entire chapter or other agreed-upon segment. Then they can rewind the tape and read along with the voice.

5. Help students to set a purpose for reading that fosters comprehension monitoring. For example, tell students that they will retell the story to a peer.

6. When beginning a new text, check students' reading and comprehension after they have listened to part of the tape. If comprehension and fluency are adequate, students can continue on their own.

for pleasure and from a fairly difficult textbook. Read each excerpt silently for under-standing, and record the number of seconds it took to read it. Calculate your rate, using the formula and guidelines in Box 5.6. What is your rate of reading in each text? Now compare the differences in your silent and oral reading rates, using different excerpts from the same texts.

Repeated reading is not enough, however. Because of the complexity of reading in the older grades, varied strategies are important. Many of the approaches described in this chapter are built upon repeated reading for authentic purposes.

Reading Performance

The most successful and motivating fluency builder we have found is reading perfor-mance. Students rehearse a poem, joke, story, Readers' Theater script, speech, or other appropriate text until they can read it with fluency, and then they perform it in some way. In most classrooms, where performance is limited to special occasions, struggling readers are rarely given speaking parts—a situation that reinforces their already low self-confidence. When reading performance becomes a regular part of the reading pro-gram, as in the classroom described in Box 5.7, all students have an opportunity to practice and to perform successfully. Self-confidence and motivation are "fueled by

---

BOX 5.6. Calculating and Evaluating Reading Rate

Measuring Reading Rate in Words per Minute

Count the number of words in the passage. Using a stopwatch or a watch with a second hand, re-cord the number of seconds taken to read the passage. Use the following formula to calculate words per minute:

$$\text{Words per minute} = \frac{\text{Number of Words} \times 60}{\text{Number of seconds}}$$

Note: If your stopwatch registers minutes and seconds, convert the minutes to seconds before cal-culating the rate. For example, 1 minute and 24 seconds equals 84 seconds.

**Guidelines for Silent Reading Rates in Instructional-Level Text
(Reading Levels 1–6)**

Reading level	Vacca, Vacca, & Gove (2000)	Guszak (1998)*
1	80	60
2	90	70
3	110	80
4	140	90 (fourth
5	160	and up)
6	180	

*Guszak's suggested rates for *independent*-level text are 20 points higher (e.g., level 1 = 80).

BOX 5.7. Performance Activities in Dora Jarrard's Sixth-Grade Class

Dora Jarrard, a middle school teacher in Georgia, values fluency development in all her sixth-grade students. Each week Mrs. Jarrard includes authentic activities in which students can practice their oral reading. Sometimes these activities are not connected to any particular thematic study. For example, students may be divided into small groups to practice reading and to perform selections from *Fables* (Lobel, 1980) just for enjoyment. At other times, these activities are connected to topics the class is studying. For example, when they studied traditional and contemporary fairy tales, Mrs. Jarrard's students were captivated by *Roald Dahl's Revolting Rhymes* (Dahl, 1983), a poetry collection that parodies old favorites such as "Cinderella" and "Little Red Riding Hood and the Wolf," and that begs to be read aloud. As a way to practice fluent reading, to enjoy these hilarious poems, and to include these selections in their larger fairy tale study, Mrs. Jarrard divided her class of 30 students into groups of 5, and each group was responsible for presenting one poem to the class. Students had 3 days (approximately 15 minutes each day) to prepare for the performance. Each group presented its poem to the laughter and applause of the rest of the class.

The experience and the class's response were especially gratifying for the struggling readers in the class, who were able to read and interpret for their classmates a relatively difficult and very entertaining text. But in this activity and others, average and high-achieving readers also benefit from fluency practice and the opportunity to make personal decisions about how a character might be portrayed. Some of the most confident and accurate readers in Mrs. Jarrard's class tend to read too quickly, with little expression and little attention to punctuation. Practice and performance gives these students a chance to refine and season their oral reading, emphasizing the importance of fluency.

successful experiences" (Measley, 1990, p. 598). Performance is an inherently meaningful, purposeful vehicle for fluency improvement and instruction, and it incorporates explicit instruction, modeling, and repeated reading. Effective performances are built upon positive social interactions focused on reading, in which modeling and feedback are natural components of rehearsals. Thus repeated reading becomes a meaningful and motivating activity. Reading performance encourages students to read at an *appropriate* rate rather than simply to read indiscriminately faster without regard to the text's meaning. When students are able to interpret and read texts with appropriate expression, their comprehension is clear. When they read and interpret texts regularly and listen to others' reading and interpretations, they make progress in all aspects of reading.

In Readers' Theater, students perform a play (a book or other text adapted in script form) by reading it aloud to an audience. Props are used sparingly, as the focus is on reading fluently to convey meaning. Because the level of difficulty of different parts within a script can vary widely, Readers' Theater is an excellent activity for grouping students by interest rather than reading level. It is critical, however, for students to take parts that they can read successfully.

Preparing for Performances

It is important that students practice until they can read their parts with fluency. Ample rehearsal time makes the difference for struggling readers in any kind of performance, as they can decide when they are ready to perform. Some struggling readers or reserved students initially may not want to perform in front of a group, but most lose their fear with opportunities to practice a script with a teacher, tutor, or friends in a safe atmosphere. Each success leads to increased self-confidence and to motivation to repeat the success. Shown in Box 5.8 is a possible sequence of rehearsal that can be used by elementary (Martinez, Roser, & Strecker, 1998) and middle school (Ivey, 1999) teachers. The students plan, practice, and perform new texts as often as every week. The sequences incorporate all of our suggested practices for fluency instruction, as well as the important instructional features of demonstration, guided practice, independent practice, feedback, and performance. It is also important to remember that, as in all group and independent work, students and teachers will need time to plan and establish routines and appropriate behavior. It may take several weeks of explaining, role modeling, and guided practice before such activities run smoothly. As students learn what is needed to prepare for a successful performance, they are motivated to work and practice together productively. This frees the teacher to move around from group to group, listening and offering feedback as students practice.

Readers' Theater *can* be a structured activity, as described in Box 5.8; however, it is also important for students to participate in less structured dramatic activities that do

---

BOX 5.8. Preparing for Performances

A 5-day cycle for elementary school

Advanced preparation: Teacher and students select or write scripts (one for each group), based on children's interests, topics of study in the classroom, and reading levels.

Day 1: Teacher reads aloud the books for enjoyment and discussion, and to provide a model of fluency. Scripts are handed out. Students read scripts in class with teacher support and take them home to practice.

Day 2: Students read through the scripts orally in small groups, using scripts with specific parts highlighted. Each student takes a different part for each reading. Teacher moves from group to group, giving feedback on fluency and interpretation.

Day 3: Students practice with their groups. At the end of this day, students in each group choose parts for the performance and rehearse their own parts at home.

Day 4: Students rehearse their own parts and decide how to present the performance. Teacher is available for support and advice.

Day 5: Groups perform for the class and/or for other audiences.

A 3-day cycle for middle school

Advanced preparation: Students choose or write scripts, poems, or other texts. Teacher advises small groups in selecting texts to perform.

Day 1: Students meet in small groups and read texts several times individually or in pairs. If necessary, each group decides how to divide the text into parts for individual reading, and students practice their parts silently. Teacher is available for consultation and support.

Day 2: In small groups, students read their assigned parts orally in preparation for performance, offering one another constructive feedback and help with difficult words. Teacher also gives feedback to each group on fluency and interpretation.

Day 3: Students are given additional practice time, and then each group performs.

not necessarily culminate in formal performances. Informal performance can take a variety of forms. For example, Grace Young gives her third graders time once a week to experiment with performance in small groups. Some groups spend the time reading aloud favorite or new scripts; others develop their own ways of performing texts, including role playing and improvisation.

Choosing and Writing Texts for Performance

There are several books and Web sites devoted to Readers' Theater. Many teachers start with these resources, but soon find that they need to supplement what is currently available by writing their own scripts. According to Martinez et al. (1998), texts chosen for performance should have straightforward plots that present characters working through dilemmas. It is also helpful to use books from a series or by the same author, to capitalize on familiar plot structures, language, and characters. Many scripts practically "write themselves" when they are based on books with dialogue interspersed with short segments of narration. Good examples are Edward Marshall's *Fox* books (e.g., *Fox at School*—Marshall, 1983) and James Marshall's *George and Martha* books (e.g., *George and Martha Back in Town*—Marshall, 1984). Picture book versions of folk and fairy tales, such as Galdone's (1973) *The Little Red Hen*, also provide a straightforward framework when dialogue is turned into speaking parts and description into narration. Tales written in verse, such as Zemach's (1969) *The Judge* and Minters's (1994) *Cinder-Elly* can be read straight from the books or turned into scripts. As the teacher reads the book aloud, the illustrations provide a context, which allows students to understand the setting of the story and provides support for interpreting characterization.

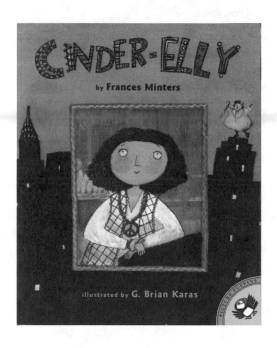

Poetry and speeches also provide performance-ready formats and meaningful contexts in which to focus on fluency. Both lend themselves to rhythmic choral reading as well as to independent and group performance. It is also important for students to hear models on tape of gifted speakers such as Maya Angelou and Martin Luther King, Jr., as well as to be exposed to speeches and debates during election times. Commercials, sports announcers, and actors also provide models for expressive speaking. Through studying these performances, students learn how a speaker conveys meaning and inspiration through carefully chosen words and prosodic language, and how an effective speaker can influence emotions and votes. Box 5.9 shows performance-ready and easy-to-script sources for performance reading, categorized by sophistication of text and

BOX 5.9. Performance-Ready and Easy-to-Script Resources for Performance

Performance-Ready Materials

Dahl, R. (1983). *Charlie and the chocolate factory: A play*. New York: Puffin. (Fifth grade and up.)

Niccol, A. (1998). *The Truman show: The shooting script*. New York: Newmarket Press. (Middle school and up.)

Pugliano, C. (1997). *Easy to read folk and fairy tale plays*. New York: Scholastic. (Easy and short; first- to third-grade reading levels.)

Shepard, A. (1997, April 14). *Aaron Shepard's RT page*. http:/www.aaronshep.com. (Written on a range of difficulty levels, from third grade to high school.)

Soto, G. (1997). *Novio boy: A play*. New York: Harcourt Brace. (Fifth grade and up.)

Books for All Ages

Allard, H. (1985). *Miss Nelson is missing*. Boston: Houghton Mifflin.

Brown, M. (1989). *Arthur's teacher trouble*. Boston: Little, Brown.

Fox, M. (1986). *Hattie and the fox*. New York: Bradbury Press.

Galdone, P. (1973). *The little red hen*. New York: Seabury Press.

Hall, D. (1994). *I am the dog, I am the cat*. New York: Dial.

Hoose, P., & Hoose, H. (1998). *Hey, little ant*. Berkeley, CA: Tricycle Press.

Klise, K. (1998). *Regarding the fountain: A tale, in letters, of liars and leaks*. New York: Avon.

Lester, H. (1988). *Tacky the penguin*. Boston: Houghton Mifflin.

Marshall, E. (1983). *Fox at school*. New York: Dial.

Marshall, J. (1984). *George and Martha back in town*. Boston: Houghton Mifflin.

Minters, F. (1997). *Cinder-Elly*. New York: Viking.

Raschka, C. (1993). *Yo! Yes?* New York: Scholastic.

Thaler, M. (1989). *The teacher from the black lagoon*. New York: Scholastic.

Scieszka, J. (1992). *The stinky cheese man and other fairly stupid tales*. New York: Viking.

Van Laan, N. (1998). *With a whoop and a holler: A bushel of lore from way down south*. New York: Atheneum.

Zemach, H. (1969). *The judge*. New York: Farrar, Straus, Giroux.

Books for Middle School and Above

Avi. (1991). *Nothing but the truth*. New York: Orchard.

Draper, S. M. (1994). *Tears of a tiger*. New York: Atheneum.

Noyes, A. (1981). *The highwayman* (ill. C. Keeping). New York: Oxford University Press.

---

concepts. As you gain more confidence in writing scripts, you may choose to adapt less straightforward books for performance, condensing the narration and inserting dialogue where appropriate. With initial support from the teacher, students can and should write their own scripts for Readers' Theater, song lyrics, raps, and poetry for performance. For example, Gay Ivey's eighth-grade students enjoyed developing Readers' Theater scripts for favorite scenes from novels they read. Other students presented excerpts from novels, using Readers' Theater as a way to recommend books to their classmates. Documentary novels for older students, including *Regarding the Fountain* (Klise, 1998), *Nothing But the Truth* (Avi, 1991), and *Tears of a Tiger* (Draper, 1994)—which contain mock documents like transcripts, memos, letters, and newspaper articles—can also be transformed into a Readers' Theater format.

Books and poetry related to content area topics in science, history, and math are excellent for improving fluency as well as for supporting growth of conceptual knowledge. Fleischman's (1988) book of poetry about insects, *Joyful Noise: Poems for Two Voices*, is tailor-made for reading performance, as are speeches such as Martin Luther King's "I Have a Dream" speech. Hutchins's (1986) *The Doorbell Rang*, an introduction to fractions; *Math Curse* (Scieszka, 1995); and Cole's *The Magic School Bus* books (e.g., *The Magic School Bus inside the Human Body*—Cole, 1989) can be easily adapted for performances. Books consisting of diary entries and letters, including *Letters from a Slave Girl* (Lyons, 1992) and *The Diary of a Young Girl* (Frank, 1995), also lend themselves to performance scripts and help to bring historical topics to life for students. Content area resources, in order of reading difficulty and sophistication of content, are shown in Box 5.10.

Write your own performance script. Choose a fairy tale or other book (see suggestions in Boxes 5.9 and 5.10) and write a script. Enlist some friends, colleagues, and/or students to help you perform it. Congratulations! You've started your Readers' Theater library. Gather other Readers' Theater resources to include in your library, and get your colleagues and students involved in writing and performing.

BOX 5.10. Resources for Performance in Content Areas

Mathematics

Pinczes, E. J. (1993). *100 hungry ants*. Boston: Houghton Mifflin.
Hutchins, P. (1986). *The doorbell rang*. New York: Greenwillow.
Scieszka, J. (1995). *Math curse*. New York: Viking.

Social Studies

Frank, A. (1995). *The diary of a young girl: The definitive edition*. New York: Doubleday.
King, M. L., Jr. (1997). *I have a dream*. New York: Scholastic.
Lyons, M. E. (1992). *Letters from a slave girl: The story of Harriet Jacobs*. New York: Scribner.
Stevens, L. (1978). *Cesar Chavez: A mini-play*. Stockton, CA: Relevant Instructional Materials.

Science
Carle, E. (Ed.). (1989). *Animals, animals*. New York: Scholastic.
Cole, J. (1989). *The magic school bus inside the human body*. New York: Scholastic.
Fleischman, P. (1985). *I am Phoenix: Poems for two voices*. New York: Harper & Row.
Fleischman, P. (1988). *Joyful noise: Poems for two voices*. New York: Harper & Row.
Koss, A. G. (1987). *Where do fish go in the winter and answers to other great mysteries*. Los Angeles: Price Stern Sloan.

Reading Aloud to Younger Children or to Peers

Mrs. Hammond's fourth-grade class and Mrs. García's first-grade class are "reading buddies." They meet together every Friday afternoon for an hour, during which time the students share books together. On Mondays, students in both classes carefully choose the books they will read with their buddies. They practice reading the chosen texts with partners and independently all week. When Friday comes, the fourth graders go to the primary hall, where their buddies greet them with smiles and hugs. They move right into their special book-sharing time, huddled in pairs around Mrs. García's classroom.

The practice of "buddy reading" encourages even the most reticent students to read out loud, as young beginning readers are nonthreatening. Reading to younger children also opens up more possibilities for choice in literature, allowing older learners to read easy books designed for young children without losing face. This is an especially important time for struggling readers in the older grades, who have an opportunity to read practiced texts with supportive friends and to experience the role of experts in supporting their younger buddies' reading. Students should choose books that they can easily read and that are appropriate and interesting for their younger buddies. To ensure a successful experience, it is essential for students to prepare carefully, with teacher input, before performing a read-aloud (see Box 5.11). It is also essential that older students be paired with students whose reading skills are significantly less ad-

---

BOX 5.11. A Story of the Importance of Practice for Buddy Reading (by Jo Worthy)

During my first year of teaching, I arranged for my third graders to read out loud to a kindergarten class, thinking I was doing a great favor for the teacher. Each afternoon after lunch, one of my students would choose a book and head down to the kindergarten wing. After a week, the teacher told me she wanted to discontinue the Friday readings. To my chagrin, she said that the kindergartners were bored and misbehaved during the readings. After talking to the teacher and my students about the problems, I realized that I had left out the two most crucial steps: (1) helping my students to choose appropriate books; and (2) giving them the time and support to practice their "performances" so they could read fluently. I learned to check with the kindergarten teacher for suggestions of books that would be appropriate and engaging for young children, and to keep the books short and fun to guard against fidgety behavior.

---

vanced than their own. Many a struggling reader has been mortified by not having enough preparation and/or by having a younger buddy correct his or her reading.

Teachers can make special arrangements for middle school students to have this experience as well. Shawn, a seventh-grade student, needed to read easy, repetitive texts to build fluency, but his classroom situation rarely offered opportunities to do so. Shawn's teacher arranged for him to read to a second-grade girl in a nearby elementary school. In preparation, he read and reread books he thought his student might enjoy. Shawn's reading improved drastically, and his mother was thrilled when he began reading voluntarily to his preschool-age sister.

Sharing favorite books with peers is also appealing, especially to less successful and reluctant readers, whose prior experiences with public reading may have consisted mainly of whole-class, round-robin reading of frustrational-level texts. When students have a chance to choose the books, short stories, or poems, they will share, and to rehearse before they read aloud, even struggling readers can feel like competent, valued members of their classroom literacy communities. A related activity is to make a class library of books on tapes by having students choose books, practice them, and then record them on tape. To prepare a tape that is polished enough to be placed in the classroom library, students will naturally want to practice, edit, and reread until they have a "perfect" final copy.

Reading Series Books and Thematically Related Texts

We have found that reading books in a series provides experiences and benefits similar to those of rereading the same text. With the recent proliferation of series books on a multitude of topics and difficulty levels, even reluctant readers can usually find a series that they are willing and able to read (Worthy, 1996). Series books also provide excellent

vehicles for helping students move toward reading longer books for sustained periods of time. Thus they have great potential for improving attitudes toward reading, as well as for increasing voluntary reading, engagement, and fluency. Information series should be included as well (e.g., Parsons's [1990] *Amazing Poisonous Animals* from the *Eyewitness Juniors* series). See Chapter 2 for further discussion of the benefits of series books and other light reading. As long as students are exposed to a broad range of other materials for read-alouds and instruction, teachers should feel free to encourage students to read light materials for free reading. However, remember that many series books and other light materials have sophisticated plots, vocabulary, and characterization, and usu-

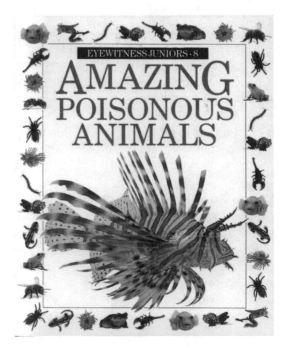

ally lead students to more complex materials (see Chapter 2). In discussing the early reading habits of adult avid readers, Carlsen and Sherrill (1988) concluded that "[light] materials seem to be as much a part of one's literary maturation as are the children's classics" (p. 16).

Like series books, books on the same topic or theme provide repeated exposure to challenging vocabulary, sophisticated concepts, and important details, which transfer to the reading of new texts. Thus reading widely in thematic materials is a good strategy for improving fluency, independent reading, and comprehension in the content areas. It is also important to include other fluency activities when pursuing thematic studies in the classroom, since fluency is so closely tied to comprehension. Approaches such as Readers' Theater give students opportunities to critically examine content material, including interpreting characters' motives in a historical context.

Making the Transition to Independent Reading through Sustained Reading in Manageable Texts

When students read fluently in a variety of appropriate texts, they will have better attitudes toward reading, will choose to read more on their own, and will make more rapid progress. Oral reading fluency sets the stage for students to become independent readers who can learn from and find enjoyment in reading. Silent sustained reading, monitored by teachers, provides a bridge to independent reading (Manning & Manning, 1984; Mullis, Campbell, & Farstrup, 1993). When we interviewed sixth-grade teachers about sustained reading (Worthy, Turner, & Moorman, 1998), many pointed out that simply reading during class was viewed by some parents and administrators (and even other teachers) as enrichment rather than instruction. According to this view, lower-achieving students could not afford to use instructional time for "just reading." As one teacher explained:

> "I remember in my first year of teaching, I didn't do a whole lot of silent reading because I felt like it was wasted time or something. I had this traditional feeling: '15 minutes of just reading? I'm sorry, not in middle school.' "

Another spoke of the pressure of covering skills and preparing for achievement tests:

> "I think what's so hard about this is you think there's not enough time to read . . . then get your grammar and test skills stuff in, and that's what's tough. It's the push for time."

Through reading research, observing their students, and conferring with other literacy professionals, these teachers came to realize that reading in connected text is *the most essential* activity for students' progress, and that grammar and skills practice are a waste of time if not connected to real reading. "Just reading," as discussed in Chapter 4, is not enrichment; rather, it is the center of reading instruction.

Students should read every day in texts that are interesting and manageable, on their independent or instructional reading level. That is, students should be able to easily read approximately 95% or more of the words correctly, and should be able to understand the text without difficulty. Although these criteria may sound simple, typically only the highest-achieving students have abundant access to the types of materials that they can easily read and understand, and that further improve their ability to read independently. In many classrooms, students who read below grade level or who have limited fluency do not have many materials that they can easily read (Lipson & Lang, 1991). Thus, rather than improving reading, sustained reading can be a frustrating experience that can lead to anxiety and avoidance of reading. Box 5.12 describes sustained reading time in a third-grade classroom. Box 5.13 lists the components of an effective independent reading time (Bintz, 1993; Palmer, Codling, & Gambrell, 1994; Worthy et al., 1998). See Chapter 4 for more discussion on independent reading.

BOX 5.12. Sustained Reading Time in Susan Buchanan's Third-Grade Classroom

It is self-selected reading time in Susan Buchanan's third-grade classroom. Several of the students are sitting at tables, reading books from displays corresponding to topics the class is studying (fairy tales and dogs). Susan is supporting two students as they read *The Important Book* (Brown, 1949) for the first time. Later they will reread the book independently. Other students are reading at their desks, under their desks, or lying on the rug with pillows. They are reading a variety of self-selected materials, including *Sports Illustrated for Kids*, short chapter books, series books, information picture books, poetry collections, novels, and a homemade book containing stories written by last year's students. Alana and Jamie are huddled together on a couch; both are reading *There's a Boy in the Girls' Bathroom* (Sachar, 1987). The students are deeply involved in their reading, and the room is mostly quiet for the 35-minute reading time. When she finishes with her *The Important Book* group, Mrs. Buchanan will move around the room asking students about the books they are reading, suggesting books to a resistant reader, and assessing students as they read a page of their book aloud.

Mrs. Buchanan, who is in her second year of teaching, explains that her sustained reading time did not always look like it does now: "It didn't happen overnight. I started by assessing my students' reading strengths and challenges, and found, as most teachers do, that there was a wide range of reading levels." With the help of the librarian and other colleagues, Mrs. Buchanan gathered materials to add to her own growing classroom library. She adds:

"I like reading easy, fun things, and I know how important it is for students to experience success, especially at the beginning of the year. In addition to interesting grade-level texts, I gathered many fun, easy books that everyone could read fluently, and also high-interest books in every genre possible, including old favorites that I knew they had read in second grade. I also established routines for choosing books and for behavior. At first, I helped them choose manageable books. Now they can choose their own books and they do a good job [see Chapter 1]. We began with a 10-minute reading time and gradually increased the time to 35 minutes. Everyone is reading at their level, and improving their fluency and love of reading every day. At the end of every reading time, I give them a few minutes to share the books they are reading with their friends. I also share what I am reading with them, and I make a point of gathering and introducing books that I think they will like. They often choose to read the books that they have heard about from their friends or from me."

BOX 5.13. Components of an Effective Sustained Reading Time

1. Assess students' reading levels and interests.
2. Provide a wide range of materials (levels, genres, and topics), and let students choose the materials they read.
3. Give students informal time to share the books they are reading with their peers.
4. Introduce books to students that you think they will like.
5. Share your enthusiasm about reading with your students.
6. Provide time every day (20 to 45 minutes) for reading.
7. Keep follow-up assignments to a minimum, and give students choices of purposeful response activities rather than busywork.
8. Confer with and support individual students as they read (see Chapter 4).

Note: If you think you do not have time for daily sustained reading, ask yourself this question and answer it honestly: "What am I doing that is *more* important for students' reading development?"

ASSESSING FLUENCY

There are many important reasons for assessing students' fluency in reading. Traditionally, assessment of fluency has been limited to measuring *reading rate* (words per minute) in combination with *accuracy* (words read correctly). As this chapter has shown, there is far more to fluent reading than speed or accuracy. Some students can read quickly and accurately without understanding and/or without appropriate phrasing or expression. However, measuring reading rate can be useful for determining whether a student's reading speed falls within suggested guidelines, what further assessments are appropriate, and whether intervention may be warranted (see Box 5.6). It is important to know that rates can and should vary widely according to the type and difficulty of the text, the context in which the reading takes place, whether the reading is silent or oral, and the purpose for reading. For example, most people find that information text takes more time to read, especially when it contains new information and vocabulary or when the reader's background knowledge does not match the conceptual demands of the text. In addition, many readers have more experience reading narrative than other text structures.

For a more meaningful assessment of fluency, we recommend using a fluency scale or rubric with multidimensional components of fluency. We have based ours (Box 5.14) on the scale produced by the National Assessment of Reading Progress (National Center for Education Statistics, 1995). Another advantage of using a fluency rubric rather than simply a measure of rate and accuracy is that it corresponds to observable reading behaviors and is specific, yet leaves room for teacher judgment. The rubric should be used as a starting point; teachers should consider the text and context in making judgments about fluency. Teachers should explain to students the purpose and procedures for the fluency rubric so that they can use it in self-assessment. Use the scale several times a year to assess students' fluency, and keep records in the students' portfolios. After you have had practice using the scale, you will be able to assess students' fluency in-

---

BOX 5.14. An Oral Reading Fluency Scale
(Modified from the National Assessment of Educational Progress)

- *Level 4*. The student reads with expression throughout most of the text, reading in larger, meaningful phrase groups. Repetitions, hesitations, or mistakes are rare. The student appears very comfortable reading the text.
- *Level 3*. The student reads primarily in longer phrases that preserve the author's syntax. Although there may be occasional hesitations, repetitions, and miscues, most words are identified or decoded automatically. The student is beginning to read with expression and more comfort.
- *Level 2*. The student is beginning to identify more words automatically and to read in short phrases. Some word-by-word reading continues. The student reads with little or no expression, and there may be long pauses and frustration with unfamiliar words.
- *Level 1*. The student reads slowly and word by word, with many pauses and with little or no expression. Few words are identified automatically. The student may seem frustrated.

Remember, fluency depends on the difficulty of the text for the reader.

Note. Adapted from the National Center for Education Statistics (1995).

---

formally during meaningful oral reading activities, such as practicing for performance. It is also important to observe students' reading as another check for whether the text is appropriate for fluency building and for independent reading. Students who are bored or frustrated are probably not reading an appropriate text; students who are having fun and asking to read more probably are. Remember, fluent reading always assumes adequate comprehension, so always check comprehension, using retelling, reader response, and/or discussion. Practice using the fluency rubric to assess all of your students' oral reading in various texts.

EPILOGUE

Remember John Mendoza from the beginning of the chapter? After trying out almost every form of fluency instruction and every reading series she could find, John's teacher finally discovered his hidden talent: Shy, inhibited, uncommunicative John was a closet performer. After reading a script based on *The Teacher from the Black Lagoon* (Thaler, 1989), John asked to take it home. This previously reluctant reader proceeded to read his way through his teacher's entire collection of scripts and some borrowed from other teachers. He read them with friends in class, took them home to practice with his cousin, and eventually began writing his own scripts. At the end of the year, in front of an audience of more than 60 children, teachers, and families, John was the Stinky Cheese Man in a performance of Jon Scieszka's (1992) fractured fairy tale of the same name. He read more quickly, accurately, and with better phrasing and more expression than his teacher had ever heard him read. John thoroughly enjoyed the experience and grinned from ear to ear when he received the first standing ovation of his life.

CHILDREN'S BOOK REFERENCES

Avi. (1991). *Nothing but the truth*. New York: Orchard.

Allard, H. (1977). *Miss Nelson is missing*. Boston: Houghton Mifflin.

Blume, J. (1972). *Tales of a fourth grade nothing*. New York: Dutton.

Brown, M. W. (1949). *The important book*. New York: Harper.

Cole, J. (1989). *The magic school bus inside the human body*. New York: Scholastic.

Dahl, R. (1983). *Roald Dahl's revolting rhymes*. New York: Knopf.

Draper, S. M. (1994). *Tears of a tiger*. New York: Atheneum.

Fleischman, P. (1988). *Joyful noise: Poems for two voices*. New York: Harper & Row.

Frank, A. (1995). *The diary of a young girl: The definitive edition*. New York: Doubleday.

Galdone, P. (1973). *The little red hen*. New York: Seabury Press.

Hutchins, P. (1986). *The doorbell rang*. New York: Greenwillow.

Klise, K. (1998). *Regarding the fountain: A tale, in letters, of liars and leaks*. New York: Avon.

Konigsburg, E. L. (1996). *The view from Saturday*. New York: Atheneum.

Lester, H. (1988). *Tacky the penguin*. Boston: Houghton Mifflin.

Lobel, A. (1980). *Fables*. New York: Harper & Row.

Lyons, M. E. (1992). *Letters from a slave girl: The story of Harriet Jacobs*. New York: Scribner.

Marshall, E. (1983). *Fox at school*. New York: Dial.

Marshall, J. (1984). *George and Martha back in town*. New York: Houghton Mifflin.

Minters, F. (1994). *Cinder-Elly*. New York: Viking.

Parsons, A. (1990). *Amazing poisonous animals* (Eyewitness Juniors, No. 8). New York: Knopf.

Sachar, L. (1987). *There's a boy in the girls' bathroom*. New York: Knopf.

Scieszka, J. (1992). *The stinky cheese man and other fairly stupid tales*. New York: Viking.

Scieszka, J. (1995). *Math curse*. New York: Viking.

Silverstein, S. (1974). *Where the sidewalk ends*. New York: Harper & Row.

Silverstein, S. (1981). *A light in the attic*. New York: Harper & Row.

Taylor, M. D. (1976). *Roll of thunder, hear my cry*. New York: Dial.

Thaler, M. (1989). *The teacher from the black lagoon*. New York: Scholastic.

Zemach, H. (1969). *The judge*. New York: Farrar, Straus, Giroux.

REFERENCES

Aaron, P. G. (1989). *Dyslexia and hyperlexia: Diagnosis and management of developmental reading disabilities*. Dordrecht, The Netherlands: Kluwer Academic.

Adams, M. J. (1990). *Beginning to read: Thinking and learning about print*. Cambridge, MA: MIT Press.

Allington, R. L. (1977). If they don't read much, how they ever gonna get good? *Journal of Reading, 21*, 57–61.

Allington, R. L. (1983). Fluency: The neglected goal. *The Reading Teacher, 36*, 553–561.

Anderson, R. C., Wilson, P. T., & Fielding, L. G. (1988). Growth in reading and how children spend their time outside of school. *Reading Research Quarterly, 23*, 285–303.

Barr, R., & Johnson, B. (1991). *Teaching reading in elementary classrooms*. New York: Longman.

Bear, D. R. (1991). "Learning to fasten the seat of my union suit without looking around": The synchrony of literacy development. *Theory into Practice, 30*, 145–157.

Bintz, W. P. (1993). Resistant readers in secondary education: Some insights and implications. *Journal of Reading, 36*, 604–615.

Carlsen, G. R., & Sherrill, A. (1988). *Voices of readers: How we come to love books*. Urbana, IL: National Council of Teachers of English.

Carver, R. P., & Hoffman, J. V. (1981). The effect of practice through repeated reading on gain in reading ability using a computer-based instructional system. *Reading Research Quarterly, 16,* 374–390.

Chall, J. S. (1979). Learning to read: The great debate (3rd ed.). New York: Harcourt Brace.

Chomsky, C. (1978). When you still can't read in third grade: After decoding, what? In S. J. Samuels (Ed.), *What research has to say about reading instruction* (pp. 13–30). Newark, DE: International Reading Association.

Clay, M. M., & Imlach, R. H. (1971). Justice, pitch, and stress as reading behavior variables. *Journal of Verbal Learning and Verbal Behavior, 10,* 133–139.

Dowhower, S. L. (1987). Effects of repeated readings on selected second grade transitional readers' fluency and comprehension. *Reading Research Quarterly, 22,* 389–406.

Dowhower, S. L. (1991). Speaking of prosody: Fluency's unattended bedfellow. *Theory into Practice, 30,* 165–175.

Ehri, L. C., & Wilce, L. S. (1983). Development of word identification speed in skilled and less skilled beginning readers. *Journal of Educational Psychology, 75,* 3–18.

Guszak, J. (1998). *Reading for students with special needs* (2nd ed.). Dubuque, IA: Kendall Hunt.

Hoffman, J. V. (1987). Rethinking the role of oral reading in basal instruction. *Elementary School Journal, 87,* 367–374.

Hoffman, J. V., & Isaacs, M. E. (1991). Developing fluency through restructuring the task of guided oral reading. *Theory into Practice, 30,* 185–194.

Holdaway, D. (1979). *Foundations of literacy.* Sydney, Australia: Ashton Scholastic.

Ivey, G. (1999). A multicase study in the middle school: Complexities among young adolescent readers. *Reading Research Quarterly, 34,* 172–193.

Johnston, P., & Allington, R. L. (1991). Remediation. In R. Barr, M. L. Kamil, P. B. Mosenthal, & P. D. Pearson (1991). *Handbook of reading research* (Vol. 2, pp. 984–1012). New York: Longman.

Samuels, S. J. (1994). Toward a theory of automatic information processing in reading, revisited. In R. Ruddell, M. Ruddell, & H. Singer (Eds.), *Theoretical models and processes of reading* (4th ed., pp. 816–837). Newark, DE: International Reading Association.

Lipson, M. Y., & Lang, L. B. (1991). Not as easy as it seems: Some unresolved questions about fluency. *Theory into Practice, 30,* 218–227.

Manning, G., & Manning, M. (1984). What models of recreational reading make a difference? *Reading World 23,* 375–380.

Martinez, M. G., Roser, N. L., & Strecker, S. (1998). "I never thought I could be a star": A Readers Theater ticket to fluency. *The Reading Teacher, 52,* 326–337.

Measley, D. (1990). Understanding the motivational problems of at-risk college students. *Journal of Reading, 33,* 593–601.

Mullis, I., Campbell, J., & Farstrup, A. (1993). *NAEP 1992: Reading report card for the nation and the states.* Washington, DC: U.S. Department of Education.

National Center for Education Statistics. (1995). *Listening to children read aloud.* Washington, DC: U.S. Department of Education.

National Reading Panel. (2000). *Teaching children to read: An evidence-based assessment of the scientific research literature on reading and its implications for reading instruction.* Bethesda, MD: NICHD.

Palmer, B. M., Codling, R. M., & Gambrell, L. B. (1994). In their own words: What elementary students have to say about motivation to read. *The Reading Teacher, 48,* 176–178.

Pikulski, J. J. (1991). The transition years: Middle school. In J. Flood, J. M. Jensen, D. Lapp, & J. R. Squire (Eds.), *Handbook of research on teaching the English language arts* (pp. 303–319). New York: Macmillan.

Rasinski, T.V. (1986). *Developing models of reading fluency.* Newark, DE: International Reading Association. (ERIC Document Reproduction Service No. ED 269 721)

Schreiber, P. A. (1987). Prosody and structure in children's syntactic processing. In R. Horowitz & S. J. Samuels (Eds.), *Comprehending oral and written language* (pp. 243–270). New York: Academic Press.

Stanovich, K. E. (1980). Toward an interactive–compensatory model of individual differences in the development of reading fluency. *Reading Research Quarterly, 16,* 32–71.

Stanovich, K. E. (1986). Matthew effects in reading: Some consequences of individual differences in the acquisition of literacy. *Reading Research Quarterly, 24,* 7–26.

Strecker, S. K., Roser, N. L., & Martinez, M. G. (1999). Toward understanding oral reading fluency. *Yearbook of the National Reading Conference, 48,* 295–310.

Vacca, J. A., Vacca, R. T., & Gove, M. K. (2000). *Reading and learning to read* (4th ed.). New York: Longman.

Worthy, J. (1996). Removing barriers to voluntary reading: The role of school and classroom libraries. *Language Arts, 73,* 483–492.

Worthy, J., & Invernizzi, M. (1996). Linking reading with meaning: A case study of a hyperlexic reader. *Journal of Reading Behavior: A Journal of Literacy, 27,* 585–603.

Worthy, J., Turner, M., & Moorman, M. (1998). The precarious state of free-choice reading. *Language Arts, 75,* 293–304.

Zutell, J., & Rasinski, T. (1991). Training teachers to attend to their students' oral reading fluency. *Theory into Practice, 30,* 212–217.

CHAPTER 6

Guiding Students to Read as Writers

Bones. My first experience with bones is eating one. In my family of older sisters, we still tell the story of being given holy relics from Rome, by an uncle of mine who is a priest. Each ornate case was rumored to contain the bone of a saint. My sisters convinced me, the youngest, that if I smashed my case and swallowed the tiny bone inside, I would be holy forever. Without hesitation, I smashed the jeweled case and swallowed the tiny bone. I don't know that it made me holy! But, it did begin my fascination with bones, with things that once were. (McDonald, 2000, p. 22)

A fascination with bones. Years later, author Megan McDonald used the inspiration from this childhood experience to write a completely new story, *The Bone Keeper* (1999). Take a careful look at the beginning of her picture book. Consider how McDonald re-creates the sights and sounds of the desert as an old woman sifts through the sand for bones. Where do you see hints of folklore?

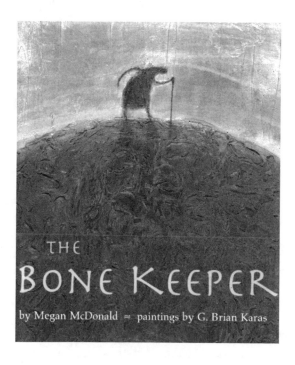

If you listen to the desert,
if you listen,
you may hear
a laughing,
a chanting, a singing.

They call her Owl Woman.
They call her Rattlesnake Woman.
They call her Bone Woman.

Bone Woman is old,
older than the Joshua tree.
She is bent and stooped,
closer to earth than sky.
Her hands are withered
like some ancient oracle.
Through a wrinkle in the sole of her
    foot,
she feels everything.

Some say she has three heads,
past, present, and future.
Some say she carries the snake,
walks with the wild hare.

Some say Bone Woman brings the dead back to life. (McDonald, 1999)

Will the dead live again? There is mystery, yet the passage works on many other levels. The reader's senses come alive through the sounds of words, through placement and repetition. Strong writing begins with an interest in a topic—a fascination with details—and a willingness to play with words. In *The Bone Keeper*, McDonald uses her own personal experiences, references to folktales about bones from around the world, and her research in nonfiction books about bones. Think about how McDonald's work provides a model for reading and writing instruction in the middle grades. As a teacher, you will be supporting students' continued development of reading comprehension strategies as you focus explicitly on how authors use prior experiences, reading, and research to create varied forms of writing.

In this chapter, we describe how students in the middle grades can explore two important sources for writing: personal experience and models from reading. We have chosen to explore these sources for writing for practical reasons. First, connecting personal experience with writing can be a key factor in promoting student engagement and developing writing fluency. Second, models from other pieces of student writing and from literature provide resources for students to see how form and content work together. In Chapter 8, we will look at a third source for writing—the information students discover through the research process. We also explore record keeping and assessment.

WHAT'S IN THIS CHAPTER?

Tapping Personal Experience as a Source for Writing
Thinking as an Author: Using Models from Literature
Engagement and Writing: Developing Independence

TAPPING PERSONAL EXPERIENCE AS A SOURCE FOR WRITING

Developing Students' Voices in Writing

How can we help students to develop clear voices in their writing? What makes middle grades students analyze and respond to text as writers? One strategy is to guide students to discover personal connections to their reading. When a teacher uses a group process of reading and responding to literature, such as a think-aloud (see Chapter 3), the resulting discussion demonstrates how an author's writing sparks a wide array of personal associations. Likewise, in their own writing, students need to recognize that they have areas of expertise that provide useful resources. In *Inside Out: Developmental Strategies for Teaching Writing*, Kirby and Liner (1988) offer the following advice about setting priorities in writing instruction:

> When you teach the new student–writer, the immature writer, you begin with only two real at-
> tainable objectives—to help the student find a voice in writing and to build a feeling of confi-
> dence in students that they *can* write. Too often we demand that students write about things they
> care little about (and sometimes know less), and forbid them to use their own natural voices. And
> then we immediately search out every mistake, large and small, that they make writing within
> these narrow restrictions. And we worry that our students don't seem to have anything interest-
> ing to say, that they despise writing. (p. 41)

Guiding students to use personal experience as they gain mastery of basic writing
skills has two distinct advantages. First, the students avoid the problem of lack of information. Writing based on personal experience is more interesting in terms of specific
content. Second, the act of reflecting on one's own experiences is engaging. The students are more likely to develop the personal motivation to write, and, as a result, to
practice writing. This combination of finding interesting content and spending time
writing is essential in developing writing fluency. Students need to explore subjects
that they understand and to develop their ease with the process of writing before exploring topics that are less familiar.

Focusing on the Details

Connecting Life Experiences with Different Forms of Writing

Using personal experience in writing does not mean that the style of writing must be a
memoir. Writers often use their own background experiences to make descriptions realistic and compelling. It is this fascination with details—real information that a writer
gathers from personal experience and research—that makes text come alive. For example, in *The Bone Keeper*, McDonald began her research by exploring visual details. In an
interview with one of us (Karen Broaddus), she recalls: "I spent a lot of time looking at
Georgia O'Keeffe's studies of bones. She sees skulls and bones as art, as form, as composition. O'Keeffe's work inspired me and reaffirmed the connection between *bones*
and *desert*." McDonald points out that her own experiences also served as a rich source
for her description of the desert landscape:

> "A single story comes not from one place, but many. To write *The Bone Keeper*, I had
> to draw not only from mythology, folklore, and imagery, but from experience. I
> had never seen the desert before moving to California. To get there, my husband
> and I crossed Nevada in our rattletrap of a truck in an August so hot the heat
> looked shimmery, as if we were about to see a mirage. The road we came across
> had a sign calling it The Loneliest Road in America. In that landscape, I found the
> setting for my story. But even more important than finding the setting was experi-
> encing for myself the starkness, the silence, the haunting loneliness of a place so
> desolate one welcomes the errant movement of a tumbleweed across the unbroken
> surface of rock and sand."

Even when writing in another genre such as fantasy, this type of personal memory provides an author with specific sensory images to recreate a scene. These details help to
create a bridge for readers to draw upon their own experiences and make personal connections to their reading. In an interview with Karen Broaddus in Box 6.1, McDonald

BOX 6.1. An Interview with Author Megan McDonald
(Conducted by Karen Broaddus)

What gave you the idea for the story of The Bone Keeper?

Bones. As a child, I was famous for collecting. Bones, skulls, fossils, shells, skins of snakes and bugs, charcoaly leaf-prints pressed between layers of Pennsylvania shale. Even scabs and baby teeth I could not surrender to the tooth fairy. I began thinking about bones. What do we know, or think, of bones in our culture? The Halloween skeleton, the Thanksgiving turkey wishbone, the museum dinosaur. Scary. Wishful. Old. Bones to me are anatomy and history, haunting and lonely and lovely.

Your story is original, but does it have roots in mythology or folklore?

Yes. *The Bone Keeper* is not based on any one individual tale. I had heard storytellers tell oral tales in which bones come back to life. I consulted a friend of mine, who excitedly informed me that these bone stories appear in virtually every culture around the world. My curiosity had me racing to the library, heading first for mythology and folklore. To my surprise, I discovered tales of bones coming to life from Africa to India, Greenland to New Guinea, Australia to Iran. From the American Sonoran and Chihuahuan deserts to the Arabian Rub'al Khali and the Taklimakan of China. I found bones that jump from fires and leap from wells, animals that leap from skeletons, earths and mountains created, heroes born from a single swallowed bone.

What other types of books did you read while you were writing? How did this new information fit in your book?

Wow. I must have looked at a hundred books. Aside from mythology, I read everything I could get my hands on about deserts all over the world, discovering a unique ecosystem in the extreme that I knew little about, where strange rock shapes loom, where pink sands exist, where sand blowing across dunes sounds like singing. I researched desert animals and plants, learning everything I could about the saguaro cactus or the catclaw, imagining a place where mammoths, camels, and sloths once roamed. I pored over books with skeletons, studying animal bones and their names. For example, the small collarbone of an owl is called a *wishbone* and snakes have 400 vertebrae! I made lists! Lists of trees and nighttime creatures. Lists of oddities I came across. Lists of interesting or unfamiliar terms, like *dust devil* and *taproot*, *jird* and *jerboa*. Lists of nicknames for deserts. The Rub'al Khali is called the "empty quarter." The Takla Makan is called "place from which there is no return." These became part of the poetry of the story.

How did you come up with the single character of an old woman?

It had to be someone wise! I never knew my own grandmothers, so I invented an old woman, an "every grandmother." Images of the archetype of the old woman are ancient and many: the crone, grandmother, wise woman, the Greek deity Hecate, the Russian witch Baba Yaga, Italy's Strega Nona, India's Kali, the Hopi Spider Woman, to name just a few. I borrowed their attributes from mythology—the wrinkle in the sole of the foot and the milky eye. For example, Hecate, in Greek mythology, is said to have three heads; tames wild animals; turns invisible; and can see past, present, and future.

Your book looks like a poem. Were you trying to write poetry?

Not intentionally, but as a writer, I can't help but love the sounds of words and word play, so I did consciously play with language and sound. Researching a book is, for me, like learning a new and foreign language. Once I knew the language of the desert, sounds began forming to create lines like "one by one by one/she collects/each lonely bone." I did a lot with the repetition of sounds, such as echoing "bones, bones" throughout the text or repeating a particular vowel sound in passages like "Bone Woman/calls to bat and badger,/kit fox and kangaroo rat,/rattlesnake and ring-tailed cat." This gives the story its poetic rhythm, emphasizing that mysterious, other-worldly quality.

describes how she makes use of personal experience, models from literature, and research in her writing.

Keeping a Writer's Notebook

Teachers can provide students with a structure to collect interesting details about everyday life by using the model of a *writer's notebook*. Take a look at Megan McDonald's writing notebook that she kept while she was working on *The Bone Keeper* (see Box 6.2). See how information from lists and other small details are used in the picture book itself. A writer's notebook is any type of personal log where students can record types of information that might be useful in their writing. Donald Murray (1999) uses the terms *daybook* and *process log* to describe this collection of facts, quotes from reading, lists, conversations, articles from a newspaper or magazine, pictures, letters, or just bits of personal writing. Students can jot down ideas or details that they are not quite ready to use—an interesting title for a poem, an outline for a fantasy story, the first line for an editorial, a question about bats, or a description of what the sea looks like at night. It is a good idea to get students in the habit of adding brief entries each day. Sometimes it is interesting for students to focus a writer's notebook on a particular project. In such a case, the notebook becomes a place to record research on a topic, along with the author's ideas about writing. Later, these notes become the framework for pursuing more focused research.

Connecting Thinking with Writing: A Focus on Fluency

Learning Logs

Collecting information is not only beneficial for young authors preparing to write. In content area classrooms, personal writing can be an important activity to promote thinking through writing. Exploring real experiences in science or math through writing not only creates a firm base for writing about the subject, but also provides a personal context—a voice—for writing. *Learning logs* are journals students use to record different types of information they have collected on a topic that they are studying in school, including personal observations and further questions. Books such as *Three Days on a River in a Red Canoe* (Williams, 1981) demonstrate how a journal can contain much more than narrative writing. This book contains directions for pitching a tent and tying two half hitches, a map of where events took place, recipes for cooking outdoors, and illustrations of different types of fish and ducks. A social studies log on a historical topic might include hand-drawn maps, a timeline, lists of important facts, vocabulary terms, a comparison chart of past and present, a letter written from the perspective of a historical figure, a response to reading a play about the time period, and notes for a final research paper. A science learning log could be set up as a data entry journal to record weather patterns or the results of a long-term experiment. Drawing and labeling can also be helpful for students in content area studies. It allows them to visualize the data or the setting and the vocabulary terms being used.

Learning logs provide a valuable alternative to traditional assessment of student learning. In *Math Is Language Too: Writing and Talking in the Mathematics Classroom* (Whitin & Whitin, 2000), samples of student writing about problem solving reveal what

BOX 6.2. A Writer's Notebook

Entries in author Megan McDonald's Writer's Notebook	Final text from *The Bone Keeper*, using information from her writer's notebook
Joshua tree (200–300 years old, American southwest, Mexico) Easy place to find bones and other remains because few plants cover them up; winds blow away topsoil	Bone Woman is old, older than the Joshua tree.
List of cacti/trees: Ironwood Yucca Barrel cactus Smoke tree Catclaw Saguaro (starts as a seed smaller than a grain of sand, thorns called spines, needles, stickers, points, silvery spines) Taproot (fat tuber/root that grows down to collect water) [Choose words for sound and atmosphere: catclaw, smoke tree]	She goes where the barrel cactus points south . . . It pierces the night, sharper than a thousand thorns. She knows. She sees things smaller than a grain of sand. Bone Woman chews on the taproot of the smoke tree, rubs it on her brow, pricks her finger with the needle of the cat claw.
Dust devil (strong winds in desert, swirls, few plants to slow them down, sandstorms, wind picks up dust and makes column of whirling sand, sky darkens)	At last it is time. A dust devil blows and swirls, a whirlwind of sand. The final bone is found at her feet.
Desert pack rat (collects seeds, stems, rocks, bones) Harvester ant, kangaroo rat (gatherers) Harvester ant (collects seeds to eat, takes to its nest in a cave cluttered with bones, bones; stores bushels underground)	Like the desert pack rat, the harvester ant, Bone Woman lives deep in a cave, a cave cluttered with bones, bones.
List of animals: Sand viper or sidewinder rattlesnake (moves sideways in "S" shape) Vulture Bat Badger (North America, Europe, Asia) Kit fox (Mojave) Kangaroo rat (Sonoran, Mojave) Rattlesnake Ring-tailed cat (SW deserts, Central America) Lizard Owl Hawk (known for backstanding, one on top of the other, on top of the saguaro) [Choose animals' names for sounds/internal rhymes]	She goes . . . where the sidewinder leaves its track, where the vulture flies. By night Bone Woman calls to bat and badger, kit fox and kangaroo rat, rattlesnake and ring-tailed cat. It rises and floats up, up, up into the night, higher than hawk upon hawk perched atop the saguaro.

(continued)

Death Valley, CA (known for cracked salt beds; mammoths, camels, sloths once roamed) Sonora, Chihuahuan, Mojave Rub'al Khali (Arabian desert) "empty quarter" Takla Makan (China) "place from which there is no return" Sahara (rocky desert) Wadi Rum (Jordan, also rocky)	She walks in death's valley, where the mammoths once roamed, the empty quarter, the place from which there is no return.
It takes 3 years for cactus to bloom. Seeds are scattered by wind and birds. There is a legend that coyote scatters the seeds.	Bones, bones are everywhere and nowhere. Wind tosses them across dunes and bare rock, into dry washes and arroyos, the way seeds are scattered on the sides of hills waiting years to become cactus.

Note. *The Bone Keeper* text is from McDonald (1999). Copyright 1999 by Megan McDonald. Reprinted with permission of Dorling Kindersley Publishing, Inc. The writer's notebook entries are used with permission of Megan McDonald.

students understand and what they have not mastered. Thompson (1990) found math letters in learning logs to be an excellent way to communicate with fifth graders about the subject matter. She notes that "fifth grade mathematicians tell me, better than any score on any test, how they are doing in math. They chronicle their breakthroughs, mastery of new concepts, discoveries of tricks of the math trade, personal satisfaction and accomplishments, and genuine pleasure in mathematics" (p. 90). Teachers often comment that using learning logs becomes central to the teaching process (Blake, 1990; Chard, 1990). Not only do the logs provide a long-term record of student learning, but also student feedback allows the teacher to individualize instruction through personal response.

Quick Writes

Moffett (1992) capitalizes on the natural connection between personal experience and more formal writing assignments in his book *Active Voice: A Writing Program across the Curriculum*. In order to establish a fluent base in writing, Moffett begins by having students complete a *quick write* about immediate thoughts or observations. This sequence allows students to explore thinking through writing about what they know well. Here are directions for an early fluency assignment as a quick write:

> Choose a place away from school that you would like to observe, go there with paper and pencil, and write down for fifteen minutes what you see, hear, and smell. Think of what you write as notes for yourself later.... Don't worry for now about spelling or correct sentences; write in whatever way allows you to capture on paper what you observe during that time. (p. 33)

A quick write is a way of brainstorming thoughts—getting specific details down on paper—that can be the source for other writing. Quick writes can be rewritten as a *com-*

posed observation or used to create a *found poem*, a technique of creating poetry from prose that is described in Chapter 7. The quick-write procedure encourages students of varying abilities to write with fluency, from those who fear a blank page of paper to those who are overly concerned with creating the perfect paper. It can also be a useful technique to allow students to collect their personal responses to a read-aloud before they participate in a discussion.

Personal Journals

You can explore narrative writing with your students by providing time for writing in personal journals. To help students move beyond producing a simple record of events, use models from literature that demonstrate varied forms. Keep the focus of personal journal writing on fluency—generating details about experiences and observations with ease. Students will need examples and focused minilessons to incorporate features of narrative writing such as dialogue. For example, Sharon Creech's (1990) book *Absolutely Normal Chaos* is set up as a school assignment—a required summer journal that is written by 13-year-old Mary Lou Finney. She writes her entries in varied styles, including character sketches of family members, scripts of conversations that she has with her friends, and lists of synonyms for words her mother says she should stop using (e.g. *stupid*: asinine, apish, moronic, beefbrained; *stuff*: material, substance, constituents, pith). Mary Lou also includes hilarous commentary on selections from her summer reading of the Greek epic *The Odyssey*. She addresses everything from her disbelief that Odysseus is truly a hero ("I think he'd be put in jail if he were alive today," p. 116) to Homer's style of writing ("Homer also has a strange way of putting things. . . . It reminds me of the preacher at Aunt Radene's church in West Virginia," p. 61). She decides to try out this descriptive style in some of her journal entries: "Little did I know when rosy-fingered Dawn (child of morning) crept over the horizon today that it would be such a good day. Where shall I begin Muse?" (p. 82).

What makes Mary Lou's journal entries such good models is that she actually comments on the process of writing. Early in the journal she writes, "After our last exam, Christy came slinking up to Alex and said, 'Welllll, Alex, see you tonight.' (I am going to try some dialogue here.)" (p. 7). A few pages later, she decides that she needs to make some changes in how she is using dialogue. Here is an example of a conversation between Mary Lou and Alex Cheevy, a boy she has run into on the street who lives across town. She asks if he is visiting someone on her street:

> He said, "Oh. No."
> I said, "On Winston?" Winston is the next street over.
> He said, "Oh. Yeah."
> I said, "Who?"
> I am getting tired of writing "I said" and "he said." Sometimes you don't have to put those words just to know who is talking, so I'm not going to.
> "Oh. The Murphys." (That's Alex talking.) (p. 10)

For examples of journals for younger students, use the illustrated *Amelia* series by Marissa Moss, or the notebooks of the *Katie Roberts* series by Amy Hest.

THINKING AS AN AUTHOR: USING MODELS FROM LITERATURE

Why Use Other Authors' Models for Writing?

Encouraging Students to Experiment with Their Writing

Personal experience is a wonderful source for writing. However, even Nancie Atwell (1998), whose book *In the Middle: New Understandings about Writing, Reading, and Learning* is widely used as a model for teaching students about personal writing in the middle grades, has struggled with the question of balance between personal writing and other forms of writing. Where does personal experience fit in the writing process? How does a teacher guide students to explore diverse types of writing? Atwell recalls what happened in her early years of teaching, when much of her instruction focused exclusively on personal writing:

> But for my students, my nudges toward the ubiquitous personal experience narrative began, like a slow leak, to sap their pleasure in writing. They grew bored telling what happened to them and bored listening to stories about other kids' experiences. . . . I realize now that what I viewed as the easiest jumping-off point for a beginning writer was, in fact, the easiest place for a beginning teacher of writing to jump from. If I didn't yet know how to teach the features of genres—how to identify, name, exemplify, demonstrate, and respond to the elements of different literary forms—I stood on safe ground when kids and I focused on little stories about moments from their lives. . . . Bringing fiction and nonfiction literature into the writing workshop—reading it aloud, reading it together with my kids, reacting to it with them, and naming what we noticed—changed me, changed us, and changed the workshop. (pp. 370–371)

Experimenting with the different ways to approach a topic stretches a developing writer to try new forms. By encouraging students to read widely and to share and discuss what they are reading, you will be exposing them to *content*, or new information to include in their writing. At the same time, your class will be studying examples of *format*, or models for structure and style of writing. Fletcher and Portalupi (1998) use this principle of modeling in their book *Craft Lessons: Teaching Writing K–8*. This book is set up as a series of *minilessons*, or short, focused teaching sessions with students about specific techniques in writing. Each minilesson is based upon analyzing contemporary children's and adolescent literature, and reproducible copies of student writing are included as an additional resource. Here is an example of how they suggest teaching a minilesson on finding a focus in a piece of writing by using two picture book memoirs—*Bigmama's* (Crews, 1991) and *Shortcut* (Crews, 1992)—as models:

> First, I read *Bigmama's* by Donald Crews, a collection of Crews' memories of the summers he spent at his grandparents' home. This picture book is more like the whole summer. I tell students that after Crews wrote *Bigmama's*, he decided to write about one piece of his summer, one specific memory. He chose to tell about the time he and his cousins took a shortcut along the train tracks. *Shortcut* is a moment in time that Crews captures with detail, sound effect, and suspense. It reminds kids of the times they dared to do (or at least thought about doing) something dangerous. It's about fear, relief, and keeping a lifelong secret. With my students I call these "the bigger issues" and they become used to that distinction—underlying feelings and ideas that run through our experiences rather than the simple happenings of our lives. The next day I read *Shortcut* and we talk about the differences between the two books. Why did Crews choose this moment in time to zoom in on? (p. 78)

Notice how these two picture book models allow students to explore different ways to focus their own personal experiences. The teacher guides students to consider options that provide a structure for their storytelling.

Using Visual Resources and Wordless Picture Books to Inspire Writing

Another way to encourage students to experiment with form and genre is to provide illustrations as an impetus for writing. Box 6.3 lists examples of illustrated books that encourage students to develop new techniques as writers. For starters, wordless picture books engage students' imaginations. The storyline is already provided; students can create a text that answers the many questions raised by detailed illustrations. This is a fun way to introduce students to writing narratives in a new genre such as fantasy. In David Wiesner's visual adventures—*Tuesday* (1991), *June 29, 1999* (1992), and *Free Fall* (1988)—readers are forced to explain events that seem impossible. Still, the illustrations are firmly anchored in parts of the real world just as fantasy is based on reality. For older students, illustrations help spark brainstorming and critical thought before writing begins. At the same time, it engages their interest in drawing techniques used by artists. Chris Van Allsburg's (1984) *The Mysteries of Harris Burdick* is set up to use as a series of "story starters." Each page includes a black-and-white fantasy illustration, a title, and a caption. The detailed drawings include the fantastic (a house on Maple Street blasting off), the humorous (a nun sitting in a chair high above the cathedral floor), and the mysterious (a lump approaching under the rug). Students enjoy using the captions as either the first line or the last line of their piece of writing. For examples of poetry based on pictures, have students look at two books by Walter Dean Myers, *Brown Angels: An Album of Pictures and Verse* (1993) and *Glorious Angels: A Celebration of Children* (1995). Myers collected old photographs as the inspiration for his poetry about children. These books provide an excellent model for teachers and students to pursue a similar project—searching for family photographs and collecting old pictures at antique shops and yard sales to use as sources for writing. Try taking your class on a field trip to an art gallery or sculpture garden to explore writing about works of art. Be sure to have them take notepads to jot down details and begin their writing as they are looking at the artwork. Box 6.4 shows two excerpts from an eighth-grade student's *simulated journal*—a journal set in a historic period. Erin decided to focus on the perspectives of two young girls shown in Renoir's painting "The Luncheon of the Boating Party."

BOX 6.3. Using Illustrations to Support Fluency in Writing

Wordless Picture Books and Other Illustrated Books to Use to Inspire Writing

All Ages

Anno, M. (1978). *Anno's journey.* New York: Philomel.
Baker, J. (1991). *Window.* New York: Greenwillow.
Banyai, I. (1995). *Zoom.* New York: Viking.
Bang, M. (1980). *The grey lady and the strawberry snatcher.* New York: Simon & Schuster.
Jenkins, S. (1995). *Looking down.* Boston: Houghton Mifflin.
Maizlish, L. (1995). *The ring.* New York: Greenwillow.
Mayer, M. (1974). *Frog goes to dinner.* New York: Dial.
Rohmann, E. (1994). *Time flies.* New York: Crown.
Turkle, B. (1976). *Deep in the forest.* New York: Dutton.
Wiesner, D. (1988). *Free fall.* New York: Lothrop, Lee & Shepard.
Wiesner, D. (1991). *Tuesday.* New York: Clarion.
Wiesner, D. (1992). *June 29, 1999.* New York: Clarion.

Older Students

Feelings, T. (1995). *The middle passage: White ships/black cargo.* New York: Dial.
Sendak, M. (1993). *We are all in the dumps with Jack and Guy: Two nursery rhymes.* New York: HarperCollins.
Van Allsburg, C. (1984). *The mysteries of Harris Burdick.* Boston: Houghton Mifflin.

Books Inspired by Art and Photography to Use as Models for Writing

Conrad, P. (1991). *Prairie visions: The life and times of Solomon Butcher.* New York: HarperCollins.
Hamanaka, S. (1990). *The journey: Japanese Americans, racism, and renewal.* New York: Orchard.
Lawrence, J. (1993). *The great migration: An American story.* New York: HarperCollins.
Mattaei, G., & Grutman, J. (1995). *The ledgerbook of Thomas Blue Eagle* (ill. A. Cvijanovic). Charlottesville, VA: Thomasson-Grant.
Myers, W. D. (1993). *Brown angels: An album of pictures and verse.* New York: HarperCollins.
Myers, W. D. (1995). *Glorious angels: A celebration of children.* New York: HarperCollins.
Panzer, N. (Ed.). (1994). *Celebrate America: In poetry and art.* New York: Hyperion.

In content area classrooms, visual sources can provide the structure for research in a text. Whether these are the historical photographs of the West from Pam Conrad's (1991) *Prairie Visions: The Life and Times of Solomon Butcher,* or the mural on Japanese internment that inspired Sheila Hamanaka's (1990) *The Journey: Japanese Americans, Racism, and Renewal,* illustrations force students to think more carefully about a time period and the types of research sources available. Books such as *Celebrate America: In Poetry and Art* (Panzer, 1994) pair artwork with writing. These poems explore diverse scenes in America's past and present and provide an excellent model for student writing about art. For mature students in the upper middle grades, interpretations of historical incidents such as *The Middle Passage: White Ships/Black Cargo* by Tom Feelings (1995) can present visual details that move far beyond the information provided in textbooks.

**BOX 6.4. Simulated Journal Entries Based on Renoir's Painting
"The Luncheon of the Boating Party"**

Luncheon of the Boating Party: A Perfect Fit

July 2, 1845 Marie Clavel

I saw her again today. Watching from a distance, of course, not daring to approach. She sat with her legs crossed and her hands folded delicately in her lap. How I envied that navy blue party dress she had on. It had red trimming and a lace collar, the same dress I had seen in the window of Tiffany's store so many times. I would press my face against the display case so hard it would leave traces of mist in round circles on the glass.

I can imagine the girl bustling into Tiffany's and trying on my dress to find it fit her perfectly. How I wish my family had enough money to buy me a decent dress. With my mother gone and my father only working a few hours a week, I am expected to bring home enough money to feed us all. For a few hours every day, I work at the Browns' house washing laundry and hanging it out to dry. I even cook and clean sometimes. Often I go to bed with an empty stomach, so I know it's foolish to be dreaming of a dress so extravagant.

Sometimes I wonder if the girl ever watches me. Surely she has seen me working at the Browns' house. I know this is a silly thought because what would be so interesting about a poor servant girl?

July 2, 1854 Madeline Ross

I saw Marie today at the luncheon. Her body stuck out from behind a tall boxwood. My mother's friend mentioned her name in a discussion about trying to find a new maid. She says Marie is hardworking, but is known to daydream and linger off her task. I caught sight of her during our main course. She was looking longingly at my roast beef and potatoes. Marie looked so hungry, I almost thought of slipping some into my napkin for her, but if mother found out she would have a fit. Her clothes looked as though they might fall off. She was wearing a shirt and long skirt about three sizes too big. Her bony face was framed by tangled wisps of brown hair. As I looked in her direction, she averted her eyes, and quickly dived back behind the bush. After the meal I looked for her behind the group of shrubs. Nothing was there, not even a trace.

Black-and-white illustrations of daily events on a slave ship are powerful testimonies about the atrocities that took place as Africans were transported to the New World. Illustrated books can provide a direct link from history to literary elements studied in the language arts curriculum. For example, Feelings uses symbolism throughout his drawings. In his rendition of a slave ship, the hold appears as a coffin. Visual interpretations provide a model in which students can easily understand literary elements (e.g., tone and mood, satire) before experimenting with their use in creative writing.

Getting Down to the Specifics of Writing: Using Multiple Texts as Models

Looking at How Words are Used

When you are introducing a technique or structure for writing, carefully orchestrate how students learn about a concept and how they practice this new form. Within this type of structure, reading and writing integrate naturally. First, let's look at some of the choices an author makes about wording. Often a writer begins with a quick draft that gets the message across. Later, as the author rereads and reconsiders, word choice is an important area of focus. Consider the example of finding specific terms shown in Box 6.5. Megan McDonald began with a draft from the information collected in her writer's notebook, then fine-tuned the wording after further research about specific bones. Look at the change in the writing. The final draft has images that are much more specific and, as a result, easier for the reader to visualize. These distinct images create mood—a feeling that allows the reader to become involved in the story.

Although not all writing requires this type of research, careful attention to how words are used is essential to any writing. In Chapter 7, we go into more detail about how vocabulary and word play hold a powerful place in inspiring developing writers. Teacher read-alouds are an excellent way to highlight specific points about wording in writing. After a discussion of the technique being introduced in the read-aloud text, paired reading or independent reading in new texts allows students to look closely across models. This exposure to print is essential, because it forces students to examine the conventions of the form they will be asked to use. Box 6.6 shows the beginning of a story written by Dana for her third-grade book project. She was interested in mysteries. She read and compared the features of different mysteries before she began writing. Look at the content of her story. Notice how setting works and how dialogue is used. Now look at the mechanics of her writing. Dana is not quite sure about how to use punctuation with dialogue, but you can see that she is using different speakers and quotes with ease. She is ready to learn about how to use commas with dialogue and how to indent for new speakers. Later, Dana set up each paragraph on a separate page, illustrated her mystery, and presented it at an author reading and signing in her classroom. Parents were invited to attend the signing to see the picture books created by their children at the end of the school year.

How do you guide students to examine different models before writing? For example, if students are going to write a narrative, they need to explore how to set up dialogue and how to vary the oral speech of different characters. A study of language us-

---

BOX 6.5. Selecting Specific Words in Writing

First draft of writing about skeleton building in *The Bone Keeper*	Final draft after research on individual bone names of certain animals
One by one by one, Jawbone, cheekbone, neckbone. One by one by one A skull, a tooth, a tiny piece of rib.	One by one by one, Spine of snake, skull of lizard. Bone by bone by bone, claw of badger, wishbone of owl, wing bone of bat. Skeleton Maker.

Note. The Bone Keeper text is from McDonald (1999). Copyright 1999 by Megan McDonald. Reprinted with permission of Dorling Kindersley Publishing, Inc. The first draft is used with permission of Megan McDonald.

BOX 6.6. The Beginning of a Third-Grade Student's Mystery Book

The Mystery of the Missing Purse

Chapter 1

Rosy and I raced down the stairs of the hotel. I was staying with Rosy's family for a week! We had gone to a hotel called the Comfort Inn. As Rosy and I ran outside, I thought of something. "We could make a mystery club and you and I will be the only members." "O.K." said Rosy. "Let's start by going into the ice cream store, getting an ice cream and think about it.

Chapter 2

Rosy and I went into the ice cream store. "Hello" said Mrs. Kooshman, the owner of the store. "What can I get you?" "I'll have a strawberry slurpee" I said. I'll have a rocky roll" said Rosy. "Coming right up" said Mrs. Kooshman.

   We slurped down our ice cream. I said "So how should we start our mystery club?" "Well" said Rosy, "We need to have cards, don't we?" "Good idea!" I said. We raced back to the hotel.

   We were inside the hotel room in a dash. "Girls?" said Mrs. Shackter, Rosy's mom, "Have you seen my purse?" "No, why?" I asked. "It's gone" she said. Looks like a job for our mystery club we thought. We'll call ourselves the googles. "Where did you last see your purse?" I asked. Mrs. Shackter said "In the bathroom." "Oh, no!" I said. "What!" said Rosy. "The cat lives in the bathroom!"

Continued

---

age across several texts guides students to consider the types of decisions authors make when writing dialogue. Let's look at how one teacher taught her students about writing dialogue in a narrative. Ms. Melville started with a read-aloud in the picture book *The Watertower* (Crew, 1998) to examine the type of language students might use themselves in everyday conversation. In this mysterious adventure set in Australia, Crew uses informal dialogue—the slang that comes up in a conversation between two boys:

> One summer afternoon, Spike Trotter met Bubba D'Angelo by the service station and together they went up to the tower for a swim.
>   Spike led the way, as usual.
>   "My mother says it's dangerous up there," he said, "but it's worth it, hey?"
>   Bubba puffed on behind. His mother couldn't have cared less where he went.
>   At the summit, Spike stopped to look down on the sweltering town. "Suckers," he grinned, and headed for the tower.
>   Last summer, a security fence had kept trespassers out, but now the metal posts were twisted and flattened and barbed wire lay coiled on the ground.
>   "You reckon vandals done that?" Bubba asked, recovering his breath.
>   But Spike was already on the top. "Hurry up," he yelled, throwing open the access hatch. "It's scorching up here."
>   He pulled his shirt over his head, dropped his shorts and clambered down into the tank.

   After a group discussion of how plot works with dialogue in *The Watertower*, students worked in pairs to read other picture books with distinctive dialogue and style. Choices for this type of parallel reading included *Ruby* (Emberley, 1990), *Pink and Say*

(Polacco, 1994), *Chato's Kitchen* (Soto, 1995), *Mirandy and Brother Wind* (McKissack, 1988), *Willy and Hugh* (Browne, 1991), *Smoky Night* (Bunting, 1994), and *The Boy and the Ghost* (San Souci, 1989). Using a variety of texts allowed Ms. Melville to match books with students. Although all of the texts modeled the use of dialogue and strong characterization, reading levels varied greatly. A straightforward text with casual conversation, like *Willy and Hugh*, could be handled by students reading at the second- to third-grade levels; a more complex text with a heavy use of dialect, such as *Pink and Say*, was more appropriate for students reading at the fifth- to sixth-grade levels. As students read these books together, Ms. Melville guided their reading by providing a chart for them to fill out that looked at writing features across the books. Box 6.7 shows an example of how you might connect this

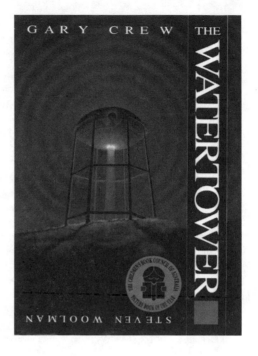

type of graphic analysis of language with a study of basic literary elements. Later, students used this same graphic format to brainstorm ideas before they began their own writing. We will look at this sequence in greater depth in Chapter 8 as we explore the steps of the writing process.

Considering Beginnings and Endings

A careful look at language usage helps students to begin to consider the choices they make in their own writing. This process can be extended to examine how a piece of writing is framed. How do beginnings and endings work? For example, if students are studying narrative writing, it makes sense to look at story leads as a way to hook the reader's interest. Consider the opening lines of the novels shown in Box 6.8. What engages the reader in the story? Often it is a sense of mystery. An aunt vanishes. A murder will occur. Sometimes a lead hooks the reader with a refreshing, humorous perspective. A girl forced to keep a journal during the Middle Ages complains of both fleas and her family in one sentence. A narrator speaks of borrowing a brain. In the case of *The Wild Kid* (Mazer, 1998), the opening forces the reader to consider what is different about this situation. Why has the main character been locked out? In this book, readers will discover the realities of day-to-day life through the eyes of the main character, Sammy, a 12-year-old boy with Down syndrome. Later, when Sammy is kidnapped and held in the woods by a teenage delinquent, his unique yet simplistic perspective about the situation makes this adventure narrative both unusual and straightforward.

This same type of analysis technique can be used with forms of expository writing. If students are going to write book reviews for a class newsletter, have them look critically at a number of published reviews of similar types of books. Categorize opening lines. Students will discover that strong openings to book reviews include many differ-

BOX 6.7. Graphic Analysis of Literary Elements across Picture Books

Title, author, illustrator	Type of narrative and setting	Language usage and dialogue	Illustrations and style	Effect
The Watertower by G. Crew (1998) (ill. S. Woolman)	Mystery and adventure/Small town in Australia	Informal conversation with slang; descriptive words in text help build suspense	Heavy use of black, varied page formats to show changes in perspective and to give clues about the meaning of the ending	Hints of the supernatural as an explanation for unexpected changes in one of the characters
Ruby by M. Emberley (1990)	Inner-city version of Little Red Riding Hood with animals as the characters (mouse, cat, and dog as rescuer)	From street slang to conventional English, depending upon the character portrayed	Exaggerated cartoon drawings; style works well to represent hectic city life	Humorous version of Little Red Riding Hood that plays off traditional cat and mouse tales
Pink and Say by P. Polacco (1994)	Civil War story about Polacco's family/Battlefield in Georgia	First-person narration, dialogue with dialect from the time period; strong and realistic	Expressive figures, dark pictures, symbolic use of hands	Wrenching portrayal of friendship, race, and war
Chato's Kitchen by G. Soto (1995) (ill. S. Guevara)	Cat and mouse tale set in the barrio, East Los Angeles	Spanish terms and street slang; talk of Mexican food	Bold, colorful drawings of characters; strong facial expressions	Humorous commentary on difference and getting along
Mirandy and Brother Wind by P. McKissack (1988) (ill. J. Pinkney)	Story handed down orally in McKissack's family/rural South	Story told in traditional oral form with Southern dialect spoken	Light-hearted, colorful pictures of a family celebration	Warm feeling of a family storytelling; uplifting

ent types of leads: a question, a quote from the book, the reviewer's point of view, a connection to previous writing by the author, a fact about the book. Use a simple analysis chart to have students collect information about the subject of the book reviewed, the opening lines used, and the effect. Afterward, they can try several of these forms out in their own reviews and discuss the effect with other students.

Studying Variants of Tales

An explicit way to focus students on how language is used in writing is to look carefully at how the same story is told in different versions. Using a traditional tale that is

BOX 6.8. Examining Strong Opening Lines in Novels
for Older Students

Opening line	Book information
I never had a brain until Freak came along and let me borrow his for a while, and that's the truth, the whole truth.	Philbrick, R. (1993). *Freak the mighty*. New York: Blue Sky Press.
The door was locked, and he was outside. It had taken both of them to put him out. His mother couldn't move him alone. He'd clung to the door, and she'd had to call Carl.	Mazer, H. (1998). *The wild kid*. New York: Simon & Schuster.
Around 5:00 a.m. on a warm Sunday morning in October 1953, my Aunt Belle left her bed and vanished from the face of the earth.	White, R. (1996). *Belle Prater's boy*. New York: Farrar, Straus, Giroux.
One summer day Amanda Woods traded her right hand for Lyle Leveridge's. Years later, she would think of that day as the beginning of a new life. At the time, though, she only knew it was the end of something.	Cameron, A. (1998). *The secret life of Amanda K. Woods*. New York: Foster.
The house looked strange. It was completely empty now, and the door was flung wide open, like something wild had just escaped from it. Like it was the empty, two-story tomb of some runaway zombie.	Bloor, E. (1997). *Tangerine*. San Diego, CA: Harcourt Brace.
Not every thirteen-year-old girl is accused of murder, brought to trial, and found guilty.	Avi. (1990). *The true confessions of Charlotte Doyle*. New York: Orchard.
Fanny Swann popped the only red balloon, pretending it was her father's heart.	Henker, K. (1995). *Protecting Marie*. New York: Greenwillow.
12th Day of September I am commanded to write an account of my days: I am bit by fleas and plagued by family.	Cushman, K. (1994). *Catherine, called Birdy*. New York: Clarion.
I got the idea to run away the night Uncle Homer beat me for spilling a glass of milk.	Hahn, M. D. (1996). *The gentleman outlaw and me, Eli: A story of the old west*. Boston: Houghton Mifflin.
I was fourteen the summer Mama took off for the Birdcage Collectors' Convention and we had ourselves what is now known in this town as the Adrienne Dabney Incident.	Nolan, H. (1996). *Send me down a miracle*. San Diego, CA: Harcourt Brace.
I've never told this to anyone before, at least not all of it. All through the Sheriff's investigation and the court proceedings, I only told what they wanted to know, the facts—what I saw, what I did. I never told all that happened or how I felt about it. A murder comes hard to anyone, especially a twelve-year-old, mixes him up so's it can take years to get straight again.	Staples, S. F. (1996). *Dangerous skies*. New York: HarperCollins.

told across cultures is an effective strategy to begin a discussion of style. Picture books also provide visual support to help students handle this type of analysis for the first time. For example, students can examine setting, language, illustrations, and cultural differences in versions of the Cinderella story, such as San Souci's (1998) *Cendrillon: A Caribbean Cinderella*, Schroeder's (1997) *Smoky Mountain Rose: An Appalachian Cinderella*, and Martin's (1992) *The Rough-Face Girl*, an Algonquin Indian tale. See Worthy and Bloodgood (1992–1993) for further information about how graphic analysis of text variants of Cinderella can support reading comprehension. This technique can be particularly effective when you ask students to analyze the same passage across stories, considering use of language and the mood that is created with any set of variants. Look at Box 6.9 for examples of how setting and language work together to create mood in two humorous versions of the Little Red Riding Hood tale. Your students' interpretations will be supported by the distinctive, cartoon-like drawings in each version.

Books that are transformations or continuations of traditional fairy tales also provide a good starting place for a discussion on style. Look at a familiar storyline with a distinctive perspective. Author Jon Scieszka is a master of fractured fairy tales, or stories that lend a new and often humorous twist to traditional versions. Look at Scieszka's (1991) introduction to *The Frog Prince Continued*, a modern sequel to the classic fairy tale about a young girl who kisses a frog and ends up with a prince. Scieszka clearly pokes fun at the fairy tale concept of "happily ever after." Students are quick to see the distinct stance the narrator has taken to retell this story. Other Scieszka books that "fracture" tales to create an entirely new slant on old stories include a hilarious retelling of the story of the three little pigs from the wolf's perspective in *The True Story of the Three Little Pigs* (1989). After comparing original versions with other renditions of

BOX 6.9. Looking across Variants of a Familiar Folk Tale

Version of Little Red Riding Hood	Quote from the picture book
Red Riding Hood by James Marshall (1987)	Before long she was in the deepest part of the woods. "Oooh," she said. "This is scary." Suddenly a large wolf appeared. "Good afternoon, my dear," he said. "Care to stop for a little chat?" "Oh, gracious me," said Red Riding Hood. "Mama said not to speak to any strangers."
Little Red Riding Hood: A Newfangled Prairie Tale by Lisa Campbell Ernst (1995)	As the edge of town disappeared, and the prairie began, Little Red Riding Hood zig-zagged between the crops, taking the shortcut to Grandma's house. . . . But who should be cutting through that same field—and up to no good, I might add—but a very hungry wolf.

Note. The first version is from *Red Riding Hood* by James Marshall. Copyright 1987 by James Marshall. Used by permission of Dial Books for Young Readers, a division of Penguin Putnam, Inc. The second version is reprinted with the permission of Simon & Schuster Books for Young Readers, an imprint of Simon & Schuster Children's Publishing Division, from *Little Red Riding Hood: A Newfangled Prairie Tale* by Lisa Campbell Ernst. Copyright 1995 by Lisa Campbell Ernst.

familiar tales, students will have ideas about how they might adapt a similar tone in their own modern tales. See Box 6.10 for some examples of humorous, diverse forms of retellings and ideas for traditional versions to use as models for comparison.

Examining Structure and Perspective

Writing fractured fairy tales is one technique to encourage students to focus on the framework of the tale, or the structure of a narrative, and the perspective taken, or the viewpoint. As students begin writing narratives, there are numerous models in contemporary realistic fiction and historical fiction of events told from different perspectives. A good place to start is with Anthony Browne's (1998) picture book *Voices in the Park*. This seemingly simple story about a park visit has a complexity in structure that makes it perfect for use in teaching writing in the middle grades. The format is clearly

---

BOX 6.10. Modern Perspectives on Traditional Forms

Fractured version	Format	Model for comparison
The Jolly Postman, or, Other People's Letters by J. Ahlberg & A. Ahlberg (1986)	Letters from the perspectives of fairy tale characters (younger students)	*The Helen Oxenbury Nursery Story Book* by H. Oxenbury (1985)
Yo, Hungry Wolf!: A Nursery Rap by David Vozar (1993), ill. by B. Lewin	Rap (third-person retelling) about the wolf's adventures with the three little pigs and others (all ages)	*Red Riding Hood* and *The Three Little Pigs* by J. Marshall (1987, 1989)
The Frog Prince Continued by J. Sciesczka (1991), ill. by S. Johnson	Sequel to a fairy tale (all ages)	*The Frog Prince*, by The Brothers Grimm (1990), retold by J. Ormerod & D. Lloyd
The True Story of the Three Little Pigs by J. Sciesczka (1989), ill. by L. Smith	1st person retelling through the wolf's perspective (all ages)	*The Three Little Wolves and the Big Bad Pig* by E. Trivias (1993), ill. by H. Oxenbury
The Stinky Cheese Man and Other Fairly Stupid Tales by J. Scieszka (1992), ill. by L. Smith	Fractured retellings of traditional fairy tales (all ages)	*A Handful of Beans: Six Fairy Tales* by J. Steig (1998), ill. by William Steig
Squids Will Be Squids by J. Scieszka (1998), ill. by L. Smith	Fables about humorous issues (older students)	*Fables* by A. Lobel (1980)
Roald Dahl's Revolting Rhymes by Roald Dahl (1983), ill. by Q. Blake	Poems about fairy tale characters, fractured tales (older students)	Versions of traditional tales (see J. Marshall & P. Zelinsky)
The Inner City Mother Goose by E. Merriam (1969), ill. by L. Ratzkin	Retellings of nursery rhymes with contemporary issues (mature students)	*The Glorious Mother Goose* by C. Edens (1998)

laid out in four unique perspectives. The reader can see shifts in point of view through changes in perspective on the ongoing events, the type of language used, the typeface selected, and the color and focus of the illustrations. Another interesting example for older students is the graphic novel *Making Up Megaboy* (Walter, 1998). This book relates how 17 different individuals try to understand the meaningless shooting of an elderly shopkeeper by a 13-year-old boy, Robbie. Each double-page spread has a distinct style of text, a unique voice, and an accompanying graphic that fits the narrator. This book is not only a wonderful example of perspective in writing, but also a visually engaging piece that is easy to read yet challenging in the issues that it raises. Students will be drawn to the complex look at popular culture and violence.

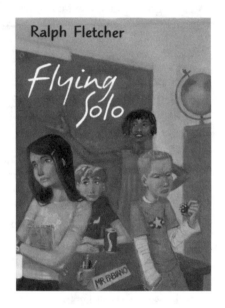

When you explore the types of books available for models of telling a story through different perspectives, you will see that there are many uses for these books in the classroom. School stories are always popular for independent reading and at the same time provide worthwhile models for writing about real experiences. The humorous yet poignant story of the members of a sixth-grade class who are *Flying Solo* (Fletcher, 1998) when the substitute teacher does not appear is just such a book. One series that will quickly be passed around the classroom is *The Friendship Ring* by Rachel Vail (e.g., *If You Only Knew*—Vail, 1998). This is a unique format for a series, with each small-sized book telling the same story from a new point of view. These types of models can serve as an inspiration for group writing projects in the classroom. Students can decide upon a setting, characters, and the problem at the beginning of the story, and then write about the details from different characters' voices. There are also models of collaborative writing projects to show to students. Look at the personas shown through the letters of Elizabeth and Tara* Starr, best friends separated by a move, taken on by popular authors Paula Danziger and Anne Martin in *P.S. Longer Letter Later* (1998). With more mature students, examine alternating male and female perspectives in a teenage drama about the end of the world, *Armageddon Summer* (Yolen & Coville, 1998).

Forms of writing can also be explored in books with varied perspectives. Whether it is the fifth-grade class in *Regarding the Fountain: A Tale, in Letters, of Liars and Leaks* (Klise, 1998) or the high school classrooms of *Tears of a Tiger* (Draper, 1994) and *Nothing but the Truth* (Avi, 1991), different documents can be used to tell a story. Memos, letters, newspaper articles, student writing, and telephone conversations are just a few of the ways students will find that these authors show perspective with primary sources. In history and social studies classrooms, these types of books can force students to think about the different perspectives individuals can have on the same situation. Whether these are the viewpoints on a single Civil War battle by members of the Union and Confederacy in Paul Fleischman's (1993) *Bull Run*, or the explanations of a racial incident after World War II at a sixth-grade girls' softball tournament game in Virginia E. Wolff's

(1998) *Bat 6*, these books bring out the different stances of individuals during events in history. It allows readers to think through why certain events took place, and the books provide excellent models for student writing about nonfiction topics.

Looking at Models in the Content Areas

Models become particularly useful as you are teaching students to write about new information that they are studying in classes such as math, social studies, or science. In order for students to include content in creative writing, they must have a thorough grasp of the subject matter. By reading across different models, students improve their own understanding of the topic and related vocabulary as they link content information with memorable stories and poems. For this reason, *topical collections* of materials, often called *text sets*, are effective for supporting reading comprehension. Vary the materials by reading level and genre; include different types of visual sources; and be sure your collection contains recently published nonfiction books that are both accurate and interesting. Find the very best materials on the topic with the most engaging formats. See Box 6.11 for an example of a topical set of books that can be used with Megan Mc-Donald's *The Bone Keeper* to explore the mysteries of bones. Appendix C includes samples of other text sets to use across the content areas. A topical collection of books also allows you to address the needs of diverse students in your classroom, because you can match individual students with books that they find interesting and can read with fluency. You can also consider students' background knowledge on the topic and their ideas about what they would like to write.

Even in subject areas that are not typically connected with creative writing instruction, such as mathematics, there are excellent resources available to use as models for these types of projects. Jon Scieszka's (1995) picture book *Math Curse* provides a hilarious example of how math problems are part of everyday life, as do Jack Prelutsky's (1994) poems in *A Pizza the Size of the Sun*, or Lee Bennett Hopkins's (1997) poetry collection *Marvelous Math*. In *Math Talk*, Pappas (1991) presents mathematical concepts in poems for two voices that are perfect for performance. Traditional tales such as *One Grain of Rice: A Mathematical Folktale* (Demi, 1997) also turn upon a mathematical model. The cunning heroine of this picture book, Rani, asks for a simple reward from the raja for her honesty in returning rice that had fallen from the raja's baskets during a famine. She is given a single grain of rice that day, then, for 30 days, double the rice given the day before. When students calculate Rani's reward, they discover that she received more than 1 billion grains of rice, enough to feed the starving people from the raja's storehouse. *Melisande* (Nesbit, 1999) is a folktale that works on a similar principle. Much like the Sleeping Beauty, Melisande is cursed at her birth—in Melisande's case, with baldness. When she is a young woman, her father the king grants her a single wish, and she replies, "I wish I had golden hair a yard long, and that it would grow an inch every day, and grow twice as fast every time it was cut" (p. 17). After several failed attempts, a prince manages to find a solution to this mathematical problem. Other models for writing about math include examining factorials in *Anno's Mysterious Multiplying Jar* (Anno & Anno, 1983); looking at probability in *Socrates and the Three Little Pigs* (Mori, 1986); applying logic in *Sideways Arithmetic from Wayside School* (Sachar, 1989) and *More Sideways Arithmetic from Wayside School* (Sachar, 1994); or understanding big numbers in *How Much Is a Million?* (Schwartz, 1985). Nonfiction books such as *Cool*

BOX 6.11. Exploring the Mysteries of Bones: A Topical Collection of Books across Genres

Folk Tales and Picture Books

Barner, B. (1996). *Dem bones*. San Francisco: Chronicle.

DeFelice, C. (1989). *The dancing skeleton* (ill. R. A. Parker). New York: Aladdin.

Johnston, T. (1996). *The ghost of Nicolas Greebe* (ill. S. D. Schindler). New York: Dial.

McDonald, M. (1999). *The bone keeper* (ill. G. B. Karas). New York: Dorling Kindersley.

Simms, L. (1997). *The bone man: A Native American Modoc tale* (ill. M. McCurdy). New York: Hyperion.

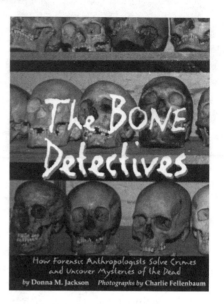

Novels and Stories

Conrad, P. (1989). *My Daniel*. New York: Harper & Row.

Dickinson, P. (1992). *A bone from a dry sea*. New York: Delacorte.

Lasky, K. (1988). *The bone wars*. New York: Morrow.

Olson, A. N. (Ed.). (1999). *Ask the bones: Scary stories from around the world* (ill. D. Linn). New York: Viking.

Nonfiction/Facts about Bones

Jackson, D. M. (1996). *The bone detectives: How forensic anthropologists solve crimes and uncover mysteries of the dead*. Boston: Little, Brown.

Jones, C. F. (1999). *Fingerprints and talking bones: How real-life crimes are solved* (ill. D. G. Klein). Bantam Doubleday Dell.

Kahney, R. (1992). *The glow-in-the-dark book of animal skeletons* (ill. C. Santoro). New York: Random House.

Legg, G. (1994). *X-ray picture book of amazing animals* (ill. D. Salariya). New York: Franklin Watts.

Presnall, J. J. (1995). *Animal skeletons* (ill. K. Kest). New York: Franklin Watts.

Simon, S. (1998). *Bones: Our skeletal system*. New York: Morrow.

Thomas, P. (1995). *Talking bones: The science of forensic anthropology*. New York: Facts on File.

Nonfiction/Archeology

Giblin, J. C. (1999). *The mystery of the mammoth bones*. New York: HarperCollins.

Goodman, S. (1998). *Stones, bones, and petroglyphs: Digging into Southwest archeology*. New York: Atheneum.

Wilcox, C. (1993). *Mummies and their mysteries*. Minneapolis, MN: Carolrhoda Books.

Biography

Anholt, L. (1998). *Stone girl, bone girl: The story of Mary Anning* (ill. S. Moxley). New York: Orchard.

Fradin, D. (1998). *Mary Anning: The fossil hunter* (ill. T. Newsom). Parsippany, NJ: Silver Press.

Math (Maganzini, 1997), or novels such as *The Number Devil: A Mathematical Adventure* (Enzensberger, 1997) and *Weirdo's War* (Coleman, 1999), round out such a collection by providing more in-depth information on mathematical topics in engaging adventure formats. Box 6.12 shows examples of other books that use content information in creative formats such as a diary, a newspaper, interviews, or poetry. The professional resources in the right-hand column provide extensive modeling of using writing techniques across subject areas.

ENGAGEMENT AND WRITING: DEVELOPING INDEPENDENCE

Promoting Engagement in Writing in the Classroom

Keep in mind that your end goal is to create engaged, independent writers. If you assign rather than model writing, students will quickly lose interest and refuse to take risks. If the examples from literature that you use do not engage your students' interests as free reading, then the models are unlikely to inspire writing. Although teacher read-alouds are a good way to begin to focus students on new techniques, the best exposure is through student reading of multiple texts. Looking directly at format and language is what supports the developing writer. Since engagement is so important to developing readers and writers, some of your time as a teacher will need to be spent finding materials that demonstrate these different forms of writing for your students. Think back to Chapter 2, which covers the types of materials that are important to use in your classroom. When you are teaching any new technique to students, be sure to include high-interest reading. Magazines are an excellent source to analyze different forms of writing. For example, an issue of *American Girl* might include historical fiction, feature articles, interviews, and mysteries. Picture books, such as Brian Pinkney's (1997) *The Adventures of Sparrowboy* or Arthur Yorinks's (1995) *The Miami Giant*, provide models of fantasy adventure stories in graphic, comic-book-style formats. Nonfiction can include high-interest formats in series such as the *Eyewitness Juniors* (e.g., *Amazing Poisonous Animals*—Parsons, 1990). For individual students, engaged reading can directly influence purposes for writing. Take a look at Box 6.13, where a preservice teacher describes her experience teaching a student who was having difficulty reading

fluently and often refused to write. When the student's interests were considered and a context was created in which she could read fluently, writing no longer proved an issue.

Be sure to integrate purposeful reasons for writing throughout the school day. A class newspaper is a great outlet for publishing students' writing about their own interests. Many teachers find that after initial modeling and guided practice, even elementary students can learn to do virtually all of the work involved in publishing a newspaper. Possible jobs include managing ed-

BOX 6.12. Creative Writing across the Content Areas

Content areas	Models from literature	Professional resources
Science	• Baker (1995), *The Story of Rosy Dock* • Florian (1996), *On the Wing: Bird Poems* • Leedy (1993), *Postcards from Pluto: A Tour of the Solar System* • Talbott & Greenberg (1996), *Amazon Diary: Property of Alex Winters* • George (1997), *Look to the North: A Wolf Pup Diary*	• Chancer & Rester-Zodrow (1997), *Moon Journals: Writing, Art, and Inquiry through Focused Nature Study* • Harvey (1998), *Nonfiction Matters: Reading, Writing, and Research in Grades 3–8*
Social studies and history	• Bowen (1994), *Stranded at Plimoth Plantation 1626* • Edwards (1997), *Barefoot: Escape on the underground railroad* • Fleischman (1996), *Dateline: Troy* • King & Osborne (1997), *Oh, Freedom!: Kids Talk about the Civil Rights Movement with the People Who Made It Happen*	• Edinger & Fins (1998), *Far Away and Long Ago: Young Historians in the Classroom* • Wolf, Craven, & Balick (1996), *More Than the Truth: Teaching Nonfiction Writing through Journalism*
Language arts	• Blackwood (1998), *The Shakespeare Stealer* • Munsch (1980), *The Paper Bag Princess* • Klise (1998), *Regarding the Fountain: A Tale, in Letters, of Liars and Leaks* • Nye & Janeczko (1996), *I Feel a Little Jumpy Around You* • Yolen (1992), *Encounter*	• Fletcher & Portalupi (1997), *Craft Lessons: Teaching Writing K–8* • Grossman (1982 and 1991), *Getting from Here to There* and *Listening to the Bells* • Tompkins (2000), *Teaching Writing: Balancing Process and Product*
Math	• Cushman (1996), *The Mystery of King Karfu* • Ledwon (2000), *Midnight Math* • Schwartz (1998), *G is for Googol* • Wakeling (1992), *Lewis Carroll's Games and Puzzles*	• Atwell (1990), *Coming to Know: Writing to Learn in the Intermediate Grades* • Cullinan, Scala, & Schroder (1995), *Three Voices: An Invitation to Poetry Across the Curriculum*
Integrated curriculum	• Adler (1999), *The Babe and I* • Hesse (1996), *Out of the Dust* • Jackson (1996), *The Bone Detectives: How Forensic Anthropologists Solve Crimes and Uncover Mysteries of the Dead* • Sis (1996), *Starry Messenger* • Yolen (1998), *Here There Be Ghosts*	• Freeman & Person (1998), *Connecting Informational Children's Books with Content Area Learning* • Tchudi & Huerta (1983), *Teaching Writing in the Content Areas: Middle School/Junior High*

BOX 6.13. A Preservice Teacher Talks about a Fourth Grader Who Was Reluctant to Read or Write (by Julee Hart)

Jillian began by reading a story to me from Alvin Schwartz's delightful scary book, *In a Dark, Dark Room* (1985). The book is below her instructional reading level, but I wanted to work on her fluency and enjoyment. She read with no real problem except that her fluency was choppy, and once again, she lacked voice inflection and expression. I read the next story to her, and she followed along patiently and listened better this time than I have ever noticed before. Usually she gets distracted easily, and I was pleased to see that the story had captured her attention. I asked her if she thought the stories were scary, and she looked at me and laughed. When I suggested that we read them as if we were characters, her eyes lit up and she squealed. I was shocked to see such a dramatic reaction from the same girl who normally runs screaming from any sort of acting. We read a script created from the story "The Green Ribbon." Jillian came alive like I have never seen before; she read her part with flourish and fever. After reading it once, we switched characters and read again, this time trying funny voices to make the parts even more interesting. Jillian was so enamored by her part that she literally fell out of her chair when she was trying to act frightened. She clearly comprehended the material and was fluent and proficient with her use of the text. Jillian read with a clear, confident voice that I knew she had in her all along. Most importantly, she enjoyed herself. Normally, when it comes to writing, Jillian groans a little and is reluctant to offer suggestions. Today, I asked her to write about how Jenny, the main character in "The Green Ribbon," lost her head in the first place and then found her green ribbon. I left the room, then peeked back in to see Jillian working diligently. When I returned, she read her story to me. Her writing was directly connected to the story. As she was reading, she picked out her own mistakes in her writing. Jillian has improved so much in our time together. I noticed that she checked out a mystery book on a third-grade reading level. Normally she marches straight for the beginning readers, but she is beginning to accept ownership and challenge herself. Her self-esteem has also increased, as shown by her ease with Reader's Theater. Jillian is starting to see herself as a reader, a writer, and a good thinker.

---

itor, copy editor, reporters, typists, printers, distributors, and illustrators. Students should rotate jobs so that everyone has a chance to learn the whole business. An example of a class newspaper is shown in Box 6.14.

Class newspaper articles are usually student-initiated and written and can be about virtually anything. Articles we have seen have focused on such diverse topics as popular culture (movie, television, and music reviews), jokes, personal interests, advertisements, announcements, book reviews, sports schedules, interviews, gossip, bios, advice columns, letters to the editor, and current news reports. Also, be sure that your free-reading shelf has books that provide examples of students writing for their own purposes, from historical sources such as *Anastasia's Album* (Brewster, 1996) or *I Never Saw Another Butterfly: Children's Drawings and Poems from Terezin Concentration Camp* (Volavkova, 1993) to contemporary journals such as *Amelia's Notebook* (Moss, 1995) or *Anni's Diary of France* (Axworthy, 1994).

Promoting Writing Outside of School: Underground Literacy

As teachers, we hope that students will take some of what they learn about literacy in school and use it for their own purposes at home, whether it is to learn more about a topic of interest or just for personal entertainment. Your students can write scripts for

BOX 6.14. Student Newspaper

NEWS and VIEWS April 14, 1998

Published twice a month by Mr. Li's 3/4/5 multiage class.

Movie Review

"Tarzan"
review by Linda
Have you seen the new "Tarzan" movie? The animation is great. It's a love story (duh!), but there's a lot of action and adventure. My mom hates Disney movies, but she loved Tarzan. I think you'll like it.

Music Review

"Just the Two of Us" by Will Smith
review by James W.
I have been hearing this song on the radio and I love it. Will Smith sings about being a father. His real, son, Trey talks on the song. Will Smith is cool!

Yo-Yo Tricks

by Jun
I have five yo-yos and I can do tricks like Walk the Dog, Eiffel Tower, Around the World, the Creeper, and many others. If you would like to learn some tricks, see me after school. Also, check out this web site: http:/www.yo-yo.com

Joke Time!

by Aisha and Jared
Where can you find the most cows?
In Moo York
What do you get from a nervous cow?
A milk shake
How can you tell when you're near a chicken farm?
By the fowl smell!!!!
Knock-knock.
Who's There?
Police
Police who?
Police stop telling those silly jokes!

The Real "Stone Cold"

by Omar
Stone Cold is a wrestler who was born on December 18, 1965 in Austin, Texas. When he was in fifth grade he started watching wrestling. He was a football player in college, but he did not graduate from college. He has two daughters and a step daughter. He is 32 years old now.

About Lasers

by John C.
I am curious about lasers because I like the way the red dot looks. I've seen lasers at Laser Quest, at the Erwin Center, and at the grocery store. Some teachers use lasers to point to the board in class. Some kids bring lasers to school, but teachers are always taking them away. When my teacher took my pointer away, I decided to find out why she says they are dangerous. I found out that lasers are concentrated light that can burn you. I also found out that there are different kinds of lasers. Some are so powerful they can drill through strong medal. Some lasers are used to do surgery. Lasers cut with heat, so there is very little blood. Laser beams are used in phone conversations. The voice is turned into a laser signal and sent through fiber optic lines. Some printers use a laser beam to burn the image on paper. This newspaper was printed using a laser printer.

Soccer/Fútbol

by Jacinta
Soccer is my best sport. I play forward on a soccer team with boys and girls. I score a lot of goals. So far we have won 3 games and tied one. When I speak Spanish I call soccer fútbol. My favorite pro team is from Mexico. My favorite player is Luis Hernandez. Soccer is an action-packed game.

The Contest

by Vivian and Jaleel
We are reading *The Candy Corn Contest* by Patricia Reilly Giff. We decided to have our own contest. If you guess the number of jelly beans in the jar, you win them all. The contest will end on April 22. Do you want to make a guess? See Vivian!

Editors: Ahmed, Sharon, and Tom
Calling all reporters. Would you like to see your article printed in News and Views? Submit your article to Ahmed as soon as you write it.

their favorite television shows, share scary stories with each other, exchange their own comic strips, talk with each other nightly by e-mail, and publish their own magazine. Box 6.15 provides an example of this type of underground literacy. If you expose students to varied writing and reading experiences at school that they truly enjoy, you can help create lifelong readers and writers.

BOX 6.15. An Example of Underground Literacy (by Jo Worthy and Her Daughter Jenna)

Jo's Introduction

My fifth-grade daughter, Jenna, announced one day that she wanted me to borrow a camcorder so she could film a movie. It turned out that she had been working on a script entitled "Family Murders" (don't ask) every day after school for a month, and it was now ready for filming. The script included stage directions, as well as lines, and was pretty sophisticated (see excerpt below). She printed the script, chose five boys and five girls for actors, gave out the scripts at school, and told the actors to memorize and practice their parts. The filming was scheduled for a no-school Monday. I was pretty surprised that only two kids didn't show up (they were out of town), and that everyone else came right on schedule ready to make the movie. They had all memorized their parts and were very serious (well, most of the time). Jenna played the part of the temperamental director beautifully, arguing with actors about script and wardrobe changes, and she really kept those kids moving through the scenes. They worked for almost 3 hours straight and would have kept going, except that it was pizza time and some had to leave after lunch. So about half of the movie got made. Part two was scheduled for the following weekend, but, unfortunately, the director got sick. I guess it's pretty tough making a movie. I was impressed that this complex activity requiring writing, reading, and acting was done entirely outside of school, with no adult input.

An Excerpt from "Family Murders" by Jenna

STACEY: Mom I'm going to take a shower!
MOM: Okay, Honey.
{Door shuts}
MOM: Come on everybody, she's in the shower. We can set up her surprise birthday party now.
{A crowd of people come in and throw streamers everywhere.}
{Two girls are in a car talking.}
DIANE: Thanks Mrs. Mason for driving me home! And thanks Katherine for coming to my sister's birthday party.
KATHERINE: Well, you talked me into it.
DIANE: Stacey doesn't care whom you are if you brought her a present.
{Back at the house}
MOM: Hmm, 30 minutes. I wonder what's taking her so long? I'm going to see if she's all right.
{She walks into the bathroom which has blood all over the walls and screams. Stacey is lying on the floor dead and in bloody writing it says "red rum"}
{In the car}
DIANE: Just one more minute. I hope we make it.
KATHERINE: Do we have to stay at the party the whole time? I hear Marty's having a mob at his house.

CHILDREN'S BOOK REFERENCES

Adler, D. (1999). *The Babe and I*. San Diego, CA: Harcourt Brace.

Ahlberg, J., & Ahlberg, A. (1986). *The jolly postman, or other people's letters*. Boston: Little, Brown.

Anno, M., & Anno, M. (1983). *Anno's mysterious multiplying jar*. New York: Philomel.

Avi. (1991). *Nothing but the truth*. New York: Orchard.

Axworthy, A. (1994). *Anni's diary of France*. Watertown, MA: Charlesbridge.

Baker, J. (1995). *The story of Rosy Dock*. New York: Greenwillow.

Blackwood, G. (1998). *The Shakespeare stealer*. New York: Dutton.

Bowen, G. (1994). *Stranded at Plimoth Plantation, 1626*. New York: HarperCollins.

Brewster, H. (1996). *Anastasia's album*. Toronto: Madison Press.

Browne, A. (1991). *Willy and Hugh*. New York: Knopf.

Browne, A. (1998). *Voices in the park*. New York: Dorling Kindersley.

Bunting, E. (1994). *Smoky night* (ill. D. Diaz). San Diego, CA: Harcourt Brace.

Coleman, M. (1998). *Weirdo's war*. New York: Orchard.

Conrad, P. (1991). *Prairie visions: The life and times of Solomon Butcher*. New York: HarperCollins.

Creech, S. (1990). *Absolutely normal chaos*. New York: HarperCollins.

Crew, G. (1998). *The watertower* (ill. S. Woolman). New York: Crocodile.

Crews, D. (1991). *Bigmama's*. New York: Greenwillow.

Crews, D. (1992). *Shortcut*. New York: Greenwillow.

Cushman, D. (1996). *The mystery of King Karfu*. New York: HarperCollins.

Dahl, R. (1983). *Roald Dahl's revolting rhymes* (ill. Q. Blake). New York: Knopf.

Danziger, P., & Martin, A. M. (1998). *P.S. longer letter later*. New York: Scholastic.

Demi. (1997). *One grain of rice: A mathematical folktale*. New York: Scholastic.

Draper, S. (1994). *Tears of a tiger*. New York: Atheneum.

Edens, C. (1998). *The glorious Mother Goose*. New York: Atheneum.

Edwards, P. D. (1997). *Barefoot: Escape on the underground railroad* (ill. H. Cole). New York: Harper-Collins.

Emberley, M. (1990). *Ruby*. Boston: Little, Brown.

Enzensberger, H. M. (1997). *The number devil: A mathematical adventure*. New York: Holt.

Ernst, L. C. (1995). *Little Red Riding Hood: A newfangled prairie tale*. New York: Simon & Schuster.

Feelings, T. (1995). *Middle passage: White ships/black cargo*. New York: Dial.

Fleischman, P. (1993). *Bull Run*. New York: HarperCollins.

Fleischman, P. (1996). *Dateline: Troy*. Cambridge, MA: Candlewick.

Fletcher, R. (1998). *Flying solo*. New York: Clarion.

Florian, D. (1996). *On the wing: Bird poems and paintings*. San Diego, CA: Harcourt Brace.

George, J. C. (1997). *Look to the north: A wolf pup diary* (ill. L. Washburn). New York: HarperCollins.

Grimm, The Brothers. (1990). *The frog prince* (retold by J. Ormerod & D. Lloyd). New York: Lothrop, Lee & Shepard.

Hamanaka, S. (1990). *The journey: Japanese Americans, racism, and renewal*. New York: Orchard.

Hesse, K. (1997). *Out of the dust*. New York: Scholastic.

Hopkins, L. B. (Ed.). (1997). *Marvelous math* (ill. K. Barbour). New York: Simon & Schuster.

Jackson, D. M. (1996). *The bone detectives: How forensic anthropologists solve crimes and uncover mysteries of the dead* (ill. C. Fellenbaum). Boston: Little, Brown.

King, C., & Osborne, L. B. (1997). *Oh, freedom!: Kids talk about the civil rights movement with the people who made it happen*. New York: Knopf.

Klise, K. (1998). *Regarding the fountain: A tale, in letters, of liars and leaks*. New York: Avon.

Ledwon, P. (2000). *Midnight math: Twelve terrific math games* (ill. M. Mets). New York: Holiday House.

Leedy, L. (1993). *Postcards from Pluto: A tour of the solar system*. New York: Holiday House.

Lobel, A. (1980). *Fables*. New York: Harper & Row.

Maganzini, C. (1997). *Cool math*. New York: Price Stern Sloan.

Marshall, J. (1987). *Red Riding Hood.* New York: Dial.

Marshall, J. (1989). *The three little pigs.* New York: Dial.

Martin, R. (1992). *The rough-face girl* (ill. D. Shannon). New York: Putnam.

Mazer, H. (1998). *The wild kid.* New York: Simon & Schuster.

McDonald, M. (1999). *The bone keeper* (ill. G. B. Karas). New York: Dorling Kindersley.

McKissack, P. (1988). *Mirandy and Brother Wind* (ill. J. Pinkney). New York: Knopf.

Merriam, E. (1969). *The inner city Mother Goose* (ill. L. Ratzkin). New York: Simon & Schuster.

Mori, T. (1986). *Socrates and the three little pigs* (ill. M. Anno). New York: Philomel.

Moss, M. (1995). *Amelia's notebook.* Berkeley, CA: Tricycle.

Munsch, R. (1980). *The paper bag princess* (ill. M. Martchenko). Buffalo, NY: Annick Press.

Myers, W. D. (1993). *Brown angels: An album of pictures and verse.* New York: HarperCollins.

Myers, W. D. (1995). *Glorious angels: A celebration of children.* New York: HarperCollins.

Nesbit, E. (1999). *Melisande* (ill. P. J. Lynch). Cambridge, MA: Candlewick.

Nye, N. S., & Janeczko, P. B. (Eds.). (1996). *I feel a little jumpy around you: A book of her poems and his poems collected in pairs.* New York: Simon & Schuster.

Oxenbury, H. (1985). *The Helen Oxenbury nursery story book.* New York: Knopf.

Panzer, N. (Ed.). (1994). *Celebrate America: In poetry and art.* New York: Hyperion.

Pappas, T. (1991). *Math talk: Mathematical ideas in poems for two voices.* San Carlos, CA: Wide World.

Parsons, A. (1990). *Amazing poisonous animals* (Eyewitness Juniors, No. 8; ill. J. Young). New York: Knopf.

Pinkney, B. (1997). *The adventures of Sparrowboy.* New York: Simon & Schuster.

Polacco, P. (1994). *Pink and Say.* New York: Putnam.

Prelutsky, J. (1994). *A pizza the size of the sun.* New York: Greenwillow.

Sachar, L. (1989). *Sideways arithmetic from Wayside School.* New York: Scholastic.

Sachar, L. (1994). *More sideways arithmetic from Wayside School.* New York: Scholastic.

San Souci, R. D. (1989). *The boy and the ghost* (ill. J. B. Pinkney). New York: Simon & Schuster.

San Souci, R. D. (1998). *Cendrillon: A Caribbean Cinderella* (ill. B. Pinkney). New York: Simon & Schuster.

Schroeder, A. (1997). *Smoky Mountain Rose: An Appalachian Cinderella.* New York: Dial.

Schwartz, A. (1985). *In a dark, dark room* (ill. D. Zimmer). New York: Harper & Row.

Schwartz, D. M. (1985). *How much is a million?* (ill. S. Kellogg). New York: Lothrop, Lee & Shepard.

Schwartz, D. M. (1998). *G is for googol: A math alphabet book* (ill. M. Moss). New York: Scholastic.

Scieszka, J. (1989). *The true story of the three little pigs* (ill. L. Smith). New York: Viking.

Scieszka, J. (1991). *The frog prince continued* (ill. S. Johnson). New York: Viking.

Scieszka, J. (1992). *The stinky cheese man and other fairly stupid tales* (ill. L. Smith). New York: Viking.

Scieszka, J. (1995). *Math curse* (ill. L. Smith). New York: Viking.

Scieszka, J. (1998). *Squids will be squids* (ill. L. Smith). New York: Viking.

Sis, P. (1996). *Starry messenger.* New York: Farrar, Straus, Giroux.

Soto, G. (1995). *Chato's kitchen* (ill. S. Guevara). New York: Putnam.

Steig, J. (1998). *A handful of beans: Six fairy tales* (ill. W. Steig). New York: HarperCollins.

Talbott, H., & Greenberg, M. (1996). *Amazon diary: Property of Alex Winters* (ill. M. Greenberg). New York: Putnam.

Trivias, E. (1993). *The three little wolves and the big bad pig* (ill. H. Oxenbury). New York: McElderry.

Vail, R. (1998). *If you only knew.* New York: Scholastic.

Van Allsburg, C. (1984). *The mysteries of Harris Burdick.* Boston: Houghton Mifflin.

Volavkova, H. (Ed.). (1993). *I never saw another butterfly: Children's drawings and poems from Terezin concentration camp.* New York: Schocken.

Vozar, D. (1993). *Yo, hungry wolf!: A nursery rap* (ill. B. Lewin). New York: Doubleday.

Wakeling, E. (Ed.). (1992). *Lewis Carroll's games and puzzles.* Mineola, NY: Dover.

Walter, V. (1998). *Making up megaboy* (ill. K. Roeckelein). New York: Dorling Kindersley.

Wiesner, D. (1988). *Free fall.* New York: Lothrop, Lee & Shepard.

Wiesner, D. (1991). *Tuesday.* New York: Clarion.

Wiesner, D. (1992). *June 29, 1999.* New York: Clarion.

Williams, V. B. (1981). *Three days on a river in a red canoe.* New York: Morrow.

Wolff, V. E. (1998). *Bat 6.* New York: Scholastic.

Yolen, J. (1992). *Encounter* (ill. D. Shannon). San Diego, CA: Harcourt Brace.

Yolen, J. (1998). *Here there be ghosts.* San Diego, CA: Harcourt Brace.

Yolen, J., & Coville, B. (1998). *Armageddon summer.* San Diego, CA: Harcourt Brace.

Yorinks, A. (1995). *The Miami giant* (ill. M. Sendak). New York: HarperCollins.

REFERENCES

Atwell, N. (Ed.). (1990). *Coming to know: Writing to learn in the intermediate grades.* Portsmouth, NH: Heinemann.

Atwell, N. (1998). *In the middle: New understandings about writing, reading, and learning* (2nd ed.). Portsmouth, NH: Heinemann.

Blake, M. (1990). Learning logs in upper elementary grades. In N. Atwell (Ed.), *Coming to know: Writing to learn in the intermediate grades* (pp. 53–60). Portsmouth, NH: Heinemann.

Chancer, J., & Rester-Zodrow, G. (1997). *Moon journals: Writing, art, and inquiry through focused nature study.* Portsmouth, NH: Heinemann.

Chard, N. (1990). How learning logs change teaching. In N. Atwell (Ed.), *Coming to know: Writing to learn in the intermediate grades* (pp. 61–68). Portsmouth, NH: Heinemann.

Cullinan, B. E., Scala, M. C., & Schroder, V. C. (1995). *Three voices: An invitation to poetry across the curriculum.* York, ME: Stenhouse.

Edinger, M., & Fins, S. (1998). *Far away and long ago: Young historians in the classroom.* York, ME: Stenhouse.

Fletcher, R., & Portalupi, J. (1998). *Craft lessons: Teaching writing K–8.* York, ME: Stenhouse.

Freeman, E. B., & Person, D. G. (1998). *Connecting informational children's books with content area learning.* Boston: Allyn & Bacon.

Grossman, F. (1982). *Getting from here to there: Writing and reading poetry.* Portsmouth, NH: Boynton/Cook.

Grossman, F. (1991). *Listening to the bells: Learning to read poetry by writing poetry.* Portsmouth, NH: Boynton/Cook.

Harvey, S. (1998). *Nonfiction matters: Reading, writing, and research in grades 3–8.* York, ME: Stenhouse.

Kirby, D., & Liner, T. (1988). *Inside out: Developmental strategies for teaching writing* (2nd ed.). Portsmouth, NH: Boynton/Cook.

McDonald, M. (2000). Bones of a story. *Book Links, 9*(4), 22-26.

Moffett, J. (1992). *Active voice: A writing program across the curriculum* (2nd ed.). Portsmouth, NH: Boynton/Cook.

Murray, D. M. (1998). *Write to learn* (6th ed.). Fort Worth, TX: Harcourt Brace.

Tchudi, S. N., & Huerta, M. C. (1983). *Teaching writing in the content areas: Middle school/junior high.* Washington, DC: National Education Association.

Thompson, A. (1990). Letters to a math teacher. In N. Atwell (Ed.), *Coming to know: Writing to learn in the intermediate grades* (pp. 88–93). Portsmouth, NH: Heinemann.

Tompkins, G. E. (2000). *Teaching writing: Balancing process and product* (3rd ed.). Upper Saddle River, NJ: Merrill.

Whitin, P., & Whitin, D. (2000). *Math is language too: Writing and talking in the mathematics classroom.* Urbana, IL: National Council of Teachers of English.

Wolf, D. P., Craven, J., & Balick, D. (Eds.). (1996). *More than the truth: Teaching nonfiction writing through journalism.* Portsmouth, NH: Heinemann.

Worthy, J., & Bloodgood, J. W. (1992–1993). Enhancing reading instruction through Cinderella tales. *The Reading Teacher, 46,* 290–301.

CHAPTER 7

Exploring Words

"Sometimes I have trouble with the words and stuff, and it gets me all frustrated." Sixth grader Phoebe was sure about her biggest problem with reading. Although she was motivated to learn, enthusiastic about the texts used in her classroom, and generally interested in her school subjects, difficulties with word identification and limited vocabulary hindered her independent reading and writing. Phoebe eagerly listened when the teacher read aloud, asked critical questions in class, read fluently in easy-to-read picture books, and thrived in oral reading performances when she was given opportunities to practice repeatedly before reading to the class. However, her growing knowledge about the world, her developing social and emotional maturity, and her curiosity for learning new information were often masked and inhibited by her problems with reading the words. For instance, Phoebe loved historical fiction, but she could not get through the first page of *Shades of Gray* (Reeder, 1989), a book about the Civil War. There were a significant number of unfamiliar words in the first couple of paragraphs that she could not decode, such as *monotonous*, *motionless*, and *florid*, and even simpler one-syllable words, such as *sigh*, *brim*, and *scarce*. The results of an informal reading inventory indicated that Phoebe was reading at a third-grade level for word identification. It was not surprising that Phoebe resisted required reading in class. As she put it, "Sometimes it's better for me just to listen." The bottom line, however, is that Phoebe needs to be able to read on her own.

How would you help Phoebe build her word knowledge while keeping her engaged in meaningful, age-appropriate reading and writing experiences? A balanced approach to literacy in the middle grades includes opportunities for students to examine the structure of words, consider syntax, apply principles of spelling, and learn more about word meanings. How to support and structure this type of analysis of language, however, can be confusing for teachers. As with other areas of literacy, engagement is a key issue. Often students have been asked simply to memorize vocabulary or spelling words, rather than to think critically about the sounds in words, their spelling patterns, and connections with meaning.

In this chapter, we discuss how to engage students in an examination of language, including word usage, vocabulary, syntax, and spelling, through word analysis and language play. We focus on three areas of English orthography, or how letters are sequenced in our writing system, that have been identified by researchers of developmental spelling (Bear, Invernizzi, Templeton, & Johnston, 2000; Henderson, 1990; Templeton & Morris, 1999). These include exploring language and spelling through *sound* (alphabetic or letter–sound relationships), *pattern* (sound–pattern relationships within or across syllables), and *meaning* (meaning–spelling relationships despite changes in sound). We conclude by discussing how to support students to apply their developing knowledge about words to their spelling and writing.

WHAT'S IN THIS CHAPTER?

Encouraging Language Play
When Do I Teach Grammar?
What about Spelling?
Using Students' Knowledge about Words to Guide Instruction

ENCOURAGING LANGUAGE PLAY

Focusing on the Sounds of Language in Oral Reading

Listening to the Music of Words

Students are naturally drawn to the sounds of language. Consider the power of music to engage response on many levels. Words can function much the same way. In Chris Raschka's (1992) tribute to jazz musician Charlie Parker, the picture book *Charlie Parker Played Be Bop*, language represents musical sounds. With careful placement, Raschka uses commonplace and nonsense words to create hip hop in an amusing, melodic beat. Words form the rhythm of improvisational jazz through rhyme (*be bop, bus stop, lollipop*) or sound (*zznnzznn*). This type of picture book begs to be read aloud or even to be performed. Literature that plays with the sounds, the patterns, and the meaning of language is most effective when readers are able to hear the language and see the written words. This is particularly true with poetry. Performing text is a key strategy to use to focus middle grades students on language. The act of interpreting a poem orally requires students to use sound to represent meaning. Group performance can be done in the Readers' Theater format that we have presented in Chapter 5 or through a dramatic presentation (Anderson, 1998; Gardoqui, 1998; Hancock, 2000). This is an engaging activity that helps students to focus on the varied elements of language and interpret, or infer, the meaning of the text.

   In addition to poetry, books that present musical content through language are excellent sources to begin a close examination of words and written form. For example, the picture book *Zin! Zin! Zin! A Violin* (Moss, 1995) makes the transition from the printed word to the sound of music in a visually seamless fashion by presenting melodic waves of print on the page. In *I See the Rhythm*, illustrator Michelle Wood and author Toyomi Igus (1998) create a vivid history of African American music through art, prose poems, and songs. Different forms of typeface heighten the impact of the words, which represent musical topics as diverse as slave songs and the birth of the blues. A timeline at the bottom of each page provides detailed information about historical events taking place during each musical period. Language works on multiple levels in these types of books to create an emotional impact through form and style.

Taking a Closer Look at an Author's Words

Students can also be encouraged to look more closely at language by reading short poems about familiar things. Valerie Worth's (1987) *All the Small Poems* and Karla Kuskin's (1980) *Dogs and Dragons, Trees and Dreams* both contain sharp observations on objects in everyday life. Look at the following excerpt from the poem "Pleitos" by Gary Soto (1995), in which he describes his cat.

> Pleitos, my *gatito*
> With all nine lives,
> Wrestles socks, bullies
> A spool of yellow thread,
> Boxes a potted
> Plant in the corner,
> And now sleeps in sunlight.
> His whiskers twitch,
> And his ears, left
> First, then right,
> Also twitch, His
> Breathing comes and goes,
> Comes and goes,
> As the motor inside
> His belly idles. (pp. 23–26)

Notice the strong verbs Soto uses: *wrestles, bullies, boxes, twitch*. Consider how he pairs nouns with the verbs (*motor with idles*). What pictures does he create? Read the excerpt aloud. How does the rhythm of the poem change as Soto focuses on different topics?

Authors can also create meaning by using words in varied formats. For example, concrete poetry is visual word play. The shape of the poem is closely tied to meaning. Jack Prelutsky's (1994) "I Was Walking in a Circle" reads in an endless round, and some of Douglas Florian's (1998) poems in *Insectlopedia* such as "Inchworm" and "The Anteater," actually take on the shapes of creatures. In *Sweet Corn*, James Stevenson (1995) experiments with how varying typeface and word placement creates visual settings for his poetry. The format of the writing also affects the impact of the language. Consider Alice Schertle's (1995) powerful nature poem "Secretary Bird," which be-

INSECTLOPEDIA

POEMS AND PAINTINGS BY
DOUGLAS FLORIAN

gins with the phrase "Take a letter," and continues in the form of a dictation: "Say that/ the ancient trees are falling." Judith Viorst's *Sad Underwear and Other Complications* (1995) groups poems into categories such as "Questions," "Stuff You Should Know," and even "Knock Knocks."

Form is just one way to encourage students to experiment with words. Authentic dialects and uses of other languages can represent both regional and international cultures and draw students into a particular setting. Battle (1996) provides an annotated list of books that celebrate this type of language variety. For example, in the picture book *Working Cotton*, Sherley Anne Williams (1992) writes a first-person account from a young girl's perspective of a day of picking cotton with other migrant workers. The use of dialect, coupled with the description of the changes in the morning, is both musical and poignant. The language creates a clear sense of setting:

> We gets to the fields early, before it's even light. Sometime I still be asleep.
> It be cold, cold, cold.
> The field fire send up a gray trail to the hazy sky. Everyone speak in smoky whispers . . .
> Cotton smell like morning, sometime, kind of damp. It smell dusty now it's warm, like if you
>   get too close, you sneeze.
> The rows of cotton stretch as far as I can see.

Compare the mood created in the simple dialect above to the humorous tone of the language in *Whitefish Will Rides Again!* (Yorinks, 1994). When unemployed sheriff Will takes up the harmonica to fill his free time, this is the description of his playing: "Soooooooey! What a ruckus. Worse than a bobcat caught on a cactus. Yup, coyotes learned how to howl just to drown out that stinkweed serenade." Diane Stanley's (1996) *Saving Sweetness* is another exaggerated tale about an orphan in the Wild West, told from the sheriff's perspective with colorful language. Box 7.1 provides other examples of books that will engage students to think closely about language.

Using Double-Entry Journals to Record Student Responses to Language

Having students create a *double-entry journal* of quotes and responses is one way to formalize this examination of language usage. As their name indicates, double-entry journals are set up in two columns. On the left side, students list quotes to analyze. In the right column, students reflect on the quotes selected. In challenging reading, the teacher can preselect quotes for students to consider as they read. These reflections can include different topics. Students can take a careful look at comments about a character's motivations, or write predictions about what will happen in the story, or discuss personal connections with the text. Students can also consider finer points for discussion: how a character makes a statement, hidden meanings in words, or different char-

BOX 7.1. Books That Encourage Language Play and Word Analysis

Poetry in Unusual Forms

Florian, D. (1994). *Beast feast.* San Diego, CA: Harcourt Brace.
Florian, D. (1996). *On the wing: Bird poems and paintings.* San Diego, CA: Harcourt Brace.
Florian, D. (1997). *In the swim: Poems and paintings.* San Diego, CA: Harcourt Brace.
Schertle, A. (1995). *Advice for a frog* (ill. N. Green). New York: Lothrop, Lee & Shepard.
Stevenson, J. (1995). *Sweet corn: Poems.* New York: Greenwillow.
Viorst, J. (1995). *Sad underwear and other complications* (ill. R. Hull). New York: Atheneum.

Thinking about Words and Syntax

Clements, S. (1996). *Frindle* (ill. B. Selznick). New York: Simon & Schuster.
Gwynne, F. (1970). *The king who rained.* New York: Windmill.
Heller, R. (1987). *A cache of jewels and other collective nouns.* New York: Grosset & Dunlap.
Heller, R. (1995). *Behind the mask: A book about prepositions.* New York: Grosset & Dunlap.
Price, R., & Stern, L. (1996). *Grab bag! Mad libs.* New York: Price Stern Sloan.
The Scholastic dictionary of synonyms, antonyms, homonyms. (1965). New York: Scholastic.
Terban, M. (1987). *Mad as a wet hen! And other funny idioms.* New York: Clarion.
Terban, M. (1992). *Funny you should ask: How to make up jokes and riddles with wordplay* (ill. J. O'Brien). New York: Clarion.
Terban, M. (1993). *It figures: Fun figures of speech.* New York: Clarion.
Viorst, J. (1994). *The alphabet from Z to A (with much confusion on the way).* New York: Aladdin.
Wood, A. (1988). *Elbert's bad word* (ill. D. Wood & A. Wood). San Diego, CA: Harcourt Brace.

English and Spanish

Dorrows, A. (1991). *Abuela* (ill. E. Kleven). New York: Dutton.
Ehlert, L. (1997). *Cuckoo.* San Diego, CA: Harcourt Brace.
Garza, C. L. (1998). *In my family/En mi familia.* New York: Children's Press.
Soto, G. (1987). *The cat's meow* (ill. J. Cepeda). Portland, OR: Strawberry Hill.
Soto, G. (1995). *Chato's kitchen* (ill. S. Guevara). New York: Putnam.
Zamorano, A. (1996). *Let's eat* (ill. J. Vivas). New York: Scholastic.

Dialect and Setting

Del Negro, J. (1998). *Lucy Dove* (ill. L. Gore). New York: Dorling Kindersley.
McKissack, P. C. (1988). *Mirandy and Brother Wind* (ill. J. Pinkney). New York: Knopf.
Root, P. (1996). *Aunt Nancy and Old Man Trouble* (ill. D. Parkins). Cambridge, MA: Candlewick.
San Souci, R. D. (1992). *Sukey and the Mermaid* (ill. J. B. Pinkney). New York: Macmillan.
Schroeder, A. (1997). *Smoky Mountain Rose: An Appalachian Cinderella* (ill B. Sneed). New York: Dial.
Taylor, M. D. (1987). *The friendship.* New York: Dial.

acters' viewpoints. A double-entry journal is also a good place to look at quotes that relate to theme in a novel, to consider an author's style of writing, or to analyze the point of view used. A teacher can direct the style of response in a dialogue journal by modeling the selection of a quote and the type of response that can be written. Box 7.2 gives an example of a double-entry journal for the beginning of the book *Skellig* by David Almond (1999). The focus of this journal is on the author's choice of wording in the development of the main characters and the setting. However, you can see that this type of journal also allows the reader to consider personal connections to literature.

Teaching Students about Language through Writing

Discovering Language through Found Poetry

One way to focus students on the power of language is by using another author's words to create a new piece of writing, or found poetry. Hobgood (1998) gives step-by-step instructions for how to create a poem from an author's selection of prose, and then how to use a student's own informal writing as a basis for poetry. Students learn how to harvest powerful words and images to form a poem from a short selection of a narrative text or even a primary source in a nonfiction book. Later, students are able to use this same technique to select main ideas and strong words from their own journal response or *quick write* to create poetry. See Box 7.3 for directions and an example of a humorous found poem from a fifth-grade student's writing.

The keys to successful found poetry are selecting an interesting piece of writing and carefully considering word choice and line breaks. This is a good technique to focus students on the language and vocabulary of specific content areas. Classroom compilations of found poems can be produced from collections such as Kathleen Krull's (1993, 1994, 1995, 1998, 1999) humorous biographies of athletes, presidents, writers, musicians, and even psychics, or from primary sources such as *Slavery Time When I Was Chillun* (Hurmence, 1997) and *I Was Dreaming to Come to America: Memories from the Ellis Island Oral History Project* (Lawlor, 1995). Picture books that clearly describe a setting also work well, such as Faith Ringgold's description of imagining flying over a city in *Tar Beach* (1991) or Chris Van Allsburg's fantasy journeys in *The Wreck of the Zephyr* (1983) and *The Polar Express* (1985). Model how to select powerful language and determine line breaks by working through these procedures with your class. Create a found poem as a group using an excerpt from a children's book. Select a short description or a story from a novel that includes written entries by children, such as the journals kept by Sophie and her cousin Cody as they sail across the Atlantic Ocean in Sharon Creech's (2000) *The Wanderer*. Try using Sophie's description of their boat as it battled through the storm to create a found poem:

> As each wave started to build, it made me weak and queasy, not so much from the motion, but from the fear that this wave would be too big, that this one would roll us over. Off in the distance, I saw a wave that looked different from all the others. It was much bigger, at least fifty feet high it seemed, and not dark like the others. It was white—all white—and the entire wave was foam, as if it had just broken. I stared at it for a couple of seconds, trying to figure out what was up with it, and by that time it was right behind us, growing bigger and bigger, still covered with foam.
>   I shouted a warning to Cody: "Cody! Look behind—" (p. 207)

BOX 7.2. An Example of a Double-Entry Journal

Quotes selected from the beginning of *Skellig* by David Almond (1999)	Student reflections on the author's word choice in setting and character development
I found him in the garage on a Sunday afternoon. It was the day after we moved into Falconer Road. The winter was ending. Mum had said we'd be moving just in time for spring. Nobody else was there. Just me. The others were inside the house with Dr. Death, worrying about the baby. (p. 1)	This starts like a mystery, but with really simple words. It doesn't tell you who Michael found, or why they are worrying about the baby. They must think the baby will die, because why else would he call the doctor that name. Michael calls his mother "Mum." I know they do this in England. That is where this author is from.
He was filthy and pale and dried out and I thought he was dead. I couldn't have been more wrong. I'd soon begin to see the truth about him, that there'd never been another creature like him in the world. (p. 1)	It is hard to tell whether he is talking about a person. I guess you can think about an old person as dried out, but what Michael finds in the garage seems different than just someone who is old. You can tell that part of the mystery will be finding out what type of creature he is. He's different, talking to humans but not human. For some reason I think it will be good to know him, even though he looks disgusting.
"Do you think we've got more to worry about than stupid you getting crushed in a stupid garage?" "Yes." "You keep out, then! Right?" "Right. Right, right, right." Then I went back into the wilderness we called a garden and she went back to the stupid baby. (pp. 4–5)	It is weird for his mom to say stupid like that to Michael. The first sentence sounds like what a lot of parents would say (with the stupid part taken out). It changes the message to call him stupid. He found something really incredible in the garage and his mom just yells at him. I think Michael calls the baby stupid because he is really mad at his mom and because the baby has changed their family. The outside is where he feels good now and can forget the way his parents are acting.
"What are you doing there?" I whispered. He sighed, like he was sick to death of everything. "Nothing," he squeaked. "Nothing, nothing, and nothing." I watched a spider scrambling across his face. He caught it in his fingers and popped it in his mouth. (p. 18)	The creature in the garage still seems really different than other people, although he talks, or squeaks, which makes him seem like an animal. There must be something wrong with him, and he doesn't seem like he is going to explain what it is to Michael. Eating the spider sounds like a bird although he uses his fingers. It seems normal for him, just how he eats.

Creating found poems from a book presenting multiple perspectives, such as the dual journal entries of Sophie and Cody on their transatlantic journey, is one way to support students to focus on first-person narration and character development. Novels told in two voices can be sources for an effective paired writing exercise in which students work together to select passages that show different perspectives on the same issue and to create found poems of the two voices. Historical novels such as *Silent Thunder: A Civil War Story* (Pinkney, 1999) and *Steal Away* (Armstrong, 1993), which address the topic of slavery from two characters' perspectives, would be good choices for this type of exercise. To challenge more sophisticated writers, use Fleischman's (1985, 1988) models of "poems for two voices" to show students how to create single poems from two perspectives. This requires a much more careful analysis of language usage and character stance. The writer will need to select lines that both characters speak separately, as well as lines showing common views that both characters speak together.

BOX 7.3. Found Poetry

Steps for Creating a Found Poem: Directions for Students

1. Select a paragraph or short piece of text from a story, a novel, or a piece of nonfiction. A paragraph that describes a character or setting works particularly well. Primary sources, such as a journal entry or a letter from an historical period, can create powerful poetry. You can also use your own quick write or journal entry. Make a copy of the piece of the piece of writing that you can mark.

2. Circle (or list) the strongest words in the passage. Look for active verbs and specific nouns. Cross out any words that are not necessary or are repetitive.

3. Using your strongest words, begin to form a poem. Try to keep the words in the author's original order. Carefully consider line breaks. Which words do you wish to highlight at the beginnings and endings of lines? Which words should stand alone? Think about the meaning of your passage, and let the line breaks demonstrate the strength of certain words.

4. Edit your poem by looking at verb tense and how words work together. If necessary, add a few words, but keep these additions to a minimum. Title your poem.

5. Write a final draft of your poem. Be sure to include a complete citation of your source (author, title, publication information, page numbers).

A Fifth-Grade Student's Writing on an Early Memory

One of my early memories was when my mother had made a cheesecake for my grampa's and my birthday. My grampa's birthday is January 15, and mine is January 16. It was before they came. My mom got a phone call, and I (thinking no one would notice) got out a spoon, and opened up the refrigerator door. I pulled up the plastic wrap covering the cheesecake and scooped up a spoonful right in the middle. I looked out and saw my mom still on the telephone. I ate my spoonful and got another, and another, and another until there was a big hole in the middle of the cheesecake. I put the plastic wrap back on and went into the other room. The next thing I knew, "Jessica! Do you know anything about this?" My mother had discovered the cheesecake. She got very mad at me because my grandparents would be there soon and she couldn't do anything like bake a new cake. My grampa laughed though because we had to eat the cheesecake with a hole in it.

(continued)

Sample of a Found Poem Developed from Student Writing

Our Birthday

One early memory—
A cheesecake my mother made
For my grampa's and my birthday.
It was before they came.
I got out a spoon,
Opened the refrigerator,
Pulled up the wrap,
And scooped up a spoonful
Right in the middle.
Another
Another
Another
Until there was a big
Hole.
"Jessica! Do you know anything about this?"
Grampa laughed,
The cheesecake with a
Hole.

Using Dialogue to Create Readers' Theater Scripts

Another strategy to use to focus students on an author's language usage is to create Readers' Theater scripts from dialogue in text. This process allows students to look closely at the words that an author chooses to use to represent speech, whether it is examining a cultural variant of a folk tale or exploring actual documents from a historical period. Brian Lundstrom, a sixth-grade teacher in Virginia, describes how he uses this process in his social studies class to teach students how to read and write about content about World War II:

"Writing dialogue, whether it is simply copying from their book, or crafting it one-self, is a good way to develop writing skills. Blending the words and story of the author with their own writing styles is a valuable writing experience for the students. The writing of my sixth graders improves with the model of a published author. They were worried at first about having to make decisions themselves without the teacher pointing out the facts, but later they came to enjoy the idea of having to choose what is important.

"I modeled how to write a Readers' Theater [script], using a passage from a nonfiction book, *The Children of Topaz* (Tunnell & Chilcoat, 1996). I gave each student a copy of a page from the book, and I had the same page on the overhead projector. We brainstormed and considered which characters were in the passage, then we wrote the first several lines of dialogue on the board. I had them finish the passage individually at their desks, then we shared the papers orally to get a feel for the procedure. Next, I told the students that I had 24 nonfiction books (e.g., Bachrach, 1994; Durrett, 1998; Stanley, 1994) about various topics dealing with our current study of World War II. They could select a book and work individually or with a partner of their choice."

The scripts students create can then be performed publicly, using the rehearsal techniques given in Chapter 5.

Creating Text Innovations

Students can examine examples of *text innovations*, to see how the form or pattern of a poem or story can be used as a model to create new pieces of writing. Typically, the author keeps the original form of the piece but varies the content. Box 7.4 provides excerpts from the traditional version (*Mother Goose: The Old Nursery Rhymes*, 1978) and a

---

BOX 7.4. Examples of Text Innovations of "The House That Jack Built"

Traditional Version

This is the maiden all forlorn,
That milked that cow with the crumpled horn,
That tossed the dog,
That worried the cat,
That killed the rat,
That ate the malt
That lay in the house that Jack built.

Scary Story Version

This is the mummy from days of yore
that rose from the coffin under the floor
that fell on the monster whose bloodcurdling roar
startled the fearsome manticore
that wrestled the werewolf
that chased the cat
that bit the bat
that lived in the house that Drac built.

Other Text Innovations

Cole, H. (1995). *Jack's garden*. New York: Greenwillow.
Scieszka, J. (1994). *The book that Jack wrote* (ill. D. Adel). New York: Viking.
Taylor, C. (1992). *The house that crack built* (ill. J. T. Dicks). San Francisco: Chronicle.

Note. The traditional version is from *Mother Goose: The old nursery rhymes* (1978). Copyright NTC/Contemporary Publishing Group. Reprinted with permission of NTC/Contemporary Publishing Group, Inc. The scary story version is an excerpt from *The House That Drac Built*, copyright 1995 by Judy Sierra, reprinted by permission of Harcourt, Inc.

---

text innovation (Sierra, 1995) of the nursery rhyme "The House That Jack Built." This pattern also has been used to create rhymes about content as diverse as gardening (Cole, 1995), writing a book (Scieszka, 1994), and drug use (Taylor, 1992).

When students create text innovations, they write their own version of a pattern book or poem, write a new ending to a story, or change the text in another way. This is often less intimidating than starting with a blank page, and once again, it requires students to look carefully at the words that the author has chosen. In *Rose, Where Did You Get That Red?*, Kenneth Koch (1973) uses the works of classic and modern poets as sources of inspiration to encourage both word play and a focus on meaning for students. See Box 7.5 for a poem eighth grader Eliza wrote after studying the apology written by William Carlos Williams in the poem "This Is Just to Say" (the Williams poem is reprinted in Koch, 1973, p. 128). This is followed by a poem written by fourth grader James, based upon the title poem in Judith Viorst's (1981) popular collection *If I Were in Charge of the World and Other Worries*.

Creating double-entry journals, found poetry, Readers' Theater scripts, and text innovations are just a few of the strategies that you can use with your students to encourage them to look more closely at language in poetry and prose. Although this type of work supports your students' understanding of how language is used in context, it may not directly address what your students need to know about the mechanical conventions of English. We continue by demonstrating how your students can strengthen their grammatical knowledge through language study.

WHEN DO I TEACH GRAMMAR?

Learning about Syntax

Syntax refers to the ways sentences are formed in a language and "the grammatical rules that govern their formation" (Harris & Hodges, 1995, p. 249). Most children learn the syntax of their native language without formal instruction, because they hear and practice speech constantly and are naturally adept at generalizing patterns. Typically, this knowledge of oral language transfers easily when written language matches oral language. However, for students learning a language with syntax and grammatical rules that differ from the home or community language, it is necessary to make the differences explicit. For example, a native English speaker learning Spanish or vice versa will need instruction in the different rules of word order and verb forms.

Another component of syntax is *morphology*, or "the study of structure and forms of words including derivation, inflection, and compounding" (Harris & Hodges, 1995, p. 158). *Morphemes*, the smallest unit of meaning in a language, include stand-alone words (or *free morphemes*) such as simple verbs (*jump*) and nouns (*cat*), but also include word parts that change meaning when added to a root word (*bound morphemes*), such as -*s*, -*ed*, and -*ing*. Bound morphemes are difficult to grasp in English, especially for nonnative speakers and speakers of dialects such as African American vernacular. Figures of speech and idiomatic language can be difficult for native English speakers as well as for second-language learners.

The teaching of syntax in schools has traditionally been limited to what has been termed *grammar*, or "conformity to certain structural aspects of speech and writing that

BOX 7.5. Text Innovations Based on Poems

I am Sorry
(based on the poem "This is Just to Say" By William Carlos Williams)

I have taken
Your shirt
That was in
The dryer.

And which,
You were probably
Going to wear
Tomorrow.

Forgive me.
I spilt chocolate on it.
It wasn't fair.
I used to have the same one.
But, I still enjoyed,
How everyone said
I looked better in it than you.

IF I WERE IN CHARGE OF THE WORLD

(based on the poem by Judith Viorst)
If I were in charge of the world,
I'd party all weekend
Go see all the movies I want to see
Travel around the world
And have a giant zoo with endangered species in it.

If I were in charge of the world,
I'd rule my school
Not have to run the mile in gym,
Have recess all day long
And leave school at 9 a.m.

If I were in charge of the world,
I'd give all my teachers report cards
Give the principal detention
Make the teacher sit out for study hall
And make the gym teacher do 2,000 push ups.

If I were in charge of the world,
I'd play all day,
Never have to work again,
Get all the comic books I want,
And send my mom and dad to bed.

Best of all . . .
I'D BE IN CHARGE OF THE WORLD!

we judge acceptable" (Harris & Hodges, 1995; p. 99), although linguists use the term *grammar* in more complex ways (see Harris & Hodges, 1995). Students sometimes still do exercises in grammar books, diagram sentences, and learn the names for common parts of speech (e.g., *nouns*, *verbs*, *adverbs*, *adjectives*) and less well-known ones (e.g., *gerund*, *participial phrase*). Critics of traditional grammar instruction insist that such exercises have little or no effect on the quality of students' writing. A more productive system is to use students' own writing for assessment and individualized instruction in syntax during the editing process. Take a look at how Donald Graves (1983) determines when it is time to focus on mechanical conventions in a conference about a student's writing:

> Three factors should be considered before choosing the focus on skills:
>
> - The writer's intention (push for meaning).
> - Frequency of the skill problem.
> - Place of the writer in the draft.
>
> What does the writer care about in the information? If the main push of a writer's intention is blocked by a skill that stands in the way of meaning, then that skill is chosen. If there is only one instance of the problem, then the teacher will probably ignore it. On the other hand, if there are six other opportunities for a writer to generalize the skill within the same piece, then the writer can gain practice with his own writing. Rarely are mechanical skills taught in early drafts. The skill of working with information is considered in early drafts and the mechanical skills appearing only in later drafts. (p. 276)

This type of grammar instruction provides a student with explicit strategies and meaningful practice opportunities with a grammatical convention the student is already attempting to use. As a convention is mastered, it can be added to an editor's checklist in a personal writing folder. This list contains all of the mechanical conventions that the writer is able to edit without assistance from the teacher.

Introducing Grammar Instruction through Language Play

There are other high-interest methods to use to support the study of grammar. Ruth Heller's exquisitely illustrated picture books, such as *Up, Up, and Away: A Book about Adverbs* (1991), provide illustrations of parts of speech (nouns, adjectives, adverbs, prepositions). See Box 7.1 for several titles. *Mad libs*—short stories with key nouns, adjectives, verbs, and other parts of speech missing—are wonderful for providing meaningful, fun practice with parts of speech. It takes at least two people to do a mad lib. The first player asks the second player to supply the missing parts of speech, writes the words in the story blanks, and reads the finished version aloud. The results are hilarious. Roger Price and Leonard Stern have written many mad lib books about various topics (e.g., outer space, monsters, dinosaurs, sports), including *Grab Bag! Mad Libs* (1996). Magazines such as *Storyworks*, published by Scholastic, also include mad libs. Teachers and students can also use published stories and information books to construct mad libs or write their own.

Marvin Terban's illustrated books (see Box 7.1 for several titles) are also wonderful for analyzing and playing with parts of speech (e.g., "funny real words," "tricky verbs," and "tricky nouns"). He has also written books about figures of speech (similes, metaphors, onomatopoeia, alliteration, hyperbole, and personification), idioms (e.g., "mad as a wet hen," "ants in his pants," "punching the clock"), and puns. *The Scholastic Dictionary of Synonyms, Antonyms, Homonyms* (1965) is another useful tool for studying language.

Grammar Study in Middle School and Beyond

Purser (1996) provides another alternative to traditional grammar instruction by guiding upper grades students to consider the functions of different parts of speech through a color-coded graphic organizer containing all of the topics (and appropriate word lists) that have been addressed in class. Students use this personal grammar sheet as a reference as they are writing and editing. For additional study, Tchudi and Thomas (1996) encourage upper grades students to pursue studies of grammar through creative analysis of the structure of language. Each student researches and creates her or his own "grammar" for a specific topic, such as a grammar of music, fairy tales, road signs, or Shakespeare. These articles and other discussions about grammar instruction are included in a themed issue of *English Journal*, entitled "The Great Debate (Again): Teaching Grammar and Usage" (November 1996).

Although this type of work supports your students' understanding of how language is used in context, studying language through literature and students' writing may not directly address your students' difficulties with decoding words or spelling words correctly. We continue by demonstrating how your students can strengthen their word knowledge through word analysis and word play activities.

WHAT ABOUT SPELLING?

Whenever we spend time with teachers, either informally or in presenting workshops, someone always brings up spelling. There are few topics more controversial. Like beginning reading instruction, views on spelling instruction are often categorized into two seemingly opposite camps. Camp 1 contends that to spell correctly, students need to learn the rules of correct spelling and apply them; Camp 2 argues that students will learn to spell correctly through reading, writing, and experimentation. However, like reading, there is no one best way to approach spelling. A historical look at spelling instruction and some of the parallels with reading instruction helps us to see some of the reasons for the controversy, as well as some of the nuances of the arguments.

A Brief History of Spelling Instruction:
Why We Are Where We Are Today

In this section, we discuss the following major ideas:

- Until the early 1970s, English spelling was thought to be so irregular that the only way to learn it was through rote memorization.
- Thanks to research beginning in the early 1970s, we now know that children can

write and make discoveries about spelling even before they can read, and that students learn to spell in developmental stages.

• English contains many regular spelling patterns, features, and high-frequency words that students can learn through reading, writing, and focused instruction based on their developing knowledge about words.

• Acceptance of invented or developmental spelling encourages young children to write creatively and gives them opportunities to experiment with their growing understanding of how words work. Students of all ages, even adults, may continue to invent spellings for unfamiliar words, frequently misspelled words (e.g., *necessary*), and patterns that don't see to follow a rule (e.g., words that end with *-ence/-ance*, *-ible/-able*).

• As spelling patterns and common words are learned, students should be *encouraged* to spell them correctly in drafts and *expected* to spell them correctly in published work. Spelling references, such as word walls, thematic word lists, dictionaries, books, and spell checkers, are excellent tools for helping students to spell these words correctly.

• Correct spelling is not equated with intelligence or good character!

The Whole-Word versus Phonics-First Debate

As early as the late 1800s, there were two distinct methods for teaching students to identify words. Proponents of the *whole-word* method believed that the irregularities of the English language made it futile to base instruction on sound-to-letter correspondences, so words were taught through repetition and by linking them with meaning in context. *Phonics-first* advocates, though aware that sound-to-letter correspondences were not always regular, believed that sounds were a better bridge to reading than guesses based on context. As different as these approaches were in beliefs about the teaching of reading, however, they were in agreement about spelling instruction: "In both groups, spelling was thought to require brute memory" (Henderson, 1990, p. 810). Even into the 1950s and 1960s, a particularly contentious time in the whole-word versus phonics-first debate, spelling was still a nonissue. Now we know that learning to spell by memorizing every word would not only be impractical; it would be impossible because of the tremendous number of words in the English language. Fortunately, English is not as irregular as it seems, as shown in studies of the spontaneous writing of preschoolers described in the next section.

How Students Learn to Spell: Research from the 1970s Onward

In the early 1970s, linguists Carol Chomsky (1970) and Charles Read (1971) analyzed preschoolers' writing to determine the complex phonological understandings of written language that the children had developed. On their own, with no formal instruction, these children had each discovered similar generalizations about how the sound–letter system in English works. Young children's attempts at spelling came to be known as *invented spelling* or *developmental spelling*. Paired with an idea made popular in the 1970s—that learning to read is as natural as learning to speak—developmental spelling became a hallmark of instructional approaches that stressed meaningful experiences with reading and writing, such as process writing. This movement is still underway. Whereas previously people had assumed that children could not write until they learned to read, kindergarten and first-grade teachers began to give students opportu- nities to experiment with writing. It was an exciting and productive time in writing in- struction. Freed from the constraints of correctness, and given many open-ended op- portunities to write, the change in children's writing was remarkable. In classrooms that focused on correctness, children often produced stilted writing with simple, easy- to-spell vocabulary, like the writing sample in Box 7.6 (written by a first grader). In con- trast, children who were encouraged to write without concern for spelling or form of- ten produced more interesting, personal writing, with a strong voice and varied vocab- ulary, as in the writing sample in Box 7.7 (also written by a first grader). This freedom to experiment also aided students in further developing their own knowledge about how words work, leading to progress in word identification as well as spelling and writing.

However, there were problems. Some students continued to misspell words that they could easily read, even past the early grades. Box 7.8 contains a piece written by a fourth grader, Alex. Notice the misspellings of common, familiar words and simple spelling patterns. Alex is not an isolated case; we even see students in middle school misspelling some of these words. Why does this still happen? One reason is that some teachers stop short of requiring students to edit their final papers for mechanics, and invented spellings continue to be accepted for words and patterns that have already been learned and for high-frequency words. When asked, Alex was able to easily pick out and correctly edit the misspelled words in his piece, as most students are. Another reason is that appropriate, meaningful spelling instruction is not a reality in many classrooms. However, before you target developmental spelling as the downfall of liter- acy, remember that prior to the acceptance of developmental spelling, students' writing was typically limited to known "safe" words, resulting in the kind of stilted writing produced by the first grader in Box 7.6. Educators who advocate a return to the "good old days," when students supposedly spelled correctly, are asking for a return to risk-

---

BOX 7.6. A First Grader's Writing with a Spelling and Mechanics Focus

I Love Happys and Pizza
I Love cats.
I Love dogs.
I LiKe dears.
and I LiKe me too

BOX 7.7. A First Grader's Writing with a Meaning Focus

A Big strog gie walked up
to our tent and said I have
a tent qust like youers and a
skuck got in it! so we tide
A twisty tiue around it But
Unfoush uutly hedid

averse students who produce uninteresting writing with a finite number of memorized words.

Even today, when students turn in papers with misspellings, some teachers are not sure how to respond, especially if the focus is on the content of the piece. Many ignore misspellings completely, hoping that students will learn to spell through reading and writing experiences alone. In contrast, some teachers circle every misspelling on students' papers, hoping that students will get the message and spell those words correctly next time. These same teachers often believe that good spellers are good memorizers, and they use commercial spelling programs or give students unrelated lists of words to memorize for Friday spelling tests. In our experiences, neither of these approaches seems to help students learn to spell, nor do they encourage students to take responsibility for their own published work.

Although some naturally good spellers catch on, most students need guided instruction to make accelerated progress in spelling. One point of agreement in current spelling research is that for spelling instruction to be effective, it should be based on an understanding of how students learn to read and spell and where students are working on this developmental continuum. After discussing the foundations of spelling, we return to the question of what and when students should spell conventionally.

Henderson and his colleagues extended Read's and Chomsky's work with school-age students (Henderson & Templeton, 1986), outlining instructional implications and approaches (see Bear et al., 2000). One important understanding that came from this work was that children learn to spell in developmental stages that parallel their development in reading. In a nutshell, most young children begin to spell by imitating writing in scribbles or letter-like forms. Reading at this stage consists of memorizing favorite books and making up stories or words to accompany the pictures in books (pretend reading). Gradually, with exposure to print and experiences with tracking words, they

BOX 7.8. A Fourth Grader's Writing Sample

YO YO'S

One thing I like
about yo yo's that they are
fun. You cold buy yo yo's form
store and mialls. With a yo-y
you can do different tricks /
walk the dog, around the world,
sleep the yo yo, dog bite and disco.
There are some yo-yos for beginers
who don't know how to yo-yo.
Yo yo's have ~~good~~ cool pictures
on the sides. There even is
a internet for yoyo's.
It is yo yo.com or yo yo.
Now you know how
to look up yo-yo's on the
internet. I love yo-yo's !

begin to use the sounds of letter names to represent the initial sounds in words and to recognize a few common words (e.g., *cat, dog*). They may attempt to "sound out" unknown words simply by using the first letter and guessing based on pictures or other meaning clues. As students spend more time in shared reading experiences, they start to understand the other sounds produced by letters and will begin to use their new knowledge in decoding. In turn, as students develop independence and fluency in their reading, they are able to spell chunks of words using word patterns. They also begin to attend to the syllables and word endings. Finally, students who are skilled readers apply their understanding of the meaning of words in order to spell more complicated words. Box 7.9 shows characteristics and examples of spelling at each stage.

BOX 7.9. Using Students' Developmental Spellings to Plan for Instruction

A student's developing knowledge about spelling	Sample spellings of the word *break*	Instructional strategies to support further learning
• Letter-like forms or scribbles • Random letters • Some correct initial consonants	Emergent spelling: *I/xO* *0PX13* *BLo*	• Present oral phonemic awareness activities (rhyming words, initial consonants) using pictures, songs, and poetry. • Begin to work on initial consonants in print (e.g., finding a target consonant in print and finding pictures that begin with the same letter, sorting pictures).
• Most initial consonants spelled correctly • Beginning to spell but often confusing simple digraphs (*ch* in *chin*, *th* in *this*) and blends (*st* in *stop*, *pl* in *play*, *gr* in *green*) • Using a vowel in the word that sounds like the letter's name (e.g., *lik* for *like*) • Spelling long vowel sounds using the correct vowel • Spelling short vowel sounds using the letter name that is closest in place of articulation	Spelling by sound: *Bk* *BaK* *brak*	• Teach the concept of blending letters together to make a word. Oral phonemic blending and segmentation activities can also be used. • Begin "onset and rime" or "word family" work (*r-an/p-an*). Use simple short vowel rimes. • Teach the concept of blends orally, using pictures. • Compare words with blends to words without blends (*cap/clap*). • Demonstrate how to add blends and digraphs to simple word families.
• Beginning to experiment with long vowel markers (*shaed/shade*) • Spelling short vowels, blends, and digraphs correctly most of the time • Spelling inflectional endings phonetically (*pind/pinned, jumpt/jumped, batid/batted*) • Not doubling (*bated/batted*) • Overgeneralization of doubling (*helpping/helping*) • Confusing more complex vowel patterns (*through/cough/though/thought, steak/break/hear/mean, rein/reign*)	Spelling by pattern: *baeck* *braik* *brake*	• Compare three-letter short vowel words with silent *e* words (*rat/rate, cap/cape*). • Study long vowel rimes. • Focusing on one vowel, contrast short vowel patterns with long vowel patterns. • Collect words with *-ed* and examine the meaning (the spelling stays constant despite differences in pronunciation). • Compare doubled versus nondoubled words. Teach open and closed syllables. • Compare and contrast complex vowel patterns. • For independent practice, go for vowel pattern word hunts to collect words with certain patterns from books students are reading. Play other word games (e.g., riddles, concentration).
• Confusing homophones (*plain/plane*) • Misspelling letters in reduced syllables (e.g., *defanition/definition*)	Spelling by meaning: *break*	• Work on meanings and spellings of simple prefixes and suffixes. • Work with homophones (stress how meaning determines the spelling). • Examine the constancy of meaning and spelling in Greek combining forms (e.g., *therme, tele, phono*) and Latin roots (e.g., *-tract-, -spir-*).

Strategies Students Use in Spelling

Spelling by Sound

Few preschoolers know the *sounds* of all the letters, but many know the *names*. Students first pay attention to the most salient or important *sounds* in a word and match those sounds with letter names. They begin by matching the initial consonant sound in the word with a letter. This works well for many letters, but many children have problems when a letter name does not make a similar sound, such as the letter *w*. The children usually substitute a letter name that makes a similar sound, such as *y*. Similarly, the sound made by the consonant blend *dr* (as in *drive*) matches best with the letter names *g* or *j*. The consonant digraph *ch* (as in *chop*) is often spelled with the letter *h*, which contains the /*ch*/ sound. In spelling long vowels, like the *i* in *like*, preschoolers and beginning readers may spell the word *lik*. For short vowels, children match the sound of the vowel with the vowel letter name that is closest in place of articulation (i.e., where the sound is produced in the mouth and throat). As an illustration, say the sound of short *o* in *bottle* and *chop*. Note the shape of your mouth and where the sound is produced. Your mouth should be wide open and your tongue relaxed. Now say each vowel letter *name* in turn (*a, e, i, o, u*). Which letter name is closest to the sound of /*o*/? Most children will say *i* and will use that letter in spelling *chop* (*chip, hip,* or *cip*) and *bottle* (*bitl, bidl*). See Box 7.9 for other examples.

Spelling by Pattern

Through experiences with print and/or instruction, children begin to see that English spelling is dependent on patterns in addition to sound. For example, a child using a letter name strategy could be expected to spell the words *lick* and *like* exactly the same (*lik*). In the typical developmental progression, students next begin to notice and use patterns for long vowels, and might spell the word correctly or with a different pattern (e.g., *liak, liek*). Early in this phase you may notice students overgeneralizing—that is, inserting long vowel markers where they are not necessary (e.g., *blake* for *black*). Typically, these overgeneralizations are short-lived, disappearing as students gain more experience with print. The English language is replete with long vowel patterns. Consider that the sound of long *i* can be spelled in all of the following ways: *bike, hi, high, fly, pie, height, aye*. Now consider that each of the vowels has multiple patterns, and you begin to understand the complexity of learning English spelling. However, the very fact that there *are* identifiable patterns and that our brains are programmed to detect patterns means that much of the English language can be learned through experience coupled with instruction, although in the case of less common long vowel patterns, the road to conventional spelling is long. Especially difficult are vowel patterns with variable sounds (e.g., *four/pound/though/through/cough; steak/bread/breathe/heard/fear*).

Other patterns are seen in words with more than one syllable, including when to double consonants (as in *hop* and *hopping*) or drop *e*'s (as in *hope* and *hoping*) when adding inflectional endings like *-ing, -es,* and *-ed*. Remember that there are often exceptions to generalities (see Adams, 1990; Bear et al., 2000; Henderson & Templeton, 1986). Even students who have learned the importance of pattern are often confused when trying to spell the vowel sounds in reduced syllables (i.e., the schwa sound), such as the *u* in *helpful*, the *o* in *conserve*, and the first *i* in *definition*. The schwa sound in these words could be spelled with any vowel and still sound correct.

Spelling by Meaning

In multisyllabic words, meaning usually overrides sound in spelling. When students learn the role that meaning plays in spelling, they become aware that the word *dear*, for example, can also be spelled *deer*, depending on its meaning and the context in which it is used. Another example of the importance of meaning is in derivations. The words *define* and *definition*, for example, come from the same root. Students who understand the role that meaning plays in spelling know that the reduced or schwa sound in *definition* must be spelled with an *i*, rather than with an *e*, *o*, *a*, or *u*. Even college students regularly misspell *definition* and other similar words, such as *composition* (where the second *o* is a reduced sound, but can be remembered if the root word, *compose*, is recalled). Words that have silent letters (e.g., *hasten*, *sign*, *condemn*) can also be spelled correctly if students know words from the same root in which the silent letter is heard (*haste*, *signal*, *condemnation*). When students are studying the role of meaning in the spelling of homophones, derivations, and Greek and Latin roots, they are also learning important principles for vocabulary study.

USING STUDENTS' KNOWLEDGE ABOUT WORDS TO GUIDE INSTRUCTION

Henderson and his colleagues have stressed that to learn to spell conventionally, most students need instruction based on their developing knowledge about words. The spellings that you observe in regular classroom writing activities are windows into your students' developing knowledge about words. Determining the different features that your students have mastered in their spelling will allow you to design instruction that is based on your students' strengths. Studying the features that your students are *attempting* to use as they spell will suggest the areas in which your students are ready to learn more. As a resource for considering developmentally appropriate instruction, see the third column in Box 7.9.

Learning about words is not a step-by-step sequence in which students master features one at a time. In many cases, students who are working on spelling one-syllable words may be considering several features at the same time, such as consonant blends (*bl*, *tr*, *sn*), consonant digraphs (*ch*, *sh*, *th*), and word families (*-at*, *-ot*, *-it*). On the other hand, students who are comfortable spelling most long and short vowel patterns may still be working on spelling one-syllable words with unusual vowel patterns (*caught*, *rough*, *reign*, *juice*) as well as two-syllable words (doubling consonants or dropping the *-e* when adding endings such as *-ed* or *-ing*). Sometimes students will appear to take a step backward as they try to make sense of a new concept. For example, a student who has regularly represented short vowel sounds in one-syllable words such as *bed* may "forget" the short vowel *e* when trying to spell a two-syllable compound word such as *bedtime*, writing *bdtime*. At the same time, an awareness of how students typically develop word knowledge in reading and spelling will help you consider how you might want to individualize instruction or how you might group students for focused study of a feature. In the next sections, we present instructional ideas for students who are learning about sounds and patterns, followed by meaning. Students can keep a word study notebook or folder, including assessments and all word study lists and activities, for reviewing and tracking progress.

Supporting Early Spelling Knowledge about Sounds and Patterns

Words with One Syllable

How do readers typically identify unfamiliar words? Do they sound them out letter by letter? Do they look at the initial consonant and make a guess based on context? The answer, according to research, is neither (Gunning, 1995; Glass & Burton, 1973). Read the word *gleape*. Could you do it? How? Did you use context? Obviously not, since it's a fake word (also called a *pseudoword*), and since the context does not give any clues to what the word might mean. Did you sound it out letter by letter? Mostly likely not, since the *a* and final *-e* are silent in this word. If you are like most readers, you used the more effective strategy of dividing the word into pronounceable chunks and/or familiar patterns (*gl* + *eape*). This strategy is based on what linguists (Treiman, 1991) say are the most natural sound units of words, the *onset* and *rime*. The onset of a one-syllable word (e.g., *stop*) consists of the beginning consonant or consonant cluster (*st-* in *stop*). Consonant sounds are relatively consistent in pronunciation. The rime, which is also called a *spelling pattern*, *word family*, or *phonogram*, consists of the vowel and the letters that follow it (*-op* in *stop*). A single vowel has a multitude of different sounds in different words. For example, the letter *a* sounds different in each of these words: *cat, cape, far, ball, was, bleak*. Vowel letters within rimes are more predictable in pronunciation (Adams, 1990; Wylie & Durrell, 1970). For example, the rimes *-at, -ane, -ar, -ap, -age*, and so forth usually make the same sound when they are seen in words, as the following examples show:

-ane: *mane, pane, plane, crane*
-ag: *bag, tag, rag, flag*

In their examination of primary reading materials, Wylie and Durrell (1970) found 272 rimes with stable pronunciations (pronounced the same in three or more words). They also pointed out that almost 500 primary-level words can be derived from only 37 rimes (see Box 7.10 for the 28 most common ones) using different onsets (see Box 7.11). How many words can you make from the rimes *-ope* and *-ant*?

BOX 7.10. Common Rimes

-ack	-ail	-ain	-ake	-ale	-ame	-an
-ank	-ap	-ash	-at	-ate	-aw	-ay
-eat	-ell	-est	-ice	-ick	-ide	-ight
-ill	-in	-ine	-ing	-ink	-ap	-ir

BOX 7.11. Onsets

b-	g-	qu-*	st-
bl-	gl-	r-	str-
br-	gr-	s-	sw-
c-	h-	sc-	t-
cl-	j-	scr-	th-
cr-	k-	sh-	thr-
ch-	kn-	shr-	tr-
chl-	l-	sk-	tw-
chr-	m-	sl-	v-
d-	n-	sm-	w-
dr-	p-	sn-	wh-
f-	ph-	sp-	wr-
fl-	pl-	spl-	y-
fr-	pr-	spr-	z-

*The *u* makes the consonant sound /w/ in this onset.

Gunning recommends that students become familiar with a core of rimes that are found in common single and multisyllable words. Not all words have onsets; the word *and* consists only of the rime *and*. However, every syllable has one and only one rime. Here are some more examples of onsets and rimes:

strike	onset = str-		rime = -ike
fly	onset = fl-		rime = -y
all	onset = none		rime = -all
through	onset = thr-		rime = -ough
flying	first syllable: onset = fl-; rime = -y	second syllable: onset = none; rime = -ing	

Can you identify the onset and the rime in the following words? Remember, some words do not have onsets, but every one-syllable word (and every syllable in a multisyllable word) has one and only one rime:

jump   thrush   cry   out   through   bringing   Neptune

An effective spelling program should include attention to the concepts of onset and rime. However, when teaching the concept, it is most helpful to use the label *spelling pattern* rather than *rime*.

Building Words

The majority of teachers beyond the primary grades will not need to systematically teach two- and three-letter spelling patterns, unless assessments show that some students are experiencing confusion in basic spelling. However, for all students who have not participated in word study instruction, teachers should review how words are blended together and how spelling patterns work. For students who are still depending upon the sounds of letters to spell words, Gunning (1995) recommends a technique called *building words* to introduce the concept of spelling patterns to students. Starting with a simple spelling pattern (e.g., *-at*), the teacher guides students in blending onsets with the pattern to form other words. It is helpful to begin with words that have single-consonant onsets (e.g., *pat, mat, sat, rat*), followed by words that begin with consonant blends (e.g., *flat, brat*) and with digraphs (*chat, that*). If students need more review or teaching, or if you would like to read some excellent discussions of the concepts discussed here, see Gunning's (1995) article and the books *Words Their Way* (Bear et al., 2000) and *Phonics They Use* (Cunningham, 2000). *The Scholastic Rhyming Dictionary* (1994) is a helpful tool for both teachers and students in studying simple spelling patterns.

"Real Books" with Spelling Patterns

A good way for students to practice and review what they have learned through word study is to read materials containing many examples of words that fit the studied patterns. Currently, there is a resurgence of books that are written specifically for practicing patterns, called *decodable books*. However, they can be very expensive. We have found that some schools have old sets of decodable books from the 1960s and 1970s stuck away in storage areas. Although decodable books can be useful for practice and for word hunts (described in a later section), we prefer that students read "real books," which are more interesting and meaningful. Many excellent reading materials contain regular spelling patterns. Probably the best examples for easy two-letter (e.g., *-op*) and three-letter (e.g., *-ake, -ick*) patterns are in the *I Can Read It All by Myself* series, which include many books by Dr. Seuss such as *The Cat in the Hat* (Seuss, 1957). Other easy Dr. Seuss books with many regular patterns include *One Fish, Two Fish, Red Fish, Blue Fish* (1960) and *Hop on Pop* (1963). The Shel Silverstein poems "Drats" (Silverstein, 1974, p. 72) and "Spoiled Brat" (Silverstein, 1996, p. 89) are examples of text that contain regular patterns in the context of a wonderful poem. Poetry is also excellent for long vowel patterns, as are easy chapter and series books (e.g., in the book *Too Perfect Eek! Stories to Make You Shriek* series—Heiligman, 1999; *Triplet Trouble and the Field Day Disaster*—Dadey & Jones, 1996). Usually, books on students' independent or instructional reading levels will provide many examples of appropriate spelling patterns. Although the major focus should be on appreciation, these books and poems will provide natural, engaging spelling pattern practice for students. Students can also write their own silly stories made of studied spelling patterns.

Spelling Pattern Riddles

What do you call a dog who has just had a bath? A *wet pet*. What's another word for a star? A *night light*. What do you call a riddle that is answered with two rhyming words? A *hink-pink*. An activity that addresses both spelling patterns and critical thinking skills, hink-pinks are a big hit with students (Bromley, 1992). To write a hink-pink, first think of two words that rhyme and have the same pattern. Then think of a riddle that describes the word pair. You can start by giving students a list of hink-pinks and have them match each one up with the riddle that makes sense. Later, students can make up their own hink-pink riddles. Here are some examples:

glad dad   *dime grime*   *old gold*   *kid lid*   *book nook*

What do you call a father who just got a new sports car?
What do you call a cap worn by a young goat?
What do you call your great-great-grandmother's wedding ring?
What is another name for a library?
What is another name for dirt on a 10-cent piece?

A hink-pink can also be made of rhyming word pairs with different spelling patterns (Cunningham, 2000), such as *great weight*, to illustrate that rhyming words do not always have similar spellings. The book *One Sun: A Book of Terse Verse* (McMillan, 1990) is filled with rhyming word pairs illustrated by photographs. Here are some other examples:

loud crowd   *cheap sheep*   *red bread*   *great date*

For more challenging word play, try *hinky-pinkys* (two-syllable rhyming words) and *hinkety-pinketys* (three-syllable rhyming words, and much more difficult). Examples (Buchoff, 1996) are shown below:

Hinky-pinkys: *funny bunny*   *mellow fellow*   *pretty kitty*
Hinkety-pinketys: *resident president*   *confession obsession* *pollution solution*

Addressing Spelling Generalizations and Meaning in Upper-Level Spelling and Reading

When students understand spelling patterns in one-syllable words and simple two-syllable words, they have a foundation for reading and spelling words with more syllables. Teach students to look for pronounceable word parts (consonants, consonant units, and spelling patterns), and also for other familiar patterns, such as word endings (e.g., the *-tion* in words such as *national* and *action*) when they are reading words. Similarly, when they are attempting to spell long or unfamiliar words, encourage students to say and spell each syllable. Word sorts and other activities described above are also appropriate for upper-level word study. *Words Their Way* (Bear et al., 2000) provides additional explanation and suggestions for instruction, independent games, and other activities for all of the word study discussed in this chapter. Students should continue to update word study notebooks as they study new features.

What about Teaching Spelling Rules?

Many spelling programs begin by teaching rules or generalizations and expecting students to memorize and apply them. For several reasons, this strategy rarely works. First, generalizations are often only understood if the learner already has a working knowledge of them. Second, of the 45 generalizations analyzed by Clymer (1963), only 20 "work" more than 80% of the time. For example, the rule "When there are two vowels side by side, the long sound of the first one is heard and the second is usually silent" (more commonly stated as "When two vowels go walking, the first one does the talking") works only 45% of the time! It works in words like *bean* and *pie*, but not in *steak* and *chief*. Finally, when students play an active rather than a passive role in learning, they are more likely to remember and apply what they have learned. We do not mean to say that generalizations are useless. Rather, when students have guided practice in examining words, rather than starting with a rule to memorize and apply, they can make their own hypotheses and test them out through reading and writing.

One way of guiding students to discover principles about spelling is to start with examples of words that fit a pattern, and then to help students to exercise their brainpower in deducing the generalizations or rules. In this way, students exercise the natural tendency to detect patterns, use their own words to explain the patterns, and are likely to remember them better. For example, a very common rule states that when a one-syllable word ends in the letter -*e*, the first vowel sound always "says its name." Although this generalization works only 63% of the time in general (Clymer, 1963), it teaches the concept of long and short vowels, which is useful in understanding how more complex words work (Adams, 1990). A simple activity to guide students in deducing this rule might start with a list of words with a two-letter spelling pattern, contrasted with the same spellings where -*e* has been added—changing the sound, the visual pattern, and the meaning of the words.

hat	*hate*
rip	*ripe*
hop	*hope*
man	*mane*

Discuss with students the vowel sounds that they hear and the pattern that they can observe in each row of words, being sure to model how to break a word down into parts in case students have difficulty hearing the vowel sound. To do this, first take off the initial consonant or blend sound. Second, take off the ending, then say the vowel sound. For instance, you would break down the word *track* as /track/, /ack/, /a/; and the word *shape* as /shape/, /ape/, /a/. Next, ask students to talk about the differences in pattern and sound between the two rows, and to make a rule that fits the pattern. Most students will see that adding -*e* changes the short vowel sound to the long vowel sound. Next, introduce a few words in which the rule doesn't work (e.g., *some*, *have*). We call these "exceptions" or "oddballs," and we find that students love to be the first to find them. "Oddballs" help students to see that while many patterns and generalizations are useful, they do not always work. This activity may seem unnecessarily easy for upper elementary and middle school students. However, for students who have never engaged in word study, it can be a brief, straightforward introduction to the strategy of analyzing words. A wonderful activity for older students is to present generalizations and have students test them out by looking for examples and nonexamples in their reading. Rule-generating demonstrations such as this one are precursors to *word analysis sorts*—a related activity that aids students in analyzing words and patterns.

Word Analysis Sorts

Word analysis sorts are valuable because they provide students with guidance and practice in analyzing how words work. Students also develop an analytical mindset and become "word detectives" who can continue to learn on their own as they read and write. Remember first to introduce word study topics according to what students are representing in their spelling. Students who are ready to contrast long and short vowel patterns, for example, are correctly spelling simple beginning and ending consonants. They usually know consonant blends and digraphs, particularly at the beginnings of words. They spell most one-syllable short vowel words correctly, and they are making some mistakes as they attempt to "mark," or add a second vowel, to long vowel patterns (e.g., *scait* for *skate*). Start with what students know (short vowel patterns), and contrast that knowledge with what students are attempting (long vowel patterns).

As students begin to experiment with patterns in their writing, they need opportunities to compare and contrast how vowel patterns work in different words. A word analysis sort (hereafter called simply a *word sort*) is a hands-on activity in which students categorize words under exemplars (words that provide models of the vowel sounds that they are studying). This type of work allows students to gain fluency in recognizing the sounds vowel patterns make and in associating spelling patterns with sounds. When you first teach students about word sorts, begin by contrasting two distinct sounds of one letter, such as the long and short sounds of a single vowel.

Let's walk through a simple word sort, contrasting short and long *i* vowel patterns by the sounds they make. Select two words that clearly demonstrate the two different vowel sounds to use as models, such as *sit* and *like*. Avoid exemplars with consonants that make the vowel sound more difficult to distinguish, such as *l* (*pill*) or *n* (*pin*). Provide students with about 16 cards on which you have printed the words clearly in lower-case letters. Provide examples of the two vowel patterns (e.g. *fit, dive, ride, lip, chin, time, hide, dig, list, wish, five, fire, mice, pin*), and add a couple of "oddball" words that do not fit either pattern (*girl, dirt*). Be sure to use only words that students can read automatically; set aside any other word cards. You may need to demonstrate how to sort with several words, comparing the words to be sorted to the exemplars, and then monitoring students and providing feedback as they begin to sort the words. Have the students read each of the words aloud as they sort the cards under the two exemplars so that they can clearly hear the differences in sounds. It is helpful to have students say the exemplars out loud as they say the new word if they are having problems determining the category. Set up an "oddball" category for words that do not fit either pattern. The final sort should look like this:

sit	like	"oddballs"
fit	dive	dirt
lip	ride	girl
chin	time	
list	five	
wish	fire	
pin	mice	
dig	hide	

After students have finished sorting, ask them to read each column aloud, starting with the exemplar, to check their work by listening to the sound of the short and long *i* vowel patterns. If there are still errors, read the list to the students or give a clue as to how many errors are in each column. When the words are correctly sorted, ask the students to discuss the pattern shown in each column. They should be able to see the clear difference between the short *i* pattern (consonant–vowel–consonant, or CVC) and the long *i* pattern with a silent -*e* marker (consonant–vowel–consonant–silent -*e*, or CVC*e*). Repeat the process by having students complete one or more quick sorts to gain automaticity with the process. When students are able to sort with speed and accuracy, test their spelling knowledge with a *writing sort*. Before you put away the sorting cards, ask the students to copy the two exemplars at the top of their papers. Call out words they have sorted and new words with the same pattern, and have the students sort the words as they write them under the exemplars in their word study notebooks. This will give you a written record of how the students are internalizing the word sorting process in their own spellings.

Box 7.12 and Box 7.13 provide examples of a more difficult vowel pattern sort that begins with sorting words by sounds, then continues by having students distinguish different long and short vowel patterns. Students' automaticity with distinguishing word patterns and correctly representing those patterns in their spelling can be supported by having students read texts that contain words with the patterns, combining word sorts with word hunts in text, word study games, and word play in writing.

Word Hunts and Word Games

A more explicit activity that helps students learn and practice spelling patterns is the *word hunt* (Henderson, 1990), in which students look through books and other print

---

BOX 7.12. Step 1: Sorting Words by the Sound of Short e and Long e

fed	beat
pet	chief
send	speed
chest	heat
tell	sea
pen	thief
dead	beet
breath	sneak
bent	meal
stem	bleed
sled	me
slept	sleep
death	feed
head	grief
yes	we
stretch	teeth
deaf	she

BOX 7.13. Step 2: Sorting Words by Short and Long e Vowel Patterns

Short e			Long e		
fed	dead	feed	beat	we	chief
pet	head	speed	sneak	she	thief
stretch	breath	teeth	meal	me	grief
tell	death	beet	heat		
send	deaf	feed			
yes		sleep			
slept		bleed			
sled					
pen					
bent					
stem					
chest					

materials for words that follow a target pattern or patterns. Students record the words by pattern in their word study notebooks (see example in Box 7.14). Although most students in grades 3–8 will not need to focus on simple rimes and patterns, they are helpful for initially teaching the concept of word hunts. Word hunts are ideal for independent or small-group practice with already taught patterns after initial teaching through word sorts and other more explicit instructional activities. Before doing a word hunt, students should read and enjoy the books and should be very familiar with the spelling patterns to be found. It's important to preview materials to be sure there are many examples. Box 7.14 shows a word hunt with one short and two long *a* vowel patterns. For less experienced readers and for more complex spelling features, use only one or two patterns. Commercially published word games such as Scrabble and Boggle give stu-

BOX 7.14. Spelling Pattern Word Hunt

Directions for students: Copy the words below in your notebook or on a sheet of paper. Get an easy chapter book. Go through the books and list all of the different *one-syllable* words you can find with these spelling patterns. You can also add words that you can think of.

back	safe	pain
sack	bake	bait
track	flake	raid
_____	_____	_____
_____	_____	_____
_____	_____	_____
_____	_____	_____
_____	_____	_____
_____	_____	_____

dents practice in manipulating letters to form patterns and words. Educational supply stores stock other word games and activities.

Spelling Generalizations in Upper-Level Spelling

You can also address upper-level spelling issues through word analysis by working on a few useful generalizations. Look at Box 7.15 for a word study activity in which students are examining the principles of doubling and -*e* drop when adding an -*ing* ending to a verb (notice that the CVCC pattern can signal either a short vowel or long vowel sound). This sort is not for beginners. Even older students will need to be guided through less complex sorts before attempting a sort with this many patterns. Keep in mind that your purpose is to guide students to voice the principle behind the spelling of the words in each column after they sort, not to "teach" the rule before you begin working with the words. To study the different sounds of *c*, have students generate a list of words that begin with a hard *c*- and a list of words that begin with a soft *c*- (e.g., *canter, coast, college, cut, category, copy, card, carry, catalog, cave, caught, cash* vs. *center, cell, cement, cereal, cent, central, certain, central, certify, ceremony, ceiling, cemetery, century*). Write the list on the board. What differences do they see in the vowels used after the hard *c* and the soft *c*? How does this inform spelling? You can use this type of approach

---

BOX 7.15. Learning to Spell Words with -*ing* Endings

With your students, generate a list of words with *o* vowel patterns and -*ing* endings. Write the words on the board. Write down the base word beside each word. A sample list is given below:

topping (top)	hoping (hope)	stopping (stop)	coping (cope)	coating (coat)
voting (vote)	holding (hold)	mopping (mop)	mowing (mow)	locking (lock)
moaning (moan)	coach (coaching)	knock (knocking)	plotting (plot)	floating (float)
popping (pop)	plotting (plot)	bombing (bomb)	loading (load)	phoning (phone)
shopping (shop)	shocking (shock)	hosing (hose)	smoking (smoke)	hopping (hop)
stroking (stroke)	posting (post)	growing (grow)	coaching (coach)	

Sort all of the base words with short vowel patterns under the exemplars below, then match with the -*ing* form of the word:		Sort all of the words with long vowel patterns under the exemplars below, then match with the -*ing* form of the word:		
CVC:	CVCC:	CVCe:	CVVC:	CVCC:
top (topping)	lock (locking)	vote (voting)	load (loading)	hold (holding)
stop (stopping)	shock (shocking)	smoke (smoking)	float (floating)	post (posting)
hop (hopping)	knock (knocking)	hose (hosing)	coach (coaching)	
shop (shopping)	bomb (bombing)	stroke (stroking)	coat (coating)	Other patterns:
plot (plotting)		phone (phoning)	moan (moaning)	go (going)
mop (mopping)		cope (coping)		mow (mowing)
pop (popping)		hope (hoping)		

to look for patterns in spelling different word endings that sound the same, including -*or* and -*er*, -*le* and -*el*, -*ible* and -*able*, -*tion* and -*sion*, and other frequently misspelled features that you or students may find. Keep in mind that even though students will often not find straightforward generalizations for all of their word study quests, they will be reading and studying many words and developing a tendency to study words closely, which will be likely to transfer to their spelling and reading.

Vocabulary in Upper-Level Word Study

As students develop more independence in reading and writing, the spelling features they encounter will become more complex and will focus more on meaning than on patterns and sound. Meaning becomes increasingly important in determining how words are spelled. According to Templeton (1983), spelling and vocabulary become increasingly integrated as reading and writing become more sophisticated. *Homophones* (also called *homonyms*), words that sound alike but have different meanings and spellings, are excellent examples of this integral relationship between spelling and meaning. Even after students have a handle on sound and pattern, it is impossible to be sure how to spell words like *break* and *brake* without knowing the context or meaning of the words. After introducing the concept of homophones through several examples of familiar words (e.g., *to/two/too*, *rode/road*, *pear/pear*) and books, students can begin to look for others on their own or in small groups. Gwynne's *The King Who Rained* (1970) and *A Little Pigeon Toad* (1988) provide hilarious illustrations of homophones. Terban's *Eight Ate* (1982) is a book of homophone riddles. Students can use these books as models to write their own riddles and make books or posters.

Homophone games are easy to make. For Homophone Concentration, collect 20 or more homophone pairs and write each word on an index card. Turn all of the cards face down and have each player in turn pick a pair of cards. To be able to keep the cards, the player must use each homophone in a sentence. Another fun way to practice spelling and understanding the meaning of homophones is to include drawing contests similar to the popular game Win, Lose, or Draw. Set up two teams with two students on each team. Create a deck of homophone cards that list two homophones (e.g., *rain/rein*) on one side. A player on the first team takes a card, but does not show it to anyone else. After turning over an egg timer, this  player begins to illustrate the two homophones. To win a point and continue playing, his or her partner must spell the two homophones correctly within the time limit. If the partner is unable to guess what the homophones are and spell them correctly, then the other team gets a chance to try. See *Words Their Way* (Bear et al., 2000) for a list of homophones and instructions for how to play Homophone Rummy.

Working with affixes (prefixes and suffixes) and word roots is essential at this stage of word study. Start with a study of simple prefixes and suffixes (e.g., *re-*, *un-*, *dis-*, *pre-* and *-er*, *-ing*, *-ed*, *-able*), gathering words with familiar roots in which the meaning is obvious. For example, in studying the prefix *un-*, start with words like those below:

Row 1: *unhealthy*   *unable*   *unpaid*   *unfair*   *unequal*
Row 2: *undo*   *unwrap*   *unbend*   *uncross*   *unmask*

Assist students in identifying and defining the root words and deciding how the prefix changes the meaning of each word. What does *un-* mean in the first row? ("Not.") In the second? (To reverse an action or to undo.). As they look for more examples, students will see that there are other words in which *un-* is not a prefix (e.g., *under*, *uncle*) or is part of a different prefix (e.g., *undergo* or *uniform*). Beginning a study of prefixes and suffixes in this way guides students' thinking as they analyze more difficult affixes. For example, the meaning of the prefix *re-* ("back" or "again"), which is obvious in words like *redo* and *reuse*, is less clear in words that include Latin roots (e.g., *retract*, *revise*). This procedure also works to explore the meaning of more complex word beginnings and endings, such as *inter-*, *over-*, *-able*, and *-ful*. See Box 7.9, third column, for other features that can be taught through word sorts and other instructional activities.

Silent Consonants and Shifting Vowel Sounds

Students are fascinated by the fact that meaning from other forms of a word can give them clues for spelling words with a silent consonant. For example, the word *sign* seems to be a strange spelling, since the letter *g* is not heard. The relationship between meaning and spelling becomes clear when students realize that *signal*, in which the *g* is heard, comes from the same root. Other word pairs in which a silent letter is only heard in some forms include the *m* in *mnemonic* (a memory aid) and *amnesia* (the loss or absence of memory), and the *b* in *bomb* and *bombard*. Similarly, when a multisyllable word contains a schwa or reduced vowel sound in one of the syllables (e.g., the second syllable of *definition*), it is impossible to know which vowel letter to use in the spelling (we have seen adults often spelling this *defanition*, *defenition*, etc.). A word derived from the same root will usually contain a clue to the spelling of the reduced syllable. In *define*, the tricky vowel makes the sound of long *i*, which makes the spelling obvious. Other examples of words having these relationships are *competition/compete*, *opposition/ oppose*, *major/majority*, *confidence/confide*, and *brutal/brutality*. Words like these are frequently misspelled even by adults. Students can collect such words in their notebooks.

Borrowed Forms, Roots, and Words

Greek combining forms and Latin roots also provide examples of the constancy of spelling when words are related in meaning. Start with Greek forms, which are easier to define. Collect examples of related words, and help students to define them and isolate the meaning of the Greek form. For example, many words, including *telephone*, *phonograph*, *phonic*, and *homophone* (meaning "same sound") are derived from the Greek form *phon*, meaning "sound." *Thermometer*, *speedometer*, and *barometer* are all measuring instruments derived from the Greek form *meter*, meaning "measure." As students examine the Greek origins of these and other sets of related words such as *thermal* (*therme*, "heat"), they can collect and attempt to define related words such as *thermometer*, *thermos*, *thermostat*, *thermodynamic*, *thermography*, *thermoelectricity*, *thermoregulation*, *thermolysis*, *thermomagnetic*, and *thermosphere*. Other Greek forms include *photo* ("light"), *graph* ("drawn, written"), *hyper* ("over, above, beyond"), and *aster/astr* ("star"). Be sure to begin with familiar words when doing this kind of study. Students can be made aware of these connections by collecting similar words in content area studies to display in the classroom in a mobile or on a bulletin board.

Next, study Latin roots that have fairly stable meanings and spellings (*uni-*, *-spect-*, *-press-*, *-port-*, *-form-*, *-pose-*, *-tract-*, *-spir-*, *-dict-*). Templeton (1983) has noted that the point in such word study is for students to gain an understanding of Greek forms and Latin roots as stable elements in words. Examine a few forms and roots carefully rather than attempting to cover a large number. Word hunts and word games such as Latin Root Jeopardy are engaging ways to solidify this knowledge. See this and other games, along with lists of words for analysis, in *Words Their Way* (Bear et al., 2000). The English language includes borrowed words, forms, and patterns from many different languages. Several books are available for teachers and students who wish to pursue the history of English and the origins of words (e.g., Bryson, 1994; Sarnoff & Ruffins, 1981; *Webster's Dictionary of Word Origins*, 1992).

Organizing Classroom Instructional Time to Teach Spelling Features

Before you set up a program for spelling instruction, you will need to determine the features that your students are ready to study. We have given you some suggestions about how to collect this information from your students' writing and word play activities. Another strategy is to administer a *developmental spelling inventory*, or a list of words that is arranged by spelling features. Box 7.16 provides an example of an inventory taken from *Words Their Way* (Bear et al., 2000). Box 7.17 walks you through an analysis of students' spelling.

The first way to analyze a developmental spelling inventory is by considering the most simple information—the words students spelled correctly and those words that were misspelled. Use this information to put the papers from your classroom in three to four general piles of similar numbers of errors. The next step is to examine the features that each student is able to represent and the features that the student is attempting to use. Look back at Box 7.9 and consider what types of information the student is using to spell words. Is spelling based on sound? Is the student beginning to experiment with patterns? Is the student making errors that are based on meaning? Use this information to reconsider the groupings you did by number of errors. Set up three to four word study groups that examine particular features. For example, after administering an inventory in a sixth-grade classroom, a teacher might initially set up three groups: one group studying long and short vowel patterns, a second group looking at doubling, and a third group exploring Greek and Latin roots. Remember that students may need to move in and out of groups as they work on different features. Box 7.18 describes a weekly spelling program set up by Brandy McCombs, a fourth-grade teacher in Oklahoma, using flexible word study groups.

BOX 7.16. Developmental Spelling Inventory

Elementary Spelling Inventory 1

This is a short spelling inventory to help you learn about your students' orthographic knowledge. The results of the spelling inventories will have implications for reading, writing, vocabulary, and spelling instruction.

Instructions: Let the students know that you are administering this inventory to learn about how they spell. Let them know that this is not a test, but that they will be helping you be a better teacher by doing their best.

Possible script: "I am going to ask you to spell sbme words. Try to spell them the best you can. Some of the words will be easy to spell; some will be more difficult. When you do not know how to spell a word, spell it the best you can; write down all the sounds you feel and hear."

Say the word once, read the sentence, and then say the word again. Work with groups of five words. You may want to stop testing when students miss three out of five words. See Chapter 3 for further instructions on administration and interpretation.

Have students check their papers for their names and the date.

Set One

1. bed	I hopped out of bed this morning.	*bed*
2. ship	The ship sailed around the island.	*ship*
3. when	When will you come back?	*when*
4. lump	He had a lump on his head after he fell.	*lump*
5. float	I can float on the water with my new raft.	*float*

Set Two

6. train	I rode the train to the next town.	*train*
7. place	I found a new place to put my books.	*place*
8. drive	I learned to drive a car.	*drive*
9. bright	The light is very bright.	*bright*
10. shopping	Mother went shopping at the grocery store.	*shopping*

Set Three

11. spoil	The food will spoil if it is not kept cool.	*spoil*
12. serving	The restaurant is serving dinner tonight.	*serving*
13. chewed	The dog chewed up my favorite sweater yesterday.	*chewed*
14. carries	She carries apples in her basket.	*carries*
15. marched	We marched in the parade.	*marched*

Set Four

16. shower	The shower in the bathroom was very hot.	*shower*
17. cattle	The cowboy rounded up the cattle.	*cattle*
18. favor	He did his brother a favor by taking out the trash.	*favor*
19. ripen	The fruit will ripen over the next few days.	*ripen*
20. cellar	I went down to the cellar for the can of paint.	*cellar*

Set Five

21. pleasure	It was a pleasure to listen to the choir sing.	*pleasure*
22. fortunate	It was fortunate that the driver had snow tires during the snowstorm.	*fortunate*
23. confident	I am confident that we can win the game.	*confident*
24. civilize	They had the idea that they could civilize the forest people.	*civilize*
25. opposition	The coach said the opposition would give us a tough game.	*opposition*

Note. From *Words Their Way: Word Study for Phonics, Vocabulary, and Spelling Instruction* (2nd ed.) by Bear, Invernizzi, Templeton, and Johnson. Copyright 2000. Reprinted by permission of Prentice-Hall, Inc., Upper Saddle River, NJ.

BOX 7.17. Analyzing the Developmental Spelling Inventory

Qualitative Spelling Checklist

Student _____ Observer _____

Use this checklist to help you find what stages of spelling development your students are in. There are three gradations within each stage—early, middle, and late. The words in parentheses refer to spelling words on the first Qualitative Spelling Inventory.

This form can be used to follow students' progress. Check when certain features are observed in students' spelling. When a feature is always present check "Yes." The last place where you check "Often" corresponds to the student's stage of spelling development.

Dates: _____ _____ _____

Emergent Stage

Early
- Does the child scribble on the page?   Yes _____   Often _____   No _____
- Do the scribbles follow the conventional direction?
  (left to right in English)   Yes _____   Often _____   No _____

Middle
- Are there letters and numbers used in pretend writing? (*4BT for ship*)   Yes _____   Often _____   No _____

Late
- Are key sounds used in syllabic writing? *(P for ship)*   Yes _____   Often _____   No _____

Letter Name–Alphabetic

Early
- Are beginning consonants included? *(B for bed, S for ship)*   Yes _____   Often _____   No _____
- Is there a vowel in each word?   Yes _____   Often _____   No _____

Middle
- Are some consonant blends and digraphs spelled correctly?
  (ship, when, float)   Yes _____   Often _____   No _____

Late
- Are short vowels spelled correctly? *(bed, ship, when, lump)*   Yes _____   Often _____   No _____
- Is the *m* included in front of other consonants? *(lump)*   Yes _____   Often _____   No _____

Within Word Pattern

Early
- Are long vowels in single-syllable words "used but confused"?
  (FLOAT for *float*, TRANE for *train*)   Yes _____   Often _____   No _____

Middle
- Are most long vowels in single-syllable words spelled correctly
  but some long vowel spelling and other vowel patterns "used
  but confused"? (SPOLE for *spoil*)   Yes _____   Often _____   No _____
- Are most consonant blends and digraphs spelled correctly?   Yes _____   Often _____   No _____
- Are most other vowel patterns spelled correctly?
  (spoil, chewed, serving)   Yes _____   Often _____   No _____

Syllables and Affixes

Early
- Are inflectional endings added correctly to base vowel
  patterns with short vowel patterns? (*shopping, carries*)   Yes _____   Often _____   No _____
- Are consonant doublets spelled correctly? (*cattle, cellar*)   Yes _____   Often ___   No _____

Middle
- Are inflectional endings added correctly to base words?
  (chewed, marched, shower)   Yes _____   Often _____   No _____

Late
- Are less frequent prefixes and suffixes spelled correctly?
  (confident, favor, ripen, cellar, pleasure)   Yes _____   Often _____   No _____

Derivational Relations

Early
- Are most polysyllabic words spelled correctly? (*fortunate, confident*)   Yes _____   Often _____   No _____

Middle
- Are unaccented vowels in derived words spelled correctly?
  (confident, civilize, opposition)   Yes _____   Often _____   No _____

Late
- Are words from derived forms spelled correctly? (*pleasure, civilize*)   Yes _____   Often _____   No _____

Note. From *Words Their Way: Word Study for Phonics, Vocabulary, and Spelling Instruction* (2nd ed.) by Bear, Invernizzi, Templeton, and Johnson. Copyright 2000. Reprinted by permission of Prentice-Hall, Inc., Upper Saddle River, NJ.

BOX 7.18. A Weekly Spelling Program in a Fourth-Grade Classroom (by Brandy McCombs)

Ideas for Developing a Classroom Spelling Program

I developed this program when I was asked to teach spelling to different groups of fourth graders during my first year of teaching. I usually work with about 75 students in three different classes. Their reading abilities range widely; my students are able to read books from early elementary to high school levels. This spelling program allows all of my students to analyze word patterns at appropriate, yet challenging levels. Students also are able to work together to create projects with their classmates. For my students who are just beginning to recognize and apply patterns in words, this approach works well because they pick up information about the construction of words that they missed in previous years at school. However, for my students who have more knowledge about the principles of spelling, this approach is effective because they are challenged with more than just "longer" words. They discover information that they can apply to understanding spelling and new vocabulary in other areas at school, such as science, reading, and writing. I have also found that I can integrate words from two other subjects I teach, Spanish and mathematics, by including Spanish words and mathematical terms.

Getting Started

I begin the year by administering the spelling-by-stage assessment from *Words Their Way* (Bear et al., 2000) to place students in word study groups. I work with up to three groups in a classroom, but students are able to move between groups as they experience success over time with their level of study. I have to educate my parents at the beginning of the year and continue to communicate with them about our goals for spelling. I describe how we break words down (analyze patterns), build new words (apply concepts), and search for more examples of patterns in actual literature (practice). Parents are supportive because they notice substantial growth in their children's knowledge about spelling that is not dependent upon memorizing words. They also comment on the consistency in how spelling is approached at school. Students are being challenged while learning varied concepts, applying valuable writing and editing techniques, and practicing integrated dictionary skills. When I first started teaching, it took me a month or two to establish my program, to discover what worked the best for my students, and to collect the resources that I needed to teach. At this point, it is easy to adapt to make accommodations for students who have an individual education plan (IEP).

Weekly Spelling Plan

Monday: Introduction and Analysis of Word Patterns

Students are introduced to a new spelling pattern through a word sort. They are given the words listed on a sheet for their word analysis group. Students copy two separate lists to cut and sort (one set stays at school and one set is taken home)

Tuesday: Research and Practice

Students practice word sorts then work in dictionaries to examine pronunciation, definitions, and other forms of each word.

(continued)

Wednesday: Applications to Reading and Writing

Students go for "word hunts" in books they are reading, to find patterns related to the words on their lists. Students write stories, poems, commercials, or riddles using these words. Riddles are a huge success; spelling words are used in the description and in the answer.

Thursday: Automaticity and Review

Each group reviews the words (sometimes in game form) and practices sorting.

Friday: Assessment

A spelling test is administered to each group (spelling words on the list, underlining roots when applicable, writing definitions in their own words if appropriate). There are five challenge words, so students have the opportunity to apply the word analysis concept being studied to new vocabulary. Students are also assessed about their understandings of word usage through creative writing (poems, stories, riddles, commercials).

Other Engaging Activities with Spelling Words

- *News Show:* Write a script for a news show about current, high-interest topics, using spelling words and related patterns.
- *Shape-Roos.* Create art drawings that include spelling words as lines in a drawing.
- *Crossword Puzzles:* Design word puzzles for parents and classmates to solve.

Learning to Spell High-Frequency Words

High-frequency words are words that occur frequently in print. Many common words are phonetically irregular; that is, they do not follow a regular sound-to-letter pattern. For example, if *what* was phonetically regular, it would rhyme with *bat. Some* would rhyme with *home, have* with *wave, one* with *zone, are* with *care,* and *many* with *zany. Sure* would begin with *sh-, cough* would end with *-ph* or *-f,* and *one* would begin with *w-.* Confusing? Certainly. However, one good thing about these common words is that they *are* common. They come up in reading and writing constantly, so students see them repeatedly. In fact, although there are more than 80,000 words in the English language, 100 of the most common words account for 50% of written material (Fry, Fountoukidis, & Polk, 1985). If students learn to spell these and other common words, the majority of what they write will be spelled correctly.

Students learn to spell through reading and writing as well as through instruction, so these words should be easy to learn to read and spell. Although they are often difficult for beginning readers to remember, students who have developed some reading fluency can usually *read* these words automatically. Spelling is often a different story, however. For students like Alex (see Box 7.8), and he is far from alone, years of misspelling words that should be easy have led to bad habits. Surely it takes more time to unlearn a bad habit built over many years than to build a good habit. Automaticity in reading means being able to read words quickly so that students can focus on meaning. Being able to write these same words correctly without thinking leads to automaticity in writing. When high-frequency words can be spelled without having to stop and think, students are free to focus on what's most important—the content.

We understand and agree with the argument that an excessive focus on spelling can interfere with students' creativity and thinking about ideas. We agree that if teachers insist that students spell even unfamiliar words correctly, they may respond by using only familiar, easily spelled words in their writing. Students *must* be given the freedom to take risks and use new vocabulary in their writing. However, the story is different with common words when students have learned them and have resources such as word walls to use as references. Common words are not unfamiliar vocabulary. When students have to think about how to spell a familiar common word that should be automatic, it can slow down writing and thinking. Furthermore, many high-frequency words are not spelled like they sound, so invented spellings, which are usually based on *phonetics* (sound) and regular spelling patterns, are usually wrong (Cunningham, 2000). Based purely on sound, *what* would typically be spelled *wut*, *said* would be spelled *sed*, *friend* would be *frend* or *frind*, and *because* would be *becoz*.

What can teachers do to help students learn to spell common words? The best way to learn common words is repeated exposure through lots of reading and writing. Drilling with flash cards and asking student to copy words are not effective techniques, but there are other ways to bring students' attention to individual words outside the context of reading. Word hunts are an excellent way to give students repeated exposure to common words. By their nature, common words are very easy to find in any kind of text. Another approach to learning common words that supplements reading is Cunningham's (2000) *word wall*. A word wall is an alphabetized collection of words. It may be a large bulletin board or piece of butcher paper attached to a wall that every student can see. Cunningham recommends that the words be written with a black Magic Marker on scraps of different-colored construction paper. The teacher introduces four or five high-frequency words per week, discusses the meanings with students, places the words on the alphabetized word wall, and guides students in daily practice activities with the words. When words follow a regular pattern, one of the activities will be finding words that have the same pattern, as shown below:

and → *hand*	*stand*	*band*
in → *pin*	*spin*	*grin*
each → *peach*	*teach*	*preach*

New words are added to the wall each week until, by the end of the year, the word wall contains about 100–120 words. The words used for first graders will contain the easiest of the high-frequency words; the second-grade teacher will use slightly more difficult words, along with some of the more difficult first-grade words; and so on. Many elementary classrooms now have word walls based on Cunningham's books and articles. However, as Cunningham (2000) points out, it is not enough to *have* a word wall; the word wall must be *used*. Using a word wall means introducing the words, engaging students in instructional activities, and reviewing (and holding students accountable for) the words that are on the wall. Even if students initially have to slow down to look at the word wall to find the spelling of a high-frequency word, repeatedly spelling the words correctly will help make them automatic.

Beyond the primary grades, the class word wall should consist of words that students often misspell in writing, including words with multiple syllables and doubled letters (e.g., *necessary, tomorrow*), homophones (a picture can distinguish one homophone from its pair), tricky patterns (e.g., *-ough, -ea-*), contractions, and so forth (Cunningham, 2000; Henderson & Templeton, 1986). Teachers should observe and examine students' writing and add common words as needed. We have found it helpful for upper elementary and some middle school students to use a personal word wall or dictionary. This alphabetized list of high-frequency words can be updated regularly, kept in a writing folder, and used as a reference for spelling high-frequency words when writing and editing. See *The New Reading Teacher's Book of Lists* (Fry et al., 1985) for the most common 1,000 words, which account for approximately 90% of written material.

Helping Students to Move toward Conventional Spelling

The main purpose of writing is to communicate ideas. Coherence and well-formed ideas are the backbones of communication, but these are aided by spelling. Word play and analysis help students not only to spell, but also to read more quickly and automatically. You may still be wondering how and when to hold students accountable for spelling. One way to think about it is to consider that there are both private and public contexts for writing. Assigned work and papers that others will read are public writing, and students should hold themselves accountable for spelling common and familiar words. Personal journals and learning logs are mainly private, even though you as the teacher may read them. Although it is still important that students establish the habit of

---

BOX 7.19. Spelling in Different Writing Contexts

Context	Recommendations for attending to students' writing
Personal journal	Spelling is not emphasized. However, students should be reminded and encouraged to spell known words correctly. Monitor students' journals and work with students who habitually misspell common words.
Learning logs	Same as for the personal journal, except that students should spell content vocabulary correctly when it is readily available (e.g., in books currently in use, books displayed in the room, or teacher-prepared materials).
General schoolwork, including classroom assignments and homework	Students should be expected to spell common words and patterns that have been taught, especially in published work. Make spelling references and resources (e.g., word walls, lists of content words, dictionaries, spell checkers), readily available. Students should attempt unfamiliar words and check their attempts in the dictionary.
Published writing	Teach students a structure for conducting careful edits (several editing checklists are shown in Appendix B). Before publishing, the teacher should complete final edits, consulting with students when appropriate.

spelling common and known words so that they can develop fluency in writing, you will usually not mark spelling errors in private writing. However, you will not want a student to consistently misspell high-frequency words or content vocabulary in a learning log, since this writing will be used as a resource for studying the material. Therefore, displaying common words and content vocabulary in the classroom during writing times, and expecting students to use them, will aid in correct spelling of these words. Consider the goals for each writing assignment, share your expectations for correct spelling with your students, be sure that spelling resources are readily available (common-words list, word study notebook, word wall, list of content vocabulary, content textbooks, dictionary), and model how to use those resources for particular assignments. Box 7.19 shows different writing contexts and provides recommendations for attending to students' spelling.

CHILDREN'S BOOK REFERENCES

Almond, D. (1999). *Skellig*. New York: Delacorte.

Armstrong, J. (1993). *Steal away*. New York: Scholastic.

Bachrach, S. (1994). *Tell them we remember: The story of the Holocaust*. Boston: Little, Brown.

Cole, H. (1995). *Jack's garden*. New York: Greenwillow.

Creech, S. (2000). *The wanderer*. New York: HarperCollins.

Dadey, D., & Jones, M. T. (1996). *Triplet trouble and the field day disaster*. New York: Scholastic.

Durrett, D. (1998). *Unsung heroes of World War II: The story of the Navajo code talkers*. New York: Facts on File.

Fleischman, P. (1985). *I am phoenix: Poems for two voices* (ill. D. Nutt). New York: Harper & Row.

Fleischman, P. (1988). *Joyful noise: Poems for two voices* (ill. E. Beddows). New York: Harper & Row.

Florian, D. (1998). *Insectlopedia: Poems and paintings*. San Diego, CA: Harcourt Brace.

Gwynne, F. (1970). *The king who rained*. New York: Windmill.

Gwynne, F. (1988). *A little pigeon toad*. New York: Simon & Schuster.

Heiligman, D. (1999). *Too perfect (Eek! Stories to make you shriek)*. New York: Grosset & Dunlap.

Heller, R. (1991). *Up, up, and away: A book about adverbs*. New York: Grosset & Dunlap.

Hurmence, B. (Ed.). (1997). *Slavery time when I was chillun*. New York: Putnam.

Igus, T. (1998). *I see the rhythm* (ill. M. Wood). San Francisco: Children's Book Press.

Krull, K. (1993). *Lives of the musicians: Good times, bad times (and what the neighbors thought)* (ill. K. Hewitt). San Diego, CA: Harcourt Brace.

Krull, K. (1994). *Lives of the writers: Comedies, tragedies (and what the neighbors thought)* (ill. K. Hewitt). San Diego, CA: Harcourt Brace.

Krull, K. (1995). *Lives of the artists: Masterpieces, messes (and what the neighbors thought)* (ill. K. Hewitt). San Diego, CA: Harcourt Brace.

Krull, K. (1998). *Lives of the presidents: Fame, shame (and what the neighbors thought)* (ill. K. Hewitt). San Diego, CA: Harcourt Brace.

Krull, K. (1999). *They saw the future: Oracles, psychics, scientists, great thinkers, and pretty good guessers* (ill. K. Brooker). New York: Atheneum.

Kuskin, K. (1980). *Dogs and dragons, trees and dreams: A collection of poems*. New York: Harper & Row.

Lawlor, V. (Ed.). (1995). *I was dreaming to come to America: Memories from the Ellis Island oral history project*. New York: Viking.

McMillan, B. (1990). *One sun: A book of terse verse*. New York: Holiday House.

Moss, L. (1995). *Zin! Zin! Zin! A violin* (ill. M. Priceman). New York: Simon & Schuster.

Mother Goose: The old nursery rhymes (ill. A. Rackham). (1978). New York: Weathervane.

Prelutsky, J. (1994). *A pizza the size of the sun* (ill. J. Stevenson). New York: Greenwillow.

Pinkney, A. D. (1999). *Silent thunder: A Civil War story*. New York: Hyperion.

Price, R., & Stern, L. (1996). *Grab bag! Mad libs*. New York: Price Stern Sloan.

Raschka, C. (1992). *Charlie Parker played be bop*. New York: Orchard.

Reeder, C. (1989). *Shades of gray*. New York: Macmillan.

Ringgold, F. (1991). *Tar Beach*. New York: Crown.

Schertle, A. (1995). *Advice for a frog* (ill. N. Green). New York: Lothrop, Lee & Shepard.

Scieszka, J. (1994). *The book that Jack wrote* (ill. D. Adel). New York: Viking.

Seuss, Dr. (1957). *The cat in the hat*. New York: Random House.

Seuss, Dr. (1960). *One fish, two fish, red fish, blue fish*. New York: Random House.

Seuss, Dr. (1963). *Hop on Pop*. New York: Random House.

Sierra, J. (1995). *The house that Drac built* (ill. W. Hillenbrand). San Diego, CA: Harcourt Brace.

Silverstein, S. (1974). *Where the sidewalk ends*. New York: HarperCollins.

Silverstein, S. (1996). *Falling up*. New York: HarperCollins.

Soto, G. (1995). *Canto familiar* (ill. A. Nelson). San Diego, CA: Harcourt Brace.

Stanley, D. (1996). *Saving Sweetness* (ill. G. B. Karas). New York: Putnam.

Stanley, J. (1994). *I am an American*. New York: Crown.

Stevenson, J. (1995). *Sweet corn: Poems*. New York: Greenwillow.

Taylor, C. (1992). *The house that crack built* (ill. J. T. Dicks). San Francisco: Chronicle.

Terban, M. (1982). *Eight ate: A feast of homonym riddles*. New York: Clarion.

Tunnell, M. O., & Chilcoat, G. W. (1996). *The children of Topaz: The story of a Japanese-American internment camp based on a classroom diary*. New York: Holiday House.

Van Allsburg, C. (1983). *The wreck of the Zephyr*. Boston: Houghton Mifflin.

Van Allsburg, C. (1985). *The polar express*. Boston: Houghton Mifflin.

Viorst, J. (1981). *If I were in charge of the world and other worries* (ill. L. Cherry). New York: Atheneum.

Viorst, J. (1995). *Sad underwear and other complications* (ill. R. Hull). New York: Atheneum.

Williams, S. A. (1992). *Working cotton* (ill. C. Byard). San Diego, CA: Harcourt Brace.

Worth, V. (1987). *All the small poems* (ill. N. Babbitt). New York: Farrar, Straus, Giroux.

Yorinks, A. (1994). *Whitefish Will rides again!* (ill. M. Drucker). New York: HarperCollins.

REFERENCES

Adams, M. J. (1990). *Beginning to read: Thinking and learning about print*. Cambridge, MA: MIT Press.

Anderson, A. P. (1998). Doing poetry. *Voices from the Middle, 6*, 28–33.

Battle, J. (1996). Celebrating language variety. *Language Arts, 73*, 204–211.

Bear, D. R., Invernizzi, M., Templeton, S., & Johnston, F. (2000). *Words their way: Word study for phonics, vocabulary, and spelling instruction* (2nd ed). Upper Saddle River, NJ: Merrill.

Bromley, K. (1992). *Language arts: Exploring connections*. Boston: Allyn & Bacon.

Bryson, B. (1994). *Made in America: An informal history of the English language in the United States*. New York: Morrow.

Buchoff, R. (1996). Riddles: Fun with language across the curriculum. *The Reading Teacher, 49*, 667–668.

Chomsky, C. (1970). Reading, writing, and phonology. *Harvard Educational Review, 40*, 288–309.

Clymer, T. (1963). The utility of phonic generalizations in the primary grades. *The Reading Teacher, 16*, 252–258.

Cunningham, P. (2000). *Phonics they use: Words for reading and writing* (3rd ed.). New York: Harper-Collins.

Fry, E. B., Fountoukidis, D. L., & Polk, J. K (1985). *The new Reading Teacher's book of lists*. Englewood Cliffs, NJ: Prentice-Hall.

Gardoqui, K. E. (1998). Double-dutch, hopscotch, b-ball, and . . . poetry!: Using children's games to create performances of rhythmic poems. *Voices from the Middle, 6*, 11–18.

Glass, G. G., & Burton, E. H. (1973). How do they decode?: Verbalizations and observed behaviors of successful decoders. *Education, 94*, 58–65.

Graves, D. (1983). *Writing: Teachers and children at work.* Portsmouth, NH: Heinemann.

Gunning, T. (1995). Word building: A strategic approach to the teaching of phonics. *The Reading Teacher, 48,* 484–488.

Harris, T. L., & Hodges, R. E. (Eds.). (1995). *The literacy dictionary: The vocabulary of reading and writing.* Newark, DE: International Reading Association.

Hancock, M. R. (2000). *A celebration of literature and response.* Upper Saddle River, NJ: Merrill.

Henderson, E. H. (1990). *Teaching spelling* (2nd ed). Boston: Houghton Mifflin.

Hobgood, J. M. (1998). Found poetry. *Voices from the Middle, 5*(2), 30.

Henderson, E. H., & Templeton, S. (1986). A developmental perspective of formal spelling instruction through alphabet, pattern, and meaning. *Elementary School Journal, 86,* 305–316.

Koch, K. (1973). *Rose, where did you get that red?: Teaching great poetry to children.* New York: Vintage.

Purser, D. (1996). Grammar in a nutshell. *English Journal, 85,* 108–114.

Read, C. (1971). Preschool children's knowledge of English phonology. *Harvard Educational Review, 41,* 1–34.

Sarnoff, J., & Ruffins, R. (1981). *Words: A book about word origins of everyday words and phrases.* New York: Scribner.

The Scholastic dictionary of synonyms, antonyms, homonyms. (1965). New York: Scholastic.

The Scholastic rhyming dictionary. (1994). New York: Scholastic.

Tchudi, S., & Thomas, L. (1996). Taking the g-r-r-r-r out of grammar. *English Journal, 85,* 46–54.

Templeton, S. (1983). Using the spelling/meaning connection to develop word knowledge in older students. *Journal of Reading, 27,* 8–14.

Templeton, S., & Morris, D. (1999). Questions teachers ask about spelling. *Reading Research Quarterly, 34,* 102–112.

Treiman, R. (1991). The role of intersyllabic units in learning to read. In L. Rieben and C. A. Perfetti (Eds.), *Learning to read: Basic research and its implications* (pp. 149–160). Hillsdale, NJ: Erlbaum.

Webster's dictionary of word origins. (1992). New York: Smithmark.

Wylie, R. E., & Durrell, D. D. (1970). Teaching vowels through phonograms. *Elementary English, 47,* 788–791.

CHAPTER 8

Guiding Students to Act as Researchers

It helps me to think of research as the skeleton upon which the flesh of a historical novel is built. A skeleton without blood or muscle and skin is not a complete human being; but without the bones, the rest has no form or strength. Similarly, facts alone don't make a story; yet historical fiction that isn't based on fact simply won't stand up. (DeFelice, 1998, p. 30)

Research is the heart of meaningful writing. In her own historical writing, Cynthia DeFelice describes how she sees facts embedded in creative ideas. Any form of writing has a framework of specific details. By teaching students how to use different resources for research, you will provide them with strategies to collect the facts that make their writing realistic and engaging. In the process, student authors will find themselves hooked by the information they are reading. Consider these comments from students and their teacher about their class research on topics about World War II. These projects culminated in the writing and performance of Readers' Theater scripts based upon nonfiction trade books that they had read.

Emma: "I like doing creative things. I want to be a news broadcaster, and so it was fun to do that. . . . I like when we do projects, but it's really fun when we 'present' them."

Todd: "I really enjoyed doing Readers' Theater because I enjoy writing plays, and it was *much* more interesting than just reading out of a book, and it wasn't terribly difficult. I learned a lot and paid attention. Usually when reading out of history books, I lose interest and start to daydream."

Carrie: "*The Children of Topaz* [Tunnell & Chilcoat, 1996] play was my second favorite—next to *Tell Them We Remember* [Bachrach, 1994]. . . . It was fun because we got to learn about World War II while getting to write and star in plays."

Teacher: "Having the format of a script brings the point to the students that real live people took part in their area of study—something not always gleaned from the standard text. To become a class expert, students realize that they better have a pretty good idea of what it is they are talking about. . . . Selecting what is important attaches ownership to the process, and the results spoke for themselves."

Students need to develop their skills in writing with fluency, accuracy, and meaning. At the same time, engaging students' interest in a topic is always a primary concern. When students are writing a script from a nonfiction text, they must read carefully to select sections that not only are interesting to read aloud, but also present key points about the time period. In addition, when performance becomes the means of publication, students work to share an exciting and creative product with their peers.

In this chapter, we focus on the connections between reading for information and purposeful writing. Performing Readers' Theater scripts written from nonfiction materials, using primary sources for research, and conducting interviews or surveys are just some of the activities that help immerse students in the process of reading and writing. This interactive work with different types of content engages students' interest as they learn about new topics. However, keep in mind that personal choice in research topics is a key factor for promoting engagement in long-term projects in the language arts classroom. We explore how teachers can introduce varied topics and strategies for conducting research in short-term projects; then we consider how to set up more extensive research activities that allow students to investigate areas of personal interest.

WHAT'S IN THIS CHAPTER?

Why Focus on Research?
Learning about the Research Process
Setting Up Clear Steps for Research and the Writing Process
Revisiting the Topic of Engagement in Research

WHY FOCUS ON RESEARCH?

Even when teachers actively explore models of different forms of writing with their classes, students will occasionally struggle with the problem of what to write. Personal experience can provide a basis for their writing, but as you may remember from Nancie Atwell's (1998) comments on the writing workshop in her classroom (see Chapter 6), relying on students' memories and hands-on activities as their primary sources for content will certainly limit what they choose to write. By demonstrating to your students how to conduct research as authors, you will be guiding them to read for information in a purposeful way. In fact, the principles behind teaching writing have similarities to the principles we have discussed in teaching reading. Read the guidelines Stephanie Harvey (1998) uses to organize her research program in *Nonfiction Matters: Reading, Writing, and Research in Grades 3–8*. Where do you see similarities between what we have discussed about strategies for teaching reading and what Harvey suggests about guiding writing and research?

- Teachers can demonstrate how to engage in nonfiction inquiry by going through the process themselves.
- Teachers need to share their passion and curiosity about inquiry and research.
- Research begins with a question.
- Research projects take time.

- To write nonfiction, read nonfiction.
- Writers write best about things they know about, care about, and wonder about.
- Writers need to own their topics and projects.
- Writers need opportunities to share their products.
- Nonfiction inquiry must be authentic whenever possible. (pp. 6–7)

Notice that Harvey focuses on areas you might not initially consider part of the research process. Student engagement is an important point, as well as allowing time for students to work in class with guidance from the teacher. Harvey also suggests that models are needed; students should be reading examples of the format in which they are writing. Here you see a clear fit with issues that we have been discussing about the teaching of reading.

Comprehension is not the only reading issue that you should consider as you structure research and writing. Reading fluency goes hand in hand with reading comprehension. Be sure that you provide students with opportunities to read fluently in research materials. Focused reading on one topic, or *thematic reading*, provides support for fluency because of the continued repetition of vocabulary, details, and related concepts. As a teacher, you can provide even more support by introducing this type of thematic reading with teacher read-alouds from nonfiction materials. Varying the level of difficulty of the reading materials available for research is also important. Providing easy materials on the topic, or reading that is slightly below a student's reading level, also supports comprehension of unfamiliar materials. Using performance techniques such as Readers' Theater supports fluent reading through repetition, but it also creates an emotional context that helps students understand and remember the information. Box 8.1 provides examples of books that not only are excellent sources for studying content area writing, but also can be easily scripted for Readers' Theater.

As an added benefit, this type of nonfiction reading takes students far beyond the basic information that typically is presented in textbooks. For example, many historical trade books focus on the perspectives of groups underrepresented in textbooks: children, women, religious groups, ethnic minorities, and the poor. The primary sources—speeches, advertisements, letters, maps, and diary entries—that are often used in nonfiction trade books to illustrate a historical time period can also be used as models for student writing. In areas such as the sciences, nonfiction can promote a deeper understanding of the materials through the extensive use of photographs and illustrations. Students need this depth of understanding to write comfortably about a topic.

LEARNING ABOUT THE RESEARCH PROCESS

How to Use Different Types of Information

As you can see, teaching students about writing about content topics requires planning on the part of the teacher. Students need to be shown effective ways to read and write about real issues. Box 8.2 outlines basic steps to keep in mind as you guide students to become independent researchers. If you are planning a long-term project, try to collaborate in teams to teach students about resources available in your school and in the community. Projects can be completed across disciplines (e.g., science/language arts poetry projects, history/technology research projects), with the support of school staff

**BOX 8.1. Combining Research with Reading Fluency:
Books with Content Information that are Ready
for Oral Performance or Easy to Script**

Bode, J., & Mack, S. (1996). *Hard time: A real life look at juvenile crime and violence.* New York: Delacorte.

Brown, T. (1998). *Children of the midnight sun: Young native voices of Alaska.* Anchorage, AK: Alaska Northwest Books.

Bruchac, J. (1997). *Lasting echoes: An oral history of Native American people.*

Bruchac, J., & London, J. (1992). *Thirteen moons on Turtle's back: A Native American year of moons.* New York: Philomel.

Bunting, E. (1997). *I am the mummy Heb-Nefert.* San Diego, CA: Harcourt Brace.

Cummings, P. (Ed.). (1999). *Talking with artists* (Vol. 3). New York: Clarion.

Cummings, P., & Cummings, L. (Eds.). (1998). *Talking with adventurers.* Washington, DC: National Geographic Society.

Dunphy, M. (1996). *Here is the wetland* (ill. W. McLaughlin). New York: Hyperion.

Fleischman, P. (1988). *Joyful noise: Poems for two voices* (ill. E. Beddows). New York: Harper & Row.

Florian, D. (1998). *Insectlopedia: Poems and paintings.* San Diego, CA: Harcourt Brace.

Greenfeld, H. (1993). *The hidden children.* New York: Ticknor & Fields.

Hopkins, L. B. (Ed.). (1994a). *Hand in hand: An American history through poetry* (ill. P. M. Fiore). New York: Simon & Schuster.

Hopkins, L. B. (Ed.). (1994b). *Weather* (ill. M. Hale). New York: HarperCollins.

Hopkins, L. B. (Ed.). (1997). *Marvelous math* (ill K. Barbour). New York: Simon & Schuster.

Hopkins, L. B. (Ed.). (1999). *Spectacular science: A book of poems* (ill. V. B. Halstead). New York: Simon & Schuster.

Igus, T. (1998). *I see the rhythm* (ill. M. Wood). San Francisco: Children's Book Press.

Hurmence, B. (Ed.). (1997). *Slavery time when I was chillun.* New York: Putnam.

Lawlor, V. (Ed.). (1995). *I was dreaming to come to America: Memories from the Ellis Island oral history project.* New York: Viking.

Lawrence, J. (1968). *Harriet and the promised land.* New York: Windmill.

Lincoln, A. (1995). *The Gettysburg Address.* Boston: Houghton Mifflin.

Maynard, C. (1999). *Micro monsters: Life under the microscope.* New York: Dorling Kindersley.

Ousseimi, M. (1995). *Caught in the crossfire: Growing up in a war zone.* New York: Walker.

Panzer, N. (Ed.). (1994). *Celebrate America: In poetry and art.* New York: Hyperion.

Pappas, T. (1991). *Math talk: Mathematical ideas in poems for two voices.* San Carlos, CA: Wide World.

Parker, D. L., Engfer, L., & Conrow, R. (1998). *Stolen dreams: Portraits of working children.* Minneapolis, MN: Lerner.

Platt, R. (1999). *Plants bite back!* New York: Dorling Kindersley.

Rochelle, B. (1993). *Witnesses to freedom: Young people who fought for civil rights.* New York: Penguin.

Rosenberg, M. B. (1994). *Hiding to survive: Stories of Jewish children rescued from the Holocaust.* New York: Clarion.

Royston, A. (1998). *Fire fighter!* New York: Dorling Kindersley.

Sandler, M. W. (1995). *Immigrants.* New York: HarperCollins.

Viola, H. (1998). *It is a good day to die: Indian eyewitnesses tell the story of the Battle of the Little Bighorn.* New York: Crown.

Warren, A. (1996). *Orphan train rider: One boy's true story.* Boston: Houghton Mifflin.

BOX 8.2. Basic Steps in Guiding Students to Become Independent Researchers and Writers

1. Begin by sharing books that model how students conduct research.

    Cole, H. (1998). *I took a walk*. New York: Greenwillow.
    Heiligman, D. (1998). *The New York Public Library kid's guide to research*. New York: Scholastic.
    Nixon, J. L. (1996). *Search for the Shadowman*. New York: Delacorte.
    Osborne, W., & Osborne, M. P. *Magic tree house research guides* (series). New York: Random House.

2. Show samples of how authors collect information. Have your students begin to record information in a writer's log or learning log (see Chapter 6).

    King, C., & Osborne, L. B. (1997). *Oh, freedom!: Kids talk about the civil rights movement with the people who made it happen*. New York: Knopf.
    Sayre, A. P. (1997). *Put on some antlers and walk like a moose: How scientists find, follow, and study wild animals*. Brookfield, CT: 21st Century.
    Wright-Frierson, V. (1999). *A North American rain forest scrapbook*. New York: Walker.

3. Support students in reading for content with a visual organizer to collect information. Provide a graphic aid that analyzes the way this information is organized (e.g., relationships web, sequence map, timeline, cause–effect graphic organizer, comparison chart, data chart). As students become experienced readers of content texts, they can design their own graphic organizers. Appendix A provides samples of graphic organizers.

    Lauber, P. (1995). *Who eats what?: Food chains and food webs* (ill. H. Keller). New York: HarperCollins.

4. As students are recording information, continue to explore books that provide both sources of content information and creative models for writing. For short-term reading and research projects, consider formats in which students can write one brief piece (e.g., haiku, simulated journal entry, editorial), engage in interactive writing with a partner (e.g., letter correspondence between two individuals, written interview), or contribute one page to a class book (e.g., ABC book, historical newspaper, multiple perspectives on one event). Use lengthier models (e.g., folk tale, picture book, biography) when you are planning more extensive time for reading, writing, and research.

    Fletcher, R. (1997). *Ordinary things: Poems from a walk in early spring* (ill. W. L. Krudop). New York: Atheneum.
    Schwartz, D. M. (1998). *G is for googol: A math alphabet book* (ill. M. Moss). New York: Scholastic.
    St. George, J. (2000). *So you want to be president?* (ill. D. Small). New York: Philomel.
    Yue, C., & Yue, D. (2000). *The wigwam and the longhouse*. Boston: Houghton Mifflin.

---

members such as the librarian, the technology teacher, a content area teacher, and the language arts teacher.

First, be sure that your students have a strong basic grounding in how to conduct research. Deborah Heiligman's (1998) accessible guide, *The New York Public Library Kid's Guide to Research*, is a great starting place for both teachers and students. Beginning with how to choose a topic, this book highlights all the steps along the way—from

learning what is available in the public library (reference books, books on a particular topic, magazines and newspapers, visual resources, and the Internet) to the reliability of each piece of information. Heiligman also gives invaluable advice about active ways to gather research information, such as visiting a site, conducting an interview, developing a survey, or performing experiments. These types of activities are often overlooked in classroom research projects, even though they provide a direct means to promote student engagement in the process.

An interesting way to have students focus on how research is conducted is to read aloud and discuss a story that brings the research process to life. Joan Lowery Nixon's *Search for the Shadowman* (1996) follows 12-year-old Andy as he unwillingly undertakes a school project on his family history. His interest is sparked when he discovers that no one in his family wants to talk about one questionable relative, Coley Joe Bonner, and what happened in the past. His research process includes diverse sources, such as visiting a cemetery, conducting interviews, using library resources, and exploring geneological sites on the Internet. Another book for mature students, *Burning Up* (Cooney, 1999), explores 15-year-old Macey's school research project about a barn that burned across from her grandparents' house in the late 1950s. No one wants to answer Macey's questions, and the mystery begins. Nonfiction books also model the inquiry process. *The Bone Detectives: How Forensic Anthropologists Solve Crimes and Uncover Mysteries of the Dead* (Jackson, 1996) uses an appealing format to present how research investigations have solved both ancient and modern mysteries. Box 8.3 provides a list of engaging books that model the process of scientific investigation or historical research. These types of books portray the heart of research for students in the middle grades—finding answers to real questions.

Examining an Author's Research Sources

With your class, study the sources provided in books to determine how real authors find ideas and collect information. Jane Yolen's collections of folk tales, poetry, and stories—*Here There Be Ghosts* (1998), *Here There Be Unicorns* (1994), and *Here There Be Dragons* (1993)—are perfect for this type of analysis. At the beginning of each collection, Yolen describes her inspirational sources; these are usually combinations of personal experience, reading, and research. These collections provide short, high-interest read-alouds that set students up to discuss how a writer uses background resources. In non-fiction trade books, guiding students to examine an author's or editor's introduction, final notes, and the description of research sources creates a sample road map for how they might conduct their own research on a similar topic. For example, in *Slavery Time When I Was Chillun* (1997), Belinda Hurmence describes the roots of her book in the "slave narratives" (Rawick, 1972)—oral histories of former slaves compiled by workers

BOX 8.3. Middle Grades Books That Engage Students
to Think like Researchers

Arnosky, J. (1998a). *Crinkleroot's visit to Crinkle Cove.* New York: Simon & Schuster.

Arnosky, J. (1998b). *Watching desert wildlife.* Washington, DC: National Geographic Society.

Beattie, O., Geiger, J., & Tanaka, S. (1992). *Buried in ice.* New York: Scholastic.

Cone, M. (1992). *Come back, salmon: How a group of dedicated kids adopted Pigeon Creek and brought it back to life* (ill. S. Wheelwright). San Francisco: Sierra Club Books.

Duke, K. (1997). *Archeologists dig for clues.* New York: HarperCollins.

Facklam, M. (1997). *Tracking dinosaurs in the Gobi.* Boston: Little, Brown.

George, L. B. (1995). *In the snow: Who's been here?* New York: Greenwillow.

Giblin, J. C. (1990). *The riddle of the Rosetta Stone: Key to ancient Egypt.* New York: Crowell.

Gillette, J. L. (1997). *Dinosaur ghosts: The mystery of coelophysis* (ill D. Henderson). New York: Dial.

Goodall, J. (1989). *The chimpanzee family book* (ill. M. Neugebauer). Saxonville, MA: Picture Book Studio.

Goor, R., & Goor, N. (1986). *Pompeii: Exploring a Roman ghost town.* New York: Crowell.

Jarrow, G., & Sherman, P. (1996). *The naked mole-rat mystery: Scientific sleuths at work.* Minneapolis, MN: Lerner.

Johnson, R. L. (1997). *Braving the frozen frontier: Women working in Antarctica.* Minneapolis, MN: Lerner.

Kovack, D., & Madin, K. (1996). *Beneath blue waters: Meetings with remarkable deep-sea creatures.* New York: Viking.

Lasky, K. (1995). *Pond year* (ill. M. Bostock). Cambridge, MA: Candlewick.

Lasky, K. (1997). *The most beautiful roof in the world: Exploring the rainforest canopy* (ill. C. G. Knight). New York: Gulliver.

Lauber, P. (1985). *Tales mummies tell.* New York: HarperCollins.

Lessem, D. (1996). *Dinosaur worlds.* Honesdale, PA: Boyds Mill Press.

Luenn, N. (1994). *Squish! A wetland walk* (ill. R. Himler). New York: Atheneum.

Martin, J. B. (1998). *Snowflake Bentley* (ill. M. Azarian). Boston: Houghton Mifflin.

Montgomery, S. (1999). *The snake scientist* (ill. N. Bishop). Boston: Houghton Mifflin.

Pringle, L. (1990). *Saving our wildlife.* Springfield, NJ: Enslow.

Pringle, L. (1991). *Batman: Exploring the world of bats* (ill. M. Tuttle). New York: Scribners.

Reeves, N. (1992). *Into the mummy's tomb: The real-life discovery of Tutankhamun's treasures.* New York: Scholastic.

Simon, S. (1988). *How to be an ocean scientist in your own home* (ill. D. A. Carter). Philadelphia: Lippincott.

Sis, P. (1996). *Starry messenger.* New York: Farrar, Straus, Giroux.

Skurzynski, G. (1991). *Almost the real thing: Simulation in your high-tech world.* New York: Bradbury Press.

Steger, W., & Bowermaster, J. (1997). *Over the top of the world: Explorer Will Steger's trek across the Arctic.* New York: Scholastic.

Swanson, D. (1994). *Safari beneath the sea: The wonder world of the north Pacific coast.* San Francisco: Sierra Club Books.

Tunnell, M. O., & Chilcoat, G. W. (1996). *The children of Topaz: The story of a Japanese-American internment camp based on a classroom diary.* New York: Holiday House.

Wick, W. (1997). *A drop of water: A book of science and wonder.* New York: Scholastic.

for the Federal Writers' Project in 1936. Hurmence looks carefully at how these interviews were conducted, including the specific directions the interviewers were given,
such as being told to be "moderate" in how they portrayed the speech dialects of former slaves. Since few of these participants were literate, Hurmence considers the
power of having this group finally represented by their own words. However, as you
can see below, she also notes her concerns about accuracy and providing broad perspectives:

> A number of considerations affected the selection of narratives for this book—age of the former
> slave, for one. I looked for stories from those who had been at least ten years old when Freedom
> came in 1865. A ten-year-old's perceptions are fresh and shrewd, especially when related to direct
> experience. From a source younger than ten, the stories sound vaguer and are more apt to be
> tainted by hearsay.
>
>   I chose from a dozen states, to show both differences and similarities of slave experience;
> and for gender, since I wished to present the experience of both male and female slaves. Above
> all, I selected for content and for the natural gifts of these storytellers who afford us a glimpse
> into our inescapable past. (p. xii)

I Was Dreaming to Come to America: Memories from the Ellis Island Oral History Project
(Lawlor, 1995) provides a similar model of using interviews to provide a range of viewpoints on a topic.

Interviews are just one type of resource for writing. A book such as Pam Conrad's
(1991) *Prairie Visions: The Life and Times of Solomon Butcher* shows how visual sources
such as photographs can inspire research. Historical fiction can also have a clear connection to research. In Kristiana Gregory's (1989) *Jenny of the Tetons*, fifteen-year-old
Carrie Hill describes her new life with trapper Beaver Dick and his Shoshone wife after
losing her parents in an Indian attack. At the beginning of each chapter, an original
journal entry from Beaver Dick, complete with his invented spelling, provides a firm
grounding for each fictional episode in historical fact. The combinations of primary
sources—documents, photographs, letters—in some children's books such as *Anastasia's Album* (Brewster, 1996) provide visual references for how to collect and use information on a topic. Brewster uses the picture albums, drawings, and letters of
Anastasia, the daughter of Tsar Nicholas II, to allow readers to see the imperial family's
everyday life and the events leading to their deaths during the Russian Revolution. Box
8.4 lists books that demonstrate how authors use specific sources such as field journals,
interviews, and visual records to collect information and write about a topic.

SETTING UP CLEAR STEPS FOR RESEARCH
AND THE WRITING PROCESS

Understanding the Writing Process

Research can be conducted by individual students, in pairs, in groups, or even as a
class project. Plan the research process to fit with the final product being created by students. If you share instructional goals with your students, and clearly teach each part of
the process rather than assign products, you will be well on your way. Many teachers
set up steps to help their students navigate the process of writing. Tompkins (2000)

BOX 8.4. Using Books as Models for Collecting Information for Writing

Observations and Field Journals

Arnosky, J. (1997). *Crinkleroot's guide to knowing animal habitats*. New York: Simon & Schuster.

Arnosky, J. (1998). *Watching desert wildlife*. Washington, DC: National Geographic Society.

George, L. B. (1998). *In the woods: Who's been here?* New York: Mulberry.

Heinrich, B. (1990). *An owl in the house: A naturalist's diary*. Boston: Joy Street Books.

Wright-Frierson, V. (1996). *A desert scrapbook: Dawn to dusk in the Sonoran desert*. New York: Simon & Schuster.

Wright-Frierson, V. (1998). *An island scrapbook: Dawn to dusk on a barrier island*. New York: Simon & Schuster.

Interviews

King, C., & Osborne, L. B. (1997). *Oh, freedom!: Kids talk about the civil rights movement with the people who made it happen*. New York: Knopf.

Cummings, P., & Cummings, L. (Eds.). (1998). *Talking with adventurers*. Washington, DC: National Geographic Society.

Cummings, P. (Ed.). (1999). *Talking with artists* (Vol. 3). New York: Clarion.

Marcus, L. S. (Ed.). (2000). *Author talk*. New York: Simon & Schuster.

Ringgold, F., Freeman, L., & Roucher, N. (1996). *Talking to Faith Ringgold*. New York: Crown.

Visual Records: Photographs, Maps, Drawings

Brewster, H. (1996). *Anastasia's album*. Boston: Little, Brown.

Conrad, P. (1991). *Prairie visions: The life and times of Solomon Butcher*. New York: HarperCollins.

Everett, G. (1991). *Li'l Sis and Uncle Willie: A story based on the life and paintings of William H. Johnson*. New York: Hyperion.

Freedman, R. (1987). *Lincoln: A photobiography*. New York: Clarion.

Haskins, J. (1992). *The day Martin Luther King, Jr., was shot: A photo history of the civil rights movement*. New York: Scholastic.

Haskins, J. (1995). *The day Fort Sumter was fired on: A photo history of the Civil War*. New York: Scholastic.

McMillan, B. (1995). *Nights of the pufflings*. Boston: Houghton Mifflin.

Matthews, T. L (1998). *Light shining through mist: A photobiography of Dian Fossey* (ill. G. Schaller). Washington, DC: National Geographic Society.

Wick, W. (1997). *A drop of water: A book of science and wonder*. New York: Scholastic.

---

identifies a five-stage process based on current research about how children learn to write. This is called the *writing process* and is often used as a framework in school settings to guide students from the early stages of writing to a finished product. Murray (1999) presents a more interactive model, which promotes students' thinking and experimenting with the content of their writing in the prewriting stage before they even begin a first draft. His areas of focus work particularly well with the research process. Box 8.5 shows examples of these areas of focus for teaching writing.

Students need to be shown the types of strategies that writers use to find their topics, collect relevant details, select points on which to focus their writing, and then de-

BOX 8.5. Steps of the Writing Process

Teaching Writing: Balancing Process and Product (3rd ed.) by Gail E. Tompkins (2000)	*Write to Learn* (6th ed.) by Donald M. Murray (1999)
These activities usually take place in order from brainstorming to published product.	These activities can take place in the order listed, but writing processes often interact or take place simultaneously.
• Prewrite	• Collect • Focus • Order
• Draft	• Develop
• Revise • Edit • Publish	• Clarify

cide upon an order in which to present that information. Murray (1999) describes several techniques that work well for students, such as making lists to collect facts, mapping how ideas are connected in a graphic form, free writing about everything known on a topic, or creating a "tree" with central ideas and related branches. Examples of methods of *brainstorming* are shown in Appendix A. Consider the following guidelines as you encourage students to collect, focus, and order information before writing a first draft.

• Keep *engagement* at the forefront by allowing students to take part in decision making as they pursue areas of interest. Students need to be able to see a clear purpose for writing.

• Collect *high-interest materials* to use as references. Use visual sources and primary sources whenever possible.

• Model varied styles of *brainstorming,* and have students consider which methods suit particular forms of writing or different topics. When students are learning about a particular type of writing for the first time, provide a graphic organizer that guides them to collect and analyze the information needed.

• Show students how to *revisit the facts* collected in brainstorming to find interesting information and to discard unimportant details. Murray (1999) suggests that you guide student writers to find (1) the connections between ideas, and (2) things that surprise them. Model how to circle strong phrases in a free write or how to draw lines between related items when mapping. Use highlighters to color-code connections and surprises.

• Demonstrate methods to *organize* information before drafting. Techniques can be as simple as numbering or crossing out items on a graphic organizer. For lengthier projects, show students how to create a new graphic organizer or a detailed outline to use as a reference while writing.

• Have students start to *develop* their topics by writing first drafts. Encourage the students to write as much as they can, with the clear understanding that they can always go back and discard parts of their writing as they are working on clarifying their focus.

Providing Instructional Support for Writing across the Content Areas

Methods of Teaching Writing

Even when students are familiar with the basic steps of the writing process, they still will need your support. As a writing teacher, you must demonstrate how to use the writing process when students are attempting new forms of writing or trying to apply new content information in their writing. The following strategies provide instructional support for students as they are experimenting with form and content.

- *Modeled writing.* The teacher models the thought processes used when creating a new piece of writing, actually thinking out loud and composing in front of the students on a chart or using an overhead projector. Modeled writing is usually part of a minilesson to demonstrate a new technique to the whole class or to a small group, although teachers can effectively use this strategy with less skilled writers to provide focused, individualized instruction. Use modeled writing to introduce concepts such as *content editing*, or clarifying the content of a piece of writing, by showing how a writer revisits what has been written to see whether the information is clear and the wording is appropriate.
- *Shared writing.* The teacher still models the writing process in this technique, but students actively participate in creating the text. Shared writing can incorporate some of the activities covered in Chapter 7, such as *found poetry* or *text innovations*; the teacher does the actual writing while incorporating students' ideas. This technique works well in combination with instructional reading strategies that activate prior knowledge, encourage student participation, and support critical thinking. For example, the teacher writes as students dictate in a *language experience approach* (LEA) activity (Stauffer, 1970), or the teacher creates a chart in the K-W-L method (Ogle, 1986) to determine what students *know*, what they *want* to know, and what they have *learned*. Shared writing is an effective technique to guide a group of students through a new form of writing. It is also an excellent method to use to support an individual student who will not attempt an assignment. The teacher serves as the recorder, brainstorming with the student and taking a dictation to begin the piece of writing, then handing the paper over for the student to complete.
- *Interactive writing.* In this technique, the teacher and the students actually take turns writing, or two students share the responsibility for writing. Interactive writing provides a focus on perspective, content, and how language is used. Paired work encourages fluent writing through activities such as creating and writing dialogue (two students take on the personas of two characters), writing letters back and forth, or conducting e-mail correspondence with another class. Students can also share written predictions for a directed reading–thinking activity (DR-TA; Stauffer, 1969). Show your students published models of interactive writing, such as interviews (Cummings & Cummings, 1998; King & Osborne, 1997) or novels written in different perspectives by two authors (Danziger & Martin, 1998; Yolen & Coville, 1998). This instructional technique is engaging for students and often encourages reluctant writers to try new forms.

Remember that your end goal is to create independent writers. The amount of support that you will need to provide for your students depends upon their personal experience with the writing procedures you have outlined, as well as their familiarity with the subject matter. Use modeled writing or shared writing when the writing task is un-

familiar, and try interactive writing in groups or pairs when students have been introduced to a topic but have not had much time to practice using the information.
Tompkins (2000) provides step-by-step directions on how teachers plan instruction for
modeled, shared, and interactive writing.

Using Models from Literature to Support Writing

As you teach any new technique, always provide models of other students' writing and
models from literature. In Figure 8.1, we outline an organizational format for integrating content area reading and writing (Crook & Broaddus, 1992) that works well for
supporting students to develop the knowledge that they need to respond creatively to
subject matter.

In this process, students begin a project by looking at varied models of writing
about the content being explored. Resources can include high-interest materials (such
as picture books, magazines, or novels) that provide background information, new perspectives about the topic, or models of how to write about a subject. As they read, students begin to form questions about the topic or related subjects. The next step is to
search for new information in nonfiction trade books. As students find answers and

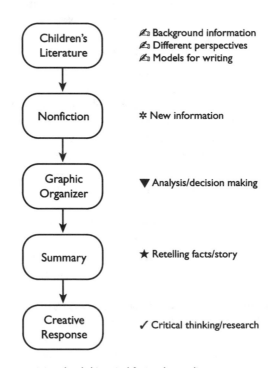

FIGURE 8.1. An organizational format for integrating content area reading and writing. From
Crook and Broaddus (1992). Reprinted with permission of the authors.

think of new questions, they collect ideas and details in a graphic organizer. To reconsider their topics and check for missing details, students summarize the points on the graphic organizer orally with peers or the teacher, or they write a short synopsis. For the final presentation of the material, students use the information that they have collected to write creative responses, such as diary entries, interviews, letters, or how-to manuals. At this point, sometimes it is necessary for students to take a second look at the models from literature for ideas about structuring the writing. Students may also realize that they need to collect more information from nonfiction sources as they begin to focus on a particular topic.

Creating a Framework for Independent Research

Research projects provide the opportunity for a teacher to be strategic in reading and writing instruction. With careful planning, the structure that you use to support reading comprehension will also guide your students to collect the details that they need for meaningful writing. Remember that every writing exercise need not be published. Students should be given plenty of time to practice thinking and learning about information by using prewriting strategies (collecting, focusing, ordering) or developing first drafts. Editing and publication are best used selectively. Collect this type of "process work" in student writing folders, or *writing portfolios*, so that they can self-select items to extend and to edit for publication. Let's consider some of these strategies that teachers use to support both comprehension and writing.

Graphic Organizers

Visual support can be particularly successful for group and individual projects. Venn diagrams, timelines, sequence maps, and comparison charts are just a few of the visual forms that can help students read for specific information as they record interesting details. Use graphic organizers of the different types of expository writing (sequence, comparison, description, problem and solution, cause and effect) to demonstrate to your students how to use the structure of text to determine key information. Appendix A provides examples of graphic organizers that your students can use to record and analyze data from their reading. These types of visual aids become easy references for students to use to frame their own expository writing or to find details for creative forms of writing.

For larger research projects, you can guide students to search for specific information by creating a *data chart* to record research sources they have consulted and the information they will use in their writing. For example, Ms. Jacobs teaches both language arts and science to third graders. She decided that she wanted to show her students how they could use the science content that they had studied in their poetry writing. To provide models, she had her students work in groups or pairs to rehearse and perform poems from *Dinosaurs* (Hopkins, 1987), *Insectlopedia* (Florian, 1998), and *Advice for a Frog* (Schertle, 1995). She also provided illustrated poetry books on varied levels for shared and independent reading, such as *Space Songs* (Livingston, 1988), *Weather* (Hopkins, 1994), *Antarctic Antics: A Book of Penguin Poems* (Sierra, 1998), *Joyful Noise: Poems for Two Voices* (Fleischman, 1988), and *Cool Melons—Turn to Frogs!: The Life and Poems of Issa* (Gollub, 1998). Next, Ms. Jacobs demonstrated how a writer could collect information about a scientific topic on a data chart. She selected three books about snakes: *Slinky, Scaly Snakes!* from the *Eyewitness Readers* series (Dussling, 1998), *All about Rattlesnakes* (Arnosky, 1997), and *Sea Snakes* (Souza, 1998). Then she asked the class to help her consider the types of information that they wanted to know about different snakes. To keep track of these details as they read sections of each book, they recorded notes on the data chart shown in Box 8.6. For headings on the chart, she included vocabulary words that her class had been studying, such as *habitat*, *protection*, and *reference*. When Ms. Jacobs put out nonfiction books for her students to start their research, she made sure that she included ones containing vivid photographs and drawings. *Red-Eyed Tree Frog* (Cowley, 1999) and *Crocodiles and Alligators* (Simon, 1999) provided excellent visual resources for students as they brainstormed descriptive terms. When the students were ready to write poems about their topics, they consulted the data chart for details and interesting vocabulary.

Organizing Instruction for Research and Writing

As you teach your students the basics of writing about information, be sure to model all procedures and to designate time for students to pursue their own research on topics of personal interest. Take a look at the following guidelines for supporting individual research and writing in a classroom setting. You can adapt these procedures to provide a structure for any reading and writing for a class research project that will be published.

BOX 8.6 Data Chart for Collecting Information to Write Poetry about Different Types of Snakes

Type of snake	Habitat	Food sources	Protection	Unusual facts	Reference

- *Read aloud.* Introduce the research project with a teacher read-aloud. Use an engaging piece of nonfiction writing to spark interest in the types of subjects students can choose to research (e.g., read a selection about vampire bats), or read several selections to give students ideas about different topics they might pursue.

- *Share models.* Show examples of creative writing (from literature, magazines, or student work) that is based upon content information from research. Keep these references handy as students pursue their own projects.

- *Create a group-level graphic organizer.* Set up a visual way for a group to analyze the type of information used in the models of writing. This can be a whole-class shared writing activity guided by the teacher with younger students, or a small-group activity for older students. This graphic organizer should analyze the type of form and the use of information. For a class newspaper, provide separate types of organizers for different forms (editorial, advertisement, feature story). Again, see Appendix A for examples of types of graphic organizers.

- *Model analyzing new information.* Be sure your students understand how to use the framework of the graphic organizer you have created to record new information about their topics. Read a short nonfiction piece to the students. As a class, work together in a shared writing exercise to demonstrate how to collect and organize facts on the graphic chart, using an overhead projector, a poster, or the chalkboard. With older students, this can be a small-group exercise that is shared with the whole class when completed. Add new features as necessary.

- *Read nonfiction.* Have students read nonfiction materials on their topics for new information. This type of reading can be done independently in easy materials or in pairs for support with instructional reading. For more challenging selections, use techniques such as Readers' Theater to support fluent reading.

- *Analyze information on an individual-level graphic organizer.* Have students, as individuals, fill out graphic organizers that collect details about their topics. This can be done independently, in pairs, or in small groups, depending on the focus of the project. For a research paper using multiple sources, a data chart (see Box 8.6) listing facts and citing sources would be helpful.

- *Model writing.* Show how to begin drafting the piece of writing, using information from the graphic organizer. As a teacher, you can revisit the graphic organizer you made as a class or group. Put a copy up for everyone to see; then do a modeled writing demonstration of how you would choose where to begin writing and why you made that choice. For example, you can show several different types of *leads* to students. Revisit the leads in the models you have shown students, and determine how different authors chose to begin writing (e.g. question, quote, description, data). Demonstrate writing the first paragraph on an overhead projector, and talk about the decisions you make as an author. Concentrate on content and style—what you are trying to say and how you are saying it. When working with more experienced writers, allow them to take turns doing this type of modeling for the rest of the class. You can also allow them to try writing group paragraphs on chart paper and compare the different paragraphs when they are finished.

- *Provide time for developing writing in first drafts.* Have students begin drafting their own pieces of writing. Be sure that their graphic organizers, the information books they read, and the models of prior projects are readily available as references. Use this time for one-on-one work with students who have difficulty writing fluently.

Examine each student's graphic organizer and create a plan for how to present the information in writing. Some students may need to create a detailed outline before drafting. If necessary, take a dictation from a student for the beginning of the piece, then hand over the writing to the student once the process is underway.

• *Set up conferences focused on content.* Discuss the writing process with individual students as they are working. Ask each student to read to you from his or her current writing, then ask the student to describe plans for completing the assignment. Be sure to point out how content is working in the piece of writing—where nonfiction details are used effectively, where you learned something new, or how the student took a creative approach to writing about the topic. If you feel more direction is needed, guide students to consult the information on their graphic, look at their nonfiction resources again for necessary details, or reconsider the models for questions about structure or content. You can also set up time for group conferences for peer advice while students are writing.

• *Use editing checklists.* Set up content and mechanics checklists for students to use to guide them to clarify and edit their own writing. Be sure that the content checklist includes the points you have emphasized in your modeling of the writing process and research for information. A mechanics checklist should include grammatical conventions and spelling features that have been taught in your class or another course. Provide computer editing resources, or books such as a dictionary, a thesaurus, and a grammar text, for students to use as they edit. It is effective to have a checklist that several editors can initial. For example, first have the student author edit carefully; then have the student share the writing with one or two peers; and then do a final edit as a teacher. See Appendix B for samples of editing checklists.

• *Publish student writing.* Be creative. Work can be published on a Web homepage for the classroom, in a newsletter for the grade, on a hallway bulletin board, or in a class book. Performances are an especially rewarding way to publish. Try having students write scripts to record a radio show, present a Readers' Theater production for another class, or perform a play.

Let's look at how a research project might be structured in an eighth-grade history class to support students' reading fluency and comprehension while they gather information for writing. For example, if you were planning a Civil War assignment involving simulated journal writing (i.e., writing journal entries from the perspective of a person living during the Civil War), you would need to guide your students to search for details about lives of different individuals during that time period. One way to explore these perspectives would be to have students perform Readers' Theater scripts developed from nonfiction books. This type of rehearsed reading would improve students' fluency with the language used during that time period. At the same time, their familiarity with the types of issues that affected individuals during the Civil War would develop as they listened to the performances of the scripts. As a teacher, you would be setting the stage for your students to think about character development in their own writing as they interpreted characters' motivations in their scripts and listened to how others chose to perform their parts. Consider the multiple perspectives on the Civil War presented in nonfiction trade books such as *The Boys' War: Confederate and Union Soldiers Talk about the Civil War* (Murphy, 1990), *Till Victory Is Won: Black Soldiers in the Civil War* (Mettger, 1994), *A Separate Battle: Women and the Civil War* (Chang, 1991), *Lincoln: In His own words* (Meltzer, 1993), and *Voices from the Civil War: A Documentary History of the Great American Conflict* (Meltzer, 1989). A graphic organizer that carefully analyzed character would be useful for collecting details from this reading about a person (name, age, gender, race, place of residence, occupation, present circumstances), his or her beliefs (position on Confederacy and Union, family background, other beliefs or loyalties), and the event experienced (time, place, significance to the Civil War, interesting details). Later, this same graphic organizer could be used as a prewriting exercise before beginning the Civil War journal. The primary sources from this type of nonfiction reading could be compared with examples from historical fiction that recreate the viewpoints of individuals about specific events during the Civil War. These could include the multiple first-person perspectives of one battle given in *Bull Run* (Fleischman, 1993) or views from the Union and the Confederacy in *With Every Drop of Blood* (Collier & Collier, 1994). The diary format of *Weep Not for Me, Dear Mother* (Roberson, 1996) provides a model of an actual Civil War journal. See Lott and Wasta's (1999) article for an interesting discussion about how to teach perspective with Civil War books. Box 8.7 provides the framework for a study that involves writing first-person narratives from children's perspectives, using primary sources and recollections about World War II.

Publishing a Research Project

What does a final research project look like? We have given examples of extensive reading and writing projects that connect language arts with other areas of the curriculum, such as history and science. In addition, we have considered process activities such as learning logs and graphic organizers. Students can also apply research skills to their writing in a variety of nontraditional formats, such as riddles, poetry, newspaper articles, letters, or comic strips. Familiarize your students with diverse models that demonstrate how they might share their new knowledge. Using these shorter formats allows you to integrate reading and writing even when you have limited time to spend on a topic. Settling on a specific structure for the final product also helps students organize information and focus on key points. As a teacher, this will mean that you will need to collect examples of different types of research publications from student work and published sources. See Figure 8.2 for an example of a timeline created by a student who was studying the Cold War and the Korean War. This foldout poster included a map of North and South Korea with the timeline on the front, then a written summary and related vocabulary terms on the back. Figure 8.3 shows an example of a vocabulary wheel of important terms and events created by students studying the 1930s. Such wheels were displayed on the ceiling of the classroom while the students were reading about the Great Depression.

There are some excellent books to use as models of types of publications. Remember that many of these forms can be class or small-group writing projects. Paul Erickson wrote *Daily Life in a Covered Wagon* (1994) as a teenager; this book describes the overland journey to Oregon for one family. Erickson's illustration of this journey through different resources (such as photographs, maps, and journals) makes it a particularly useful model for student authors. As you study a model such as this one, it is worthwhile to show students other creative ways authors have used to portray the westward journey. In *Pioneer Girl: Growing Up on the Prairie*, author Andrea Warren (1998) uses the memoirs of Grace McCance Snyder and interviews with her family to write an engag-

BOX 8.7. Writing Historical Fiction from a First-Person Perspective: A World War II Study

Guiding student reading and writing	Teaching points and materials
Read aloud. Teacher reads the picture book *Rose Blanche* by Gallaz and Innocenti (1985). Classroom discussion includes looking at the dramatic change in perspective at the middle of the story.	This begins as a first-person narration by a young German girl, then changes to a third-person narration when she discovers a concentration camp. The story ends with her death during the liberation.
Share models. Students read (independently or in pairs) picture books about World War II written in first person.	*Passage to Freedom*, K. Mochizuki (1997); *Star of Fear, Star of Hope*, J. Hoestlandt (1995); *Let the Celebrations Begin!*, M. Wild (1991); *The Lily Cupboard*, S. Oppenheim (1992).
Create a graphic organizer. Small groups complete charts to analyze common features across picture books.	Features considered in charts include the date, place, age of the person, ethnicity, background, beliefs, key event, outcome, and theme.
Model analyzing new information from primary sources. The teacher reads a short selection and models how to collect information on the chart.	Using a selection from the nonfiction book *We Remember the Holocaust* by Adler (1989), fill in a segment of the chart for an individual.
Read nonfiction. Students read (independently or in pairs) from nonfiction books that provide first-person accounts.	*Hiding to Survive: Stories of Jewish Children Rescued from the Holocaust*, M. Rosenberg (1994); *We Remember the Holocaust*, D. A. Adler (1989); *No Pretty Pictures: A Child of War*, A. Lobel (1998); *Ten Thousand Children: True Stories Told by Children Who Escaped the Holocaust on the Kindertransport*, A. L. Fox & E. Abraham-Podietz (1999); *Kinderlager: An Oral History of Young Holocaust Survivors*, M. J. Nieuwsma (1998) (for mature students).
Analyze information on a graphic organizer. Teacher models using categories from the chart to brainstorm writing about an event from a first-person perspective, using nonfiction resources for content.	Each student fills in her or his chart by researching one person (or compiling facts about similar people), using the information found in nonfiction resources. Point out that in historical fiction details that are historically accurate are sometimes compiled to form a portrait of a fictional individual.
Model writing. Teacher demonstrates how to move from the group-level model graphic organizer of information to drafting a first-person narrative.	Referring back to one of the original models, *Let the Celebrations Begin!* by Wild (1991), the teacher uses an overhead projector to demonstrate a writer's thought processes while drafting. These include several examples of leads and how the story might be told.
Provide time for independent writing. Students work on first drafts, consult informally with each other and the teacher, and pursue further research.	The teacher moves around the room, consulting with students about content and focus, while keeping a checklist of current progress (see Appendix B). The teacher helps each student locate information needed for the writing.

(continued)

Guiding student reading and writing	Teaching points and materials
Set up conferences. When students have completed a first draft, they meet in small groups to share their manuscripts and discuss current content.	The teacher sets up content conference groups (three students) to help students focus on what is working in their writing and to share additional information needed to make the writing accurate and easy to understand.
Use editing checklists. Students edit separately for content and mechanics.	Each writer works with a peer to complete two checklists on their manuscripts: accurate content (based on the original graphic and models) and mechanics (based on resources available and spelling features taught). The teacher serves as the final editor.
Publish student writing. Students create a final draft to include in a classroom publication.	Student complete edits and bind manuscripts in a classroom historical fiction collection of first-person memoirs about the Holocaust.

ing nonfiction story about growing up in Nebraska. Remember that writing historical fiction is another way to recreate information in a new context. Expose students to formats such as letters, poetry, and diaries as models of ways to write about nonfiction topics. Excellent examples of this type of historical fiction based on research about the westward journey include the poetry journals in *Mississippi Mud: Three Prairie Journals* (Turner, 1997), the letters in *Dear Levi: Letters from the Overland Trail* (Woodruff, 1994), the memoir in *My Daniel* (Conrad, 1989), and the diary format in *My Prairie Year* (Harvey, 1986) or *Across the Wide and Lonesome Prairie: The Oregon Trail Diary of Hattie Campbell.* (Gregory, 1997). Box 8.8 lists books that provide models of using alternative forms of writing.

As you can see, not all of the research in your classroom needs to result in students' writing research reports or book-length publications. In fact, the amount of time your students have to spend on publishing from their reading and research will often be limited. Fortunately, short pieces of writing can be an effective way to summarize and apply information learned during brief periods of focused reading and writing. In fact, students can compile their writings into a class anthology. This type of product becomes an inviting resource for a free-reading shelf in your classroom. ABC books can be a fun way to help students write about new information. An ABC book can focus on the vocabulary of a historical period, such as the Middle Ages in *Illuminations* (Hunt, 1989); can address culture and geography in another part of the world, such as Asia in *A Is for Asia* (Chin-Lee, 1997); or can look at science and the creatures in a particular environment, such as the underwater world in *Under the Sea from A to Z* (Doubilet, 1991).

Poetry is also a wonderful way to study content, word meanings, and style when you have limited class time. Figure 8.4 shows idioms with drawings that a third grader completed for a language arts class book of figurative sayings. Brief forms such as the three-line haiku (five syllables, seven syllables, five syllables) offer a focused way to look at nature and language. *Cool Melons—Turn to Frogs!: The Life and Poetry of Issa* (Gollub, 1998) and *Shadow Play: Night Haiku* (Harter, 1994) provide unique models. Try

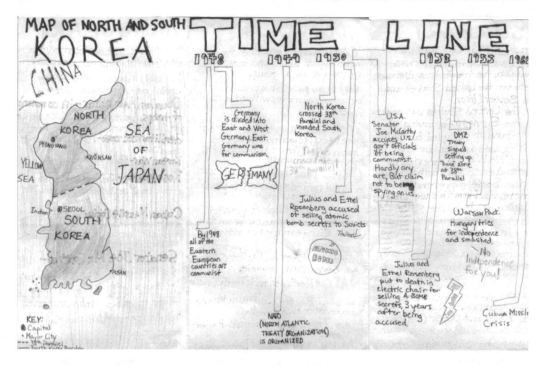

FIGURE 8.2. Foldout poster on the Cold War and the Korean War (two sides).

FIGURE 8.3. Two vocabulary wheels for the 1930s.

BOX 8.8. Providing Models of Varied Writing Forms
for Publishing Research

Diaries

Axworthy, A. (1992). *Anni's India diary.* Watertown, MA: Charlesbridge.

Axworthy, A. (1994). *Anni's diary of France.* Watertown, MA: Charlesbridge.

Harvey, B. (1986). *My prairie year: Based on the diary of Elenore Plaisted* (ill. D. K. Ray). New York: Holiday House.

Filopovic, Z. (1994). *Zlata's diary: A child's life in Sarajevo.* New York: Viking.

George, J. C. (1997). *Look to the north: A wolf pup diary* (ill. L. Washburn). New York: HarperCollins.

Lasky, K. (1998). *Dreams in the golden country: The diary of Zipporah Feldman, a Jewish immigrant girl, New York City, 1903.* New York: Scholastic.

Talbott, H., & Greenberg, M. (1996). *Amazon diary: Property of Alex Winters.* New York: Putnam.

Whiteley, O., & Boulton, J. (1994). *Only Opal: The diary of a young girl* (ill. B. Cooney). New York: Philomel.

Journals

Bowen, G. (1994). *Stranded at Plimoth Plantation, 1626.* New York: HarperCollins.

Cushman, K. (1994). *Catherine, called Birdy.* New York: Clarion.

Hopkinson, D. (1997). *Birdie's lighthouse* (ill. K. B. Root). New York: Atheneum.

Knight, A. S. (1993). *The way west: Journal of a pioneer woman* (ill. M. McCurdy). New York: Simon & Schuster.

Krull, K. (1997). *Wish you were here: Emily's guide to the 50 states.* New York: Doubleday.

Matthaei, G., & Grutman, J. (1997). *The ledgerbook of Thomas Blue Eagle.* New York: Lickle.

Mullen, F. (1997). *The Donner party chronicles: A day by day account of a doomed wagon train.* Reno, NV: Nevada Humanities Committee.

Roop, P., & Roop, C. (1993). *Off the map: The journals of Lewis and Clark* (ill. T. Tanner). New York: Walker.

Turner, A. (1997). *Mississippi mud: Three prairie journals* (ill. R. J. Blake). New York: HarperCollins.

Letters

Brisson, P. (1990). *Kate heads west* (ill. R. Brown). New York: Bradbury Press.

Hesse, K. (1992). *Letters from Rifka.* New York: Holt.

Leedy, L. (1991). *Messages in the mailbox: How to write a letter.* New York: Holiday House.

Lyons, M. E. (1992). *Letters from a slave girl: The story of Harriet Jacobs.* New York: Scribner.

Turner, A. (1987). *Nettie's trip south* (ill. R. Himler). New York: Simon & Schuster.

Woodruff, E. (1994). *Dear Levi: Letters from the overland trail* (ill. B. Peck). New York: Knopf.

Postcards

Arnold, H. (1996). *Postcards from France.* Austin, TX: Steck-Vaughn.

Leedy, L. (1993). *Postcards from Pluto: A tour of the solar system.* New York: Holiday House.

Willard, N. (1997). *The magic cornfield.* San Diego, CA: Harcourt Brace.

Williams, V. (1988). *Stringbean's trip to the shining sea.* New York: Scholastic.

(continued)

Poetry

Fleischman, P. (1985). *I am phoenix: Poems for two voices* (ill. K. Nutt). New York: Harper & Row.

Fleischman, P. (2000). *Big talk: Poems for four voices* (ill. B. Giacobbe). Cambridge, MA: Candlewick.

Florian, D. (1994). *Beast feast.* San Diego, CA: Harcourt Brace.

Hesse, K. (1997). *Out of the dust.* New York: Scholastic.

Michelson, R. (1999). *A book of flies* (ill. L. Baskin). New York: Cavendish.

Provensen, A. (1997). *The buck stops here: The presidents of the United States.* San Diego, CA: Harcourt Brace.

Siebert, D. (1988). *Mojave* (ill. W. Minor). New York: Crowell.

Simon, S. (Ed.). (1995). *Star walk.* New York: Morrow.

Thomas, J. C. (1998). *I have heard of a land* (ill. F. Cooper). New York: HarperCollins.

Newspapers

Dowswell, P. (1997). *The Egyptian Echo.* San Jose, CA: EDC.

Dowswell, P., & Tomlins, K. (1998). *The Roman Record: Hot news from the swirling mists of time.* San Jose, CA: EDC.

Langley, A., De Souza, P., Steele, P., & Powell, A. (1996). *The Roman News.* Cambridge, MA: Candlewick.

Powell, A., & Steele, P. (Eds.). (1996). *The Greek News.* Cambridge, MA: Candlewick.

Stedman, S. (Ed.). (1997). *The Egyptian News.* Cambridge, MA: Candlewick.

Steele, P., Batemen, P., & Rosso, N. (Eds.). (1997). *The Aztec News.* Cambridge, MA: Candlewick.

Questions and Answers

Funston, S. (1992). *The dinosaur question and answer book.* Boston: Little, Brown.

MacDonald, F. (1995). *How would you survive as an Aztec?* (ill. M. Bergen). New York: Franklin Watts.

MacDonald, F. (1997). *How would you survive in the Middle Ages?* New York: Franklin Watts.

Morley, J. (1996). *How would you survive as an ancient Egyptian?* (ill. J. James & D. Salariya). New York: Franklin Watts.

Parker, N. W. (1987). *Bugs* (ill. J. R. Wright). New York: Morrow.

Innovative Picture Book Formats

Cushman, D. (1996). *The mystery of King Karfu.* New York: HarperCollins.

Edwards, P. D. (1997). *Barefoot: Escape on the underground railroad* (ill. H. Cole). New York: HarperCollins.

George, L. B. (1999). *Around the world: Who's been here?* New York: Greenwillow.

Gerrard, R. (1998). *The Roman twins.* New York: Farrar, Straus, Giroux.

Macaulay, D. (1985). *Baaa.* Boston: Houghton Mifflin.

Macaulay, D. (1992). *Black and white.* Boston: Houghton Mifflin.

Maynard, C. (1999). *Micro monsters: Life under the microscope.* New York: Dorling Kindersley.

Parker, N. W., & Wright, J. R. (1990). *Frogs, toads, lizards, and salamanders* (ill. N. W. Parker). New York: Morrow.

creating a classroom collection that features haiku based upon art. Figure 8.5 provides five examples of haiku inspired by student illustrations or collages. Students can also apply historical content and literary studies to forms of poetry. Figure 8.6 shows two character poems based on *The Diary of a Young Girl* (Frank, 1995).

Group research projects can create interesting collections. What began as student interviews for a civil rights project in Casey King's fourth-grade classroom turned into a 7-year research study with more than 500 children. The final book, *Oh, Freedom!: Kids Talk About the Civil Rights Movement with the People Who Made it Happen* (King & Osborne, 1997), includes actual interviews conducted by these students with neighbors, friends, or family members who talked about their experiences during the civil rights movement. Each student–interviewee pair is pictured, along with an original picture from the time period.

Creating a group newspaper or magazine is another engaging way to publish student work on a topic of research. This approach works equally well for covering current issues such as environmental concerns, or recreating historical events such as Sherman's "march to the sea" during the Civil War. For middle school readers, Paul Fleischman's *Dateline: Troy* (1996) makes a direct comparison between the past and the present by presenting the story of the Trojan War paired on each double-page spread with a related clipping from actual newspapers published between World War I and the Persian Gulf War. The effect is striking; here is a direct connection between how events took place in the past and what is happening in modern times. It is easy to find resources for teaching your students about journalism. "How-to" books such as *Extra!*

FIGURE 8.4. Eight illustrated idioms.

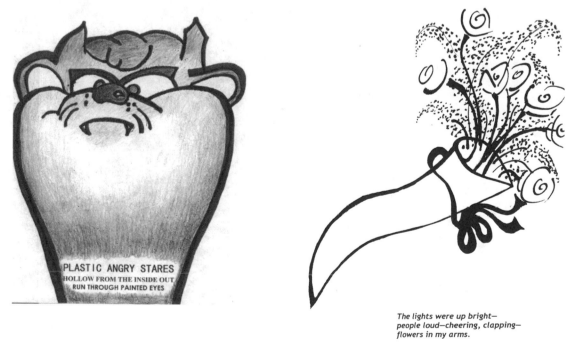

FIGURE 8.5. Five illustrated Haiku.

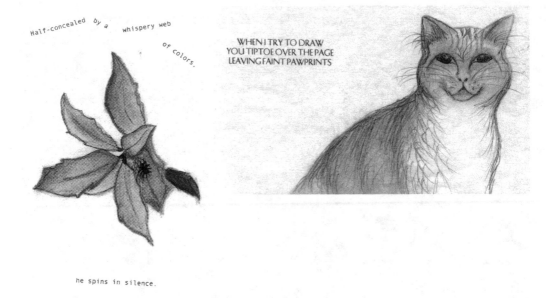

Half-concealed by a whispery web of colors,

WHEN I TRY TO DRAW
YOU TIPTOE OVER THE PAGE
LEAVING FAINT PAWPRINTS

he spins in silence.

FIGURE 8.5. *(continued)*

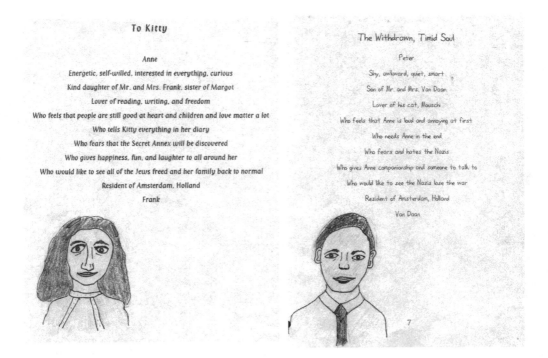

To Kitty

Anne

Energetic, self-willed, interested in everything, curious
Kind daughter of Mr. and Mrs. Frank, sister of Margot
Lover of reading, writing, and freedom
Who feels that people are still good at heart and children and love matter a lot
Who tells Kitty everything in her diary
Who fears that the Secret Annex will be discovered
Who gives happiness, fun, and laughter to all around her
Who would like to see all of the Jews freed and her family back to normal
Resident of Amsterdam, Holland

Frank

The Withdrawn, Timid Soul

Peter

Shy, awkward, quiet, smart
Son of Mr. and Mrs. Van Daan
Lover of his cat, Mouschi
Who feels that Anne is loud and annoying at first
Who needs Anne in the end
Who fears and hates the Nazis
Who gives Anne companionship and someone to talk to
Who would like to see the Nazis lose the war
Resident of Amsterdam, Holland

Van Daan

FIGURE 8.6. Two character poems from *The Diary of a Young Girl* (Frank, 1995).

Extra!: The Who, What, Where, When and Why of Newspapers (Granfield, 1994) and *The Furry News: How to Make a Newspaper* (Leedy, 1990) outline what goes into publishing a newspaper. For your own teacher resource, take a look at *More Than the Truth: Teaching Nonfiction Writing through Journalism* (Wolf, Craven, & Balick, 1996). Newspapers and magazines for students can provide useful models for different types of writing: editorials, advertisements, obituaries, feature stories, sports articles, book reviews, letters to the editor, and fashion news. Familiarize your students with national magazines written by middle grades students, such as *Merlyn's Pen, Blue Jean Magazine,* and *New Moon Magazine*. These publications not only include high-quality models of student writing, but also provide resources for your students to send out their own work for review and publication. See Appendix D for suggestions for magazines for students.

Keeping Records of Student Progress and Evaluating Writing

Evaluating student work is a demanding process that is linked to ongoing assessment and instruction. It is essential to plan carefully and to share your evaluation criteria with your students before they even begin to write. If you place a grade on everything that your students write, they will stop taking risks. They will also focus on the grade on the paper, not on the feedback that you include for improving their writing. On the other hand, if you only grade final products, you will have limited items to evaluate. These samples of formal writing will not always reflect the progress that your students have made with process writing activities. As you design an evaluation program, be sure to include ways to document and evaluate the different types of learning in your class. Look at the examples provided of forms that can be used for record keeping and evaluation in Appendix B. As you set up your own procedures for evaluating student work in your classroom, keep the following guidelines in mind.

• *Set up a writing portfolio for each student.* Keep a separate folder for each student, with dated samples of writing. In this way, you are able to document the types of writing each student has explored and to provide examples of individual development at parent conferences. Be sure to have students evaluate their own portfolios periodically. They can do this by writing a statement, by filling out an evaluation form, or by having an individual conference with you. As you review a portfolio of student work, be sure to assess gains a student has made in writing fluently, learning about different genres, using appropriate spelling and grammar, and applying content information. Provide individual feedback for each student. A writing portfolio is an important means by which to document and give students credit for the process writing activities that occupy a substantial part of your classroom writing time.

• *Provide contract sheets for research projects.* When students are engaged in long-term projects, you need to have them keep records that allow you to evaluate their reading, research, and process writing, as well as the final products that they create. You can provide students with a contract sheet that lists each step in the research process, provides a line for the date each step is completed, and includes the type of documentation the students must provide to show that each step has been completed. This might include items such as a data chart, a reflection on an Internet site, field notes from an interview, a graphic organizer about the topic, an outline of the research paper, an edited draft, and an editing checklist.

• *Keep records of daily work.* Create your own classroom chart to record students' progress as you are supervising work on writing projects. This is an informal assessment method that allows you to record information from your observations and conferences with students through anecdotal records. Document what students are learning from activities that do not have a written product, such as participating in peer conferences. This chart also provides you with the data that you need to plan for individualized or small-group instruction the next day. Use this information as your reference point when you are considering students' self-evaluations of progress.

• *Provide students with editing checklists that allow them to evaluate their own writing.* Let students know the criteria that you will be using for evaluation of a formal writing project, and create an editing checklist that guides them to revisit and improve their writing before they submit a final paper. Involve your students in creating this checklist. Students can help determine the criteria used, and they can take care of most of the paperwork involved in using a checklist. Editing checklist items should include areas that students have mastered on previous assignments or areas that you have addressed for this assignment through modeled, shared, or interactive writing instruction.

• *Give students specific feedback, not just a grade.* Even when it is necessary to grade students, it is not appropriate to mark every "mistake" with a red pen. Focus your evaluation on predetermined points. Noting every error on a paper results in an overwhelming amount of feedback for a developing writer, and certainly takes away any pride a student had in the content of the writing. Instead, create a feedback chart (see Appendix B) that allows you to rate a short list of areas where you have focused instruction. Use specific terms (e.g., *strong, adequate, needs development, not present*) on a checklist to rate student work, and write a short comment that documents your evaluation of each area on a particular paper. As you record this information, be sure to create a planning sheet for yourself that lists topics you will address in future instruction to reinforce concepts for the whole class, for small groups, or for individuals.

You will find that the evaluation of student work is an area that you will need to continue to read and collaborate with other teachers to grow professionally. Box 8.9 lists books about writing that provide useful strategies for keeping records of assessment and instruction and for evaluating student work.

REVISITING THE TOPIC OF ENGAGEMENT IN RESEARCH

Sometimes when we consider a complex process such as teaching writing, it is difficult to keep our end goals in mind. First, we recognize that engagement is essential to lifelong literacy. Second, we want to provide students with the skills to be independent writers and strategic readers. As we reconsider these goals, two areas come to the forefront as vital components for developing student engagement: technology and personal choice.

Technology as a Bridge to Student Engagement

One of the greatest challenges of literacy instruction in the 21st century will be to make effective use of the current technology and the wealth of information on the Internet for

BOX 8.9. Resources for Designing Assessment and Evaluation Procedures for a Writing Program

Atwell, N. (1998). *In the middle: New understandings about writing, reading, and learning* (2nd ed.). Portsmouth, NH: Heinemann.

Calkins, L. M. (1998). *The art of teaching writing* (3rd ed.). Portsmouth, NH: Heinemann.

Graves, D. H. (1983). *Writing: Teachers and children at work.* Portsmouth, NH: Heinemann.

Jenkins, C. B. (1996). *Inside the writing portfolio: What we need to know to assess children's writing.* Portsmouth, NH: Heinemann.

Kirby, D., & Liner, T. (1988). *Inside out: Developmental strategies for teaching writing* (2nd ed.). Portsmouth, NH: Boynton/Cook.

Routman, R. (2000). *Conversations: Strategies for teaching, learning, and evaluating.* Portsmouth, NH: Heinemann.

Tchudi, S. (Ed.). (1997). *Alternatives to grading student writing.* Urbana, IL: National Council of Teachers of English.

Tierney, R., Carter, M., & Desal, L. (1991). *Portfolio assessment in the reading-writing classroom.* Norwood, MA: Christopher-Gordon.

Tompkins, G. E. (2000). *Teaching writing: Balancing process and product* (3rd ed.). Upper Saddle River, NJ: Merrill.

---

student research. Leu (2000) notes the unprecedented changes that have taken place at the end of the 20th century in communication technology:

> Consider this situation: The rate at which the Internet is appearing in school classrooms in many countries far exceeds the rate at which any other technology of literacy has ever appeared in our history. The Internet is entering classrooms at a faster rate than books, newspapers, magazines, movies, overhead projectors, televisions, or even telephones.
>
> Consider this prediction: In 2 years, far more U.S. classrooms will have Internet computers than will have telephones, television sets, encyclopedias, or comprehensive classroom libraries. Moreover, the Internet provides access to far greater information than any of these resources. (p. 425)

Designing classroom instruction that successfully incorporates Internet usage requires careful planning on the part of a teacher. Rekrut (1999) notes that teachers must set specific objectives and integrate Internet use as part of their ongoing instruction. By requiring students to create some type of written product for each time they use the Internet, you encourage regular data collection and reflection. This also provides you with a written record of each student's research progress and allows you to troubleshoot when you notice a student who has not been able to narrow the focus in research and find specific Internet sites. Publishing final projects on a class homepage or through e-mail exchanges with other classrooms also promotes a feeling of accomplishment for students.

Teaching your students the basics about technology can provide them with the tools they need to pursue Internet research projects of personal interest outside school. After-school programs that are based on technology such as the Fifth Dimension (Blanton, Greene, & Cole, 1999) integrate literacy learning with varied computer activities that promote critical thinking. The game format encourages students to take an active interest in the development of their own reading and writing skills in an entertaining context.

Meeting Curriculum Requirements and Allowing for Student Choice

Even when teachers use interesting, high-quality materials and support students in writing in creative formats, there will still be some students who are not engaged by a preselected topic for a required research project. You need to consider how you can expose your students to different forms of writing and diverse research topics, yet still allow your students to have opportunities to pursue areas of interest in research. Many teachers also find themselves struggling with the pressures they feel to balance school requirements—particularly the threat of high-stakes testing—with their students' need for personal choice in literacy activities. Consider the example given in the Introduction to this book: In Ms. Washington's language arts class, many of her students were bored by the classroom research project on baseball. By selecting a single topic, Ms. Washington was able to be an expert on the subject and collect the materials students would use, but she still had difficulty finding engaging texts for a whole classroom of students. Think about what purposes you would have for instruction in a language arts classroom. In this case, there was no need for Ms. Washington to require one focus for research. Her students did not need to learn about the content presented in books about baseball. However, they did need to know how to read strategically as they conducted research and how to write effectively about a topic. This type of long-term project was an ideal setting for research on individual topics of student interest.

If students are engaged in the research process, you can provide the structure that they need to conduct research. In essence, you work as a literacy coach to help individual students meet their goals. There will be times when you need to narrow your focus in reading and writing instruction to cover specific content in depth in subject areas such as social studies or science. However, these projects certainly can be the types of process activities that we have mentioned earlier, such as creating simulated journals from different characters' perspectives in history class or writing poetry about the environment in science class. The research is short-term, and students have individual choice in selecting a focus for writing within the topic.

Keep in mind that when your goal is to improve your students' reading and writing skills, and that when you plan to spend an extended period of time on a research project, student engagement should stay at the forefront of instruction. Popular culture remains a vital aspect of students' literacy (Alvermann, Moon, & Hagood, 1999), and students' personal interests and social concerns provide an ideal platform from which to generate research questions. In Box 8.10, Colleen Fairbanks (1999) describes just such a writing program, "Write for Your Life," where students pursue hands-on research

---

BOX 8.10. Write for Your Life: A Writing Program That Combines Real Purposes for Writing with Research

As the video camera comes into focus, Jermaine introduces himself as the anchor for the WMS News program he and his classmates are producing, "My issue is life," he says, "which, as you know, is a pretty big topic." He continues, "Most people live their lives based upon their goals or their religion. They don't know what life means because they haven't experienced that much." As anchor, he will introduce his classmates and provide a tour of his classroom. The camera follows Jermaine as he points out the room's setup. "This is where we work together," he says pointing to the carpeted area where class meetings are held. "This is where we help each other," showing the round tables that serve as desks. He concludes, gesturing to the whole room, "This is where we conversate."

Jermaine's ad-libbed description accurately depicts the aims of Audrey's sixth-grade language arts classroom. It was the site of a partnership between a university and a classroom teacher involved in a nationwide project, "Write for Your Life." The project extended across the school year and led students toward the development of research questions that were personally meaningful. Beginning with personal narratives, the students identified themes emerging from their own and others' life stories. Naming these issues "kids' business," students were helped to see that the themes of their stories and experiences were worthy of continued study. The students and Audrey used these themes to define personally meaningful research questions: Why do friends treat you wrong? Why does my brother use drugs? Why did my parents get divorced? Why do kids join gangs?

The students and Audrey then constructed a process for conducting research together. Students brainstormed the multiple ways to find answers to their individual questions. The flexibility of this process created many avenues for student inquiry and, because of the deep interest these questions held for students, they willingly guided their own learning. For example, Angela, who studied fears and anxieties, interviewed doctors and patients at various mental health facilities. Juan read a recent issue of *Newsweek* to find information about gang violence, and Mario received pamphlets and study tips from a local tutoring center to help him find out how to get better grades in school. These activities encouraged students to extend their frames of reference beyond the four walls of the classroom and built camaraderie among the students as they shared their research data.

In order to document their research stories, the students kept daily records, plans, and interpretations for the information they were gathering. From these records, they also composed I-Search papers (Macrorie, 1980). As students worked to complete their essays, they appeared to be writing with a mission, often ending their essays with boldfaced, capitalized messages to their readers. Ariel ended her I-Search with the following: "**DON'T USE DRUGS!**"; Tonya offered this conclusion: "Why do people get divorced? **IT'S BECAUSE THEY DON'T LOVE EACH OTHER LIKE THEY USED TO.**" These conclusions intimate that personally meaningful inquiry may connect literacy in fundamental ways to students' lives. Moreover, through such literacy practices, students may also build a community in which they can open themselves to each other, trusting that each individual's inquiry has meaning for them all.

Note. From Fairbanks (1999). Reprinted with permission of Colleen Fairbanks.

---

projects stemming from questions about actual issues in their lives. Fairbanks notes that this type of research experience personalizes literacy and provides real reasons for writing.

Beach and Finders (1999) present a similar program, in which students are encouraged to be active investigators as they pursue ethnographies of their own social worlds. Research studies take place at familiar sites for students: a school sports team, a local workplace, an Internet fan club. Student researchers are guided to focus on artifacts, values, and assumptions. Beach and Finders suggest using published ethnographies, such as the PBS documentary *Hoop Dreams* (Twin Cities Public Television, 1995), as samples of research. This film portrays the lives of two high school basketball players as they transfer from an inner-city Chicago school to a Catholic school in the suburbs. Not only is this type of research material engaging, but it also encourages students to use research and writing to interpret their own worlds. These personal purposes for literacy—real reading and writing—are what we need to cultivate in our classrooms.

CHILDREN'S BOOK REFERENCES

Adler, D. A. (1989). *We remember the Holocaust.* New York: Trumpet Club.

Arnosky, J. (1997). *All about rattlesnakes.* New York: Scholastic.

Bachrach, S. D. (1994). *Tell them we remember: The story of the Holocaust.* Boston: Little, Brown.

Brewster, H. (1996). *Anastasia's album.* Toronto: Madison Press.

Chang, I. (1991). *A separate battle: Women and the Civil War.* New York: Lodestar.

Chin-Lee, C. (1997). *A is for Asia.* New York: Orchard.

Collier, J. L., & Collier, C. (1994). *With every drop of blood.* New York: Delacorte.

Conrad, P. (1989). *My Daniel.* New York: Harper & Row.

Conrad, P. (1991). *Prairie visions: The life and times of Solomon Butcher.* New York: HarperCollins.

Cooney, C. B. (1999). *Burning up.* New York: Delacorte.

Cowley, J. (1999). *Red-eyed tree frog* (ill. N. Bishop). New York: Scholastic.

Cummings, P., & Cummings, L. (Eds.). (1998). *Talking with adventurers.* Washington, DC: National Geographic Society.

Danziger, P., & Martin, A. M. (1998). *P.S. longer letter later.* New York: Scholastic.

Doubilet, A. (1991). *Under the sea from A to Z* (ill. D. Doubilet). New York: Crown.

Dussling, J. (1998). *Slinky, scaly snakes!* (*Eyewitness Readers*, Level 2). New York: Dorling Kindersley.

Erickson, P. (1994). *Daily life in a covered wagon.* Washington, DC: Preservation Press.

Fleischman, P. (1988). *Joyful noise: Poems for two voices* (ill. E. Beddows). New York: Harper & Row.

Fleischman, P. (1993). *Bull Run.* New York: HarperCollins.

Fleischman, P. (1996). *Dateline: Troy.* Cambridge, MA: Candlewick.

Florian, D. (1998). *Insectlopedia: Poems and paintings.* San Diego, CA: Harcourt Brace.

Fox, A. L., & Abraham-Podietz, E. (1999). *Ten thousand children: True stories told by children who escaped the Holocaust on the Kindertransport.* West Orange, NJ: Behrman House.

Frank, A. (1995). *The diary of a young girl: The definitive edition.* New York: Doubleday.

Gallaz, C., & Innocenti, R. (1985). *Rose Blanche* (ill. R. Innocenti). Mankato, MN: Creative Education.

Gollub, M. (1998). *Cool melons—Turn to frogs!: The life and poems of Issa* (ill. K. G. Stone). New York: Lee & Low.

Granfield, L. (1994). *Extra! Extra!: The who, what, where, when, and why of newspapers* (ill. B. Slavin). New York: Orchard.

Gregory, K. (1989). *Jenny of the Tetons.* San Diego, CA: Harcourt Brace.

Gregory, K. (1997). *Across the wide and lonesome prairie: The Oregon Trail diary of Hattie Campbell.* New York: Scholastic.

Harter, P. (1994). *Shadow play: Night haiku.* New York: Simon & Schuster.

Harvey, B. (1986). *My prairie year: Based on the diary of Elenore Plaisted* (ill. D. K. Ray). New York: Holiday House.

Heiligman, D. (1998). *The New York Public Library kid's guide to research.* New York: Scholastic.

Hoestlandt, J. (1995). *Star of fear, star of hope* (ill. J. Kang, trans. M. Polizzotti). New York: Walker.

Hopkins, L. B. (Ed.). (1987). *Dinosaurs* (ill. M. Tinkelman). San Diego, CA: Harcourt Brace.

Hopkins, L. B. (Ed.). (1994). *Weather* (ill. M. Hale). New York: HarperCollins.

Hurmence, B. (Ed.). (1997). *Slavery time when I was chillun.* New York: Putnam.

Hunt, J. (1989). *Illuminations.* New York: Bradbury Press.

Jackson, D. M. (1996). *The bone detectives: How forensic anthropologists solve crimes and uncover mysteries of the dead.* Boston: Little, Brown.

King, C., & Osborne, L. B. (1997). *Oh, freedom!: Kids talk about the civil rights movement with the people who made it happen.* New York: Knopf.

Lawlor, V. (Ed.). (1995). *I was dreaming to come to America: Memories from the Ellis Island oral history project.* New York: Viking.

Leedy, L. (1990). *The Furry News: How to make a newspaper.* New York: Holiday House.

Livingston, M. C. (1988). *Space songs* (ill. L. E. Fisher). New York: McElderry.

Lobel, A. (1998). *No pretty pictures: A child of war.* New York: Greenwillow.

Meltzer, M. (1989). *Voices from the Civil War: A documentary history of the great American conflict.* New York: HarperCollins.

Meltzer, M. (1993). *Lincoln: In his own words.* San Diego, CA: Harcourt Brace.

Mettger, Z. (1994). *Till victory is won: Black soldiers in the Civil War.* New York: Lodestar.

Mochizuki, K. (1997). *Passage to freedom: The Sugihara story* (ill. D. Lee). New York: Lee & Low.

Murphy, J. (1990). *The boys' war: Confederate and Union soldiers talk about the Civil War.* Boston: Houghton Mifflin.

Nieuwsma, M. J. (Ed.). (1998). *Kinderlager: An oral history of young Holocaust survivors.* New York: Holiday House.

Nixon, J. L. (1996). *Search for the Shadowman.* New York: Delacorte.

Oppenheim, S. L. (1992). *The lily cupboard: A story of the Holocaust* (ill. R. Himler). New York: HarperCollins.

Rawick, G. P. (Ed.). (1972). *The American slave: A composite autobiography.* Westport, CT: Greenwood Press.

Roberson, E. W. (1996). *Weep not for me, dear mother.* Gretna, LA: Pelican.

Rosenberg, M. B. (1994). *Hiding to survive: Stories of Jewish children rescued from the Holocaust.* New York: Clarion.

Schertle, A. (1995). *Advice for a frog* (ill. N. Green). New York: Lothrop, Lee & Shepard.

Sierra. J. (1998). *Antarctic antics: A book of penguin poems* (ill. J. Aruego Dewey). San Diego, CA: Harcourt Brace.

Simon, S. (1999). *Crocodiles and alligators.* New York: HarperCollins.

Souza, D. M. (1998). *Sea snakes.* Minneapolis, MN: Carolrhoda.

Tunnell, M. O., & Chilcoat, G. W. (1996). *The children of Topaz: The story of a Japanese-American internment camp based on a classroom diary.* New York: Holiday House.

Turner, A. (1997). *Mississippi mud: Three prairie journals* (ill. R. J. Blake). New York: HarperCollins.

Warren, A. (1998). *Pioneer girl: Growing up on the prairie.* New York: Morrow.

Wild, M. (1991). *Let the celebrations begin!* (ill. J. Vivas). New York: Orchard.

Woodruff, E. (1994). *Dear Levi: Letters from the Overland Trail* (ill. B. Peck). New York: Knopf.

Yolen, J. (1993). *Here there be dragons.* San Diego, CA: Harcourt Brace.

Yolen, J. (1994). *Here there be unicorns.* San Diego, CA: Harcourt Brace.

Yolen, J. (1998). *Here there be ghosts.* San Diego, CA: Harcourt Brace.

Yolen, J., & Coville, B. (1998). *Armageddon summer.* San Diego, CA: Harcourt Brace.

REFERENCES

Alvermann, D., Moon, J. S., & Hagood, M. C. (1999). *Popular culture in the classroom.* Newark, DE: International Reading Association.

Atwell, N. (1998). *In the middle: New understandings about writing, reading, and learning* (2nd ed.). Portsmouth, NH: Heinemann.

Beach, R., & Finders, M. J. (1999). Students as ethnographers: Guiding alternative research projects. *English Journal, 89*(1), 82–90.

Blanton, W. E., Greene, M. W., & Cole, M. (1999). Computer mediation for learning and play. *Journal of Adolescent and Adult Literacy, 43*(3), 272–278.

Crook, P., & Broaddus, K. (1992, December). *A literary model for exploring nonfiction: Creating an aesthetic response.* Paper presented at the meeting of the International Reading Association, 16th Southeast Regional Conference, New Orleans, LA.

DeFelice, C. (1998). The bones beneath the flesh of historical fiction. *Book Links, 8*(2), 30–34.

Fairbanks, C. (1999, December). Investigating "kids' business": Fostering adolescents' literacy engagements. In C. Roller (Chair), *Starting with readers and writers: New perspectives on middle school literacy engagement and instruction.* Symposium conducted at the 49th annual meeting of the National Reading Conference, Orlando, FL.

Harvey, S. (1998). *Nonfiction matters: Reading, writing, and research in grades 3–8.* York, ME: Stenhouse.

Leu, D. J. (2000). Exploring literacy on the Internet. Our children's future: Changing the focus of literacy and literacy instruction. *The Reading Teacher, 53*(5), 424–429.

Lott, C., & Wasta, S. (1999). Adding voice and perspective: Children's and young adult literature of the Civil War. *English Journal, 88*(6), 56–61.

Macrorie, K. (1980). *Searching writing.* Rochelle Park, NJ: Hayden.

Murray, D. M. (1999). *Write to learn* (6th ed.). Fort Worth, TX: Harcourt Brace.

Ogle, D. M. (1986). K-W-L: A teaching model that develops active reading of expository text. *The Reading Teacher, 40*, 564–571.

Rekrut, M. D. (1999). Using the Internet in classroom instruction: A primer for teachers. *Journal of Adolescent and Adult Literacy, 42*(7), 546–563.

Stauffer, R. G. (1969). *Directing reading maturity as a cognitive process.* New York: Harper & Row.

Stauffer, R. G. (1970). *The language-experience approach to the teaching of reading.* New York: Harper & Row.

Tompkins, G. E. (2000). *Teaching writing: Balancing process and product* (3rd ed.). Upper Saddle River, NJ: Merrill.

Twin Cities Public Television (Producer). (1995). *Hoop Dreams.* St. Paul, MN: Producer.

Wolf, D. P., Craven, J., & Balick, D. (Eds.). (1996). *More than the truth: Teaching nonfiction writing through journalism.* Portsmouth, NH: Heinemann.

CHAPTER 9

Tailoring Instruction for Individual Students

"What makes reading hard is like when you come across a word, and you don't know it 'cause you never heard of it before, and like you just try to figure it out 'cause you really want to see what happens. You get stuck on that one word." (Kayla, fourth grade)

"When I'm reading in school, I can't focus. I keep reading the words over and over, but they don't sink in. When I'm finished I can't remember what it was about. Especially science and social studies. I do my homework, but I fail the tests." (Diana, eighth grade)

"I hate to write. I am NO GOOD at writing and spelling. My handwriting stinks." (Clay, fifth grade)

"My teacher makes us all read out loud in class. I get so nervous when I know she's going to call on me. I can't get the words out. So I just sit and wait for somebody to tell me the word." (Xavier, seventh grade)

What would you say to the students quoted above? Where would you start in helping them? Literacy is central to achievement in school, and students who struggle are keenly aware of their difficulties. You can hear the frustration in the voices of the students above. Challenges in literacy can include difficulties in word recognition, spelling, comprehension, writing, and fluency. Often students who struggle in school develop problems with motivation, engagement, and behavior as well.

There are countless programs, approaches, methods and support services that claim to be the answer for students with literacy challenges. The unfortunate truth is that there is no "quick fix" (Allington & Walmsley, 1995) and no "silver bullet" (Spiegel, 1998) for students who find reading and writing difficult, because in the world of challenged readers and writers, there is no such thing as a typical student. However, with teacher expertise and patience, along with the right materials and instruction, many students with literacy challenges can make accelerated progress in the regular classroom. In this chapter, we explore various options for individualizing instruction, with a focus on what classroom teachers can do.

WHAT'S IN THIS CHAPTER?

Meeting Students' Needs in the Regular Instructional Program
Extra Assistance for Students Who Struggle
Current Views on Students Who Struggle in Literacy
School Programs for Students Who Struggle in Literacy
Instruction in Remedial and Special Education Programs
What Kinds of Instruction Do Struggling Learners Need?
A Plan for Meeting the Needs of Struggling Learners
Exploring Options for Additional Assistance
Learning More about Helping Struggling Learners

MEETING STUDENTS' NEEDS
IN THE REGULAR INSTRUCTIONAL PROGRAM

In every classroom, there will be students who have a hard time learning to read and write independently. These students will need additional support, but there are no easy answers for what support to provide or how to provide it. According to Duffy-Hester (1999), "reading programs should be designed to support the reading growth of all children, both struggling and nonstruggling readers" (p. 491). We agree. If instruction, tasks, and materials are appropriate for students in terms of needs, interests, and strengths, most if not all students should be able to make appropriate progress in reading and writing. Examine your literacy program carefully in light of the guidelines for reading and writing instruction presented in this book. Ask yourself questions like the following to determine whether you are doing everything you can to meet the literacy instruction needs of all the students you teach:

1. In what ways do you continually assess and evaluate your students in reading, writing, and thinking? How does your instruction compare to the suggestions in this book and in other books you value? Have you consulted your students' families (look again at Chapter 1, Box 1.3)?

2. What kinds of reading materials does your classroom contain? There should be many different types of materials on a wide range of levels, topics, and genres. Compare your classroom collection to the suggestions in Chapter 2.

3. How are you ensuring that all of your students receive engaging, purposeful instruction based on their challenges, strengths, and interests? Think about each of your students in light of all of the chapters.

4. How often do you read aloud to students? What kinds of materials do you choose to read aloud? You should be reading several times daily from a variety of texts that support and extend students' conceptual learning, thinking, and comprehension strategies. See Chapter 3.

5. What kinds of texts do students read themselves? All students need daily opportunities to read in instructional-level texts with support and to read independently in easy texts. See Chapters 2, 4, and 5.

6. What does your writing program look like? Do you provide daily opportunities and support for students to learn about writing and to write independently? Are students engaging daily in a variety of writing tasks and genres, including personal writing, literary writing, researching, learning logs, and responding to reading? See Chapters 6 and 8.

7. How does your language and word study program work? Do you provide opportunities for students to engage in supported and independent analysis of language and words? See Chapter 7.

8. In what ways do you ensure that your classroom is academically, socially, and personally supportive for all students? How do you involve students and their families in planning and assessing their learning?

EXTRA ASSISTANCE FOR STUDENTS WHO STRUGGLE

Even if your classroom is exemplary, you will have some students who struggle with literacy and are behind the majority of the class. These students will need to make accelerated progress, or they will continue to fall further behind with every school year. Your response to these students is critical to their future. Although a small number of students will need additional support, we feel strongly that well-educated, thoughtful classroom teachers who engage in continued learning can and should provide appropriate best instruction for students who struggle with reading and writing.

Unfortunately, teacher responsibility for struggling learners is not always supported by the structures of public schools. Teachers have responsibilities that extend beyond instruction and take away from planning and instructional time. Busy schedules leave little time for extended learning, reading, and consulting with colleagues. Furthermore, in the current era of high-stakes testing and accountability, teachers are encouraged to spend their energy, time, and attention on students who are achieving close to grade level and to hand off the education of their lower achievers to special programs (Allington, 1994; Spear-Swerling & Sternberg, 1996), because in many cases there is little or no accountability for the education of students who receive special education services (Gartner & Lipsky, 1987). An article in *The New York Times* about achievement testing in Texas describes what we have heard and seen in schools across the country with frightening accuracy:

> [S]ome teachers will tell you confidentially that they're urged to concentrate on the "bubble kids," the students who are on the borderline between passing and failing the test, and not to worry about "the kids who'll never pass." (Schrag, 2000, p. 53)

In the remainder of this chapter, we first discuss current views on students who struggle with literacy and the process of identifying students for school remedial programs. Next, we describe the ineffective instruction traditionally provided to struggling learners, and we contrast this with instructional principles that are based in current theory and practice. Finally, we present a plan that focuses on the role of the classroom teacher in supporting and taking responsibility for students who struggle.

CURRENT VIEWS ON STUDENTS WHO STRUGGLE IN LITERACY

It is important to stress that students who struggle with literacy are not a homogeneous group (Roller, 1996). In terms of family background and experience, their parents may have limited formal education or advanced graduate degrees; their homes may be brimming with books or may have almost no print material; they may have traveled the world or may never have left their neighborhood. In terms of literacy, students may have challenges with word analysis, fluency, writing, strategic reading, comprehension, and/or background knowledge. Certainly, there are many children who struggle mightily with reading and writing. However, like the majority of educators, we believe that most reading difficulties are the result of the learners' getting "off track" (Spear-Swerling & Sternberg, 1996) during the course of their literacy development due to experiential, emotional, developmental, or instructional issues, rather than problems within the children.

SCHOOL PROGRAMS FOR STUDENTS
WHO STRUGGLE IN LITERACY

Special Education Programs

A common response to literacy difficulties (and becoming more common by the minute) is to refer students for special education testing. In fact, the majority of students in the special education system, especially those identified as "learning-disabled," are there because they experience difficulty with reading and writing. Surely, most teachers who refer their students for testing do so because they feel a responsibility to be sure their students receive the help they need. In many schools, however, once a student is referred for testing, the teacher loses her or his voice in the decision-making process. A diagnostician takes over the case, administering standardized tests of intelligence along with psychological and educational tests. Teacher and parent input is often minimal once the diagnostic process has begun.

Work by Clay (1987) and by Vellutino and his colleagues (1996) illuminates the importance of considering also the student's previous educational history and response to intervention in making decisions about further instruction. Citing their own recent longitudinal investigation of more than 1,000 emerging and beginning readers, as well as Clay's work (Clay, 1985, 1987; Iverson & Tunmer, 1993; Pinnell, 1989), Vellutino et al. (1996) insist:

> To render a diagnosis of "specific reading disability" in the absence of early and labor intensive remedial reading instruction that has been tailored to the child's individual needs is, at best, a hazardous and dubious enterprise . . . (p. 632)

Nevertheless, most times the referral process proceeds with little or no information about classroom instruction or assessment, or evidence that intensive instruction has been attempted. If a significant discrepancy is found between the student's so-called "potential" (score on intelligence test) and literacy skill (score on an achievement test), the student may be labeled "learning-disabled" or "reading-disabled." The discrepancy definition continues to be used in spite of evidence that IQ is not a reliable predictor of reading potential (Siegel, 1989; Stanovich, Cunningham, & Freeman, 1984).

Another problem is the overrepresentation of certain groups. Many researchers have pointed out a referral bias toward boys, who are often seen as causing more behavior problems than girls, and toward poor and minority students, whose background experiences may not match those expected by their schools or tests (Lerner, 1993; McGill-Franzen, 1994; Spear-Swerling & Sternberg, 1996). Furthermore, teachers may be tacitly encouraged to refer struggling students to special programs so that they will be excluded from testing (and their scores excluded from district reporting), or so that their schools will receive more federal funding (Dyer & Binkney, 1995; McGill-Franzen, 1994).

Too often, teachers are given the impression that when a student has a "learning disability" or is "dyslexic," there is a "constitutional" or congenital cause and that they learn differently from other students, when this is rarely the case (Lyons, 1989; Reschly, 1987). According to many current educators and researchers, however, there are no tests or characteristics, no "unique biological or genetic profile" (Spear-Swerling & Sternberg, 1996, p. 276) that have been found to characterize reading disability as opposed to difficulty (Ellis, 1988). By the same token, as we will discuss in upcoming sections, research has shown no advantage of specialized instruction or materials over exemplary literacy instruction appropriate for all students, although the intensity, primary focus, and instructional format will vary from person to person. Students who struggle with literacy will, of course, need more instructional support in the classroom.

Yet many teachers assume, because this is what they are led to believe, that these students' reading is qualitatively different and that they must be instructed by specialists. Teachers often lose confidence in their ability to provide instruction for these students, assuming that the students need the help of specialists. This may lead teachers to feel that the literacy progress of these students is not their responsibility. When the students leave the classroom to "go down the hall" (Cunningham & Allington, 1999), teachers assume that they are in capable hands and are receiving the help they need. According to Cunningham and Allington,

> As these special programs have been added, we have led classroom teachers to believe that these children are not their responsibility and often that they are insufficiently expert to teach them. In some schools that we have studied, as many as three out of four classroom teachers told us the reading and language arts instruction of remedial and mainstreamed learning-disabled children was not their responsibility! (pp. 9–10)

Ironically, often special education teachers do not receive any specific preparation for teaching students who struggle with reading, even though reading will be the source of difficulty for most students in learning disabilities resource classes. It is often true that general teacher preparation programs do not include enough courses in reading instruction, processes, and assessment for new teachers to feel knowledgeable and confident in meeting the needs of struggling learners (Spear-Swerling & Sternberg, 1996; Worthy & Prater, 1998). However, we must realize that the same is true of special education teachers. In many colleges and universities, special education preservice teachers get the same preparation in reading as do preservice teachers in general education, or even less.

If parents give their permission, a student may be placed in a special education re-source class for part of the day or in an inclusion program, in which the special educa-tion teacher works with students within the regular classroom and (theoretically) col-laborates with the classroom teacher. If regular classroom instruction is appropriate and if the teachers indeed collaborate, inclusion programs have potential for helping to meet students' needs within the regular classroom.

As more and more students are being identified as needing special services, special education class size is ballooning. In schools in which we have worked, the special edu-cation teacher may have as many students in his or her resource class as there are in a regular classroom, or even more. Consider that within such a classroom, many students may have behavioral challenges, in addition to a range of "disabilities," each needing specialized, individualized remediation. How can any program or teacher possibly in-dividualize instruction to the extent that is needed with so many students? How can one teacher, even one who is an expert in literacy instruction, meet the needs of every student in a class where everyone needs individual attention?

Chapter I/Title I Programs

Similar problems have been found with federally funded remedial reading programs (Chapter I/Title I). Often remedial reading teachers have no more preparation in liter-acy education than their general education counterparts. Classroom teachers assume that their students are getting instruction that regular teachers cannot provide, even though, as in special education, class sizes are often very large and behavioral problems abound. When students leave to go to their special classes, they lose valuable instruc-tional time in moving from classroom to classroom, and their instruction is fragmented. Even more disturbing is the kind of literacy instruction that is typically given to stu-dents in both special education and remedial reading programs.

INSTRUCTION IN REMEDIAL AND SPECIAL EDUCATION PROGRAMS

In terms of improving the literacy of upper elementary and middle school students, pull-out special education and remedial literacy programs have been a dismal failure (Kennedy, Birman, & Demaline, 1986):

> Once children are classified as learning disabled, few ever attain academic achievement compara-ble to their peers. Few schools have developed education interventions that accelerate the literacy development of children classified as learning disabled. Few school districts evaluate special edu-cation programs in terms of accelerated student achievement. What little evidence is available suggests that most children classified as learning disabled fall further behind their peers even af-ter participating in special education programs. (Dyer & Binkney, 1995, p. 66)

Why don't such programs work? One simple answer is that often in these special classes designed to help students with reading and writing, students almost never en-gage in independent reading and writing (Allington & McGill-Franzen, 1989).

Numerous studies have shown that students identified as poor or struggling readers receive qualitatively different instruction from that afforded to higher-achieving students. Instruction that students receive in a "low-reading" group, in remedial programs, or in special education is typically characterized by isolated skills work and a focus on correct oral reading, as opposed to the purposeful, contextualized, reading instruction given to higher-achieving students (Taylor, Harris, Pearson, & García, 1995). According to Walmsley and Allington (1995),

> We know that active involvement in actual reading and writing of texts is critical to accelerated development, yet remedial and special education students are the groups least likely to be asked to read or write—in any sustained form—during instruction. (p. 23)

In particular, Chapter I/Title I programs serving students in the upper elementary grades have come under fire for an emphasis on lower-order skills and heavy use of worksheets (Johnston & Allington, 1991; Rowan & Guthrie, 1989). The net result of this differential instruction is that students who receive remedial instruction actually read far less than their higher-achieving peers (Allington, 1983). In fact, according to Walmsley and Allington (1995), "Much of the difference in reading strategy between high- and low-achievement readers can be explained by the differences in the instructional tasks emphasized" (p. 29). As early as first grade, high-achieving readers read an average of close to 2,000 words in connected text per week, while low-achieving readers read only 16 (Allington, 1983). This disparity continues to grow as students progress through the grades. In the intermediate grades, the best readers have read between 10 and 50 million words; average readers approximately 1 million; and struggling readers only 100,000 (Nagy & Anderson, 1984). How ironic that lower-achieving students are most in need of the acceleration afforded by reading in connected text, yet they typically get far fewer opportunities to read than higher-achieving readers do! This situation leads to even greater achievement gaps. Students who don't read don't get better at reading, and the reading they do is usually frustrating. Frustration leads to avoidance, which leads to slower progress (Stanovich, 1986) and even less motivation to read. According to Spear-Swerling and Sternberg (1996),

> . . . there are three negative factors in particular that affect all children with reading difficulties and greatly exacerbate their initial difficulties in reading. We have referred to these factors as the "swamp" of lowered motivation, lowered levels of practice, and lowered expectations. (p. 175)

Students in the middle grades who have been through years of the "swamp" often begin to misbehave because they are bored and frustrated. They learn to hate reading and writing, and they develop feelings of helplessness in regard to learning (Johnston & Winograd, 1985). In short, special classes intended to help students improve in reading and writing often do just the opposite, and students fall farther and farther behind.

There are surely many exceptions to these generalities, and recent efforts to restructure instruction are promising (e.g., Winfield, 1995). However, too many special education and Chapter I programs, and too many "low-reading" groups, continue to operate in ways that are ineffective for struggling learners. It is important, then, to ask yourself this: When you refer students to remedial reading programs or for special education consideration, will that "special" instruction will be more effective than, or even as effective, as your classroom instruction?

WHAT KINDS OF INSTRUCTION
DO STRUGGLING LEARNERS NEED?

> In the odd, often upside-down world of schools, we typically start in the wrong place. We start with what kids can't do and don't know. It's as if we brainstormed a list for each of them . . ., that we figured out what they *don't* understand or value, what they feel incompetent or insecure about, and we then developed a curriculum to remediate each deficiency. The curriculum is built on a deficit-model; it is built on repairing weakness. And it simply doesn't work. (Ayers, 1993, p. 31)

It is essential to focus on students' strengths and interests in all education, and it is even more important for those students who are having difficulties. There is no single program (Allington & Walmsley, 1995) that can possibly meet the complex literacy needs of all students. Struggling learners need instructional approaches that focus on enhancing motivation and providing reading and writing practice. The only principle that is now accepted for instructing struggling learners is what applies to all learners: For students with reading and writing challenges, as well as for all students, instructional plans must be based on the students' strengths and challenges, interests and goals. According to Spear-Swerling and Sternberg (1996):

> In all phases, children need a combination approach of instructional features that tend to be characteristic of different approaches. Yet precisely which features need to be emphasized change depending on the children's phase of development (as well as on other factors, of course, such as individual strengths and weaknesses). (p. 173)

In addition, teachers need to have high expectations for what they can do to assist struggling learners in the classroom, and they must have high expectations for students' learning. Nieto (2000) reviews research demonstrating that negative teacher expectations lead to negative results in student achievement. Conversely, when teacher expectations are high, student achievement is positively affected. Examine honestly your expectations for students. Do you have high expectations of students who have been designated as "slow" or "basic" learners, "poor readers," or "learning-disabled," and of students whose language, culture, and socioeconomic status are different from yours? It is hard for most of us to admit to differential treatment of such students; yet most of us do harbor biases, however unintentional they may be, and these are manifested in our teaching (Oakes, 1985; Flores, Cousin, & Díaz, 1991). In planning your instruction and in working with students, do you embrace and honor the language and culture of all students (Ladson-Billings, 1995)? The best weapons against bias and low expectations are awareness, knowledge about individual students, and the expectation that *all* students can make accelerated progress.

A PLAN FOR MEETING THE NEEDS OF STRUGGLING LEARNERS

Skilled, knowledgeable classroom teachers *can* and *should* be expected to provide good instruction for students who need additional support. To ensure that you are doing everything you can do for each of your students who struggle, we recommend using a four-step plan: (1) gathering information; (2) identifying strengths and challenges; (3) formulating a plan of action; and (4) evaluating this plan. The left column in Box 9.1 lists ideas and questions to think about as you go through the four steps; the right column presents a teacher's notes illustrating the use of the steps. This plan should not be considered a lockstep process. At any step along the way, you may need to go back to previous steps and modify plans accordingly. It is helpful to consult with colleagues every step of the way.

Below, we examine three cases of struggling learners whose challenges were serious but could be addressed through regular classroom instruction and modifications. Julie, a fifth grader, loved to write, but her teacher was worried about her reading fluency, engagement, and slow progress in reading. Nadra, a fourth grader from Iraq, was learning English as a second language. Nadra's smooth oral reading masked her difficulty with comprehension and background knowledge. Although both Julie and Nadra needed intervention, their teachers took the responsibility to seek advice, to learn about the issues involved, and to modify classroom instruction accordingly. Julie and Nadra were able to make accelerated progress within their regular classroom. The third student, Francisco, was a gifted eighth grader who was failing in school. We describe the information that we gathered and evaluated (steps 1 and 2), and then give you, our readers, the opportunity to construct a plan for Francisco. Keep in mind that there are many possible options for all students who have difficulty in school.

Julie: A Motivated Writer Who Struggles with Reading Fluency, Word Identification, and Engagement

Julie is a fifth grader in the class of Mr. Damien, a first-year teacher who teaches both language arts and social studies. Julie is shy, well behaved, and quiet—the kind of child who is easily ignored in many classrooms. In beginning-of-the-year assessments, Mr. Damien found that Julie's reading in grade-level novels and in the social studies textbook was dysfluent and filled with inaccuracies, which he at first attributed partly to her apparent shyness and anxiety. The beginning of the year has been a whirlwind for Mr. Damien; after 6 weeks, he is just beginning to reassess his students' progress. To his dismay, Julie has made virtually no progress since the beginning of the year. In the right column of Box 9.1, we illustrate briefly how Mr. Damien used the four-step plan with Julie to modify instruction and materials for her. The subsections below give more in-depth information about Mr. Damien's decision processes as he moved through the four steps.

Try it out yourself: Before you begin reading about Julie, think about what you know so far. What do you think is going on?

Step 1: Gathering Information

What do you know and what more can you find out about this student that will help in planning instruction? As in all good instruction, the place to start with struggling learners is with assessment. Examine the assessments that you have already done (see Chapter 1 and each instructional chapter). Make hypotheses as you would in a STAIR assessment (see Chapter 4, Boxes 4.8 and 4.9). Gather additional assessments to build a comprehensive picture of your student's strengths and challenges in literacy, as well as his or her interests. A good time to do additional assessments is during independent

BOX 9.1. Use of the Four Steps: Ideas and Questions to Consider, and a Teacher's Notes on a Motivated Writer Who Struggles with Reading

Ideas and questions	Mr. Damien's notes on Julie
Step 1. Gathering Information • Why are you concerned about this student? • What do you know from initial surveys, assessments and observations, and parent contacts about this student's strengths, challenges, and interests? • What is your initial hypothesis or hunch?	I'm worried because Julie is falling behind in reading. Her mom says she keeps a personal journal and writes at home about animals, but she never reads at home. Julie is struggling through her free-reading book and is reading *very* slowly. Early assessments showed that her word recognition and fluency in the social studies book were limited, but she could understand the concepts. My hunch is that Julie is reading books that are too hard for her because she doesn't want to read "baby" books in front of her friends. She is not making progress because she is always reading on her frustrational level. She is always engaged when I read aloud. I think that she will make progress if we can find the right materials for her.
Step 2. Evaluating Information • Describe both strengths and areas of concern, identifying what the student knows and can do well, and where the student's understanding breaks down. • Evaluate appropriateness of tasks and materials. • Identify the areas where support is needed.	*Strengths:* Julie has good comprehension of grade-level materials that I read aloud. She is a motivated writer and has strong personal interests. *Areas of Concern:* Julie's word analysis and fluency are limited. I need to start by helping Julie find books she can read and wants to read.
Step 3. Developing a Plan • Using the information you have gathered, formulate a plan for modifying materials and tasks so that the student will make accelerated progress. Be sure to make use of the student's strengths and interests. • Does your student need individual attention? How will you arrange this? • Document what you do, as well as the student's response.	I met with Julie during free-reading time to review how to choose appropriate books. Julie admitted that her book was too difficult and that she did not really enjoy it, but was reading it because her friends were. The librarian and I helped her make a list of books that she was comfortable reading and would enjoy (she picked information texts and short novels about dogs and cats). I also suggested that she do her research project on animals, using the same books. She dived right into her reading after that. The librarian also helped me gather a range of materials on our social studies topics, so Julie and other students wouldn't have to rely on the textbook.
Step 4. Evaluating the Plan • Continually assess and evaluate your plan. • If you don't see progress, return to step 1. • Take steps to learn more about struggling learners.	Julie is making progress. Her mom says she is reading at home every day. I still give her extra attention during independent reading and observe her closely during class, but she is on her way. My team members suggested some professional books to read and are helping me to build a classroom library with more range and variety.

reading and writing periods. Spend some additional time with your students who are struggling during these periods, paying close attention to their use of reading and writing strategies, and make sure that their tasks and materials are appropriately challenging but not frustrating. Also, observe these students more carefully during whole-class and small-group instruction, taking notes. Consult with your student's family and former teachers to gather additional information about the student's development, education, and other areas. During this step, Mr. Damien reexamined the assessments (see Chapter 1) that he did at the beginning of the year and found that Julie had a generally positive attitude toward reading, a very positive attitude toward writing, and a strong interest in animals. Her reading in the grade-level social studies book was at her frustrational level in word recognition and she read very slowly, although she was familiar with most of the concepts presented and was able to learn new information even from her frustrational-level reading. Julie always seemed engaged in Mr. Damien's read-alouds. Although her writing was filled with misspellings of sight words and visual patterns (e.g., consonant doubling, homophones), she wrote quickly and eagerly, and her responses were thoughtful and sophisticated. She did not talk much in class, but wrote extensively in her dialogue journal about her home activities (mainly the family dog grooming and breeding business, in which she is very involved).

Mr. Damien's anecdotal notes since the beginning of the year described a student who seemed uncomfortable reading grade-level materials. During free reading, she always seemed to choose books that other students were reading, although they were definitely too difficult in terms of word identification and fluency. To his chagrin, he noticed that she had started several novels but had never finished one. Like many students in the class, Julie was eager to read all of the *Harry Potter* books after Mr. Damien read the first one to the class. She had been "reading" the second book in the series, *Harry Potter and the Chamber of Secrets* (Rowling, 1999), for the past 3 weeks; however, she was becoming increasingly withdrawn, restless, and inattentive in class, and did not want to talk about the book during the Friday "pair share" days.

Step 2: Evaluating Information

Based on the information you have gathered, identify the focal areas in which the student needs assistance, asking questions such as these:

- What does the student know and do well?
- Where is the student making sense of her or his work?
- What are your concerns about the student's work?
- Where does he or she need your support to learn?

Building on students' strengths and interests ensures that students will have successful experiences even while they are working on challenges. Mr. Damien was able to pinpoint Julie's strengths and areas of concern from information he had gathered already, along with a conversation with her mother. Mr. Damien discovered that Julie was reading books that were too difficult for her word analysis and fluency skill, and that the ensuing frustration was causing her to withdraw and lose enthusiasm for reading. However, she had generally positive attitudes, strong personal interests, an interesting and supportive home life, and strong comprehension of both narrative and information text presented orally. Furthermore, she was a highly motivated writer. Mr. Damien determined to use Julie's strengths in planning instruction tailored to her needs.

Step 3: Formulating a Plan of Action

What will help this student make accelerated progress? How will you use what you have learned about your student in developing a plan tailored to this student's individual interests, motives, strengths, and areas of concern? Using the information you have gathered, formulate a plan for modifying instructional procedures and tasks; consult with colleagues. In developing your plan, it is important to remember that regardless of students' actual grade level, they should be engaging in reading and writing tasks and with materials that they can handle independently, and they should be supported in instructional-level tasks and materials. They must also hear grade-level materials presented orally, through read-alouds, taped reading, and other methods, so they will continue to learn conceptually. In addition, they must have access to materials in content areas that they can read and understand.

In our work with struggling learners, we focus on five major areas: teacher read-aloud, fluency, supported reading and writing, word study, and reading at home. These are the same areas that are part of an exemplary classroom instructional program. As you plan instruction, you may find it helpful to refer to Box 9.2, a chart explaining these five areas and giving examples of appropriate instruction for a student whose major challenge is either word recognition and fluency or comprehension. We don't mean to imply that the two are separate; they certainly are not. Nor do we mean to imply that every student's difficulty will be exclusively in one of these areas. However, the chart, in conjunction with the instruction described in this book, will provide ideas that you can use for almost any student. The ideas are appropriate for a variety of instructional formats, including whole-class, small-group, and individualized instruction. In most cases, it will be necessary to arrange to spend some additional instructional time during class (and, if possible, after school), supporting your student in areas of need. Document what you do, as well as the student's response.

Enlisting the help of the school librarian, Mr. Damien and Julie identified books that she could read in her areas of interest, mainly animals. Julie's areas of strength—writing and comprehension—provided supports for her reading as she engaged in research. For the following 6 weeks, Mr. Damien planned to try a project approach to social studies and literacy that he had been reading and talking to colleagues about. Mr. Damien had read that when students read and write about self-selected topics, they are often able to transcend their reading and writing achievement levels. Julie chose her family business for her research project. Her sources included information books, the World Wide Web, interviews with her parents and other professionals, and a visit to a county animal care facility. Her interest and background experiences, strong comprehension, and love of writing gave her the motivation and background knowledge she needed to feel more successful in reading, and she discovered a definite preference for information text.

Mr. Damien also planned short lessons on spelling features, commonly spelled words, and careless mistakes that many of the students in the class were struggling with in their writing. He and his students formulated checklists, so that students could be responsible for editing their own writing. Mr. Damien spent some extra time with

BOX 9.2. Suggestions for Working with Individual Students

General lesson components	Comprehension focus	Fluency/word recognition focus
Teacher/tutor read-aloud. Read an interesting short story, information article, poem, joke, or book chapter (see Chapter 3).	Use materials that will challenge the student's listening comprehension level. Focus on enjoyment and discussion.	Use materials that will challenge the student's listening comprehension level. Focus on enjoyment and discussion.
Fluent reading. Have the student choose an old favorite, poem, play, or segment from his or her read-at-home book to read with fluency. Model and coach fluent reading. Provide time for independent reading (see Chapter 5).	Use poetry, jokes, stories based on a familiar theme or structure, and Readers' Theater. Focus on metacognitive aspects of the reading (how a character in a story might talk, based on his or her feelings; the meaning of a poem or joke; how new stories differ from familiar ones).	Readers' Theater is one of the best activities. Model and point out prosody, phrasing, and expression in reading aloud the story. Have the student focus on reading based on your model. Provide coaching. Focus on "reading like you talk" as well as on meaning.
Supported reading and writing. *Reading.* Support the student in reading and thinking her or his way through the text. This should be challenging but not frustrating. Give as much support as needed (see Chapter 4). Keep informal records of reading (see Chapters 1 and 4).	Choose texts in which the student can understand most of the meaning. Use mainly silent reading in manageable chunks, predicting and discussing as you go. Use student read-alouds sparingly and meaningfully (e.g., reading a favorite part and telling why). Use series or topical text sets. Use a variety of text types with appropriate comprehension strategies and supports.	Choose texts that the student can read with about 95% accuracy. Focus on making meaning and enjoying reading while developing fluency through predicting and rereading. Use manageable text (series, same author, etc.). Focus on silent reading, but texts *must* be on instructional level. Analyze oral reading for use of word identification strategies, and help students to develop and refine appropriate strategies.
Writing. Decide with the student to use dialogue journals, literature response, personal narrative, research, text innovations, or a combination (see Chapters 6 and 8).	Focus on meaning. Use literature response and research to connect reading (above) to writing. Support writing with discussion, preplanning, and graphic organizers.	In addition to meaning, focus on writing fluency through text transformations, pen pal letters, quick writes, etc. Keep handy an alphabetical list of frequently used words and use it!
Look at words. Focus on language, spelling, sentence and word structure, and vocabulary through poetry, jokes, riddles, mad libs, puns, word sorts, word games, and materials that contain studied words and features. Use reading challenges and spelling errors to choose focus features. Connect to reading and writing (see Chapter 7).	Focus on meaning and vocabulary, including prefixes and suffixes, homophones, word derivations, words related by meaning, word play, and poetry. Keep a record of features and words studied.	Point out and work through spelling patterns. Add words to the personal word wall. Also do focused word study based on recurring challenges in reading and writing. Keep a record of words and patterns studied.
Checking out books. Help the student choose books on his or her independent level (see Chapter 2).	Books should be easy to understand, so that the student can focus on meaning. Encourage the student to read old favorite books in a series, books by the same author, and books on the same theme or topic.	Books should be easy to read and understand. Readers' Theater scripts are great for take-homes. Encourage the student to read books in a series, books by the same author, and/or books on the same topic or theme.

Julie to make sure his plan and the materials were appropriate and interesting for her. The school librarian also helped him to find a range of books and other materials related to the topic they were studying in social studies, so that all students would be able to read about the topic. In other words, focusing on Julie helped Mr. Damien to see that he needed to make some changes in his instructional formats, materials, and procedures.

Step 4: Evaluating the Plan

How is your plan working? Continually assess and evaluate the effectiveness of your plan in terms of student engagement and progress. If you do not see progress, gather additional information. Julie's case was relatively straightforward and required only a little extra instructional time from Mr. Damien. Although Julie was still reading more than one grade level below most of the class, she was making steady, accelerated progress, and Mr. Damien's modifications supported her in being successful in class despite not being proficient in most grade-level texts. She also steadily made progress in reading fluency and word identification, as evidenced in improvements in oral reading assessments, more engagement in reading, and increased time spent reading at home. These successes would not have occurred if Julie had continued to read books that were too difficult for her. In addition, Julie's spelling improved with the focused word study and with more attention to editing. Mr. Damien continued to spend time with Julie during free reading to be sure she was engaged. Through his in-depth work with Julie, Mr. Damien discovered that almost half of his students were struggling through the social studies textbook. His new plan of using a project approach, along with materials on a range of topics and difficulty levels, made social studies more engaging and successful for all students.

Take additional steps to learn more about meeting the needs of struggling learners, as Mr. Damien did. These additional steps may include seeking help from instructional leaders and literacy specialists, attending workshops or classes, reading in the professional journals or books referenced throughout this book, and tutoring a student (see the section on professional development at the end of this chapter). Some specific sources for learning about working with students who have literacy struggles are listed in Box 9.3.

BOX 9.3. Sources for Learning about Struggling Learners

Allington, R. L. (Ed.). (1998). *Teaching struggling readers: Articles from The Reading Teacher*. Newark, DE: International Reading Association.

Barr, R., Blachowicz, C. L. Z., & Sadow, M. W. (1995). *Reading diagnosis for teachers: An instructional approach* (3rd ed.). White Plains, NY: Longman.

Roller, C. M. (1996). *Variability, not disability: Struggling readers in a workshop classroom*. Newark, DE: International Reading Association.

Roller, C. M. (1999). *So ... what's a tutor to do?*. Newark, DE: International Reading Association.

Taylor, B., Harris, L. A., Pearson, P. D., & García, G. (1995). *Reading difficulties: Instruction and assessment* (2nd ed.). New York: McGraw-Hill.

Nadra: An English-Language Learner Who Struggles with Comprehension

Nadra moved with her family from Iraq a year ago and has just entered Mrs. Leonard's fourth-grade class. According to her parents, Nadra was a high-achieving student in her native country and had achieved grade-level proficiency in Arabic literacy. When she arrived in the United States a year ago, Nadra was placed in a third-grade English classroom, receiving 45 minutes per day of English as a Second Language (ESL) instruction. She picked up conversational English quickly.

When Ms. Leonard first heard Nadra read, she breathed a sigh of relief. Nadra read with excellent accuracy and expression, and loved to read out loud to the class. However, in the following weeks, Ms. Leonard began to notice that Nadra almost never participated in class discussions about reading. Her written responses to read-alouds and to books she read showed a superficial, often inaccurate grasp of information and of the characters and events in stories. Her personal writing was full of invented spelling and did not sound like natural English. By late September, Ms. Leonard was becoming increasingly concerned about Nadra's reading and writing. Box 9.4 shows how Ms. Leonard used the four-step plan for assessing and planning instructional modifications for Nadra.

What would you do if you had a student like Nadra in your classroom?

Ms. Leonard, an experienced teacher, went beyond what some teachers might do in this situation, because she was eager to learn how to provide appropriate instruction for Nadra and for other English-language learners in the school. With any second-language learner, however, *every* teacher should communicate with parents and make every attempt to assess native language proficiency. If the family does not speak English and the teacher does not speak the home language, it is essential to find someone in the school or community to translate during the home visit. Nadra also enjoyed advantages that not every student has: While Nadra was learning to communicate in English at school, her parents were providing many opportunities for her to learn academic concepts in her native Arabic. Often this kind of support is not available, either through the home or through school bilingual programs. In such cases, ESL instruction becomes crucial. With the growing number of non-English-speaking immigrants, it is important for all teachers to have some training in ESL instruction, which is often offered through school districts and universities. There are also many books available on teaching ESL. With any second-language learner, you will need to assess students' knowledge of new concepts and provide explanations in terms that students can understand. For more ideas on working with second-language learners, see the list of references and resources at the end of Box 9.4.

Francisco: A Gifted Student Who Is Failing in School

Francisco is an eighth-grade student in your language arts class. School has just begun, but you know Francisco by reputation, having heard many stories from your friend, his seventh-grade teacher. That teacher called Francisco "the most intelligent person I have run across in a long, long time." She continued, "He can spell anything you throw at him. He can read anything you put in front of him. He can comprehend anything." Francisco qualified for the district's gifted and talented program and was in the program for 4 years, but was dismissed in sixth grade because he was failing his regular

BOX 9.4. A Teacher's Notes on an English-Language Learner Who Decodes Well but Struggles with Comprehension

Step 1. Gathering Information

I'm concerned because Nadra doesn't seem to be making sense of what she's reading. In reading assessments during the first week of school, Nadra was able to read the words in grade-level texts, but she could only answer the literal questions. I decided to visit Nadra's home. When I called to set up the appointment, I realized that Nadra's parents only speak Arabic, so I found someone (a parent volunteer who was bilingual in Arabic and English) to go on the visit with me. During the visit, Nadra's parents informed us that she is interested in history and current events in Iraq. In addition to the books they brought with them, Nadra and her parents read an Iraqi newspaper, which they receive from relatives every week. Nadra's parents say she is continuing to make progress in Arabic literacy. The parent volunteer affirmed that Nadra reads and writes well in Arabic.

Step 2. Evaluating Information

Strengths

As is true of many second-language learners, Nadra is able to "decode" written English easily. Nadra is building her proficiency in Arabic language and literacy, and her parents are providing both language and cognitive support as they read and speak with her. She has a wealth of world experiences and knowledge, and a strong support system from a close-knit community of other Iraqi immigrants. When I talked to the ESL teacher in my school, she told me that cognitive support is extremely valuable for second-language learners, as it provides a foundation for academic learning, which will make such learning easier in the second language (Krashen, 1982; Cummins, 1994). Nadra has high expectations for herself and is a dedicated student. She is able to keep up in math and has a strong interest in hands-on science.

Areas of Concern

My ESL colleague thinks that Nadra did not have time to develop sufficient reading, writing, and learning proficiency in Arabic before she began English literacy instruction. In reading about bilingual and ESL education (see "References/Suggested Resources for ESL Instruction," below), I learned that when this happens, comprehension often lags behind decoding skill. This seems to be what happened with Nadra. My ESL colleague, along with what I read, helped to ease my worries. I learned that Nadra is following a typical progression for second-language learners. In light of the fact that she has only been in this country for 1 year, she has made tremendous progress in learning English. Given her history and the strong support from her family, Nadra should continue to make rapid progress in English literacy (Schwartzer, 2001).

Step 3. Developing a Plan

As it is with all students, I felt it was essential to involve Nadra's parents, as well as to consider Nadra's strengths and interests in developing instructional plans for her (Moll & Gonzalez, 1994). When I consulted with my bilingual and ESL colleagues, we decided there were several key areas for Nadra's continued literacy growth. The first, continued development of cognitive and literacy skills

(continued)

in Arabic, was being addressed by her parents at home. The second was developing English literacy. Toward this goal, I decided to take a workshop in bilingual/ESL instruction offered by my district to learn more. I was interested to learn that ESL instruction includes many of the same components of good literacy instruction that I already knew about, with a more intensive focus on development of concepts and vocabulary in English. I assessed Nadra's reading comprehension in English narrative and information text, found books that were comfortable for her (on her easy and instructional levels), and began spending time with her individually during "just reading" time. Knowing that reading without comprehension is not really reading, I determined to focus our instructional reading time on comprehension. Because Nadra already had an interest and an academic foundation in history, I found books about familiar topics in history that I thought she would be able to read and comprehend. I helped Nadra, as well as my other students, to prepare informal oral presentations about what they were learning in their reading and research. For easy-level text, we focused as a class on Readers' Theater, interpretation of poetry, and independent reading. Nadra was interested in a fiction series, Rylant's Henry and Mudge (see the series book bibliography in Box 2.5 of Chapter 2), written at a late first-grade to early second-grade reading level. These books have a predictable format and fairly stable vocabulary. She was able to read and understand the situations in the book and to predict events. After I guided her through the first two books by reading aloud and discussing the situations with Nadra, she was able to read other books in the series on her own and later moved to a more difficult series. She kept a reading log with predictions and responses to her reading, which showed a good grasp of the stories.

Step 4. Evaluating the Plan

So far, so good. Nadra is making steady progress in English literacy and is gaining more understanding from English reading. She is able to comprehend more difficult texts and to make logical predictions as she reads. I have learned a great deal about creating a curriculum that supports second-language learners. I will continue to watch Nadra's progress and to use my new knowledge and experience in working with all students. Although I am aware that Nadra may not be reading and comprehending on grade level even by the end of the year, I can expect that she will make accelerated progress.

References/Suggested Resources for ESL Instruction

Cummins, J. (1994). The acquisition of English as a second language. In K. Spangenberg-Urbsacht & R. Pritchard (Eds.), *Kids come in all languages: Reading instruction for ESL students* (pp. 36–62). Newark: DE: International Reading Association.

Krashen, S. (1982). *Principles and practices in second language acquisition*. New York: Pergamon Press.

Moll, L., & Gonzalez, N. (1994). Lessons from research with language-minority children. *Journal of Reading Behavior, 26,* 439–456.

Peregoy, S. F., & Boyle, O. F. (1997). *Reading, writing, and learning in ESL: A resource book for K–12 teachers* (2nd ed.). New York: Longman.

Rigg, P., & Allen, V. G. (Eds.). (1989). *When they don't all speak English: Integrating the ESL student into the regular classroom.* Urbana, IL: National Council of Teachers of English.

Schwarzer, D. (2001). *Noa's ark: One child's voyage into multiliteracy.* Portsmouth, NH: Heinemann.

classes and not attending school regularly. He barely passed sixth and seventh grades. So far, Francisco has been out of school 20 out of 65 days. When he is present, he makes A's on all tests and assignments that he "feels like doing," but because he never does homework, he is once again in danger of failing.

Read the information provided about Francisco (Box 9.5). The first two steps, gathering and evaluating information, are provided for you. Using this information and the suggestions in this book, formulate a plan for Francisco.

Even after following the suggestions outlined in this chapter and book, you may find that there are students who either are not progressing adequately and/or are so far behind the class that you need to explore options for additional assistance. Charles, a sixth grader whose literacy skills were far behind his grade level, was one such student. His teacher, Mrs. Rand, sought assistance for the intensive accelerated instruction that Charles needed, but also modified classroom instruction to support his learning. Charles's case is described briefly in the next section and more thoroughly in Appendix E.

EXPLORING OPTIONS FOR ADDITIONAL ASSISTANCE

When you are ready to seek additional assistance, begin by asking yourself these questions:

1. If you have students who are struggling, have you used the four-step plan described above?
2. Have you modified your instructional procedures and tasks accordingly, spending extra time with those students who struggle?
3. Have you taken steps to learn more about how to meet the needs of your students who struggle with literacy?

If you can honestly answer yes to every question and your student is still not making acceptable progress, it is time to seek other answers. Be advised, however, that seeking other answers is far more complex than it may seem at first glance. Although every school may have multiple avenues for student assistance, it is the teacher's responsibility to decide which will be the best for the student.

After gathering information about Charles, formulating a plan, and working with him in class for several weeks, Mrs. Rand realized that he needed additional assistance in order to make accelerated progress. She approached the school literacy specialist and found that the possible options for Charles were a federally funded remedial reading program or a referral for special education testing. Before deciding which avenue to take, Mrs. Rand did some research, as every teacher should do. She read about each of the programs in the professional literature, learning the information presented at the beginning of the chapter, and she talked to the Chapter I and special education teachers. Bear in mind that every school runs programs differently; consider the context, teachers, and students in your own school as you make decisions about literacy assistance for your struggling learners.

Fortunately, there was another option for Charles. The local university offered an

BOX 9.5. An Intellectually Gifted Student Who Is Failing in School: What Would You Do?

Step 1. Gathering Information

Looking through Francisco's records, you discover that he made A's and B's through fourth grade, but that his grades started to drop in fifth grade. Although he passed the state's basic skills competency test with flying colors, he earned a D in every class except art in sixth and seventh grades. In your first conference with Mr. and Mrs. Cruz, they told you that Francisco says he hates school and can't wait to drop out. They are very concerned because they expect him to go to college as his older sister did. Although they are not well off, their home is filled with reading materials, and they value literacy; both use reading and writing in their jobs, and both read magazines, newspapers, and novels at home.

Looking over your beginning-of-the-year assessments (see Chapter 1), you find that Francisco scored low on a Reading Attitudes Survey. However, even though he gave the lowest rating to most of the questions (e.g., "Reading is my favorite subject in school"), he rated a few questions either neutrally or positively. These included "When I find the kind of books I like, reading can be fun," and "Reading is an important part of my life." The interview revealed that Francisco has favorite magazines (*Low-Rider Bike* and *Popular Science*) and a favorite author (Stephen King). He is also interested in new inventions, which he learns about in *Popular Science* and on the Discovery Channel. His dream is to build a low-rider car with his father and enter it in a contest. Although he claims to hate reading, when you talk to him privately, you find that he actually reads a good deal at home when he has a new magazine or Michael Crichton book to read. Francisco says that he is bored when the class reads the same novel, because he rarely likes them and is frustrated by the slow pace. He doesn't like any of the materials in the classroom library, so free-choice reading time also bores him.

Step 2. Evaluating Information

Francisco is an excellent reader and writer and a gifted thinker, but he is so disenfranchised from school that he is in danger of dropping out. The Reading Attitudes Survey and your talks with Francisco reveal a clear distinction between his attitude toward school reading and his feelings about home reading. Francisco's dislike of school reading appears to hinge around a lack of opportunity to read materials in which he is interested, and around instruction that lacks purpose and relevancy for him. His unusual interests make it difficult to meet his needs. Do you have anything to add? What do you think will help Francisco become more engaged in school?

Suggested Resources

Ivey, G. (1999). Reflections on teaching struggling middle school readers. *Journal of Adolescent and Adult Literacy, 42*, 372–381.

Worthy, J. (1998). "On every page someone gets killed!": Book conversations you don't hear in school. *Journal of Adolescent and Adult Literacy, 41*, 508–517.

The two articles above are reprinted in the following book, which includes many helpful articles:

Moore, D., W., Alvermann, D. E., & Hinchman, K. A. (2000). *Struggling adolescent readers: A collection of teaching strategies.* Newark, DE: International Reading Association.

after-school tutoring program and a more intensive program during the summer. Such programs often offer financial assistance for students who need it. It is important to remember that this is not an option for everyone, and that other options may exist. Mrs. Rand, an experienced teacher, spoke with Charles's tutor regularly and kept a close watch on his instruction and progress. Although collaboration with teachers and parents is essential for the student's progress, it is not always a given. Again, you can read more about Charles in Appendix E.

According to Vellutino et al. (1996), most students identified as "dyslexic" have literacy learning difficulties due "primarily to experiential deficits, not constitutional origins, which can be remedied with intensive one-to-one tutoring and a balanced reading program" (p. 41). Short-term intensive tutoring was enough to improve the reading levels of the vast majority of the students in their study who were referred for special education testing. Similarly, Lyons (1989) found that more than 70% of children labeled "learning-disabled" were able to read at the average levels of their peers after an average of 13 weeks of intensive instruction designed to accelerate their learning. Most researched programs have focused on early literacy. Even so, it is likely that one-on-one tutoring, if carefully structured and delivered by experienced professionals, would be effective for students of any age. The major problem is that it is rarely available.

Is there a way for your student to receive tutoring from a literacy expert? Work with the school reading specialist, the student's parents, and the school administration. Perhaps there is a reading specialist who can provide this assistance; perhaps the parents can afford a tutor. Some teachers take the time and initiative to learn how to tutor students with special needs (see the next section).

LEARNING MORE ABOUT HELPING STRUGGLING LEARNERS

As you finish this chapter, you may have as many questions as answers about meeting individual needs. As teacher educators and former teachers, we know that many teachers may not feel confident and knowledgeable in meeting the needs of the struggling readers in their classrooms. Literacy learning and instruction are complex; added to their complexity are all the other things that teachers must think about and do every day within the context and constraints of schools.

You may still have students about whom you are concerned, and you may have found that the special programs in your school do not adequately meet the needs of these students. You may not find the perfect solution for your students, but we hope that you will take steps to learn how to provide the best instruction possible in your classroom and how to seek support from other professionals. Teaching is a profession that absolutely requires continued learning. The complexities of teaching literacy cannot be learned completely in teacher preparation. We recommend that teachers learn more about individual learners through hands-on professional development offered by experts in literacy intervention.

When we talk to teachers in our local areas, at state conferences, and across the country at national teacher conventions, the question we hear most frequently is "How do I help struggling readers?", followed by "How can I attend to individual needs when I am responsible for so many students at once?" The fact is that there are no simple solutions. Along with many other reading educators, we agree with Duffy and

Hoffman (1999), who argue that "reading instruction effectiveness lies not with a single program or method but, rather, with a teacher who thoughtfully and analytically integrates various programs, materials, and methods as the situation demands" (p. 11).

How do teachers develop this kind of expertise? Although we have read an extraordinary amount of information about teaching reading and have participated in many research projects, we all agree that we have learned the most from practice, particularly from working with individual students. Skilled teachers of literacy must be both knowledgeable and experienced. They must have both content knowledge about the subjects they teach and *procedural knowledge*, or the ability to put into practice what they have learned (Kagan, 1992). An excellent way of gaining both kinds of knowledge is literacy tutoring, which we incorporate into our preservice and graduate-level literacy education courses. Preservice teachers who have the opportunity to tutor one child learn a great deal about teaching *all* children (Worthy & Prater, 1998). After tutoring for one semester, a preservice teacher described how working with Sandra in an after-school reading program brought to life the theory from her reading methods class:

"By practicing firsthand every day in class with Sandra, I learned (and am still learning) how to effectively scaffold reading and writing, from doing book introductions to knowing how to help and when. I remember having soooo many questions, but the answers seem to be continually coming with more practice and time spent tutoring. I think our work in the reading club [tutoring] has been invaluable for this learning. Sandra taught me more than any textbook because I was *involved*."

Researchers have discovered similar benefits for practicing teachers (Broaddus & Bloodgood, 1999; Morris, Ervin, & Conrad, 1996) and principals (Fogg & Morris, 1997) who participated in a tutoring program under the guidance of literacy experts. According to the participants, one-on-one work with students helped them to see struggles from the perspective of the individual child, to learn new teaching strategies, and to better understand literacy development in general. Teachers noted particularly the benefits of direct participation in the tutoring, as opposed to participating in in-service workshops. As one teacher said: "I wouldn't have understood it the way I understand it now. . . . it's like hearing about something but not doing it. It's different" (Broaddus & Bloodgood, 1999, p. 287). Participants also found that students who struggled in the classroom were often more successful during focused interventions. More importantly, the teachers began to see these students in a whole new way. They got to know the strengths and needs of each student and the effects of different teaching strategies.

Most reconsidered and modified their regular classroom instruction based on what they learned through the tutoring. Even specialists with many years of experience find that they continue learning through tutoring students. Loretta Stewart, a literacy specialist in Virginia, explains:

> "Even after all these years, and all the students I have tutored, I need the continued one-on-one experience to keep my knowledge and tools honed to a sharp edge. This experience indeed carries over into regular classes."

If you are unable to tutor through a reading methods or graduate course, create opportunities for one-on-one work with your most needy students, with the guidance of a literacy expert (Ivey & Broaddus, 2000). While helping teachers to learn, this experience benefits students as well, if the tutoring is carefully structured and teachers seek the advice and support of a literacy specialist in the school or district. Use the suggestions in Box 9.2 to get started. A lesson plan based on Box 9.2 is shown in Box 9.6. How is one-on-one work with a student possible when a teacher is responsible for so many students? One first step is to restructure planning and instructional time (Ivey & Broaddus, 2000). For instance, if you are allotted two planning periods each school day, then you can use one period or at least part of that period to tutor a child, even just a couple of days each week. Also, think about ways to free yourself to work with individual students during regular instructional periods. If you only plan closed or teacher-directed activities (e. g., round-robin reading, whole-class skill lessons) in which everyone is engaged in the same task, you will never get the chance for one-on-one work with any student. Instead, you will likely spend your time doing "crowd control" to keep everyone on task. However, if you regularly engage the class in tasks (e.g., free reading, Readers' Theater repertory groups) in which students work independently or in small groups, you will have many opportunities not only to touch base with individual students, but also to spend high-quality teaching time with them. Obviously, you will not be able to tutor all of your students who need extra help. However, getting to know one student and learning how to plan appropriately for that student will help you become more cognizant of the needs of all of your students and will add to your knowledge, skill, and confidence.

CHILDREN'S BOOK REFERENCE

Rowling, J. K. (1999). *Harry Potter and the chamber of secrets.* New York: Scholastic.

BOX 9.6. A Lesson Format for Working with Individual Students (based on Box 9.2)

Lesson components	Plan and materials	Evaluation and comments
Read-aloud.		
Fluent reading.		
Supported reading and writing. Reading.		
Writing.		
Looking at words.		
Checking out books.	Book titles.	

REFERENCES

Allington, R. L. (1983). The reading instruction provided readers of differing reading abilities. *Elementary School Journal, 83,* 548–558.

Allington, R. L. (1994). What's special about special programs for children who find reading difficult. *Journal of Reading Behavior, 26,* 1–21.

Allington, R. L., & McGill-Franzen, A. (1989). School response to reading failure: Instruction for Chapter I and special education students in grades two, four, and eight. *Elementary School Journal, 89,* 529–541.

Allington, R. L., & Walmsley, S. A. (Eds.). (1995). *No quick fix: Rethinking literacy programs in America's elementary schools.* Newark, DE/New York: International Reading Association/Teachers College Press.

Ayers, W. (1993). *To teach: The journey of a teacher.* New York: Teachers College Press.

Broaddus, K., & Bloodgood, J. W. (1999). "We're supposed to already know how to teach reading": Teacher change to support struggling readers. *Reading Research Quarterly, 34,* 426–451.

Clay, M. (1985). *The early detection of reading difficulties* (3rd ed.). Auckland, New Zealand: Heinemann.

Clay, M. (1987). Learning to be learning disabled. *New Zealand Journal of Educational Studies, 22,* 155–173.

Cunningham, P., & Allington, R. L. (1999). *Classrooms that work: They can all read and write* (2nd ed.). New York: Longman.

Duffy, G. G., & Hoffman, J. V. (1999). In pursuit of an illusion: The flawed search for a perfect method. *The Reading Teacher, 53,* 10–16.

Duffy-Hester, A. (1999). Teaching struggling readers in elementary school classrooms: A review of classroom reading programs and principles for instruction. *The Reading Teacher, 52,* 480–495.

Dyer, P. C., & Binkney, R. (1995). Estimating cost-effectiveness and educational outcomes: Retention, remediation, special education, and early intervention. In R. L. Allington & S. A. Walmsley (Eds.), *No quick fix: Rethinking literacy programs in America's elementary schools* (pp. 61–77). Newark, DE/New York: International Reading Association/Teachers College Press.

Ellis, A. (1988). *Reading, writing, and dyslexia: A cognitive analysis* (2nd ed.). Hove, UK: Erlbaum.

Flores, B., Cousin, P. T., & Díaz, E. (1991). Transforming deficit myths about learning, language, and culture. *Language Arts, 68,* 369–379.

Fogg, M., & Morris, D. (1997, December). *The effects of a supervised tutoring experience on first grade teachers' beliefs and practices.* Paper presented at the National Reading Conference, Scottsdale, AZ.

Gartner, A., & Lipsky, D. (1987). Beyond special education: Toward a quality system for all students. *Harvard Educational Review, 57,* 368–395.

Iverson, S., & Tunmer, W. (1993). Phonological processing skills and the reading recovery program. *Journal of Educational Psychology, 85,* 112–126.

Ivey, G., & Broaddus, K. (2000). Tailoring the fit: Reading instruction and middle school readers. *The Reading Teacher, 54,* 68–78.

Johnston, P., & Allington, R. L. (1991). Remediation. In R. Barr, M. Kamil, P. Mosenthal, & P. D. Pearson (Eds.), *Handbook of reading research* (Vol. 2, pp. 984–1012). New York: Longman.

Johnston, P. N., & Winograd, P. H. (1985). Passive failure in reading. *Journal of Reading Behavior, 17,* 279–301.

Kagan, D. (1992). Professional growth among preservice and beginning teachers. *Review of Educational Research, 62,* 129–169.

Kennedy, M. M., Birman, B. F., & Demaline, R. E. (1986). *The effectiveness of Chapter I services.* Washington, DC: U. S. Department of Education, Office of Educational Research and Improvement.

Ladson-Billings, G. (1995). Toward a theory of culturally relevant pedagogy. *American Educational Research Journal, 32,* 465–491.

Lerner, J. W. (1993). *Learning disabilities: Theories, diagnosis, and teaching strategies.* Boston: Houghton Mifflin.

Lyons, C. A. (1989). Reading Recovery: A preventative for mislabeling young "at-risk" children. *Urban Education, 24*, 125–139.

McGill-Franzen, A. (1994). Compensatory and special education: Is there accountability for learning and belief in children's potential? In E. H. Hiebert & B. M. Taylor (Eds.), *Getting reading right from the start: Effective early literacy interventions* (pp. 13–35). Boston: Allyn & Bacon.

Morris, D., Ervin, C.. & Conrad, K. (1996). A case study of middle school reading disability. *The Reading Teacher, 49*, 368–377.

Nagy, W., & Anderson, R. C. (1984). How many words are there in printed English? *Reading Research Quarterly, 19*, 304–330.

Nieto, S. (2000). *Affirming diversity: The sociopolitical context of multicultural education* (3rd ed.). New York: Longman.

Oakes, J. (1985). *Keeping track: How schools structure inequality.* New Haven, CT: Yale University Press.

Pinnell, G. S. (1989). Reading Recovery: Helping at-risk children learn to read. *Elementary School Journal, 90*, 160–184.

Reschly, D. J. (1987). Learning characteristics of mildly handicapped students: Implications for classification, placement, and programming. In M. C. Wang, M. C. Reynolds, & H. J. Walberg (Eds.), *Handbook of special education: Research and practice* (pp. 35–58). New York: Pergamon Press.

Roller, C. M. (1996). *Variability, not disability: Struggling readers in a workshop classroom.* Newark, DE: International Reading Association.

Rowan, B., & Guthrie, L. F. (1989). The quality of Chapter I instruction: Results from a study of twenty-four schools. In R. E. Slavin, N. L. Karweit, & N. A. Madden (Eds.), *Effective programs for students at risk* (pp. 195–219). Boston: Allyn & Bacon.

Schug, P. (2000, January 9). Too good to be true. *The New York Times,* p. 53.

Siegel, L. (1989). IQ is irrelevant to the definition of learning disabilities. *Journal of learning disabilities, 22*, 469–478.

Spear-Swerling, L., & Sternberg, R. J. (1996). *Off track: When poor readers become "learning disabled."* Boulder, CO: Westview Press.

Spiegel, D. L. (1998). Silver bullets, babies, and bath water: Literature response groups in a balanced literacy program. *The Reading Teacher, 52*, 114–124.

Stanovich, K. (1986). Matthew effects in reading: Some consequences of individual differences in the acquisition of literacy. *Reading Research Quarterly, 21*, 360–406.

Stanovich, K., Cunningham, A, & Freeman, D. (1984). Intelligence, cognitive skills, and early reading progress. *Reading Research Quarterly, 19*, 278–303.

Taylor, B., Harris, L. A., Pearson, P. D., & García, G. (1995). *Reading difficulties: Instruction and assessment* (2nd ed.). New York: McGraw-Hill.

Vellutino, F. R., Scanlon, D. M., Sipay, E., Small, S., Pratt, A., Chen, R., & Denckla, M. (1996). Cognitive profiles of difficult to remediate and easily remediated poor readers. *Journal of Educational Psychology, 81*, 601–638.

Walmsley, S. A., & Allington, R. L (1995). Redefining and reforming instructional support programs for at-risk students. In R. L. Allington & S. A. Walmsley (Eds.), *No quick fix: Rethinking literacy programs in America's elementary schools* (pp. 19–44). Newark, DE/New York: International Reading Association/Teachers College Press.

Winfield, L. F. (1995). Change in urban schools with high concentrations of low-income children: Chapter I school wide projects. In R. L. Allington & S. A. Walmsley (Eds.), *No quick fix: Rethinking literacy programs in America's elementary schools.* Newark, DE/New York: International Reading Association/Teachers College Press.

Worthy, J., & Prater, S. (1998). Learning on the job: Preservice teachers' perceptions of participating in a literacy tutorial program. *Yearbook of the National Reading Conference, 47*, 485–495.

APPENDICES

APPENDIX D. Resources for Teaching Reading and Writing

APPENDIX E. Charles: A Case Study of a Less Skilled Reader in the Middle Grades

APPENDIX A

GRAPHIC ORGANIZERS FOR READING AND WRITING

APPENDIX A.1. Expository Writing: Sequence Chart

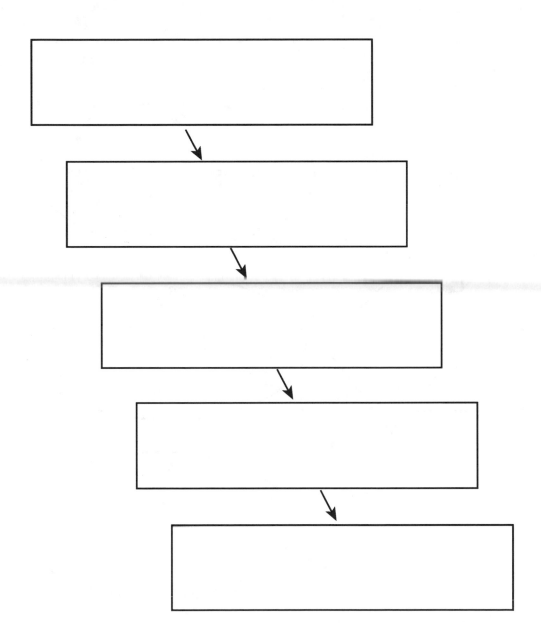

APPENDIX A.2. Expository Writing:
Cause and Effect

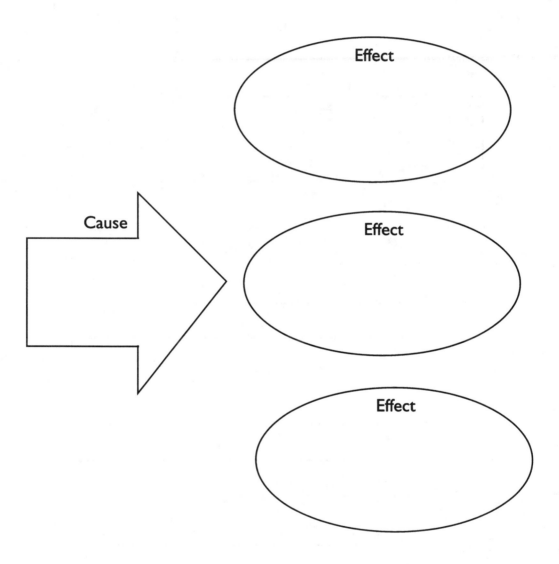

282

APPENDIX A.3. Expository Writing: Description

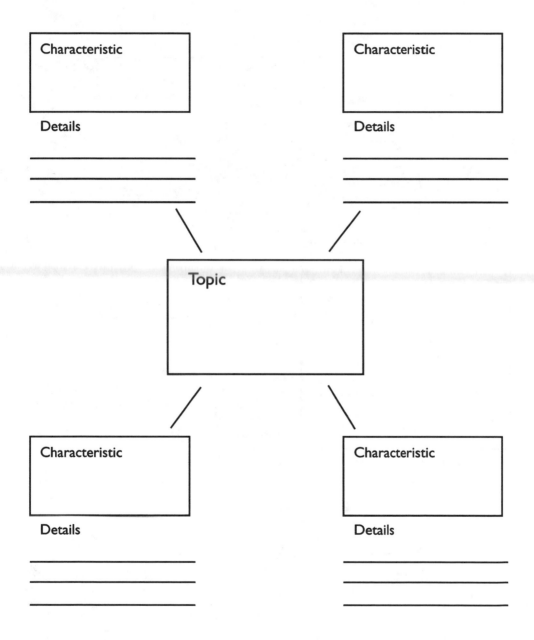

APPENDIX A.4. Expository Writing: Problem and Solution

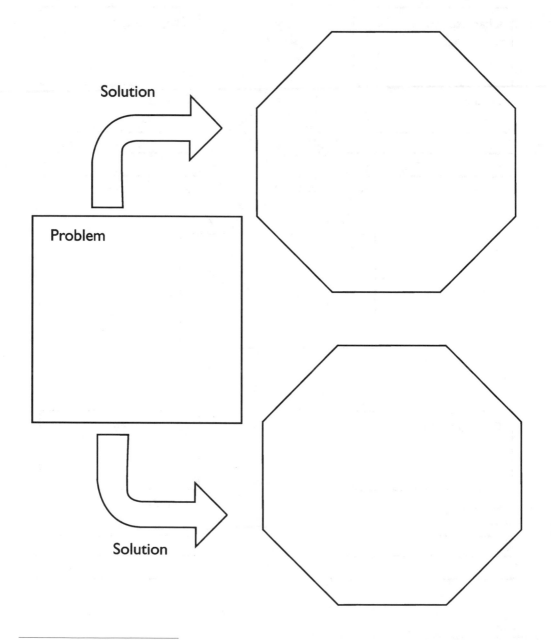

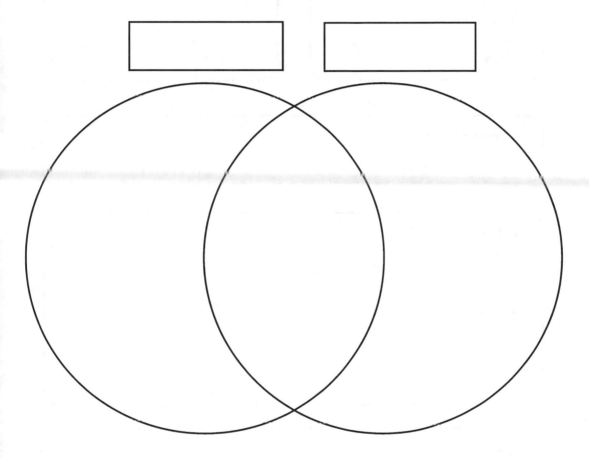

APPENDIX A.6. Narrative Writing

Setting	Characters
Time	
Place	

Beginning situation

Problem (conflict)

Events

Conclusion

APPENDIX A.7. Concept Web

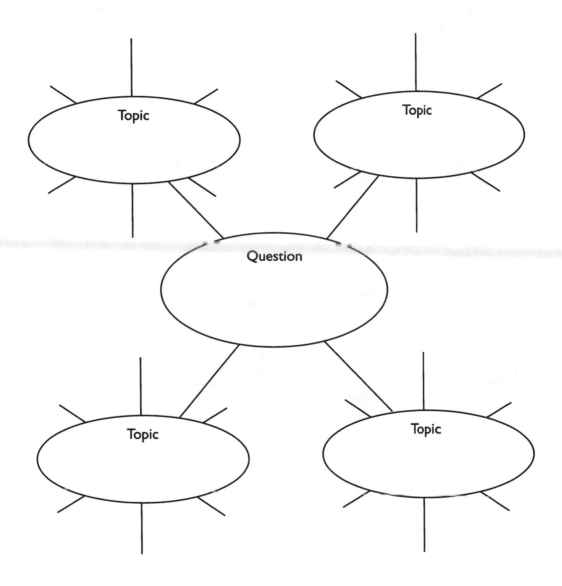

APPENDIX A.8. Persuasive Writing: Editorial

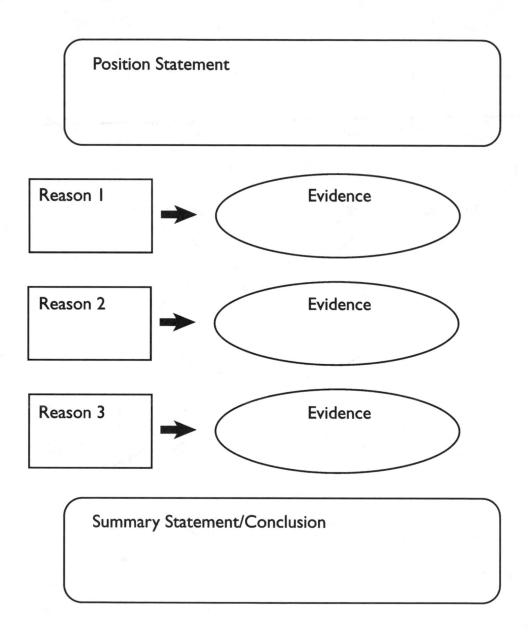

Position Statement

Reason 1 ➡ Evidence

Reason 2 ➡ Evidence

Reason 3 ➡ Evidence

Summary Statement/Conclusion

APPENDIX B

FORMS AND RECORD KEEPING

APPENDIX B.1. Interview for the First Day of School

INTERVIEW FOR THE FIRST DAY OF SCHOOL

Name: _____ Age: _____ Date: _____

Homeroom Teacher: _____ Period: _____

1. Tell me about your family.
2. With whom do you usually spend the most time?
3. How do you spend most of your time?
4. If you could be anything, what would it be?
5. If you could go anywhere, where would you go?
6. What is the best thing about you?
7. What do you think your family, your friends, or your teachers would say is the best thing about you?
8. If you could win any award, what would you most like to win?
9. If you could get someone's autograph, whose would it be?
10. Tell me about your favorite movie.
11. Tell me about the best book you have ever read. Tell me about your favorite author.
12. What types of books do you most like to read?
13. What kinds of things do you like to write about?
14. Describe the type of music you like.
15. What else would you like our class to know about you?

APPENDIX B.2. Reading Preferences Checklist

WHAT DO YOU LIKE TO READ?

Which of the following kinds of reading material would you be most interested in reading? Please listen as each item is read and discussed. Your teacher will give you some examples for each category. Then put a check by those materials that you would choose to read if they were available and you had time to read. If you have a comment or want to write in a title, you may do so underneath each item. Raise your hand if you have questions.

1. ____ Fiction adventure novels	12. ____ Poetry books
2. ____ Fiction funny novels	13. ____ Encyclopedias or books that give information about different things
3. ____ Fiction novels about things that happen to people	14. ____ Almanacs or record books
4. ____ Fiction novels about science fiction or fantasy	15. ____ Drawing books
5. ____ Scary books	16. ____ Cartoons and comics
6. ____ Biography	17. ____ Animals
7. ____ Series books	18. ____ History or historical fiction
8. ____ Books or magazines about sports	19. ____ Information books about science or math
9. ____ Magazines about people	20. ____ Picture books
10. ____ Information books and magazines about cars and trucks	21. ____ Other books or magazines. Write your favorite title(s) or author(s):
11. ____ Books that are mostly for adults Write your favorite title(s) or author(s):	

Write other comments on the back.

APPENDIX B.3. Reading and Writing Habits Survey

READING AND WRITING HABITS SURVEY

Reading

1. If you could read anything that you wanted to read, what would it be?

2. Who is your favorite author?

3. How often do you read outside of school? What kinds of things do you read at home?

4. If you could buy any book you wanted, what would it be? If you could subscribe to any magazine, what would it be?

5. To whom would you listen for book recommendations? Why?

6. Where do you usually get your reading materials (home, school library, classroom, public library, store, other)?

7. What do you do well in reading? What would you like to work on this year in your reading?

Writing

1. How often do you write outside of school other than homework?

2. What kinds of things do you write about at home? At school?

3. Do you share your writing with anyone? Tell me about that.

4. What do you like best about your writing?

5. What would you like to work on in your writing?

APPENDIX B.4. Project Checklist
for a Simulated Journal

STUDY OF AN EVENT IN HISTORY THROUGH A SIMULATED JOURNAL: PROJECT CHECKLIST

_____ Directed listening–thinking activity (DL-TA): Written predictions
_____ Free write: Response using main character's perspective
_____ Independent reading on historical period
      Book titles/authors/pages:

_____ Readers' Theater production (groups, scripts provided)
_____ Focused reading on historical event (pairs)
      Partner:
      Historical event:
      Book titles/authors/pages:

_____ Timeline of historical event (pairs)
_____ Vocabulary list of historical terms/meanings (pairs)
_____ Data chart on historical period (pairs)
      Historical event, food, clothing, work, recreation

_____ Character graphic/sequence of events (individual)
      Name, age, family background, perspective on events

_____ Simulated journal entries (individual, five entries minimum)
_____ Editing checklist (another student, teacher, self)
_____ Final draft
_____ Illustrations
_____ Self-evaluation (form provided listing parts of the project)
_____ Completed journal with project folder (all work)

APPENDIX B.5. Content Editing Checklist for Narrative Writing

CONTENT EDITING CHECKLIST: NARRATIVE WRITING

Feature/comments	Student editor	Teacher	Self
Interesting opening lead			
Clear setting (time and place)			
Well-developed characters			
Conflict and sequence of events			
Climax and resolution (twists, surprises)			
Effective use of dialogue			
Unique style of narration			

APPENDIX B.6. Blank Content Editing Checklist

CONTENT EDITING CHECKLIST

Feature/comments	Student editor	Teacher	Self

From *Pathways to Independence* by Jo Worthy, Karen Broaddus, and Gay Ivey. Copyright 2001 by The Guilford Press. Permission to photocopy this box is granted to purchasers of this book for personal use only (see copyright page for details).

APPENDIX B.7. Mechanics Editing Checklist for Narrative Writing

MECHANICS EDITING CHECKLIST: NARRATIVE WRITING

Feature/comments	Student editor	Teacher	Self
Paragraph development			
Punctuation			
Grammar features			
Spelling features			

APPENDIX B.8. Blank Mechanics Editing Checklist

MECHANICS EDITING CHECKLIST

Feature/comments	Student editor	Teacher	Self

APPENDIX B.9. Evaluation Form for Content Area Poetry Collection: Free Verse

EVALUATION FORM CONTENT POETRY COLLECTION

Name _____	Strong	Good	Needs development	Inadequate	Comments

Important features
  Title
  First line
  Last line					

Vivid language
  Specific nouns
  Strong verbs
  Descriptive terms					

Poetic features
  Simile/metaphor
  Onomatopoeia
  Alliteration					

Free verse line breaks
  Sound, rhythm
  Meaning
  Punctuation					

Creative perspective on research information					

Specific details about content
  Accuracy of information
  Use of content vocabulary					

Experimentation with new forms
  Dialogue
  Shape poem
  Poem for two voices
  Narrative poem					

Spelling feature					

APPENDIX B.10. Blank Evaluation Form

EVALUATION FORM

Name _____	Strong	Good	Needs development	Inadequate	Comments

APPENDIX C

LITERATURE FOR CHILDREN AND ADOLESCENTS

APPENDIX C.1. Poetry

PICTURE POEM BOOKS

Angelou, M. (1993). *Life doesn't frighten me* (ill. J. Basquiat). New York: Stewart, Tabori & Chang.

Baylor, B. (1985). *Guess who my favorite person is* (ill. R. A. Parker). New York: Macmillan.

Blake, W. (1993). *The tyger* (ill. N. Waldman). San Diego, CA: Harcourt Brace.

Bunting, E. (1997). *I am the mummy Heb-Nefert*. San Diego, CA: Harcourt Brace.

Frost, R. (1978). *Stopping by woods on a snowy evening* (ill. S. Jeffers). New York: Dutton.

Granfield, L. (1996). *In Flanders fields: The story of the poem by John McCrae*. New York: Doubleday.

Harter, P. (1994). *Shadow play: Night haiku* (ill. J. Greene). New York: Simon & Schuster.

Lawrence, J. (1968). *Harriet and the promised land*. New York: Windmill.

MacLachlan, P. (1995). *What you know first* (ill. B. Moser). New York: HarperCollins.

Medearis, A. S. (1990). *Picking peas for a penny* (ill. C. Shaw). Austin, TX: State House Press.

Myers, W. D. (1997). *Harlem* (ill. C. Myers). New York: Scholastic.

Noyes, A. (1981). *The highwayman* (ill. C. Keeping). New York: Oxford University Press.

Poe, E. A. (1998). *Annabel Lee* (ill. G. Tibo). Plattsburgh, NY: Tundra Books.

Service, R. (1986). *The cremation of Sam McGee* (ill. T. Harrison). New York: Greenwillow.

Service, R. (1988). *The shooting of Dan McGrew* (ill. T. Harrison). Boston: Godine.

Siebert, D. (1991). *Sierra* (ill. W. Minor). New York: HarperCollins.

Tennyson, A. (1986). *The lady of Shalott*. Oxford: Oxford University Press.

Thomas, J. C. (1998). *I have heard of a land* (ill. F. Cooper). New York: HarperCollins.

POETRY COLLECTIONS WITH FIRST-PERSON NARRATIONS

Janeczko, P. B. (1993). *Stardust 'otel* (ill. D. Leech). New York: Orchard.

Johnson, A. (1998). *The other side: Shorter poems*. New York: Orchard. (For mature students)

Rylant, C. (1984). *Waiting to waltz: A childhood* (ill. S. Gammell). Scardsale, NY: Bradbury Press.

Seabrooke, B. (1997). *Under the pear tree* (ill. R. Essley). New York: Dutton.

THEMATIC COLLECTIONS

Adoff, A. (1995). *Street music: City poems* (ill. K. Barbour). New York: HarperCollins.

Asch, F. (1998). *Cactus poems* (ill. T. Lewin). San Diego, CA: Harcourt Brace.

Bierhorst, J. (Ed.). (1994). *On the road of stars: Native American night poems and sleep charms* (ill. J. Perderson). New York: Macmillan.

Carlson, L. M. (Ed.). (1994). *Cool salsa: Bilingual poems on growing up Latino in the United States*. New York: Holt.

Fletcher, R. (1998). *Room enough for love*. New York: Simon & Schuster.

Florian, D. (1994). *Bing bang boing: Poems and drawings*. San Diego, CA: Harcourt Brace.

Greenfield, E. (1978). *Honey, I love* (ill. D. Dillon & L. Dillon). New York: Crowell.

Hopkins, L. B. (Ed.). (1987). *Dinosaurs* (ill. M. Tinkelman). San Diego, CA: Harcourt Brace. Harcourt Brace.

Hopkins, L. B. (Ed.). (1994). *Hand in hand: An American history through poetry* (ill. P. M. Fiore). New York: Simon & Schuster.

Igus, T. (1998). *I see the rhythm* (ill. M. Wood). San Francisco: Children's Book Press.

Janeczko, P. B. (Ed.). (1988). *The music of what happens: Poems that tell stories*. New York: Orchard.

Janeczko, P. B. (1998). *That sweet diamond* (ill. C. Katchen). New York: Atheneum.

Johnson, D. (Ed.). (2000). *Movin'* (ill. C. Raschka). New York: Orchard.

Kuskin, K. (1992). *Soap soup and other verses*. New York: HarperCollins.

Kuskin, K. (1994). *City noise* (ill. R. Flower). New York: HarperCollins.

Levy, C. (1994). *A tree place and other poems* (ill R. Sabuda). New York: McElderry.

Lewis, J. D. (1998). *Doodle dandies: Poems that take shape* (ill. L. Desmini). New York: Atheneum.

Livingston, M. C. (1994). *Animal, vegetable, mineral: Poems about small things*. New York: Harper-Collins.

Maples in the mist: Children's poems from the Tang Dynasty (trans. M. Ho). (1996). New York: Lothrop, Lee & Shepard.

Mora, P. (1998). *This big sky* (ill. S. Jenkins). New York: Scholastic.

Morrison, L. (Ed.). (1995). *Slam dunk: Basketball poems* (ill. B. James). New York: Hyperion.

Nye, N. S., & Janeczko, P. B. (Eds.). (1996). *I feel a little jumpy around you: A book of her poems and his poems collected in pairs*. New York: Simon & Schuster.

Panzer, N. (Ed.). (1994). *Celebrate America: In poetry and art*. New York: Hyperion.

Prelutsky, J. (Ed.). (1991). *For laughing out loud: Poems to tickle your funnybone* (ill. M. Priceman). New York: Knopf.

Provensen, A. (1997). *The buck stops here: The presidents of the United States*. San Diego, CA: Harcourt Brace.

Rosenberg, L. (Ed.). (1998). *Earth-shattering poems*. New York: Holt.

Schertle, A. (1999). *I am the cat*. New York: Lothrop, Lee & Shepard.

Smith, C. R. (1999). *Rimshots: Basketball pix, rolls, and rhythm*. New York: Dutton.

Stevenson, J. (1995). *Sweet corn: Poems*. New York: Greenwillow.

Stevenson, J. (1998). *Popcorn*. New York: Morrow.

Stevenson, J. (1999). *Candy corn*. New York: Greenwillow.

Turner, A. (1993). *Grass songs: Poems of women's journey west* (ill. B. Moser). San Diego, CA: Harcourt Brace.

APPENDIX C.2. Picture Book Sets: Literary Analysis and Teaching Writing

SETTING

Greenfield, E. (1988). *Under the Sunday tree* (ill. A. Ferguson). New York: Harper & Row.
Andersen, H. C. (1990). *The tinderbox*. Boston: Little, Brown.
Myers, W. D. (1997). *Harlem* (ill. C. Myers). New York: Scholastic.
Provensen, A., & Provensen, M. (1987). *Shaker Lane*. New York: Viking Penguin.
Turner, A. (1985). *Dakota dugout*. New York: Simon & Schuster.

CYCLICAL JOURNEYS

Gerstein, M. (1987). *The mountains of Tibet*. New York: HarperCollins.
Sendak, M. (1981). *Outside over there*. New York: Harper & Row.
Yorinks, A. (1983). *It happened in Pinsk*. New York: Farrar, Straus, Giroux.
Yorinks, A. (1986). *Hey, Al*. New York: Farrar, Straus, Giroux.

PLOT STRUCTURE

Del Negro, J. (1998). *Lucy Dove*. New York: Dorling Kindersley.
San Souci, R. D. (1989). *The boy and the ghost*. New York: Simon & Schuster.
Van Allsburg, C. (1979). *The garden of Abdul Gasazi*. Boston: Houghton Mifflin.
Yorinks, A. (1989). *Oh, brother*. New York: Farrar, Straus, Giroux.

DIALECT IN DIALOGUE

Root, P. (1996). *Aunt Nancy and Old Man Trouble*. Cambridge, MA: Candlewick.
Root, P. (1998). *Aunt Nancy and Cousin Lazybones* (ill. D. Parkins). Cambridge, MA: Candlewick.
Schroeder, A. (1997). *Smoky Mountain Rose: An Appalachian Cinderella*. New York: Dial.
Stanley, D. (1999). *Raising Sweetness*. New York: Putnam.
Yorinks, A. (1994). *Whitefish Will rides again!* New York: HarperCollins.

TONE AND MOOD

Van Allsburg, C. (1986). *The stranger*. Boston: Houghton Mifflin.
Crew, G. (1998). *The watertower*. New York: Crocodile.
Grimm, W., & Manheim, R. (1988). *Dear Mili* (ill. M. Sendak). New York: Farrar, Straus, Giroux.
Polacco, P. (1994). *Pink and Say*. New York: Scholastic.
Yorinks, A. (1980). *Louis the fish*. New York: Farrar, Straus, Giroux.
Young, E. (1989). *Lon Po Po: A Red-Riding Hood story from China*. New York: Philomel.

SATIRE

Browne, A. (1986). *Piggybook*. New York: Knopf.
Browne, A. (1992). *Zoo*. New York: Knopf.
Macaulay, D. (1985). *Baaa*. Boston: Houghton Mifflin.
Seuss, Dr. (1971). *The lorax*. New York: Random House.
Seuss, Dr. (1984). *The butter battle book*. New York: Random House.
Yorinks, A. (1988). *Company's coming*. New York: Crown.

FORMAT, PERSPECTIVE, AND ILLUSTRATION

Browne, A. (1998). *Voices in the park*. New York: Dorling Kindersley.
Gallaz, C., & Innocenti, R. (1985) *Rose Blanche* (ill. R. Innocenti). Mankato, MN: Creative Education.
Macaulay, D. (1990). *Black and white*. Boston: Houghton Mifflin.
Pinkney, B. (1997). *The adventures of Sparrowboy*. New York: Simon & Schuster.
Raschka, C. (1997). *Mysterious Thelonious*. New York: Orchard.
Scieszka, J. (1995). *Math curse*. New York: Viking.
Sis, P. (1993). *A small tall tale from the far far north*. New York: Knopf.
Yolen, J. (1992) *Encounter* (ill. D. Shannon). San Diego, CA: Harcourt Brace.

VERSIONS OF CINDERELLA

Buehner, C. (1996). *Fanny's dream*. New York: Dial.
Hooks, W. H. (1987). *Moss gown*. New York: Clarion.
Louie, A. (1982). *Yeh-Shen: A Cinderella story from China* (ill. E. Young). New York: Philomel.
Martin, R. (1992). *The rough-face girl*. New York: Putnam.
San Souci, R. D. (1989). *The talking eggs* (ill. J. Pinkney). New York: Dial.
San Souci, R. D. (1994). *Sootface: An Ojibwa Cinderella* (ill. D. San Souci). New York: Doubleday.
San Souci, R. D. (1998). *Cendrillon: A Caribbean Cinderella* (ill. B. Pinkney). New York: Simon & Schuster.
Schroeder, A. (1997). *Smoky Mountain Rose: An Appalachian Cinderella*. New York: Dial.
Steptoe, J. (1987). *Mufaro's beautiful daughters: An African tale*. New York: Lothrop, Lee & Shepard.

NEW PERSPECTIVES ON CHARACTER IN OTHER TRADITIONAL TALES

Grimm, The Brothers. (1981). *Hansel and Gretel* (ill. A. Browne). New York: Knopf.
Munsch, R. N. (1980). *The paper bag princess* (ill. M. Martchenko). Buffalo, NY: Annick Press.
Scieszka, J. (1989). *The true story of the three little pigs*. New York: Scholastic.
Scieszka, J. (1991). *The frog prince continued*. New York: Scholastic.

FOLK TALES: CHARACTER TRANSFORMATIONS

Bang, M. (1983). *Dawn*. New York: Mulberry Books.
Cooper, S. (1986). *The Selkie girl* (ill. W. Hutton). New York: McElderry.
Martin, R. (1993). *The boy who lived with the seals*. New York: Putnam.
Mollel, T. M. (1990). *The orphan boy*. New York: Clarion.

Yolen, J. (1989). *Dove Isabeau* (ill. D. Nolan). San Diego, CA: Harcourt Brace.
Yolen, J. (1990). *Tam Lin* (ill. C. Mikolaycak). San Diego, CA: Harcourt Brace.
Yolen, J. (1991). *Greyling* (ill. D. Ray). New York: Philomel.

TRICKSTER TALES

Aardema, V. (1991). *Borreguita and the coyote*. New York: Knopf.
Begay, S. (1992). *Ma'ii and Cousin Horned Toad*. New York: Scholastic.
Goble, P. (1989). *Iktomi and the berries*. New York: Orchard.
McDermott, G. (1972). *Anansi the spider*. New York: Holt.
McDermott, G. (1992). *Zomo the rabbit: A trickster tale from West Africa*. San Diego, CA: Harcourt Brace.
McDermott, G. (1993). *Raven: A trickster tale from the Pacific Northwest*. San Diego, CA: Harcourt Brace.
McDermott, G. (1994). *Coyote: A trickster tale from the American Southwest*. San Diego, CA: Harcourt Brace.

NEW VERSIONS OF TRADITIONAL VERSE: COMMENTARY ON SOCIETY (FOR MATURE STUDENTS)

Merriam, E. (1969). *The inner city Mother Goose*. New York: Simon & Schuster.
Sendak, M. (1993). *We are all in the dumps with Jack and Guy: Two nursery rhymes*. New York: HarperCollins.
Taylor, C. (1992). *The house that crack built*. San Francisco: Chronicle Books.

ILLUSTRATION AND TEXT: AFRICAN AMERICAN HISTORY

English, K. (1996). *Neeny coming, Neeny going*. Mahwah, NJ: BridgeWater.
Everett, G. (1994). *Li'l Sis and Uncle Willie*. New York: Hyperion.
Hooks, W. (1990). *The ballad of Belle Dorcas*. New York: Knopf.
Lawrence, J. (1968). *Harriet and the promised land*. New York: Windmill.
Lawrence, J. (1993). *The great migration*. New York: HarperCollins.
Williams, S. A. (1992). *Working cotton*. San Diego, CA: Harcourt Brace.

MEMOIRS

Crews, D. (1991). *Bigmama's*. New York: Greenwillow.
Crews, D. (1992). *Shortcut*. New York: Greenwillow.
Garland, S. (1993). *The lotus seed*. San Diego, CA: Harcourt Brace.
Hendershot, J. (1987). *In coal country* (ill. T. B. Allen). New York: Knopf.
McDonald, M. (1991). *The potato man* (ill. T. Lewin). New York: Orchard.
McDonald, M. (1992). *The great pumpkin switch* (ill. T. Lewin). New York: Orchard.
Smucker, A. E. (1989). *No star nights* (ill. S. Johnson). New York: Knopf.

BIOGRAPHY: PRESENTATION OF CHARACTER
THROUGH ILLUSTRATION

Bedard, M. (1992). *Emily* (ill. B. Cooney). New York: Doubleday.

Gerstein, M. (1998). *The wild boy: Based on the true story of the wild boy of Aveyron.* New York: Farrar, Straus, Giroux.

Krull, K. (1996). *Wilma unlimited: How Wilma Rudolph became the world's fastest woman.* San Diego, CA: Harcourt Brace.

Martin, J. B. (1998). *Snowflake Bentley* (ill. M. Azarian). Boston: Houghton Mifflin.

Orgill, R. (1997). *If only I had a horn: The young Louis Armstrong* (ill. L. Jenkins). Boston: Houghton Mifflin.

Pinkney, A. D. (1996). *Bill Pickett: Rodeo-ridin' cowboy.* San Diego, CA: Harcourt Brace.

Pinkney, A. D. (1998). *Duke Ellington* (ill. B. Pinkney). New York: Hyperion.

Sis, P. (1991). *Follow the dream: The story of Christopher Columbus.* New York: Knopf.

Sis, P. (1996). *Starry messenger.* New York: Farrar, Straus, Giroux.

Stanley, D. (1998). *Joan of Arc.* New York: Morrow.

Winter, J. (1991). *Diego.* New York: Scholastic.

PRIMARY SOURCES WITH ILLUSTRATIONS

King, M. L., Jr. (1997). *I have a dream.* New York: Scholastic.

Lawlor, V. (Ed.). (1995). *I was dreaming to come to America: Memories from the Ellis Island oral history project.* New York: Viking.

Lincoln, A. (1995). *The Gettysburg Address.* Boston: Houghton Mifflin.

THE GREAT DEPRESSION

Adler, D. (1999). *The Babe and I.* San Diego, CA: Harcourt Brace.

Lied, K. (1997). *Potato: A tale from the Great Depression* (ill. L. Campbell). Washington, DC: National Geographic Society.

MacLachlan, P. (1995). *What you know first* (ill. B. Moser). New York: HarperCollins.

Medearis, A. S. (1990). *Picking peas for a penny* (ill. C. Shaw). Austin, TX: State House Press.

Mitchell, M. K. (1993). *Uncle Jed's barbershop* (ill. J. Ransome). New York: Simon & Schuster.

WORLD WAR II: THE HOLOCAUST

Gallaz, C., & Innocenti, R. (1985). *Rose Blanche.* Mankato, MN: Creative Education.

Hoestlandt, J. (1995). *Star of fear, star of hope.* New York: Walker.

Mochizuki, K. (1997) *Passage to freedom: The Sugihara story.* New York: Lee & Low.

Nerlove, M. (1996). *Flowers on the wall.* New York: McElderry.

Spiegelman, A. (1986). *Maus: A survivor's tale.* New York: Pantheon. (for mature students)

Volavkova, H. (Ed.). (1994). *I never saw another butterfly: Children's drawings and poems from Terezin concentration camp.* New York: Schocken.

Wild, M. (1991) *Let the celebrations begin!* New York: Orchard.

WORLD WAR II: JAPANESE INTERNMENT

Hamanaka, S. (1990). *The journey: Japanese Americans, racism, and renewal*. New York: Orchard.
Mochizuki, K. (1993). *Baseball saved us*. New York: Scholastic.
Uchida, Y. (1993). *The bracelet*. New York: Philomel.

WORLD WAR II: WAR IN JAPAN

Coerr, E. (1993). *Sadako* (ill E. Young). New York: Putnam.
Kodoma, T. (1992). *Shin's tricycle*. New York: Walter.
Maruki, T. (1980). *Hiroshima no pika*. New York: Lothrop, Lee & Shepard.
Tsuchiya, Y. (1951). *Faithful elephants: A true story of animals, people, and war*. New York: Bantam.

APPENDIX C.3. Short Chapter Books and Short Stories

BOOKS FOR EARLY READERS

Brenner, B. (1978). *Wagon wheels* (ill. D. Bolognese). New York: Harper & Row.

Byars, B. (1996). *My brother, Ant.* New York: Viking.

Cazet, D. (1998). *Minnie and Moo go to the moon.* New York: Dorling Kindersley.

Levinson, N. S. (1992). *Snowshoe Thompson* (ill. R. Sandlin). New York: HarperCollins.

Marshall, E. (1982). *Fox in love* (ill. J. Marshall). New York: Dial.

Marshall, E. (1985). *Four on the shore* (ill. J. Marshall). New York: Dial.

Marshall, J. (1988). *Fox on the job.* New York: Dial.

McDonald, M. (1998). *Beezy.* New York: Orchard.

Rylant, C. (1990). *Henry and Mudge and the happy cat* (ill. S. Stevenson). New York: Bradbury.

Sharmat, M. W. (1998). *Nate the great and me: The case of the fleeing fang* (ill. M. Simont). New York: Delacorte.

Skofield, J. (1996). *Detective Dinosaur* (ill. R. W. Alley). New York: HarperCollins.

Schwartz, A. (1984). *In a dark, dark room* (ill. D. Zimmer). New York: Harper & Row.

Schwartz, A. (1991). *Ghosts!: Ghostly tales from folklore* (ill. V. Chess). New York: HarperCollins.

BOOKS FOR READERS GAINING FLUENCY

Adler, D. A. (1998). *Cam Jansen and the catnapping mystery* (ill. S. Natti). New York: Viking.

Avi. (1997). *Finding Providence: The story of Roger Williams* (ill. J. Watling). New York: Harper-Collins.

Brisson, P. (1997). *Hot fudge hero* (ill. D. C. Bluthenthal). New York: Holt.

Byars, B. (1996). *Tornado* (ill. D. Ben-Ami). New York: HarperCollins.

Calmenson, S., & Cole, J. (1997). *Rockin' reptiles* (ill. L. Munsinger). New York: Morrow.

Cameron, A. (1997). *More stories Huey tells* (ill. L. Toft). New York: Farrar, Straus, Giroux.

Christopher, M. (1997). *Stranger in right field* (ill. B. Dodson). Boston: Little Brown.

Clifford, E. (1997). *Flatfoot Fox and the case of the missing schoolhouse* (ill. B. Lies). Boston: Houghton Mifflin.

Dahl, R. (1966). *The magic finger* (ill. W. P. DuBois). New York: Harper & Row.

Dahl, R. (1978). *The enormous crocodile.* New York: Knopf.

Dickinson, P. (1996). *Chuck and Danielle* (ill K. de Kiefte). New York: Delacorte.

Fritz, J. (1992). *George Washington's mother* (ill. D. DiSalvo-Ryan). New York: Grosset & Dunlap.

Gauch, P. L. (1974). *This time, Tempe Wick?* (ill. M. Tomes). New York: Putnam.

Gauch, P. L. (1990). *Thunder at Gettysburg* (ill. S. Gammell). New York: Putnam.

Giff, P. R. (1991). *The war began at supper: Letters to Miss Loria* (ill. B. Lewin). New York: Bantam Doubleday.

Hall, D. (1996). *When Willard met Babe Ruth* (ill. B. Moser). San Diego, CA: Harcourt Brace.

Hesse, K. (1994). *Sable* (ill. M. Sewall). New York: Holt.

Hest, A. (1991). *Love you, soldier.* New York: Macmillan.

Hest, A. (1995). *The private notebook of Katie Roberts, age 11* (ill. S. Lamut). Cambridge, MA: Candlewick.

Hest, A. (1998). *The great green notebook of Katie Roberts: Who just turned 12 on Monday*. Cambridge, MA: Candlewick.
Hopkinson, D. (1997). *Birdie's lighthouse* (ill. K. B. Root). New York: Atheneum.
Howe, J. (1997). *Pinky and Rex and the new neighbors*. New York: Atheneum.
Kinsey-Warnock, N. (1989). *The Canada geese quilt* (ill. L. W. Bowman). New York: Dutton.
Kline, S. (1998). *Horrible Harry moves up to third grade* (ill. F. Remkiewicz). New York: Viking.
Le Guin, U. K. (1988). *Catwings* (ill. S. D. Schindler). New York: Orchard.
MacLachlan, P. (1985). *Sarah, plain and tall*. New York: Harper & Row.
Marshall, J. (1993). *Rats on the range and other stories*. New York: Dial.
Mathis, S. B. (1975). *The hundred penny box* (ill. L. Dillon & D. Dillon). New York: Viking.
Moss, M. (1995). *Amelia's notebook*. Berkeley, CA: Tricycle.
Moss, M. (1996). *Amelia writes again*. Berkeley, CA: Tricycle.
Moss, M. (1997). *Amelia hits the road*. Berkeley, CA: Tricyle.
Moss, M. (1998). *Amelia takes command*. Berkeley, CA: Tricycle.
Myers, W. D. (1996). *Smiffy Blue, ace crime detective: The case of the missing ruby and other stories* (ill. D. J. A. Sims). New York: Scholastic.
Rounds, G. (1941). *The blind colt*. New York: Holiday House.
Rylant, C. (1997). *Poppleton: Book one* (ill. M. Teague). New York: Scholastic.
Rylant, C. (1994). *Mr. Putter and Tabby walk the dog* (ill. A. Howard). San Diego, CA: Harcourt Brace.
Rylant, C. (1995). *The Van Gogh cafe*. San Diego, CA: Harcourt Brace.
Scieszka, J. (1992). *The good, the bad, and the goofy* (ill. L. Smith). New York: Viking.
Smith, D. B. (1973). *A taste of blackberries*. New York: Harper & Row.
Soto, G. (1987). *The cat's meow* (ill. J. Cepeda). New York: Scholastic.

BOOKS FOR MIDDLE-LEVEL READERS

Banks, S. H. (1993). *Remember my name*. New York: Rinehart.
Bauer, M. D. (1992). *Ghost eye*. New York: Scholastic.
Bauer, M. D. (1986). *On my honor*. New York: Clarion.
Bauer, M. D. (1993). *A taste of smoke*. New York: Clarion.
Bawden, N. (1988). *Henry* (ill. J. Powzyk). New York: Lothrop, Lee & Shepard.
Brooks, B. (1990). *Everywhere*. New York: HarperCollins.
Bulla, C. R. (1981). *A lion to guard us* (ill. M. Chessare). New York: Harper & Row.
Clements, A. (1996). *Frindle* (ill. B. Selznick). New York: Simon & Schuster.
Coerr, E. (1977). *Sadako and the thousand paper cranes*. New York: Putman.
Coman, C. (1995). *What Jamie saw*. New York: Front Street.
DeFelice, C. (1990). *Weasel*. New York: Simon & Schuster.
Dorris, M. (1992). *Morning girl*. New York: Hyperion.
Dorris, M. (1994). *Guests*. New York: Hyperion.
Dorris, M. (1996). *Sees behind trees*. New York: Hyperion.
Fleischman, P. (1980). *The whipping boy* (ill. P. Sis). New York: Greenwillow.
Hamilton, V. (1990). *Cousins*. New York: Philomel.
Klise, K. (1998). *Regarding the fountain: A tale, in letters, of liars and leaks*. New York: Avon.
Konigsburg, E. L. (1971). *Altogether, one at a time*. New York: Antheneum.
Lynch, C. (1997). *Ladies choice*. New York: HarperCollins.
MacLachlan, P. (1991). *Journey*. New York: Delacorte.
Mayerson, E. W. (1990). *The cat who escaped from steerage*. New York: Scribner.
McKissack, P. C. (1992). *The dark-thirty: Southern tales of the supernatural* (ill. B. Pinkney). New York: Knopf.

Mead, A. (1995). *Junebug*. New York: HarperCollins.

Myers, A. (1992). *Red dirt Jessie*. New York: Walker.

Naidoo, B. (1986). *Journey to Jo'burg: A South African story*. New York: Scholastic.

Peck, R. N. (1974). *Soup*. New York: Knopf.

Pinkwater, D. (1977). *The Hoboken chicken emergency*. Englewood Cliffs, NJ: Prentice-Hall.

Rylant, C. (1992). *Missing May*. New York: Orchard.

San Souci, R. D. (1987). *Short and shivery: Forty-five chilling tales*. New York: Doubleday.

San Souci, R. D. (1998). *A terrifying taste of short and shivery: Thirty creepy tales* (ill. L. Wooden). New York: Delacorte.

Schur, M. R. (1996). *When I left my village* (ill. B. Pinkney). New York: Dial.

Taylor, M. (1975). *Song of the trees* (ill. J. Pinkney). New York: Dial.

Taylor, M. (1987a). *The friendship*. New York: Dial.

Taylor, M. (1987b). *The gold cadillac* (ill. M. Hayes). New York: Dial.

Taylor, M. (1995). *The well: David's story*. New York: Dial.

Walsh, J. P. (1982). *The green book* (ill. L. Bloom). New York: Farrar, Straus, Giroux.

Yolen, J. (1996). *Hobby*. San Diego, CA: Harcourt Brace.

Yolen, J. (1996). *Passager*. San Diego, CA: Harcourt Brace.

Yolen, J. (1997). *Merlin*. San Diego, CA: Harcourt Brace.

BOOKS FOR MATURE READERS

Anderson, R. (1989). *The bus people*. New York: Holt.

Avi. (1997). *What do fish have to do with anything? And other stories* (ill. T. Mitchell). Cambridge, MA: Candlewick.

Bunting, E. (1991). *Sharing Susan*. New York: HarperCollins.

Cart, M. (1999). *Tomorrowland: Ten stories about the future*. New York: Scholastic.

Cofer, J. O. (1995). *An island like you: Stories of the barrio*. New York: Orchard.

Conford, E. (1998). *Crush*. New York: HarperCollins.

Cushman, K. (1995). *The midwife's apprentice*. Boston: Houghton Mifflin.

Doherty, B. (1990). *White Peak Farm*. New York: Orchard.

Fine, A. (1996). *Step by wicked step*. Boston: Little, Brown.

Fleischman, P. (1991). *The borning room*. New York: HarperCollins.

Fleischman, P. (1997). *Seedfolks* (ill. J. Peterson). New York: HarperCollins.

Hansen, J. (1986). *Which way freedom?* New York: Walker.

Lyons, M. (Ed.). (1991). *Raw head, bloody bones: African-American tales of the supernatural*. New York: Scribner.

Jimenez, F. (1997). *The circuit: Stories from the life of a migrant child*. Boston: Houghton Mifflin.

Johnson, A. (1993). *Toning the sweep*. New York: Orchard.

MacLachlan, P. (1993). *Baby*. New York: Delacorte.

Matas, C. (1993). *Daniel's story*. New York: Scholastic.

Matas, C. (1996). *After the war*. New York: Simon & Schuster.

Mazer, H. (Ed.). (1997). *Twelve shots: Outstanding stories about guns*. New York: Delacorte.

Mazer, H. (1998). *The wild kid*. New York: Simon & Schuster.

O'Dell, S. (1970). *Sing down the moon*. Boston: Houghton Mifflin.

Park, B. (1995). *Mick Harte was here*. New York: Knopf.

Paulsen, G. (1993). *Nightjohn*. New York: Delacorte.

Paulsen, G. (1998). *Soldier's heart: Being the story of the enlistment and due service of boy Charley Goddard in the First Minnesota Volunteers*. New York: Delacorte.

Peck, R. (1998). *A long way from Chicago: A novel in stories*. New York: Dial.

Salisbury, G. (1992). *Blue skin of the sea*. New York: Delacorte.

Shreve, S. (1996). *The goalie*. New York: Morrow.

Singer, M. (Ed.). (1998). *Stay true: Stories for strong girls*. New York: Scholastic.

Smith, C. R. (2000). *Tall tales: Six amazing basketball dreams*. New York: Dutton.

Soto, G. (1993). *Local news*. San Diego, CA: Harcourt Brace.

Soto, G. (1998). *Petty crimes*. San Diego, CA: Harcourt Brace.

Walter, V. (1998). *Making up megaboy* (ill. K. Roeckelein). New York: Dorling Kindersley.

Woodson, J. (1994). *I hadn't meant to tell you this*. New York: Delacorte.

Wynne-Jones, T. (1995). *Some of the kinder planets*. New York: Orchard.

APPENDIX C.4. Text Sets for Thematic Studies

SLAVERY

Picture Books

Edwards, P. D. (1997). *Barefoot: Escape on the underground railroad* (ill. H. Cole). New York: HarperCollins.

Hooks, W. H. (1990). *The ballad of Belle Dorcas* (ill. B. Pinkney). New York: Knopf.

Hopkinson, D. (1993). *Sweet Clara and the freedom quilt*. New York: Knopf.

Turner, A. (1987). *Nettie's trip south*. New York: Macmillan.

Winter, J. (1988). *Follow the drinking gourd*. New York: Knopf.

Nonfiction

Hamilton, V. (1993). *Many thousand gone: African Americans from slavery to freedom* (ill. L. Dillon & D. Dillon). New York: Knopf.

Hurmence, B. (Ed.). (1997). *Slavery time when I was chillun*. New York: Putnam.

Lester, J. (1968). *To be a slave* (ill. T. Feelings). New York: Dial.

McKissack, P. C., & McKissack, F. L. (1994). *Christmas in the big house, Christmas in the quarters* (ill. J. Thompson). New York: Scholastic.

McKissack, P. C., & McKissack, F. L. (1996). *Rebels against slavery: American slave revolts*. New York: Scholastic.

Meltzer, M. (Ed.). (1984). *The Black Americans: A history in their own words 1619–1983*. New York: Crowell.

Myers, W. D. (1991). *Now is your time!: The African-American struggle for freedom*. New York: HarperCollins.

Biography/Autobiography

Douglass, F. (1973). *Narrative of the life of Frederick Douglass: An American slave*. New York: Bantam.

Everett, G. (1993). *John Brown: One man against slavery* (ill. J. Lawrence). New York: Rizzoli.

Hamilton, V. (1988). *Anthony Burns: The defeat and triumph of a fugitive slave*. New York: Knopf.

McCurdy, M. (Ed.). (1994). *Escape from slavery: The boyhood of Frederick Douglass in his own words*. New York: Knopf.

McKissack, P. C., & McKissack, F. (1992). *Sojourner Truth: Ain't I a woman?* New York: Scholastic.

Folktale Collections

Hamilton, V. (1985). *The people could fly: American black folktales* (ill. L. Dillon & D. Dillon). New York: Knopf.

McKissack, P. C. (1992). *The dark-thirty: Southern tales of the supernatural* (ill. B. Pinkney). New York: Knopf.

Historical Fiction

Beatty, P. (1991). *Jayhawker*. New York: Morrow.

Blos, J. W. (1979). *A gathering of days: A New England girl's journal, 1830–32*. New York: Scribner.

Collier, J. L., & Collier, C. (1981). *Jump ship to freedom*. New York: Delacorte.
Fox, P. (1973). *The slave dancer*. Scarsdale, NY: Bradbury Press.
Fritz, J. (1987). *Brady* (ill. L. Ward). New York: Penguin.
Hansen, J. (1994). *The captive*. New York: Scholastic.
Lasky, K. (1996). *True north*. New York: Scholastic.
Lyons, M. E. (1992). *Letters from a slave girl: The story of Harriet Jacobs*. New York: Scribner.
Paterson, K. (1996). *Jip: His story*. New York: Dutton.
Paulsen, G. (1993). *Nightjohn*. New York: Delacorte.
Reeder, C. (1997). *Across the lines*. New York: Simon & Schuster.

Fantasy and Realistic Fiction

Hamilton, V. (1968). *The house of Dies Drear* (ill. E. Keith). New York: Macmillan.
Hamilton, V. (1987). *The mystery of Drear House*. New York: Greenwillow.
Hurmence, B. (1982). *A girl called Boy*. Boston: Houghton Mifflin.

Poetry

Greenfield, E. (1978). Harriet Tubman. In E. Greenfield, *Honey, I love* (ill. D. Dillon & L. Dillon). New York: Crowell.
Lawrence, J. (1968). *Harriet and the promised land*. New York: Windmill.

Art

Feelings, T. (1995). *The middle passage: White ships/black cargo*. New York: Dial.

Magazines

Cobblestone. (1994). Vol. 15, No. 5.
Cricket. (1995). Vol. 22, No. 6.

TOPICAL STUDY OF INSECTS

Picture Books

Egielski, R. (1995). *Buz*. New York: Geringer.
Egielski, R. (1998). *Jazper*. New York: Geringer.
McDonald, M. (1995). *Insects are my life* (ill. P. B. Johnson). New York: Orchard.
Parker, N. W. (1987). *Bugs* (ill. J. R. Wright). New York: Morrow.
Ryder, J. (1991). *When the woods hum* (ill. C. Stock). New York: Morrow.
Talbott, H., & Greenberg, M. (1996). *Amazon diary: Property of Alex Winters* (ill. M. Greenberg). New York: Putnam.
Van Allsburg, C. (1988). *Two bad ants*. Boston: Houghton Mifflin.

Fiction

Fletcher, R. (1997). *Spider boy*. Boston: Houghton Mifflin.
James, M. (1990). *Shoebag*. New York: Scholastic.
James, M. (1996). *Shoebag returns*. New York: Scholastic.

Poetry

Demi. (1993). *Demi's secret garden*. New York: Holt.

Fleischman, P. (1988). *Joyful noise: Poems for two voices* (ill. E. Beddows). New York: Harper & Row.

Florian, D. (1998). *Insectlopedia: Poems and paintings*. San Diego, CA: Harcourt Brace.

Hopkins, L. B. (1992). *Flit, flutter, fly!* (ill. P. Palagonia). New York: Doubleday.

Michelson, R. (1999). *A book of flies* (ill. L. Baskin). New York: Cavendish.

Informational Books

Dussling, J. (1998). *Bugs! Bugs! Bugs!* New York: Dorling Kindersley.

Facklam, M. (1994). *The big bug book*. Boston: Little, Brown.

Gibbons, G. (1989). *Monarch butterfly*. New York: Holiday House.

Lasky, K. (1997). *The most beautiful roof in the world: Exploring the rainforest canopy* (ill. C. G. Knight). New York: Gulliver.

Mound, L. (1993). *Amazing insects* (ill. F. Greenaway). New York: Knopf.

Pringle, L. (1997). *An extraordinary life: The story of a monarch buterfly* (ill. B. Marshall). New York: Orchard.

Still, J. (1991). *Amazing butterflies and moths* (ill. J. Young). New York: Knopf.

APPENDIX C.6. Diversity in Realistic Fiction

Bloor, E. (1997). *Tangerine.* San Diego, CA: Harcourt Brace.

Beatty, P. (1981). *Lupita mañana.* New York: Morrow.

Brooks, B. (1984). *The moves make the man..* New York: Harper & Row.

Buss, F. L. (1991). *Journey of the sparrows.* New York: Dutton.

Conly, J. L. (1998). *While no one was watching.* New York: Holt.

Conly, J. L. (1993). *Crazy lady!* New York: HarperCollins.

Crew, L. (1989). *Children of the river.* New York: Delacorte Press.

Dorris, M. (1997). *The window.* New York: Hyperion.

Fenner, C. (1995). *Yolonda's genius.* New York: McElderry.

Fine, A. (1997). *The tulip touch.* Boston: Little, Brown.

Fox, P. (1991). *Monkey island.* New York: Orchard Books.

Gantos, J. (1998). *Joey Pigza swallowed the key.* New York: Farrar Straus Giroux.

Gantos, J. (2000). *Joey Pigza loses control.* New York: Farrar ,Straus ,Giroux.

Hobbs, W. (1993). *Beardance.* New York: Macmillan.

Hobbs, W. (1996). *Far North.* New York: William Morrow & Company.

Holt, K. W. (1998). *My Louisiana sky.* New York: Holt.

Holt, K. W. (1999). *When Zachary Beaver came to town.* New York: Holt.

Jimenez, F. (1997). *The circuit.* Albuquerque: University of New Mexico Press.

Johnson, A. (1998). *Heaven.* New York: Simon & Schuster.

Lasky, K. (1994). *Memoirs of a bookbat.* San Diego, CA: Harcourt Brace.

Mead, A. (1995). *Junebug.* New York: Farrar, Straus , Giroux.

Myers, W. D. (1979). *The young landlords.* New York: Penguin Books.

Myers, W. D. (1982). *Won't know till I get there.* New York: Viking Press.

Myers, W. D. (1992). *Somewhere in the darkness.* New York: Scholastic.

Myers, W. D. (1996). *Slam!* New York: Scholastic.

Namioka, L. (1992). *Yang the youngest and his terrible ear.* Boston: Little, Brown.

Namioka, L. (1995). *Yang the third and her impossible family.* Boston: Little, Brown.

Nelson, T. (1994). *Earthshine.* New York: Orchard.

Nolan, H. (1997). *Dancing on the edge.* San Diego, CA: Harcourt Brace.

Orr, W. (1997). *Peeling the onion.* New York: Holiday House.

Oughton, J. (1995). *Music from a place called Half Moon.* Boston: Houghton Mifflin.

Paterson, K. (1978). *The great Gilly Hopkins.* New York: Crowell

Paterson, K. (1994). *Flip-flop girl.* New York: Dutton.

Philbrick, R. (1993). *Freak the mighty.* New York: Blue Sky Press.

Soto, G. (1990). *Baseball in April and other stories.* San Diego, CA: Harcourt Brace.

Spinelli, J. (1990). *Maniac Magee.* Boston: Little, Brown.

Staples, S. F. (1996). *Dangerous skies.* New York: Farrar, Straus, Giroux.

Temple, F. (1993). *Grab hands and run.* New York: HarperCollins.

Temple, F. (1995). *Tonight, by sea.* New York: HarperCollins.

Yep, L. (1995). *Thief of hearts.* New York: HarperCollins.

APPENDIX D

RESOURCES FOR TEACHING
READING AND WRITING

APPENDIX D.I. Professional Resources for Teachers

LITERACY: INSTRUCTIONAL STRATEGIES

Barr, R., & Johnson, B. (1997). *Teaching reading and writing in elementary classrooms.* New York: Longman.

Bear, D. R., Templeton, S., Invernizzi, M., & Johnston, F. (2000). *Words their way: Word study for phonics, vocabulary, and spelling instruction* (2nd ed.). Upper Saddle River, NJ: Merrill.

Harvey, S. (1998). *Nonfiction matters: Reading, writing, and research in grades 3–8.* York, ME: Stenhouse.

Keene, E. O., & Zimmerman, S. (1997). *Mosaic of thought: Teaching comprehension in a reader's workshop.* Portsmouth, NH: Heinemann.

Raphael, T. E., & Hiebert, E. H. (1996). *Creating an integrated approach to literacy instruction.* Fort Worth, TX: Harcourt Brace.

Rief, L. (1992). *Seeking diversity: Language arts with adolescents.* Portsmouth, NH: Heinemann.

Tierney, R. J., & Readence, J. E. (2000). *Reading strategies and practices: A compendium* (5th ed.). Boston: Allyn & Bacon.

Tompkins, G. E. (2001). *Literacy for the 21st century: A balanced approach* (2nd ed.). Upper Saddle River, NJ: Merrill.

LITERACY ASSESSMENT AND SPECIAL POPULATIONS

Allington, R. (Ed.). (1998). *Teaching struggling readers: Articles from The Reading Teacher.* Newark, DE: International Reading Association.

Gillet, J. W., & Temple, C. (2000). *Understanding reading problems: Assessment and instruction.* New York: HarperCollins.

Reading assessment in practice: Book of readings. (1995). Newark, DE: International Reading Association.

Roller, C. M. (1996). *Variability, not disability: Struggling readers in a workshop classroom.* Newark, DE: International Reading Association.

Rhodes, L. K. (1993). *Literacy assessment: A handbook of instruments.* NH: Heinemann.

Spear-Swerling, L. C., & Sternberg, R. (1996). *Off track: When poor readers become "learning disabled."* Boulder, CO: Westview Press.

Valencia, S. W. (1998). *Literacy portfolios in action.* Fort Worth, TX: Harcourt Brace.

TEACHING THE WRITING PROCESS ACROSS THE CURRICULUM

Atwell, N. (Ed.). (1990). *Coming to know: Writing to learn in the intermediate grades.* Portsmouth, NH: Heinemann.

Atwell, N. (1998). *In the middle: New understandings about writing, reading, and learning* (2nd ed.). Portsmouth, NH: Heinemann.

Calkins, L. M. (1991). *Living between the lines.* Portsmouth, NH: Heinemann.

Calkins, L. M. (1998). *The art of teaching writing.* Portsmouth, NH: Heinemann.

Chancer, J., & Rester-Zodrow, G. (1997). *Moon journals: Writing, art, and inquiry through focused nature study.* Portsmouth, NH: Heinemann.

Fletcher, R., & Portalupi, J. (1998). *Craft lessons: Teaching writing K–8*. York, ME: Stenhouse.

Graves, D. (1989). *Investigate nonfiction*. Portsmouth, NH: Heinemann.

Kirby, D., & Liner, T. (1988). *Inside out: Developmental strategies for teaching writing* (2nd ed.). Portsmouth, NH: Boynton/Cook.

Moffett, J. (1992). *Active voice: A writing program across the curriculum* (2nd ed.). Portsmouth, NH: Boynton/Cook.

Murray, D. M. (1999). *Write to learn* (6th ed.). Fort Worth, TX: Harcourt Brace.

Tchudi, S. N., & Huerta, M. C. (1983). *Teaching writing in the content areas: Middle school/junior high*. Washington, DC: National Education Association.

Tompkins, G. E. (2000). *Teaching writing: Balancing process and product* (3rd ed.). Upper Saddle River, NJ: Merrill.

Wolf, D. P., Craven, J., & Balick, D. (Eds.). (1996). *More than the truth: Teaching nonfiction writing through journalism*. Portsmouth, NH: Heinemann.

TEACHING POETRY ACROSS THE CURRICULUM

Esbensen, B. J. (1995). *A celebration of bees: Helping children write poetry*. Minneapolis, MN: Winston Press.

Cullinan, B. E., Scala, M. C., & Schroder, V. C. (1995). *Three voices: An invitation to poetry across the curriculum*. York, ME: Stenhouse.

Graves, D. (1992). *Explore poetry*. Portsmouth, NH: Heinemann.

Grossman, F. (1982). *Getting from here to there: Writing and reading poetry*. Portsmouth, NH: Boynton/Cook.

Grossman, F. (1991). *Listening to the bells: Learning to read poetry by writing poetry*. Portsmouth, NH: Boynton/Cook.

Janeczko, P. B. (1998). *Favorite poetry lessons*. New York: Scholastic.

Janeczko, P. B. (1999). *How to write poetry*. New York: Scholastic.

Koch, K. (1970). *Wishes, lies, and dreams: Teaching children to write poetry*. New York: Chelsea House.

Koch, K. (1973). *Rose, where did you get that red?: Teaching great poetry to children*. New York: Random House.

RESOURCES ON LITERATURE FOR CHILDREN AND ADOLESCENTS

Huck, C. S. (2001). *Children's literature in the elementary school* (7th ed.). Dubuque, IA: McGraw-Hill.

Nilsen, A. D., & Donelson, K. L. (2000). *Literature for today's young adults*. New York: Longman.

Norton, D., with Norton, S. E. (1999). *Through the eyes of a child: An introduction to children's literature* (5th ed.). Upper Saddle River, NJ: Merrill.

Sutherland, Z. (1997). *Children and books* (9th ed.). New York: Longman.

TEACHING WITH LITERATURE

Bosma, B., & Guth, N. D. (Eds.). (1995). *Children's literature in an integrated curriculum: The authentic voice*. New York: Teachers College Press.

Cullinan, B. (Ed.). (1993). *Fact and fiction: Literature across the curriculum*. Newark, DE: International Reading Association.

Freeman, E., & Person, D. (1998). *Connecting informational children's books with content area learning.* Boston: Allyn & Bacon.

Gambrell, L. B., & Almasi, J. F. (Eds.). (1996). *Lively discussions!: Fostering engaged reading.* Newark, DE: International Reading Association.

Lukens, R. J. (1999). *A critical handbook of children's literature* (6th ed.). New York: Longman.

Pappas, C. C., Kiefer, B. Z., & Levstik, L. S. (1995). *An integrated language perspective in the elementary school: Theory into action.* White Plains, NY: Longman.

Roser, N. L., & Martinez, M. G. (Eds.). (1995). *Book talk and beyond: Children and teachers respond to literature.* Newark, DE: International Reading Association.

Sorensen, M., & Lehman, B. (Eds.). (1995). *Teaching with children's books: Paths to literature-based instruction.* Urbana, IL: National Council of Teachers of English.

DIVERSITY RESOURCES FOR TEACHERS

Barbieri, M. (1995). *Sounds from the heart: Learning to listen to girls.* Portsmouth, NH: Heinemann.

Barrera, R. B., Thompson, V. D., & Dressman, M. (Eds.). (1994). *Kaleidoscope: A multicultural booklist for grades K–8.* Urbana, IL: National Council of Teachers of English.

Brown, J., & Stephens, E. (1998). *United in diversity: Using multicultural young adult literature in the classroom.* Urbana, IL: National Council of Teachers of English.

Corliss, J.C. (1998). *Crossing borders with literature of diversity.* Norwood, MA: Christopher-Gordon.

Day, F. (1994). *Multicultural voices in contemporary literature: A resource for teachers.* Portsmouth, NH: Heinemann.

Day, F. (1997). *Latina and Latino voices in literature.* Portsmouth, NH: Heinemann.

Harris, V. J. (1997). *Using multiethnic literature in the K–8 classroom.* Norwood, MA: Christopher-Gordon.

Rudman, M. K. (1995). *Children's literature: An issues approach.* New York: Longman.

Susag, D. M. (1998). *Roots and branches: A resource of Native American literature—themes, lessons, and bibliographies.* Urbana, IL: National Council of Teachers of English.

APPENDIX D.2. Professional Journals

The Reading Teacher

Journal of Adolescent and Adult Literacy

Reading Research Quarterly

SIGNAL Journal (Special Interest Group—A Network on Adolescent Literature)

International Reading Association
800 Barksdale Rd.
P.O. Box 8139
Newark, DE 19714-8139
http://www. reading.org

Language Arts

English Journal

Voices from the Middle

Research in the Teaching of English

The ALAN Review (Assembly on Literature for Adolescents of the NCTE)
National Council of Teachers of English
1111 W. Kenyon Road
Urbana, IL 61801-1096
http://www.ncte.org

The Horn Book Magazine

The Horn Book Guide

The Horn Book, Inc.
56 Roland Street, Suite 200
Charlestown, MA 02129-9975
http://www.hbook.com

Book Links: Connecting Books, Libraries, and Classrooms (American Library Association)

Book Links

434 West Downer
Aurora, IL 60506
http://www.ala.org/BookLinks

APPENDIX D.3. Magazines for Children and Young Adults

Spider (ages 6–9)

Cricket (ages 9–14)

Cicada (ages 14 and up) http://www.cicadamag.com

Cricket Magazine Group
315 Fifth Street
Peru, IL 61354
http://www.cricketmag.com

Appleseeds (grades 2–4; nonfiction reading)

Cobblestone (grades 4–9; American history)

Footsteps (grades 4 and up; African American history)

Calliope (grades 4–9; world history)

Faces (grades 4–9; people, places, cultures)

Odyssey (grades 5 and up; science)

Cobblestone Publishing Company
30 Grove Street, Suite C
Peterborough, NH 03458
http://www.cobblestonepub.com

Read

Writing!

Currrent Events

Current Health

Teen Newsweek

Current Science

Weekly Reader Corporation
200 First Stamford Place
P.O. Box 120023
Stamford, CT 06912-0023
http://www.weeklyreader.com

APPENDIX D.4. Resources on the World Wide Web

BOOK

Greenlaw, J. C. (2001). *English language arts and reading on the Internet: A resource for K–12 teachers.* Upper Saddle River, NJ: Prentice-Hall.

WEB SITES ON LITERATURE FOR CHILDREN AND ADOLESCENTS

Children's Literature Web Guide, by David K. Brown
http://www.ucalgary.ca/~dkbrown/index.html

Carol Hurst's Children's Literature Site
http://www.carolhurst.com

Young Adult Library Services Association (YALSA)
http://www.ala.org/yalsa/

Kay Vandergriff's Young Adult Literature Page
http://www.scils.rutgers.edu/special/kay/yalit.html

Multicultural Book Review Homepage (K–12)
http://www.isomedia.com/homes/jmele/homepage.html

Native American Books (directory of educational books and audiovisual material)
http://www.kstrom.net/isk/books/bookmenu.html

Center for Study of Books in Spanish for Children, by Isabel Schon
http://www.csusm.edu/cgi-bin/portal/www.book.book home?lang=SP

Young Adult Librarian's Help/Homepage
http://yahelp.suffolk.lib.ny.us/

The Author Page
http://www.ipl.org/youth/AskAuthor/

Fairrosa Cyber Library of Children's Literature
http://www.dalton.org/libraries/fairrosa

Once upon a Time . . . A Children's Literature Web Site
http://bsuvc.bus.edu/~00mevancamp/ouat.html

LITERACY WEB SITES

International Reading Association (IRA)
http://www. reading.org

National Council of Teachers of English (NCTE)
http://www.ncte.org

National Institute for Literacy (NIFL)
http://www.nifl.gov

Center for the Improvement of Early Reading Achievement (CIERA)
http://www.ciera.org/

National Research Center on English Learning and Achievement (CELA)
http://cela.albany.edu

RESEARCH WEB SITES

Kids Connect FAQs
http://www.ala.org/ICONN/kcfaq.html

AskEric (Internet-based information service on education)
http://www.askeric.org

APPENDIX E

CHARLES: A CASE STUDY OF A LESS SKILLED READER IN THE MIDDLE GRADES

Charles is a sixth grader struggling in all areas in school that require reading and writing. First, we look at different types of assessment information: background/personal information, reading, and writing. Next, we discuss this information with Janet Bloodgood, the supervisor of the summer reading program that Charles attended. We provide a graphic organizer that highlights focal issues for Charles in reading and writing: strengths Charles demonstrated and areas that he needed to develop. Finally, we share a plan for one-on-one work with Charles to use those strengths to improve his reading and writing skills. Keep in mind the following questions as you read this case:

- What can Charles do well? What does he know?
- Where is Charles making sense of his work, but making a few mistakes? Where does he need your support to learn?
- When do you see Charles stop making sense of his work? Where would teaching not be effective?

DIFFERENT TYPES OF ASSESSMENT INFORMATION ABOUT CHARLES

Background Information

At the suggestion of his teacher, Mrs. Rand, Charles was taken to a reading center for a reading assessment when he was 13 years old and in the sixth grade. Most of the information about his background came from interviews with his mother and with Mrs. Rand, a conversation with Charles, and school records. At the reading center, his mother was asked about his development. She said that although Charles developed normally as a child, he had numerous ear infections when he was a toddler. These bouts might have affected the quality of his hearing at the time and his exposure to language. Take a look at the information provided in Box E.1 from an interview with Janet Bloodgood, the supervisor at the reading clinic where Charles was tested. If you were Mrs. Rand, how could you use this type of information to guide your reading and writing instruction for Charles?

You can see that Charles has heretofore experienced little to no success at school. As a teacher, one of the first places you would need to start would be with the reading and writing tasks that Charles can accomplish with ease. He needs a chance to develop his fluency with what he is able to do, rather than to focus on tasks that seem out of reach. We continue by looking at some assessments of what strategies Charles uses as he reads.

**BOX E.1. Background Information and Assessments for Charles:
An Interview with Janet Bloodgood, Educator and Researcher
(Conducted by Karen Broaddus)**

Tell us about what you found out about sixth-grader Charles.

Since we first met Charles when he was a 13-year-old African American struggling in sixth grade (fall of the year), we in the Reading Clinic relied on background history and school information provided by his mother [and teacher], as well as the results from our own testing. We observed that Charles was a polite, mature, hard-working young man, but it was clear that he had struggled academically throughout his school career. He repeated kindergarten and second grade, and attended summer school from second through fourth grades. In middle school, he was part of a special program for students labeled "at risk." His mother continued to work with him on homework nightly, and she feared that he would drop out because of the frustration he was experiencing.

What were your hunches about his unusually slow development as a reader and writer?

Charles was one of those kids who fell through the cracks. He received speech and language services and Title I reading support for 3 years (second through fourth grades), but re-evaluation at the end of fourth grade revealed that his language abilities and achievement tested equal to his general cognitive abilities (low average), and services were discontinued. Our testing indicated that Charles was reading, spelling, and writing at a level typical of late first and early second grade. His word recognition, reading, and writing were very slow and painstaking, and he had difficulty comprehending fourth-grade material that was read to him. We suspected that language-processing difficulties contributed significantly to his troubles with reading and writing.

Reading

When Charles was asked to read lists of individual words selected from a reading series, he tended to confuse long and short vowel patterns. For example, he said *pants* for *paints*, *past* for *paste*, and *gun* for *gone*. He knew all of the primer-level words and was able to figure out many of the words on the first-grade list, but he had problems with the second-grade words. He often missed endings on words, such as *-ing*, or left off an *-s* added to make a word plural. Charles was able to read slowly from passages in first- and second-grade-level collections with reasonable accuracy. He recognized 91% of the words (remember that we have said in Chapter 1 that students become frustrated when they recognize fewer than 90% of the words in a text). Many of the mistakes he made in reading were substituting small "function" words such as *the* for *that* or *is* for *was*. When he missed content words, the substitutions that he made were guided by the meaning of the sentence. Charles was able to answer questions and discuss what he had read orally and silently in the first-grade book, but he had more problems with the second-grade-level passages. He did not understand all of the vocabulary terms in the reading. This same problem came up when Charles listened to a passage read from a fourth-grade book. Box E.2 provides a summary of what Charles did in his reading assessments.

Right away, you can see that Charles can read and understand well in very easy materials, but his reading speed is still quite slow. He does use the context of the passage to guide his reading, but his vocabulary is limited. Let's look at what we can find out from Charles's writing and spelling.

BOX E.2. Assessment Information for Charles, a Less Skilled Reader and Writer in the Middle Grades

Area of reading	Comments and analysis
Knowledge about words	• Good immediate recognition of easy words in primer books • Confuses long and short vowel patterns in first- and second-grade words • Problems with endings (-ed, -ing) and plurals
Fluency	• Substitutes function words • Substitutes content words by meaning • Reads slowly in first- and second-grade-level books • Becomes frustrated in third-grade-level books
Comprehension	• Good understanding of reading of first-grade books, but more problems with second-grade books • Difficulty with vocabulary terms and making inferences • Problems with understanding a fourth-grade book read to him

Writing and Spelling

Although Charles enjoys writing and experiences more success with writing than reading, he still has difficulty with assignments. Take a look at a piece of writing that Charles completed about himself (spelling errors are underlined, and an edited version of the piece is provided below the original for your reference). What works about the content of his writing? What does he know about spelling? What areas does he need to develop?

My name is Charles. I am 12 years old and I will turn 13 in Novemder. I live in Curchvill Md. I am in dand. I play tuda for the 6 grade band it is cuind of hard to play it dout I am geting go at it. last year I played trumpet last year I was go at that to. At my school we have 8 pired. We hav a short resess and then we go to lunch. I am not that go at math becauss of the timestables and devison. I am a fast runer in gum. I was the fast one on my team last year.

My name is Charles. I am 12 years old and I will turn 13 in November. I live in Churchville, Md. I am in band. I play tuba for the 6th grade band. It is kind of hard to play it but I am getting good at it. Last year I played trumpet. Last year I was good at that too. At my school we have 8 periods. We have a short recess and then we go to lunch. I am not that good at math because of the times tables and division. I am a fast runner in gym. I was the fastest one on my team last year.

Remember, when you first look at assessment information, to consider any positive factors. It is wonderful that Charles enjoys writing. This is a real window to his knowledge about literacy, and you can use that window to find out more about him. Charles shares some important personal information in this piece. You can see that he is confident about his abilities in music and gym. In looking for reading materials, you would want to consider these interests. His writing is clear, but it really is just a list of things about school. He needs to work on how to organize his work. You can see that Charles sometimes reverses letters (e.g., substituting *d* for *b* in *tuba*). When spelling words on a qualitative developmental spelling inventory list (see Chapter 7, Box 7.16), he often confused short and long vowel patterns (e.g., he spelled *break* as *brack*). Many of his spelling mistakes involve the endings of words, and he often just drops the last couple of letters in a word (spelling *good* as *go*, *have* as *hav*, *fastest* as *fast*).

DESIGNING AN INDIVIDUALIZED INSTRUCTIONAL PROGRAM FOR A MIDDLE GRADES STUDENT

Focusing on the Most Important Instructional Issues

You may be surprised to learn that there are 13-year-old students like Charles who are reading and writing with the same skill as some 6- and 7-year-old students. In fact, it is more challenging to teach a student like Charles than a younger student, because of the failure Charles has experienced throughout his school career. Think about his strong work effort and his interest in writing. It is amazing that he has kept trying at school with so little reinforcement. Always try to highlight these types of positive points, or literacy strengths, as well as areas that need development. Figure E.1 lists important features of this case and considers instructional approaches that might work for Charles.

Setting a Clear Focus for Instruction

Let's look at the focal issues together—word knowledge, fluency, and comprehension. Charles has a limited knowledge about the meaning and structure of words. This shows up in his lack of

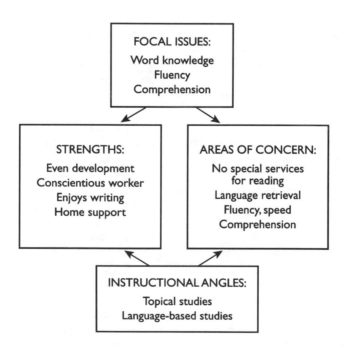

FIGURE E.I. A graphic organizer highlighting important features of Charles's case and suggesting instructional approaches.

familiarity with content vocabulary in his reading and his limited knowledge about word patterns in his spelling. Charles has also had little practice reading fluently in easy materials; his school reading assignments have been well beyond the level where he demonstrates a strong knowledge of most words (easy first-grade books). His limited comprehension of reading materials is closely related to his limited fluency and word knowledge; in his assessment at the center, he had difficulty understanding a second-grade book, where his understanding of vocabulary terms was limited and his reading speed was particularly slow. However, it is also important to note that Charles had difficulty understanding materials that were read to him, such as the fourth-grade passage. All of these issues are of particular concern when you consider that Charles is a sixth-grade student who has been retained two times, yet receives no individualized services in the school system. This is clearly a student who would benefit from attention in the regular classroom as well as one-on-one instruction to boost his developing literacy skills. One early goal would certainly be to support Charles in gaining fluency so that he can move from beginning reading to a transitional stage where he is reading with more comprehension.

Using a Student's Strengths to Find an Angle for Instruction

After narrowing down these instructional issues, it is important to reconsider what strengths a student exhibits. Charles has developed evenly in most areas of literacy. His understanding of words, his fluency in reading, and his comprehension of materials are solidly in the range of a beginning reader. He works hard and has excellent support for literacy at home. Most importantly, he has managed to keep his enjoyment of writing. As you look back across the strengths that Charles brings to literacy learning, it is clear that he can be a successful reader in easy materials. In addition, he is an obvious candidate for an instructional program that promotes reading to write—using information from reading as content for writing. We have selected two instructional angles that highlight this strength Charles demonstrates in writing: topical studies (e.g., the Civil War, weather) and language-based studies (e.g., poetry, word analysis). Both of these areas will help Charles focus on building his vocabulary. In addition, rehearsed reading of poetry and repeated reading about the same content will support both his reading fluency and his comprehension of the material. At the same time, an important component of this program will be to have Charles write about what he reads. Using graphic organizers to take notes about his reading will help him keep track of the structure of narrative and expository text as he collects important details. These graphic organizers can be used to support writing poetry, creative responses, or summaries about the reading.

Keeping Student Engagement at the Forefront

Focusing on topical studies and language-based studies does not mean that Charles will be limited to reading and writing about school topics. He will need to have opportunities to explore his own areas of interest. Sports are both a passion for Charles and an area in which he has extensive background knowledge. This sets up another opportunity to build on a strength. Reading aloud to Charles from sports magazines, biographies, or fiction would help him develop his comprehension skills while promoting his interest in reading. Sports poetry provides a wonderful, high-interest model for student writing. Books such as *Sports Pages* (Adoff, 1986), *American Sports Poems* (Knudson & Swenson, 1988), *Hoops* (Burleigh, 1997), and *Opening Days: Sports Poems* (Hopkins, 1996) can also be used for Readers' Theater to improve reading speed and expression. It would also make sense to capitalize on the interest Charles shows in music. Simple yet sophisticated picture books would be excellent sources for shared reading. Chris Raschka's (1992) innovative tribute to jazz, *Charlie Parker Played Be Bop*, is easy to read, rhythmic, and humorous. The text actually recreates the feel of music. *Ben's Trumpet* (Isadora, 1979) uses vibrant black-and-white illustrations to recreate the 1920s setting of a jazz club in the city.

Following Up on What Works for a Student

This is one way to begin to focus your instruction with an individual student such as Charles. Ongoing assessments will help you monitor changes, and you will need to keep the student's interests and engagement in reading and writing as your top priority. As a teacher, you will have to be creative to meet the needs of students like Charles who are working well below grade level while you are teaching other students with all different types of abilities. Take a look at Box E.3 to see what Janet Bloodgood can tell us about what actually worked for Charles.

Using an Individualized Lesson Plan

As you can see, teaching Charles so that he would continue to make progress in both reading and writing would require a combination of teaching about reading and writing with learning about new content. If we use the structure of the intervention lesson plan that we have introduced in Chapter 9, we can map out a plan for integrating literacy intervention with classroom studies. Look at Box E.4 for an example of the type of approach that would help Charles make progress in reading and writing.

Charles did indeed pursue some of these topics with a tutor. One school-related topic that he chose to study was the life of Frederick Douglas. To help himself keep track of the information, he used different strategies. He made a list of the ways Douglas earned other people's respect. He also kept his own notes on a story map—a graphic outline of a book about Douglas. This writing is shown in Box E.5.

After working with the information about Douglas in different formats, Charles was able to write his own short biography of the man. This piece was two pages long; it was well organized, with details about each event listed in Box E.5. Charles still struggled with spelling, but he did learn strategies to use both to read and write words. Still, even with careful planning and focused intervention, there were no easy answers. It is a balancing act to decide what a middle grades student needs and when. In her remarks about working with less skilled readers in the middle grades, Janet Bloodgood discusses those difficult decisions in Box E.6.

CHILDREN'S BOOK REFERENCES/REFERENCES

Adoff, A. (1986). *Sports pages* (ill. S. Kuzma). New York: Lippincott.

Burleigh, R. (1997). *Hoops* (ill. S. T. Johnson). San Diego, CA: Silver Whistle.

Hopkins, L. B. (Ed.). (1996). *Opening days: Sports poems* (ill. S. Medlock). San Diego, CA: Harcourt Brace.

Isadora, R. (1979). *Ben's trumpet*. New York: Greenwillow.

Knudson, R. R., & Swenson, M. (Eds.). (1988). *American sports poems*. New York: Orchard.

Let's read and find out series. New York: Harper Trophy.

New true books series. Danbury, CT: Children's Press (Grolier).

Raschka, C. (1992). *Charlie Parker played be bop*. New York: Orchard.

Rief, L. (1992). *Seeking diversity: Language arts with adolescents*. Portsmouth, NH: Heinemann.

BOX E.3. Planning an Individualized Program for Charles: An Interview with Janet Bloodgood (Conducted by Karen Broaddus)

What was most challenging about designing and monitoring a individualized program for Charles?

We knew that Charles would not receive the support he needed in the regular sixth-grade classroom; most teachers do not have the time or materials to work individually with students functioning 4 years below grade level. We asked his mother to make arrangements with the school for Charles to attend our reading clinic for an hour of tutoring four mornings a week. Barbara, his tutor, and I had a number of issues to consider as we planned a reading, writing, and word study program for Charles. The biggest challenge was to find first- and second-grade reading materials that would interest a sixth-grade boy. Whenever possible, we wanted to connect his reading and writing to topics being discussed in his classes, but our major goals were to build his reading confidence and his motivation to read. Although we believed that reading practice in easy, enjoyable material is the best way to improve reading skill, we did not give Charles reading assignments outside the tutoring time, because he was overburdened with homework in his school classes.

What types of strategies worked well for Charles?

Charles was an avid sports fan, playing football and basketball and enjoying Washington Redskins games on television. Language experience approach (LEA) dictations about sports activities helped connect reading and writing to Charles's life, and provided interesting reading passages to develop his sight word vocabulary and reading fluency. Charles's teachers [Mrs. Rand and others] gave us information about the topics they planned to cover in science and social studies during the school year. Barbara [his tutor] found easy texts (e.g., *Let's Read and Find Out* series, *New True Science* series) that covered these topics and helped Charles to read the materials and to develop strategies to build his comprehension of what he read. Some of the passages were easy enough for him to read; others required him to listen to his tutor read and make sense of what he heard. We focused on helping him learn to summarize and use graphic organizers to highlight information relationships. In the fall, Charles studied and wrote a report on weather superstitions. He investigated explorers and Frederick Douglass in the spring. Whenever possible, content-related vocabulary terms were put on cards to be used for concept sorts and writing resources. Word study was an integral part of his tutoring program. Barbara and Charles studied basic short and long vowel patterns, firming up associations between sounds and spelling patterns. They categorized words by feature, conducted word hunts for similar patterns in his reading material, and played a variety of word study games to improve his use of the features learned. These word study activities supported Charles's decoding skill and writing fluency.

As you think back, what would you do differently? What else did Charles need?

If we had the opportunity to do it over again, I would have liked to place more emphasis on building Charles's reading fluency. Remedial work with adolescents puts everyone in a double bind. Reading tutors know that unless a firm foundation of word knowledge and strategies for decoding and comprehending is in place, literacy improvement will be halting. However, there is always tremendous pressure to cover the content students are missing so that they can cope in the classroom. We tried to walk the tightrope between the reality of these two goals, and may not have been as successful as we could have been if we had focused on improving Charles's reading and writing skills. Fortunately, Charles was a patient, cooperative student who was committed to improving his own literacy; that was an important factor in the improvement he made.

BOX E.4. An Individualized Instructional Program for Charles

General lesson components	Strategies for instruction
Read-aloud	• Model fluent reading to introduce easy books that Charles might choose to read independently • Read high-interest nonfiction related to classroom studies and to writing topics
Fluent reading	• Create and rehearse Readers' Theater scripts about content area studies • Practice different ways of reading humorous poetry (paired and alone) • Reread content area dictations to support school studies
Supported reading and writing	• Pursue topical reading for school studies and for personal interests (exploration, slavery, Civil War, weather, sports) • Use graphic organizers to collect information about new topics • Take dictations that summarize information about the topic, and reread for organization and accuracy • Try structured writing tasks (experimenting with forms of poetry about content topics, writing about information collected in a graphic organizer)
Looking at words	• Use sports poetry and picture books on music as shared reading, rehearsed reading, and models for writing • Use vocabulary concept sorts (topic-related terms, root-related words) • Practice word analysis sorts and word hunts (short and long vowel patterns, homophones)
Checking out books	• Provide simple, short, humorous books for free-reading time (jokes, riddles, series books, picture books) • Explore magazines related to interests

BOX E.5. Graphic Organizer Used by Charles

Title	Frederick Douglass	
Setting	Baltimore Maryland	
Characters	slaves	Hugh Ald
	Grandma	Mr. Covy
	Miss Sophia	Mis Anna
Problem	frederick Douglass wanted to free the slaves	
Event 1	The life of a slave	
Event 2	The Biggest lesson of All (reading)	
Event 3	fight! (He got in a fight with Mr. Covey)	
Event 4	the plan That did not fail	
Event 5	The underground Railroad is running tonight!	
Solution	The slaves are finely free.	

BOX E.6. Working with Less Skilled Readers in the Middle Grades: An Interview with Janet Bloodgood (Conducted by Karen Broaddus)

In your experiences as a supervisor and tutor, what have you found to be the most essential considerations for developing strong relationships with less skilled readers in the middle grades?

When working with middle grades students with low literacy skills, I believe it's essential to respect them and to be up front about their personal strengths and weaknesses. These students know they have a problem; they often believe that they are stupid because they cannot read, and this attitude often leads them to be uncooperative or apathetic. It's important to let middle grades students know that they are not stupid, they can learn to read and write, and you are there to help them learn. Adolescents are old enough to share responsibility for their own learning; discussing their literacy problems, [talking about] their goals, and outlining strategies to help them improve allow them to be full participants in the learning process. Assessment is an important component of any instructional program, and I think that is particularly true when helping students develop reading and writing ability. Determining where students' areas of strength and weakness lie, as well as changes that are occurring across time, helps the tutor make personalized decisions about strategies, materials, and pacing that support optimal development.

Where do you feel the emphasis belongs in reading and writing instruction for older students?

I believe it is important to provide an instructional program that supports growth in all areas of literacy: word recognition, reading fluency, writing, word knowledge, and comprehension. Research suggests that the multiple strands of literacy develop in synchrony, growing from and supporting one another. Charles had limited word recognition skills. As a result, he had difficulty deciphering text beyond second-grade level, and only marginal comprehension there. His weak word knowledge limited his ability to express himself in writing; his spelling, vocabulary, and syntactic constructs were typical of second-grade writers. While we could have addressed word recognition and word knowledge as the core problems, a more comprehensive instructional program that addressed reading fluency, comprehension, and writing as well as Charles's specific areas of weakness gave him greater confidence and ensured that he continued to improve in these areas also.

What are some avenues that teachers might explore as they set up a classroom program for reading and writing?

Individualizing instruction to meet the needs of all students in the classroom is difficult if not impossible. I think that providing a balanced program of reading, writing, and word study within a workshop or contract organizational system offers the greatest chance for success. I like Linda Rief's approach to literacy instruction as outlined in *Seeking Diversity* (1992), since she recognizes and attempts to meet individual needs through a reading–writing workshop while still maintaining some common activities and experiences. Of course, this organization has the potential for chaos. It requires responsibility and cooperation from everyone, but self-direction and choice within given bounds work well with adolescents. There is a lot more work and planning for the teacher; he or she must know each student's interests and abilities, assess student progress continually, have a broad knowledge of appropriate books and their levels of difficulty, and monitor daily activities to ensure that everyone makes optimal progress.

(continued)

BOX E.6. (continued)

What practical activities can teachers emphasize to promote literacy for all readers?

Providing time for students to read materials they find interesting—sports pages, cartoons, fashion magazines, driving manuals, horror or romance novels—and taking time to read yourself demonstrates in a concrete way the value and enjoyment to be found in literacy. Whenever you can, highlight functional purposes for literacy (e.g., filling out job applications, ordering items from a catalog, reading sales brochures). Less able readers and writers need to see how literacy fits into their lives. There are also a number of activities that students can carry out with a partner or in small groups. For example, partnered students can read, time, and graph timed readings for each other to build reading fluency and expression. After modeling and some support, small groups of students can conduct literature discussion/literature circle groups independently. Cooperative learning groups allow students to research specific interests within a broader topic. Peer conferencing for revision and editing of written drafts work well once guidelines are established. Once students have been assessed and grouped by their levels of word knowledge development, and after the teacher has introduced the features to be sorted at the beginning of the week, many word study activities (e.g., word study notebook, timed sorts, word hunts, reinforcement games) can be done independently.

What might these teachers encourage parents to do to support their child's literacy development at home?

The best way to improve in anything you do is to practice, but there are innumerable distractions for middle grades students that keep them from practicing reading. If reading and writing are difficult, the desire to do it diminishes even more. The best thing that parents can do at home to help their adolescent develop improved literacy is to set a good example. Reading the daily newspaper and discussing news features and sports items (and perhaps leaving parts of the discussion hanging so the teen is tempted to read more about it) not only help to maintain positive family relations, but also encourage reading and model a literacy habit. Consistent routines are important for all children; setting a structured time for homework, and showing interest in it even when parents can't be there to supervise, let kids know that this is important. Some parents read the same book their teens are reading and discuss their favorite parts and issues of concern. If the opportunity is present, parents can encourage their adolescents with low reading ability to read and rehearse picture books to share when they go babysitting or to read to a younger sibling—a good reading performance and the appreciation of an audience do wonders for reading confidence and the desire to read more!

INDEX